1L OF A RIDE:

A WELL-TRAVELED PROFESSOR'S ROADMAP TO SUCCESS IN THE FIRST YEAR OF LAW SCHOOL

By

Andrew J. McClurg

Herbert Herff Chair of Excellence in Law
Cecil C. Humphreys School of Law
The University of Memphis

THOMSON

™

WEST

Mat #40753624

© 2009 Thomson/Reuters
      610 Opperman Drive
      St. Paul, MN 55123
      1–800–313–9378

Printed in the United States of America

ISBN: 978–0–314–19483–1

TEXT IS PRINTED ON 10% POST
CONSUMER RECYCLED PAPER

To my students—past, present, and future.

*

Acknowledgements

I couldn't have written this book without the help of many people. My research assistants at the University of Memphis Cecil C. Humphreys School of Law—Shea Barker, Chelsea L. Brown, Julia M. Kavanagh, Mary L. Wagner, and Todd V. Williams—did outstanding work and shared many valuable insights about how modern law students achieve their success. Laura J. Lee took an interest in the book as a 1L and contributed excellent ideas. I'm grateful to the students who shared and allowed me to reprint their case briefs and excerpts from class notes. They include several of my research assistants, as well as William A. Roach and a student who requested anonymity.

Special thanks are owed to the 1L students in my 2006–07 and 2007–08 Torts courses at the University of Memphis for tolerating my many survey questions designed to elicit their thoughts and feelings about the 1L experience. Specifically, all of these students answered one or more sets of survey questions: Lauren M. Armstrong, Shea Barker, Jennifer M. Baum, Willem H. Bermel, Jonathan E. Bettis, Matthew K. Bishop, Anna Vergos Blair, Peter G. Bolac, Bianca F. Brasher, Chelsea L. Brown, Wilson S. Bryan, Amanda G. Carpenter, Courtney Clothier, Christopher B. Connolly, Caroline W. Crawford, Anne B. Davis, Adam R. deNobriga, Andrew S. DeShazo, Sharon A. Fortner, LaTaya Franklin, Matthew P. Gabriel, Jennifer D. Haile, Blake W. Hazlerig, Kevin P. Henson, Katherine L. Herriman, Richard T. Hoehn, Sheryl T. Hurst, Michele L. Johnson Spears, Yael Julian, Erin Kubisiak, Cloteal LaBroi, Laura J. Lee, Ashley M. Levins, Erno D. Lindner, Tanesha L. Matthews, Kevin M. McCormack, M. Elizabeth McNinch, J. Bradley Mercer, Jonathon M. Meredith, Matthew E. Miller, Kate L. Moore, Robert G. Morgan, Charles M. Molder, J. Aaron Mullis, Benjamin R. Newman, Donald P. Nicholson, Bryce H. Phillips, Galen P. Pickard, Joshua C. Powell, Adam C. Ragan, Monica R. Rejaei, William A. Roach, Schaefer K. Rowe, Erica J. Scott, Reginald E. Shelton, Lakeisha D. Sisco-Beck, John D. Smith, Dylan M. Spaduzzi, Allison J. Starnes-Anglea, Bridgett L. Stigger, Brittany L. Strung, Sarah M. Turner, Pablo A. Varela, Gregory H. Wallace, Bridget M. Warner, Rachel D. Whitaker, Chad M. Wilgenbusch, Joanna L. Williams, Smith Nall Wilson, Justin Wojciechowski, Jason J. Yasinksy, and Erin C. Young. Many of their comments are included in the book. Forgive me if I left anyone out.

I'm also indebted to many law professors. Particular thanks are owed to the five legal writing professors who graciously contributed so much of their time, expertise, and writing ability to Chapter 17: Kimberly K. Boone, Christine N. Coughlin, Joan Malmud, Sandy C. Patrick, and David Walter. Mary Pat Treuthart read and commented on a draft, offering her usual insightful, blunt, and often hilarious wisdom. Other professors who shared input or gave other help include: Thomas E. Baker, Coleen M. Barger, Sara R. Benson, Leslie Burton, Markita D. Cooper, John M.A. DiPippa, June F. Entman, Barbara Glesner Fines, Judith D. Fischer, Elizabeth P. Foley, Jose Gabilondo, Larry Howell, Barbara Kritchevsky, Nancy Levit, Ernest F. Lidge, III, Jana R. McCreary, Kathleen A. Miller, Martha M. Peters, Lawrence A. Pivnick, Janet L. Richards, Ruth Anne Robbins, Ediberto Román, David S. Romantz, Sheila J. Simon, Kevin H. Smith, Stephen Smith, Andrej Thomas Starkis, Meredith A.G. Stange, Brenda L. Tofte, Grace C. Tonner, Barbara J. Tyler, and Nicholas L. White.

Several administrative, library, and other staff members at the University of Memphis law school also provided assistance, including Howard E. Bailey, Patricia Collier Crowell, Linda H. Hayes, Yolanda D. Wesley Ingram, and Sue Ann McClellan. Administrative assistant Karol Landers helped throughout the project.

A few passages were borrowed from my satire of legal education, *The Law School Trip: The Insider's Guide to Law School* (2001).

PROLOGUE

For more than two decades as a law professor, at several schools across the country, I've watched first-year law students—"1Ls"—make the same mistakes: in their approach to studying, behavior in and out of the classroom, exam preparation, exam performance, and overall mindset toward law school. Sometimes these mistakes result from following bad advice, but more often they occur simply because students don't know what to expect or what is expected of them when they arrive at law school.

The consequences of these missteps vary. Some students flunk out, of course, but more often the mistakes prevent students from maximizing their potential, meeting their own high expectations, and living reasonably happy lives. Even students who end up excelling in law school struggle dispiritedly to cope with the stress and anxiety that come from having to compete in the high-stakes 1L race without prior training and on a route lacking clear road markers.

My partial remedy, and the goal of this book, is to provide new students with a candid, beginning-to-end roadmap to the first year of law school, along with the navigational and other tools to complete the sojourn scholastically accomplished and emotionally intact.

But if you've done any looking around, you know that a bunch of other "how to succeed in law school" books already exist. Do law students really need another one? What makes this book distinctive?

- **Written by a law professor with a wide range of experience teaching different kinds of students at different law schools.**

As you approach law school, lots of people—lawyer acquaintances, other law students, and authors of books like this one—will be giving you advice about how to succeed. Your first question to any of us should be: "So who are you to be giving me advice?"

Over a period of twenty-two years, I've taught thousands of students at six law schools, from the West Coast (San Francisco) to the East Coast (Miami), and points in between (Boulder, Little Rock, Memphis, and Winston-Salem). These include law schools in every tier of the *U.S. News & World Report* law school rankings. I have substantial experience teaching every possible kind of law student: affluent students, poor students, private-school students, public-school students, young students just out of college, older students

with families and established careers, single parents, brilliant, average, and struggling students, kids whose parents were law school
deans and those first in their family to attend college, urbanites,
ruralites, full-time day students, part-time night students, minority
students, and students with disabilities. I've taught students who
went on to become great judges and students who went on to
become great bartenders.

My teaching credentials include five teaching awards, excellent
student evaluations at six law schools, articles and book chapters
about law teaching, and presentations for organizations such as the
Institute for Law School Teaching. My scholarly publishing record
includes numerous articles and books that have been quoted and
cited by more than 300 legal scholars in roughly 200 different academic journals. As a legal expert, I've been interviewed and quoted by
sources such as National Public Radio, the *New York Times*, *Washington Post*, *Time*, and *U.S. News & World Report*.

Additionally, I once was a successful law student. In 1980, I
graduated third in my class at the University of Florida College of
Law, where I was a member of the law review and elected to the
Order of the Coif, an honor conferred on the top 10 percent of graduates at select law schools. While my memories of the first year of
law school are distant, some of them remain quite clear, which says
a lot about the impact of the 1L adventure. I still remember my first
day of law school orientation, first class, first Socratic interrogation,
and first exam. That my own law school memories still have relevance tells you something important to know about U.S. legal education: it's deeply rooted in tradition. As noted—with disapproval—by
the authors of the 2007 *Best Practices for Legal Education* report,
"[t]ypical classroom instruction at most law schools today would be
familiar to any lawyer who attended law school during the past hundred thirty years."[1]

I don't claim to have the only right answers about succeeding in
law school. Anyone who would make such a claim knows little about
the wide variations in learning and teaching styles of law students
and professors. As with the law itself, many of the relevant questions about how to succeed have more than one answer depending
on the particular student and professor. Indeed, the very definition
of "success" is subject to different answers. I base my advice on
what will be most helpful to the largest group of students.

- **Provides a candid beginning-to-end
  roadmap of what to expect in the first
  year.**

---

1. ROY STUCKEY ET AL., BEST PRACTICES FOR LEGAL EDUCATION 133 (2007).

A large part of what makes the first year of law school so stressful and frightening is not knowing what to expect. For the last few years, I've asked my entering Torts classes to answer this online poll question:

As you begin your 1L quest, what is your dominant feeling?

• Confidence

• Excitement

• Lack of confidence

• Pride

• Stress

• Fear or anxiety

• Uncertainty

"Uncertainty" is the most common answer. "Stress" and "Fear or Anxiety"—much of which is generated by uncertainty—also receive many votes. To reduce your uncertainty and enlarge your comfort zone, this book explains what to expect as a 1L and how to respond when it happens. Essentially, it answers the questions, "What's the first year of law school really like and how do I make the most of it?"

The first year is, by far, the most important year in the three-year U.S. law school curriculum. The first year is where students acquire the basic knowledge and tools of legal analysis that carry them through the rest of law school and beyond. Think of it as the foundation on which all subsequent building blocks for becoming and being a lawyer are laid. To some degree, the second and especially the third year are redundant. In the 1970s, a substantial movement existed among law professors and practitioners to abolish the third year. While the initiative lost traction, a survey twenty years later found that 43 percent of law students believed the third year is "largely superfluous."[2]

While virtually all of the advice applies to the entire first year, we'll concentrate on the all-critical first semester. The first semester is where students learn to read cases, write case briefs, take class notes, compose course outlines, deal with the Socratic teaching

---

2. Mitu Gulati, Richard Sander & Robert Sockloskie, *The Happy Charade: An Empirical Examination of the Third Year of Law School*, 51 J. LEGAL EDUC. 235, 246 (2001). The researchers surveyed 1100 third-year students at eleven schools in 1998–99. Forty-three percent agreed with the statement that "[t]he third year of law school is largely superfluous."

method, and develop either good or poor classroom, study, and exam strategies. The first semester forges the critical reasoning skills that law professors like to call "thinking like a lawyer." It is, regrettably, also the semester that ends up defining most law students, both academically and in terms of their self-esteem, and, as a consequence, the manner in which they approach the rest of law school.

I try to be candid in depicting the good, bad, and ugly of law school. To keep myself honest in that regard, I approached the book from this standpoint: If my recent college-graduate daughter decided to go to law school, what advice would I give her? I wouldn't necessarily tell her everything law professors would want her to hear. I'd be bluntly honest. It's an apt analogy because the older I get, the more I think of law students as my "kids."

- **Addresses each aspect of academic success, including the top five habits of successful law students, effective class participation, case-briefing, note-taking, outlining, exam preparation, and essay and multiple-choice exam strategies.**

You may already be aware that grades are important in and after law school, more important than in most other graduate programs and job markets. Any suggestion to the contrary would be a misrepresentation. This isn't to say that people without high grades can't or don't succeed in the legal profession. Quite the contrary is true. Some of the wealthiest and most successful lawyers in America were *C* law students. I laughed when a colleague told me her law school has a nice basketball court for students bearing a plaque that says "Donated by a *C* Student."

But it's a fact that high GPAs and class rankings open doors not available to students who lack them, both in law school and in the real-world job market. Within law school, students with good grades have better opportunities to obtain scholarships, positions as research assistants to professors, and law review and moot court positions. Outside of law school, many law firms and judges won't interview people who are not in the top quartile of their class. At the end of a recent academic year, I asked my students to name one thing they wish they had known when they started law school. One student responded: "I wish I had known how important law firms find class rank to be."

Most law schools, albeit not all, have rigorous attitudes toward grading. A 2003 survey conducted by the Association of American Law Schools showed at least 40 percent of ABA-accredited schools impose *mandatory* grading curves. Because some schools did not respond and five years have passed since the survey was conducted, the actual percentage is probably higher. Most mandatory grade policies set specific percentages regarding the number of students who can or must fall within each grade range. Even at schools without mandatory curves, law school grades in first-year courses usually follow a well-defined, bell-shaped curve.

The result of these attitudes and formal policies is that high grades in law school are much harder to come by than in most other graduate programs. Because grades play such a crucial role, a large portion of the book is devoted to helping you "make the grade." I can't promise that if you follow my advice, you will ace your courses or finish at the top of your class. Mathematics dictates that in every law school class since the dawn of time only 10 percent of students finish in the top 10 percent. Ninety percent don't. But I do firmly believe that following the advice in this book will substantially improve your chances of succeeding at a higher level than you otherwise would.

If you're looking for shortcuts to success in law school, this may not be the book for you. While it does offer important tips for being efficient—a critical attribute of successful law students—I'm sorry to report that students who make a habit of cutting corners simply do not succeed at the highest levels in law school. Most students "succeed" in law school in terms of not being academically dismissed, including many students who cut corners. But if your definition of success is something higher, cutting corners isn't a viable option for most students.

But don't take my word for it. In response to a year-ending question to list one piece of advice students would give to someone starting law school, one student wrote:

> I read some books before I started law school: [*Title omitted*] and [*Title omitted*]. Both were helpful, but it seems that most of the pre-law, self-help books are geared toward helping students find the easy way out. For example, one of the books I read had a whole chapter on book briefing and gathering outlines from others. Well, the people who book brief and don't do their own outlines usually don't do well. I would emphasize in your book that there is no easy way through law school.

And this came from a "kid" I jumped all over on the second day of class for arriving late. Law students, God love 'em.

- **Focuses on practical advice that can be followed by any student from day one.**

One of the problems with a lot of advice about how to succeed in law school is that, while it's good advice, as a practical matter, it can't be readily followed. I learned this in seeking feedback from other law professors. Reduced to its essence, much of the advice amounted to "learn to read better," "learn to write better," and "learn to think better." Easier said than done. This book focuses on practical advice that can be followed by any student from the first day of law school.

- **Addresses "emotional success" in addition to academic success.**

As important as grades are, they are by no means the only measuring sticks of law school achievement. Success also comes in the form of happiness, well-being, and a belief that one made the right decision in deciding to devote every molecule of his or her energy and resources to pursuing a law degree as opposed to doing something else.

Here's an early warning: law school takes an emotional and physical toll on a substantial percentage of students, even those who enjoy it. Studies of law student mental distress, as you will see, do not paint a pretty picture. All along the road to academic success, this book offers advice for managing stress, maintaining well-being, and leading a healthy, balanced law school life.

- ***Shows* with anecdotes and examples.**

Showing is more effective than simply telling, so this book employs many anecdotes and examples to make and illuminate points, including samples of real Socratic dialogue, real exam questions and answers, and real law student case briefs and class notes.

Nearly all of the examples come from the subject of Torts. Simplistically, Torts is the study of monetary liability for personal injuries. Torts is a good subject to use as a proxy for exploring law school's first year because it is a required first-year course at almost all schools and many of the basic principles and fact patterns of tort law are comprehensible without extensive background or explanation. It is also a subject with which many incoming students have at least some familiarity, due to the widespread coverage of tort lawsuits and the tort system in the mainstream media and blogosphere.

A cautionary note: I picked and constructed simple examples that can be followed and processed by pre-law, admitted, and new students. Don't be misled into thinking all of law is as straightforward or easy as some of the examples might make it appear.

- **Includes a student voice with comments from real 1Ls.**

To revisit the 1L experience from a student perspective, I sought input from students all along the way, including a series of survey questions administered to a group of approximately seventy-five students in a recent entering class at the University of Memphis law school as they progressed through the first year from beginning to end. The students' interesting, insightful, and frequently poignant comments add balance to (and relief from) the drone of teacher talk that will be bearing down on you for the next many pages.

Obviously, one group of students at one law school does not represent the entire universe of law students in many ways, but in terms of their reactions to the trials and tribulations of the 1L experience, they come very close. In large part, this is attributable to the remarkable uniformity in the basic structure and institutions of the first year of law school throughout U.S. legal education. In teaching at schools in different parts of the country, I've always been struck by the core likeness of law students. At schools great and small, all 1Ls struggle to learn the same material under the same teaching methodologies and evaluation formats.

- **Backs up advice with empirical research.**

Scores of studies have been conducted about law students, legal education, and teaching and learning in general, yet this research is often overlooked in giving advice to law students. To boost confidence (yours and mine) in my recommendations, I researched and discuss several of these studies. Did you know that students who sit in the front of classrooms get higher grades than those who sit in back? That women voluntarily participate in law school class discussion at lower rates than men? That the conventional wisdom to not change initial answers to multiple-choice questions is completely backwards? Some of the research on these and other points might surprise you.

- **Includes input from other law professors.**

To broaden my own view, I solicited input from other law professors all along the way. A particularly unique aspect of the book is Chapter 17, where five experienced legal writing professors from different law schools answer important questions about the required first-year course of Legal Research and Writing. As you will soon learn, no 1L course is more important, labor intensive or angst-producing. The eloquently and elegantly expressed deliberation of these five experts on this critical topic is a high-point of the book.

- **Written in a reader-friendly voice.**

Who wants to read several hundred pages of boring law professor advice? I wouldn't, so I try to keep you engaged with a lively voice and touch of humor. My credentials for attempting to occasionally amuse you include four years as the monthly humor columnist for the *American Bar Association Journal*, webmaster of lawhaha.com (an academically oriented humor site for law students and legal professionals), and author/editor of two books in the seemingly oxymoronic realm of "legal humor."

* * *

Like all roadmaps, you'll want to keep this one close by during your 1L trip. If you were taking a real one-year road trip, you wouldn't just glance at the map once before you backed out of the driveway then toss it aside. You'd review it each time you entered new territory or faced a new fork in the road. Consider this book to be a companion text to your entire first year, a handbook that should be kept handy for convenient reference.

If you haven't started law school yet, I recommend reading the whole book to get the big picture, then returning to consult particular chapters as they become more directly relevant in your 1L journey. Much of the advice is very specific. As scintillating as the subject is, reading the chapter on course outlines (Chapter 13) before law school is unlikely to permanently imprint in memory all the essential details you'll need to know when it comes time to start preparing your own outlines. The same holds true for several other chapters, including those on class participation (Chapter 8), case-briefing (Chapter 11), exam preparation (Chapter 14), exam-taking (Chapters 15 and 16), legal research and writing (Chapter 17), and dealing with the second semester (Chapter 19).

Re-scrutinize particular chapters after you're in school as the situations they address arise. Buy some highlighters and mark the heck out of key passages as you read them the first time. That's what you'll be doing with your law school books, so it will be good practice. Consult the index for answers to questions that occur to you. I made it extremely detailed for that very purpose.

I hope you enjoy reading and learning from this book as much as I enjoyed writing it. Most important, I hope you'll actually *follow* the advice.

Table of Contents

*

1L OF A RIDE:

A WELL-TRAVELED PROFESSOR'S ROADMAP TO SUCCESS IN THE FIRST YEAR OF LAW SCHOOL

*

CHAPTER 1
DESTINATION LAW SCHOOL

Get ready to embark on a wild ride unlike anything you've ever experienced, packed with thrills, chills, and probably a few spills. Being a 1L will challenge you like you've never been challenged. Law school and a law degree offer the potential for great rewards, but at a cost. The first year of law school will be one of—if not *the*—hardest year of your life. Law school will profoundly alter the way you think, view, and interact with the world around you, in ways both good and bad. Your 1L experience will literally change who you are, whether you want it to or not.

But you may already be tired of hearing or reading these kinds of dire proclamations and predictions. Perhaps you've encountered them in other prep books. Maybe they even sound like clichés to you by now. "Yeah, yeah, law school will be hard. I'll be changed. Whatever. Everyone says the same thing. I can handle it."

The best analogy I have for explaining how law school will both take you by surprise and forever alter you involves becoming a parent. When I was an expectant dad many years ago, friends and family told me the same kinds of things about becoming a parent. "It will change your life forever." "It will be the hardest thing you've ever done." "Say good-bye to your old life."

I thought they were exaggerating. It wasn't like I was uninformed. I'd read the essential books about babies and parenting. I even attended parenting classes. I cruised blissfully through my wife's pregnancy thinking, "I'm prepared. I'm prepared. I'm prepared." Then five seconds into my first

1

encounter with infant projectile vomiting, I was like, "Augh! I'm not prepared! I'm not prepared! I'm not prepared!"

Like being a parent, one can truly understand and appreciate the first year of law school only by experiencing it, so let's start by looking at some reactions from those who did. On the last page of my first-semester Torts exam, I sometimes insert this bonus question: "Write the name of a song or a song lyric that best describes your feelings about the first semester of law school." It doesn't really count for any points, so don't get your hopes up that law school exams are that easy. Below are some of the responses. Lyrics are in quotation marks.

While we can't attach deep psychological meaning to these answers, dashed off hastily and perhaps in jest, the students' spontaneous associations are nevertheless revealing. Their first-semester jukebox reflects the roller-coaster ride of emotions inherent in being a 1L, including:

Stress, anxiety:

- Help!—The Beatles
- Chalkdust Torture—Phish
- Under Pressure—Queen/David Bowie
- I Wanna Be Sedated—The Ramones
- Panic—The Smiths

Disorientation, madness:

- Highway to Hell—AC/DC
- "They won't let me out, they won't let me out (I'm locked up)"—Akon
- Basketcase—Green Day
- Welcome Home (Sanitarium)—Metallica
- Crazy Train—Ozzy Osborne

Exhaustion, frustration, hostility:

- A Hard Day's Night—The Beatles
- Welcome to the Jungle—Guns N' Roses
- "I'm gonna knock you out. Mama said knock you out."—LL Cool J
- Rat Race—Bob Marley
- We're Not Gonna Take It—Twisted Sister

Melancholy, depression:

- A Hard Rain's Gonna Fall—Bob Dylan
- The Loneliness of the Long Distance Runner—Iron Maiden
- Paint It Black—The Rolling Stones
- "Reflections of the way life used to be."—The Supremes
- Bittersweet Symphony—The Verve

Self-doubt:

- "I fought the law and the law won."—Bobby Fuller Four
- Livin' on a Prayer—Bon Jovi
- Should I Stay or Should I Go?—The Clash
- Should Have Been a Cowboy (instead of a lawyer)—Toby Keith
- Another One Bites the Dust—Queen

But don't let these answers bring you down. They were solicited at the end of a long, tough semester, seconds after students completed a grueling three-hour exam. And even then—even in the very worst of times—many students expressed excitement, hope, optimism, and pride, as in:

- I Feel Good—James Brown
- I Will Survive—Gloria Gaynor
- "Here I am, rock you like a hurricane."—The Scorpions
- Nothing's Gonna Stop Us Now—Jefferson Starship
- We are the Champions—Queen

Every time I use the song question, one or more students quote the Grateful Dead, describing the first semester as a "long strange trip." And indeed it is. So what are we waiting for? If you haven't already started, law school is probably looming on the not-too-distant horizon. It may be just months away, perhaps only a matter of weeks. You're probably wondering what you should be doing and feeling. Let's find out.

CHAPTER 2
PRE-TRIP PLANNING: WHAT TO DO BEFORE YOU ARRIVE

Incoming students naturally feel like they should be doing something to get ready for law school before they get there. They should be, but not necessarily the things they think they should be doing. Below are two pre-arrival "To Do" lists, one for intangibles and one for tangibles. Law students and law student advice usually focus on the tangibles, but the intangibles are just as important and harder to accomplish.

Pre-Arrival "To Do" List: The Intangibles
Be excited!

Be excited about going to law school. It's a big deal and you should treat it that way. Approach it with enthusiasm. Not dread (distinguishing dread from a healthy apprehension) and certainly not apathy—nothing would be worse than that. My experience observing law students has taught me that President Harry Truman got it right when he said he had studied the lives of great men and women and "found that the men and women who got to the top were those who did the jobs they had in hand with everything they had of *energy and enthusiasm*."

Law school is an entry pass to an exclusive club offering unique challenges, opportunities, and rewards. Your degree will grant you the power to single-handedly change people's lives for the better. That's what ordinary lawyers do every day.

In my original draft of this chapter, to inspire you, I talked about some big, important lawyers and how their big, important cases changed history. It was all true. Experience has shown time and again that lawyers are the only group with the conviction and courage to consistently stand up and fight for justice when it's unpopular to do so. Lawyers created the liberties we cherish and have fought to protect them for more than two hundred years. Thirty-three of the fifty-five framers of the U.S. Constitution were lawyers. Tales about lawyers who altered the path of America could fill this book.

But a conversation in the hallway with a 2L caused me to change course. As I was walking into class, he came up and recounted a dispute he'd been having with his landlord. He said he was able to resolve it because a lawyer offered to help him without charge because he was a struggling law student. The student told me: "Professor, I'm going to remember that when I become a lawyer. I'm going to remember what it felt like to have no money and no power and no voice and how that lawyer helped me."

That brought back to me the real heart and soul of what it means to be a lawyer. Big cases change history, but the smallest and simplest cases often have the biggest impact on ordinary people. I decided to cut the history lesson and tell you instead about a very tiny case I handled as a young lawyer. It was a pro bono case, meaning there was no fee involved. The Jacksonville, Florida legal aid organization called and asked if I would help an elderly man being sued by a home improvement contractor for breach of contract. I was tempted to say I was too busy—which I was, such is the life of a young litigation associate as many of you will learn—but I accepted the case.

My client was a man in his eighties whom I'll call Clarence Jackson. Mr. Jackson had shown up at the legal aid office clutching a packet of papers, explaining to the intake interviewer that he had signed a contract with a home improvement contractor to have some repairs done on his house for $1,000, a lot of money back then, especially for a man living on Social Security. He said the contractor didn't complete the work properly, so he refused to pay. The contractor hauled off and sued him and, in a letter, threatened to take his house away.

I drove out to the house on a hot, humid summer morning to meet Mr. Jackson. The house was in a neighborhood on "the other side of town" that I had never visited. Honestly, it wasn't much of a house. It was very small and very old, but exceptionally well-kept. Mr. Jackson greeted me at the door and I took an instant liking to him. He was a gentle, soft-spoken man of diminutive stature. He wore overalls and I felt ridiculous standing on the porch sweating in my lawyer power suit. He invited me in, showed me pictures of his kids and grandchildren, and gave me some iced tea. We sat in the living room looking over the contract and the legal complaint, then he took me on a tour of the premises.

He pointed out the shoddy workmanship by the contractor: bare, wrong-size fascia boards nailed haphazardly at the roof line, a toilet that poured water out the bottom every time it was flushed, a window that was inches too small for the opening, etc. I remember getting mad. The nerve of that contractor to not only do such slapdash work, but sue Mr. Jackson and scare the heck out of him by threatening to take his home away.

I took some pictures with a Polaroid camera and went back to my office to prepare an affidavit for Mr. Jackson to sign and a motion for summary judgment in the lawsuit. Summary judgment is a way for a court to dispose of a case without a trial. We had a hearing on the motion in the judge's chambers. At the end, the judge granted our motion— dismissing the case—but with all the legalese the old man misunderstood. He thought we lost. When the judge adjourned the hearing, Mr. Jackson put his hand on my shoulder and said, "Thank you, Mr. McClurg, I know you did a good job. I guess some things just can't be helped." I said, "Mr. Jackson, it's okay. We won."[3]

He couldn't believe it. Literally. Maybe he went in believing the system would be stacked against him. When the victory finally sunk in, he just kept repeating "Thank you, thank you, thank you." I was embarrassed. I was still in my twenties. Here was a man who had done and seen far more than I ever had. But for just *a little bit* of my time, I'd changed his life.

A few days after the hearing, the receptionist buzzed me and said "There's a man out here who says he's your client."

---

3. I don't recall the exact words of the conversation in this or other anecdotes sprinkled throughout the book. I recount their substance to the best of my ability.

Mr. Jackson did not fit the profile of the firm's usual well-heeled clientele. I walked out to the receptionist area and there stood Mr. Jackson, still wearing overalls. He said he wanted to pay me and pulled a wad of bills from his pocket. He said it was a hundred dollars. I explained again that his was a pro bono case and that he didn't owe me anything. But he kept insisting he had to do something for me. Finally, he said, "Mr. McClurg, I'll tell you what. You come over to my house on Saturday and I'll cook you supper." (I had insisted he call me by my first name, but he never did.)

I went. And to this day I've never felt more proud to be a lawyer than that afternoon, sitting in that old man's blazing hot kitchen—he didn't have air conditioning—eating the dinner he made for me.

America is filled with "Mr. Jacksons"—people who desperately need help with legal problems that may seem small from the outside but which dominate their lives. Our system entrusts the awesome responsibility to give that help to one group: *lawyers*. People tend to think of doctors as being the primary life-saving profession, but make no mistake: lawyers have people's lives in their hands every day.

Start law school feeling proud about becoming part of a noble and honorable profession. Don't let the people around you sour you on studying to be a lawyer. The public has a love-hate relationship with lawyers. On the one hand, they're fascinated with the law and lawyers, as shown by the nonstop supply of books, movies, and television programming about them. On the other hand, people are quick to malign lawyers. Even total strangers will feel comfortable telling you lawyer jokes.

True story: I went on a canoeing trip with a group of law professors. You can imagine what a rollicking adventure that was. The woman at the canoe rental place asked what I did and I said, "Law professor." Without hesitating, she said, "I hate lawyers." Without hesitating, I said, "I hate people who rent canoes." She was shocked and appalled I would say something so rude. Although the irony escaped her, I felt good about standing up for my profession. Plus, I really do hate people who rent canoes.

Lawyers aren't perfect, and there are rotten apples in the bin of every profession, but as a fellow named Harrison Tweed said more than half a century ago: "With all their faults, [lawyers] stack up well against those in every other occupation or profession. They are better to work with or play with or fight with or drink with than most other varieties of mankind." Trust that the haters and joke-tellers will be the first ones running to a lawyer when they get in trouble.

Let the power of the law to right wrongs invigorate you. Let the grand tradition of lawyers in America make you proud. Be excited! If you're not enthusiastic about law school before you get there, it will only get worse after you arrive.

Get your life in order.

The first year of law school is all-consuming. The workload and volume of material you will be expected to master will be unlike anything you've ever encountered. To maximize your chances for success, you need to enter law school with your full focus on it.

Life distractions should be resolved before you get there. Don't be a procrastinator when it comes to getting your housing situation or financial aid firmed up. Having to work out kinks in either while starting school will not only take away needed time and energy, it will add extra stress you don't need. Law school will provide plenty of that.

If you're in a turbulent intimate relationship that you know deep down is going to end at some point anyway, the summer before law school is a good time to say goodbye. Don't drag it out until after law school starts. Law school takes a heavy toll even on good relationships. No reason to jeopardize your success by wasting emotional energy on a relationship you know is already on life support.

For part-time evening-division students, resolving employment conflicts is the biggest challenge. Before beginning, you need to develop a clear plan for freeing up time to prepare for classes and to arrive punctually. Don't put off discussing the issue and arriving at an understanding with your employer until after you start. Employment conflicts are the most common reason for part-time students failing in law school. I've sat through countless readmissions committee meetings listening to part-time students explain how their job didn't allow enough time for them to succeed, along with their "new plan" for reducing employment hours, etc. The "new plan" needs to be worked out before you set foot in the door.

Meanwhile, if you're a full-time student, don't even think about working during the first year.

Health issues are another source of interference with law school success. Unfortunately, people have less ability to control them than many other potential life distractions. If you face serious health issues as law school approaches, consider the prognosis for the immediate future, recognizing that the stress of law school can aggravate health conditions. If the prognosis for improvement before law school starts is unclear or not good, consider postponing law school until your health issues can be resolved. Schools often will grant deferments to admitted students for health reasons, meaning you can enroll in the next academic year without having to reapply.

Do not plan weddings, extended vacations or pregnancies during the first year of law school. To the fullest extent possible, clear your calendar of major non-law school events from August through May of the first year.

Approach law school like a full-time job.

The single most important thing you should be doing prior to law school is developing the proper mindset. Transposing a classic U.S. military recruiting slogan, law school's not just an adventure—it's a job. If every law student approached law school as they would a full-time job, more would excel at it. Accept that law school is going to be a full-time endeavor marked by long, sometimes tedious hours. Accept that you're going to have to sacrifice a lot of the leisure time you enjoyed in your pre-law student life.

Think about it. Suppose instead of going to law school, you accepted a career-type job in your field of study from undergraduate school, a job offering potentially great rewards for good performance, as well as the possibility of getting canned for poor performance. Would you:

- Show up late for work?
- Browse the web and send instant messages to friends during important company meetings?
- Arrive unprepared for a meeting with your boss?
- Skip work on days when you have a conflicting social event?

- Stay out late drinking and partying on weeknights when you know you have to get up early and go to work?

- Search for ways to cut corners in completing important job assignments, rather than giving them your best effort?

Presumably the answer to each question would be *no*, yet some law students follow exactly these behavioral patterns in law school. If you approach law school as a full-time job, you will have already charted a course toward success.

Forget what you think you know about law.

You've heard the adage that a little knowledge is a dangerous thing. Nowhere is this truer than when starting law school. On the first day of Torts, I tell my students that if they think they know something about the law, *please* try to forget it. Why? Because everything people think they know about the law when they get to law school is wrong, incomplete, taken out of context, or not in the form that your professors will want you to know it.

Beginning students without any legal background are sometimes alarmed when it seems that some of their classmates already know a lot about the law. Perhaps these students took a few undergraduate law courses. Some may have worked as secretaries or paralegals at law firms. Don't worry. The latter may know something about how law is practiced in real life, but no one without a legal education really knows anything about "the law." Most importantly, no one coming to law school knows anything about law that will be useful in helping them perform academically in the first year.

Trust that law school will teach you what you need to know, or at least give you the tools to acquire that knowledge. That's why you can go to law school with an undergraduate degree in religion or art history, but can attend medical school only with a background in science. Arrive at law school imagining your brain as a fresh, new sponge, ready to absorb a whole new world of information and way of thinking.

Expect and embrace uncertainty.

New law students arrive expecting the law to be a neat and tidy catalog of rules that they can memorize and, by doing so, become successful students and lawyers. They're perplexed and frustrated to discover that so much of law is awash in shades of gray rather than black and white. "It depends" is the most accurate answer to many legal questions. Students also struggle with the fact that the complex pieces of law do not fit neatly together like a jigsaw puzzle.

Part of this indeterminacy stems from the fact that the U.S. is a "common law" legal system. Most of the rest of the world, including all of Europe and Latin America, follows what is known as the "civil law tradition." Common law is judge-made law, derived from and developed through case precedent. In civil law systems, law is derived primarily from codes—i.e., books of neatly organized statutes promulgated by legislators. In theory, judges have no power to make law in civil law systems. Their job is to follow the rules set forth in the codes. (It doesn't really work that way in practice, as all legal language requires interpretation.)

Exasperated by the indefiniteness of the law, U.S. law students frequently utter comments such as, "Why don't they just write all the rules down in one place? That way, we'd know what the law is!" Without realizing it, they're advocating for a civil law system. Someone actually tried to do that once. In the eighteenth century, Frederick the Great implemented the Prussian Code under Prussia's civil law system. The Prussian Code stands as an attempt to install what so many U.S. law students desperately wish for: a detailed compendium of rules intended to foresee and govern the entire range of human conduct. The Prussian Code contained more than 17,000 provisions setting forth specific rules designed to govern specific fact situations. It didn't work. Even 17,000 provisions proved to be insufficient to cover all varieties of human conduct. Seventeen million provisions might not be enough.

When I workshopped a chapter of this book with a group of colleagues, I asked them to name the most important traits of successful law students. Immediately, one of my colleagues blurted out, "The ability to embrace uncertainty!" Accept before you arrive at law school that much of law is vague and malleable, as it must be to address the infinite permutations of human, corporate, and governmental actions and interactions.

Students who fixate on searching for "the answer" to every legal question can drive both themselves and their professors mad. Arrive open to the idea that the answer to many legal questions is a range of possibilities, frequently dependent on the facts of the case, rather than a single rock-solid right answer. Embrace uncertainty.

Define "success" for yourself.

Figure out what you want out of law school before you get there. "Success" can mean different things to different people. For most incoming students, success means achieving at a high academic level and this book operates on the assumption that "grade success" is at least part of the goal for most readers. But not all students come to law school with the goal of graduating in the top echelon of their class. Many part-time students with existing careers, for example, attend law school to advance their lives and careers in a practical way. They're interested in getting a law degree, not necessarily a law degree with honors.

Of course, every student has a goal of succeeding at an academic level high enough to avoid being academically dismissed, so advice pertaining to academic success applies to every student at some level. Hopefully, your academic aspirations are higher than the bare minimum necessary to avoid getting booted out of law school, but if they're not, filter the advice herein in accordance with your own goals.

But success also has meaning beyond academic achievement. Many students care about *more* than just grades. In addition to academic success, they care about things like justice, exploration, enlightenment, general happiness, and becoming a "professional."

Define success for yourself. Literally. Put it in writing. Begin the sentence with "My definition of success in law school is ..." and complete the sentence. Or make a list if your idea of success includes several components. Putting it in writing will force you to think more concretely about what you really want and need out of law school. Revisit the definition as you progress through the first year. If you notice it changing, stop and consider why. As discussed later, law school has a way of changing people's goals and values.

Pre-Arrival "To Do" List: The Tangibles

Some tangible tasks also should be on your pre-law school "To Do" list, although not as many as you might think. Let's take a look.

Buy some books (but not as many as everyone wants you to buy).

Books, books, and more books. Everywhere you turn. Piles of books. Thick books. Expensive books. Complex books. Distinctively colored red, blue, and brownish-red books. If the law could have intimate relations, it would be with a book. It wouldn't be pretty, but a lot of things in law aren't. This section breaks down the different types of books associated with starting law school and offers advice on what to buy and when to buy it.

• **Law school recommended reading lists.** Law schools inadvertently perpetuate the belief among incoming students that they should be trying to learn about the law and legal analysis before getting to law school by distributing or posting on their websites recommended pre-law reading lists. Most of these lists contain at least fifty books, many of them deep, dense tomes about jurisprudence and legal history. One law school list recommends more than three hundred books.

Many of the works that appear on these lists, such as Karl Llewellyn's *The Bramblebush: On Our Law and Its Study* (1951) and Edward H. Levi's *An Introduction to Legal Reasoning* (1949), are classics that probably should be read at some point in every lawyer's life. But laboring to comprehend this dense material, especially without any context, may spike your anxiety level and fry your synapses before you ever set foot in the door.

Certainly, much good would come from reading the great books about American jurisprudence and legal history. In a perfect world with unlimited leisure time, every law student, lawyer, and law professor should read them all. We'd be smarter, better-informed, and more capable readers and thinkers. But, of course, most of us don't have that kind of time. The good news is that you don't need to read any of the heady tomes to do well in law school.

If you insist on doing serious reading, select books that offer knowledge and insight into the structure and functioning of American government, particularly the structure of and roles filled by courts. Avoid all books that purport to teach law per se.

• **"How to Succeed" books.** Many of the recommended reading lists include less lofty books from the "how to succeed in law school" genre, hopefully including this one. A variety of these books exists. Most of them offer good information and advice. Some of the books written by law professors are excellent. This one, of course, is indispensable. (Successfully fought off urge to insert smiley-face emoticon, for which I know you are grateful.)

I intentionally didn't look at any of the other law school prep books while composing this manuscript because I didn't want to be influenced by them, even if only unconsciously. After I finished a complete draft, I did flip through several of them. What I discovered was affirming. Much of the advice is not only consistent with my advice, but remarkably identical to it. Not all of it though. I read some advice in one book written by a non-law prof that was downright *scary*. Sift through all advice in law school prep books, including mine, with a discerning eye. Be wary of books that offer shortcuts to success.

• **Inspirational books.** For enjoyable inspiration about your new pursuit, check out one of these true-life page-turners about the power of lawyers and the law to change lives:

• Jonathan Harr, *A Civil Action* (1996). A tenacious, flamboyant lawyer gives his all in taking on a large corporation accused of dumping cancer-causing solvents into the groundwater in Woburn, Masschusetts. John Travolta and Robert Duvall starred in an inferior 1998 movie version.

• Anthony Lewis, *Gideon's Trumpet* (1964). A small-time criminal named Clarence Earl Gideon changes history by appealing his burglary conviction to the U.S. Supreme Court, resulting in a landmark decision establishing the right to counsel for indigent criminal defendants. Henry Fonda played Gideon in a 1979 movie version, but the book is better.

- Gerald Stern, *The Buffalo Creek Disaster* (1977). A gripping account of litigation filed on behalf of hundreds of survivors of a horrific West Virginia coal mine disaster against the company responsible for it. The only movie account is a documentary. Hollywood, what are you waiting for?

- **Study aids.** You will become very familiar with law school "study aids." A study aid is a book that, unlike your casebooks, clearly explains the law in particular subject areas, either in an outline or treatise-like format. Study aids have traveled an interesting journey through legal education. When I was in law school, our professors threatened us with mayhem if they laid eyes on a study aid in class. Professors referred to them derisively as "commercial" study aids, as if expensive casebooks are distributed by non-profit organizations. While some professors still look down on study aids, many actually recommend particular study aids to students.

The overall quality of modern law school study aids is quite high because most are written by law professors who are experts in the particular field. Study aid series come in a wide variety. Appendix A lists and briefly describes the different study aid series offered by U.S. law book publishers. If nothing else, the sheer length of the list should convince you not to rush out and start buying any study aids until you acquire more information about what you really need. That so many study aids exist should tell you something about the nature of legal education. Law may be the only educational discipline where students feel compelled to routinely buy external books to explain what they're supposed to be learning from their assigned books.

Study aids can be very helpful not only in elucidating legal doctrine but in casting what you're learning into a coherent framework that makes it easier to see the big picture. Depending on the professor, they can be a lifesaver. Frankly, some professors just aren't very good at or concerned about conveying the law they expect you to know for the exam in a complete or organized fashion.

Just don't make the mistake of substituting study aids for reading your casebook assignments and taking good notes in class. Study aids are only useful as a supplement, not a substitute. In grading exams, professors want you to present the law in the way they taught it to you. It's always obvious when students are regurgitating something they read in a study aid because the content and presentation will be different from the way the professor taught it. That doesn't mean the answer is necessarily wrong, although it can be, but it won't fit the professor's conception of how the issue should be analyzed and, thus, the professor's preconception of what he or she is looking for on the exam.

• **Books required and recommended by professors.** The only books you absolutely must buy are those your professors assign as "required." Your law school will give you the list of these books in a hard copy form and/or publish the list on the law school website. Buy required books as soon as the list is made available to avoid confronting the common snag where the law school bookstore runs out of the books you need.

Some law school texts come with paperbound supplements (sold separately, of course) containing new cases and statutes designed to keep the book up-to-date until the next edition comes out. It's easy to overlook the supplements, so take your time when reviewing the list and poking around the bookshelves.

Buy all required texts and make sure you buy the *correct edition*. Casebooks are updated in new editions every few years. Because the page numbers always will be different, an outdated edition is worthless even if 95 percent of the content stays the same. You won't be able to follow the assignments and you won't be able to follow along in class if you don't have the correct edition. When the professor says, "Let's read the case holding at the top of page 825, four lines down," you don't want to be lost. Required texts simply are not an item to skimp on.

An age-old quandary faced by higher-education students at every level is whether to buy new or used books. Law school texts are expensive. New casebooks can cost more than $150. Expect to fork out $600–plus for your first-semester books if you buy them all new. Used books cost less, but even when I was a destitute law student, I always opted for new books, and you should do the same. You want to be able to learn the law and legal analysis without the distraction of someone else's thought pattern memorialized by highlighting, underlining, and marginalia. For all you know, that someone could have flunked out of law school. But even if you could lay your hands on the used book of the person who wrote the top paper for the course, you're still better off learning from a clean slate.

Consistent with what I've already said, don't attempt to read even required books prior to starting law school (other than your first assignments). Not only will it be a waste of time, it will be counterproductive because you won't have a proper foundation or context to understand what you're reading. Nor will you remember any of it. I once had a student who spent the summer before law school reading and briefing the cases in her casebooks. When she boasted this fact to me at the beginning of the semester, I cringed. I respected her for being so motivated and diligent, but knew she had made a grave error. I told her to throw away everything she had prepared and start fresh, but she didn't listen. She attempted to rely on her pre-prepared briefs in the first semester. Sadly (because she was a dedicated student and nice person), she did not make it past the first year.

At most, skim through your casebooks to get a feel for what a casebook is. Look at the table of contents. Read the preface. Okay, I know you won't be able to resist taking a peek at some of the cases, but don't try to understand them until you get to law school.

In addition to required texts, many professors list one or more *recommended* texts. Some of them might be study aids. With regard to books that are merely recommended, even by the professor, it's generally wise to hold off buying them until you get more information. Some professors may list several recommended books, none of which you really need. Or they may list several study aids, any one of which would suffice. Since you won't need any of these books until law school starts, wait until you arrive before shelling out cash for them. The exception is if the professor has recommended a *single* study aid for the course. A professor would do that only if he or she had personally reviewed and approved of the contents as consistent with the way the prof teaches the course. Buy it.

● **Law dictionary.** Finally, buy a *Black's Law Dictionary*. This is an essential tool for any first-year student. Even experienced lawyers and law professors consult this classic reference work. At the beginning of law school, you'll be inundated with words and phrases that are foreign to you.

Some professors will expect you to look up all unfamiliar legal terms and will express disapproval if they call on you to ask the meaning of a term and you don't know the answer. A big part of the first year of law school is learning the language of the law.

The hardcover version (eighth edition as of this writing) is a worthwhile investment since it is a book you will keep even after law school. The paperbound version (third edition), however, will suit most of your needs, sells for half as much, and can be carried around. The thick hardcover version is for home use only. As with all law books, you're better off with the latest edition, but if you're on a tight budget, you can scrimp here and get by with a used, older edition. Most of the terms you'll be looking up have been around for a long, long time.

Of course, as you might imagine, legal dictionaries are also available online, but I'd stick with *Black's*. It's also available online, through Westlaw, a legal research database, but you might not be granted instant access to Westlaw at your law school.

Discover your "law-learning personality."

Most law students are bright people. Beyond that, it's hard to generalize about them. As is true of any large group of people, an entering law school class contains a wide variety of personality types. Teaching and learning styles that work best for some students don't work as well for others. Similarly, not all law school advice works equally well for all people. If you're interested in figuring out your own law-learning style, a couple of excellent tools are available to do just that.

About fifteen years ago, a college English professor who was auditing Torts introduced me to the Myers–Briggs Type Indicator (MBTI), an instrument for measuring personality preferences based on Swiss psychologist Carl Jung's research into psychological types. The MBTI is designed to help people understand certain core personality preferences that affect the way they gather information, make decisions, organize their lives, and interact with people and the world around them. If the name sounds familiar, it could be that you've already taken the MBTI in a different educational or career context. Extensively validated, the MBTI is the world's most widely administered personality measuring instrument for mentally "normal" (if there is such a thing) people. Roughly two million people take the MBTI each year.

The MBTI identifies sixteen psychological types based on eight paired personality preferences:

Extraversion vs. Introversion (how we direct and develop our energy—inward or outward—and interact with the world around us)

Sensing vs. Intuition (how we perceive and take in information upon which to make decisions)

Thinking vs. Feeling (how we make decisions)

Judging vs. Perceiving (the ways we organize our lives and operate in the world)

A person's type is a four-letter combination of their preferences as to all four pairings. For example, I'm an ENFJ (Extraverted, Intuitive, Feeling, Judging). Each type has its strengths and weaknesses for addressing different life challenges in education, employment, relationships, etc.

Several excellent books have been written about the MBTI and psychological typing, but now law students have the benefit of an outstanding MBTI book written just for them: *Juris Types: Learning Law through Self–Understanding* (2007).[4] Authors Martha and Don Peters are law faculty members and MBTI gurus who have spent decades researching the MBTI and its application to law students. *Juris Types* is filled with practical information about the learning strengths and weaknesses for each of the sixteen MBTI types in tackling the core challenges of law school: studying, classroom participation, and exam-writing.

Let's use Extraversion and Introversion as an example. The Peters' research shows that Extraverts find it easier to participate in class and enjoy working in study groups, while Introverts may not be able to access and demonstrate their knowledge as easily when called on in class and need and prefer solitary over group study. Extraverts tend to write more rather than less on exams, but may analyze problems at a superficial level due in part to an absence of any external verbal cues. Introverts may engage in deeper internal analysis, but may not write down everything they've mentally

4. MARTHA M. PETERS & DON PETERS,   UNDERSTANDING (2007).
JURIS TYPES: LEARNING LAW THROUGH SELF-

processed.[5] For each type, the Peters offer strategies about how to maximize strengths and overcome challenges. If you're curious about how your personality is cut out for learning law, take the MBTI (it's available online for a fee) or track down your old results if you've taken it before and read the Peters' book.

Even if you don't take the MBTI or read the Peters' book, it's important to recognize and be aware that students have different learning styles. As Professor Chris Coughlin recommends in Chapter 17, one way to bolster your self-understanding is to look back on your educational experiences and "determine whether there is a common denominator in the teachers, environments, situations, and subjects in which you responded most positively and successfully." While Coughlin's suggestion is directed at legal writing courses, it applies across the board. Think also about the other side of the coin: to which kinds of teachers, environments, situations, and subjects did you respond most negatively and unsuccessfully?

In addition to helping you succeed at a higher level, developing an awareness of your learning preferences can help you overcome confusion and self-doubt arising from differences between the ways you and your classmates are experiencing law school. You'll better understand, for example, why some of your classmates love the way Professor X teaches, while you find her impossible to follow, or why you love contract law and hate constitutional law when your best friend feels exactly the opposite.

Buy a notebook computer and become adept at using it.

By the time you're about to enter law school, it's too late to perfect the most important skills you will need—such as reading comprehension and writing skills—but one important ability you might still have time to hone is your computer adeptness. Notebook computers have become standard appendages for most modern law students. If I were enrolling in law school again, I wouldn't think of showing up without a notebook computer. Not everyone agrees. In fact, the use of computers in law school classrooms is quite controversial among law professors, with some professors banning them and many more talking about banning them. More about that

5. *See id.* at 26–30.

in Chapter 6. In the meantime, here's why I believe you should be toting a notebook computer wherever you go:

• **Note-taking.** A large percentage of undergraduate students already own notebook computers, but might not have used them routinely to take notes in class. Effective note-taking is essential to succeeding in most law school courses, as explained in Chapter 12. The avalanche of complex material covered in class comes at students quickly. If you can type faster than you write by hand, you'll be able to capture more of it. Computerized notes also are easier to add to, edit, and reorganize. Moreover, much of the content of your course outlines (see Chapter 13) will be inputted from your class notes. Thus, typing your notes will save you the time and effort of having to transcribe them on computer or by hand later.

• **Exam-taking.** Regardless of whether you choose to take class notes on a computer, you will want to use a computer to take exams. The same basic reasons why computers can be valuable for taking notes—faster (and, hence, more) writing and more efficient editing and reorganization—also support using a computer for exams. Accurate, complete legal analysis requires much more depth than most students allot to it on exams. While longer is not always better, as discussed in Chapter 15, in reviewing a batch of recent Torts exams, I found that the top-scoring essay-writers wrote, on average, 40 percent more words than the lowest scorers.

Using a computer to type essay exam answers also facilitates clarity and organization. Law schools use one of several types of anti-cheating software for students taking exams on computer. Basically, these software programs convert your computer into a high-tech typewriter by blocking access to files or programs. The security software gives schools the flexibility to enable or disable various word-processing functions. Most schools, for example, disable the spell-check function to avoid giving computer users an advantage over hand-writers, but they usually enable the cut-and-paste function, which is a much bigger advantage. Because organization counts on exams, being able to rearrange text is a tremendous luxury.

Taking exams on computer also avoids problems that arise from illegible handwriting. Several non-law school studies have shown that students with better handwriting get better grades than students with poor handwriting. Typed words beat the best handwriting in the world. Anything you can do to make your exams more presentable and readable gives you a boost.

In 2001, three professors at Brigham Young University published a study in which they empirically tested the proposition that computer-keyboarding gives students an advantage over handwriting on law school exams. While more data would be needed to draw reliable conclusions, the study found that computer users received higher grades than those who wrote exams by hand.[6]

• **Research and other uses.** You'll also need a computer to do online research and type your memoranda and briefs for your legal research and writing courses. Additionally, most professors maintain online course sites called "TWEN sites" (see Chapter 6) which students need to be able to readily access. Many professors use the TWEN email function to communicate with students on a regular basis, sometimes about time-sensitive matters such as changes in reading assignments. While all law schools have computer labs with desktop computers for student use, having a notebook computer gives you more flexibility and is more convenient.

• **Beg, borrow or ... well, just beg or borrow.** If you don't have the money for a notebook computer, borrow it. Look at a notebook computer as a cost of your education, no different from tuition or books. If you have a loved one who wants to contribute to your law school success, tell them you need a notebook computer. Because computers are tangible and have a fixed price, they're easier to ask for than cash.

• **A different view from a student worth listening to.** I said at the beginning that many of the questions about law school success have more than one right answer depending on the student and computer use is a good example. Having made it sound like you're doomed to failure if you

6. *See* Kif Augustine–Adams, Suzanne B. Hendrix & James R. Rasband, *Pen or Printer: Can Students Afford to Handwrite Their Exams?*, 51 J. LEGAL EDUC. 118 (2001). Reviewing 2,588 first-year exams, the authors concluded that both mean and median grades were higher for students who typed their exams over students who handwrote them. Although the difference was small (roughly one-tenth of a point on a 4.0 scale), the authors said it was enough to make a significant difference in class rank for many students at BYU. Possible explanations offered by the authors for the higher grades by computer users included the easier readability of typed exams and the ability to write longer answers.

don't own or haven't mastered a notebook computer, let's hear a dissenting view from a student who finished number one in her class after the first year:

I disagree somewhat with your treatment of computers in the book. I know that you are a strong proponent of computer use in law school, but I have equally strong views to the contrary and I think you may have come down too strongly on one side of this issue to be helpful to all students. I did not have a laptop or home computer for the first year. I used the computer lab for all assignments and tasks that required a computer. I recently bought a laptop over the summer and have already started to notice the detrimental effect it has on my study habits. On the days I do not bring my computer to campus with me, I am very efficient and am able to complete homework assignments quickly and accurately. On the days I do bring it, I usually am able to get some work done, but I spend more time compulsively checking my email or looking for obscure LPs on eBay than I do working on my case comment or doing online research.

In addition to being a distraction, I do not find computers helpful in the classroom setting either, although I'm sure I don't speak for most students. Although I now have a computer, I never use it in class. I know I am in the minority here, but I have always written much faster than I type. Even after becoming more proficient on the keyboard, I continue to retain much more information when I write. I have talked to a number of people who notice a similar difference in their retention of material when they write as opposed to type. For example, our Civil Procedure class last year did not allow laptop usage. Despite the difficulty of this class, some of my classmates did better in Civil Procedure than in their other classes where laptops were permitted. As a result, these students have made the decision to no longer use laptops to take notes in class and have indicated to me that they are already noticing an improvement in retention.

Additionally, I think there is a lot of merit to the argument that laptop usage in class gets in the way of students engaging with the material. I know that most students prefer to use computers, but I believe that there is a not-insignificant minority who learn much better by taking written notes in class and I think that these students might be misled by this section of your book. Since learning styles are largely idiosyncratic, I think it's important to emphasize that if you know you're not a computer person, don't try to be one.

Her points, which are shared by some other students and also some professors, are well-taken and hard to argue with since she performed so well. But note, significantly, her statement that she writes "much faster" by hand than by keyboard. If that is true about you as well, it undermines one of the principal advantages of computers for both note- and exam-taking. As she says, "if you know you're not a computer person, don't try to be one," at least not right out of the starting gate. Also, key to benefiting from a notebook computer is using it properly, which is discussed in Chapters 6 and 12.

Buy other essential school supplies.

In addition to books and a computer, I recommend getting:

• **A three-ring binder with tabbed dividers for each of your courses.** Three-ring binders are an efficient way to organize and keep track of all of your course materials (e.g., notes, case briefs, outlines, course handouts, research). As you might imagine, many students rely on their notebook computers as digital binders, while an increasing number use special computer note-taking programs such as Microsoft OneNote to organize and manage their course data (see Chapter 12). I work better with hard copies of things, but that may be part personal learning style and part generational. But even if you manage your case briefs, notes, and outlines on computer, you'll still need notebooks to keep track of paper materials such as course handouts and research for your legal writing courses.

• **A heavy-duty three-hole punch.** If you go the three-ring binder route, spring for a three-hole punch. You don't want to be jamming holes in the paper with the binder ring like we did back in elementary school. Get a heavy duty one. They don't call it "the paper chase" for nothing.

• **A box of highlighters.** You'll need more, but one box will get you started. I prefer monochromatic yellow, but many students use a color-coded highlighting system when reading cases.

• **A large backpack or airline carry-on-type bag with wheels.** You're going to be carting around a ton of stuff in law school. Casebooks are heavy—hardcover-bound and running between 900–1500 pages. You'll also have your computer and accessories, study aids, research for your legal research and writing course, notes, briefs, outlines (preferably neatly organized in three-ring binders as described above), and personal items to carry. Guys usually opt for backpacks, while many women go for luggage on wheels. Today's law school classrooms look like a gate area at La-Guardia.

Don't worry about style. Functionality is the key. This comment from a 1L about things she wished she knew at the beginning of law school made me smile:

> I remember the first day I brought this cute laptop bag thinking of how professional I looked. When I got to school I realized that I couldn't fit any of my books in it. And after seeing everyone with their huge backpacks the first day, as soon as I got out of class I went and bought a huge backpack of my own. I think I ended up with one of the biggest backpacks in the class!

• **A day planner.** As detailed in Chapter 10, one of the top habits of successful law students is that they are organized. That chapter explains why you need to assiduously keep track of the many events and deadlines in your new law school life. I like to do it with an old-fashioned day planner with real paper. If you follow suit, make sure you get one with pages and calendar spaces large enough to pencil in several items per day. Of course, many people keep track of their schedules on portable electronic devices, such as personal digital assistants (PDAs) and cell phones. That's fine if you're adept at using—and will use—the calendaring function.

Relax and enjoy!

Finally, here's a "To Do" task you can relate to. Surprising as it may sound, one of the best ways to prepare for law school, assuming you have your life in order, is to just kick back and enjoy your summer. Unless you plan on attending another graduate program after law school, the summer before law school may very well be your last chance until retirement to enjoy an extended break. After the first year, there will be pressure to clerk at a law firm in the summer or do an intern-or externship. Write-on competitions to become a member of the law review are held in the summer after your first year. And, of course, there's summer school, which a substantial percentage of students attend.

So take a vacation. Exercise. Eat well. Get in good physical shape. Enter law school rested and ready to go.

CHAPTER 3
FEAR FACTOR: TOP FIVE LAW STUDENT WORRIES

"Come to the edge," he said. They said, "We are afraid." "Come to the edge," he said. They came. He pushed them . . . and they flew.

Guillaume Appollinaire

If you're stressed out about beginning law school, you can at least take comfort in the fact that you have lots of company. You're all in the same boat. Every 1L you meet, whether they show it or not, will be feeling the same feelings you are. Two weeks into the first semester, I asked a group of students to name their "biggest surprise" about law school. One student wrote: "My biggest surprise is that everyone feels the same way that I do. My insecurities are shared among most of my 152 peers. That provides tremendous comfort in that I am not the only one feeling overwhelmed, scared, stressed, and excited all at once."

Not only are your new colleagues as anxious as you are, they're stressing about the same things. Law students tend to think their fears are unique, but they're not. Evidence to support this conclusion comes from a questionnaire I've been distributing to incoming students for more than a decade. One question asks: "What is your greatest fear about law school?" Everywhere I've taught, all across the country, the answers repeat themselves. From reading hundreds of these questionnaires, I've identified five of the most common worries shared by new law students:

- Failure/failing to meet personal expectations.

27

- Socratic method/getting called on in class.

- Not understanding the material.

- Detrimental impact on non-law school life, especially relationships.

- Not being able to keep up with the workload.

I'd like to assure you that all of these fears are baseless, but I can't. Each of the fears listed above has a legitimate basis in reality. The problem is that students don't properly calibrate them. They exaggerate some fears, while underestimating others. Let's look at them individually.

Failure/Failing to Meet Personal Expectations

Failure is the most common answer I receive in response to my fear question. Here I have some good news. If failure is defined to mean failing to achieve and maintain the GPA necessary to remain a student in good standing (generally a 2.0)—i.e., getting kicked out of law school—the picture isn't as bleak as most imagine. Because admissions standards at most ABA-approved law schools are high, the average attrition rate due to academic reasons is quite low.

Analysis of data compiled in the 2006 *ABA/LSAC Official Guide to ABA–Approved Law Schools* shows that in 2003–04, the average 1L attrition rate for academic reasons for all ABA-approved schools was about 3.4 percent, although the percentages vary by school. Sixty-one of the total 189 responding law schools reported no first-year attrition for academic reasons.[7]

The 3.4 percent figure is misleading, however. The real failure rate is somewhat higher, since it is common for struggling students who see the handwriting on the walls to withdraw from law school before they are academically dismissed. But even when attrition *for all reasons* is considered, analysis of the ABA/LSAC data reflects an overall average attrition rate for first-year students of only about 10 percent.

---

7. *See* ABA/LSAC OFFICIAL GUIDE TO ABA–APPROVED LAW SCHOOLS (Wendy Margolis, Bonnie Gordon, Joe Puskarz & David Rosenlieb eds., 2006). Attrition percentages are not reported. My research assistants arrived at the overall percentage figure by dividing the total number of first-year students enrolled in the 189 reporting schools in 2003–04 (48,867) by the total number of students who attritted for academic reasons after the first year (1,682).

These figures should help alleviate fears you might have about "flunking out," *assuming* you fully apply yourself. The bottom line is that in most law school courses, in a typical 1L section of seventy to eighty students, you generally have to out-perform only ten or at most fifteen students to be assured of receiving grades that will enable you to remain in law school.

A common variation on the failure fear is the fear of not living up to one's own expectations. Most students in law school have performed well academically their entire lives. For students who have been good pupils since the first grade, failure doesn't just mean flunking out. It means not excelling.

In a recent class, for example, one student answered the "greatest fear" question by saying: "Failure, not as in failing a class or performing poorly. My fear is primarily that I will not successfully meet or exceed my own expectations." Another set a specific bar: "Failing (as in anything below a *B-*)—and yes, I know that is an unreasonable standard for my first year of law school!" Yes, that is an unreasonable standard. Prepare yourself to see some *C*s on that first grade report.

The fear of not living up to high personal expectations is more well-grounded than the fear of being academically dismissed. Law schools are full of high achievers. Instead of competing against students like your undergraduate roommate who sat in his dorm room smoking a bong and listening to Pink Floyd all night, you're competing against motivated, talented people with track records of academic accomplishment.

Many fine law students who will become excellent lawyers do not get the grades they want and expect. If you come to law school expecting *A*s, you're likely to be disappointed. Generally, only about 10 percent of the students in a first-year law school class receive any form of *A* grade (i.e., *A+*, *A*, or *A-*), which translates to only seven or eight *A* grades in an average-size class. Sometimes it's fewer. Just recently, I was barraged by students complaining that one of my colleagues dished out only one *A-* in a first-year Property class of more than seventy students. Thus, if everyone's standard for success is to make *A*s or be in the top 10 percent of their class, 90 percent of students are doomed to feel like failures. The good news is that it doesn't take *A*s to be a successful law student.

I always tell my students that a *C* in law school is a certification that they have demonstrated, among a group of talented people, the ability to be a competent lawyer, which is no small feat. I go on to emphasize that any form of *B* grade (i.e., *B*+, *B* or *B*-) in law school is a cause for breaking open a bottle of champagne and celebrating. In law school, I tell them, "*B* is the new *A*." Still, they don't listen.

Once I was in my office working at my computer. I had just posted the Torts grades outside the door. Out of the corner of my eye, I could see students coming and going to check their grades. I pretended not to notice, both to give them some privacy and to avoid having to deal with their disappointment until they had time to process it.

I noticed a young man I'll call Devin standing in the hall studying the grade sheet. He stayed there a long time. I liked Devin. He overcame a lot of odds to get to law school. He participated in class, seemed well-prepared, and struck me as a serious student. After a couple of minutes, I finally turned to look at him. The disappointment on his face was palpable. He appeared to be wiping tears away. He must have flunked, I thought. I felt terrible. Our ensuing conversation went something like this:

Me: Hey, Devin, how're you doing?

Him: [disconsolately] Not too good, professor.

Me: What's wrong? [As if I didn't know.]

Him: I—I didn't do very well. I'm really disappointed in myself.

Me: [hesitantly] What grade did you get? That's if you want to tell me. You don't have to.

Him: I only got a *B*+.

Me: A *B*+? Devin, you got a *B*+? That's *B* as in boy?

Him: [hangdog face] That's right, professor.

Me: Devin, I want to jump across this desk right now both to give you a hug for doing so well and also to strangle you for scaring the bejeezus out of me.

Lower your performance expectations or you'll drive yourself insane even if you're a good student. Since students don't listen to this advice when I give it, maybe it will help to hear this "forget your expectations" advice from a 1L:

It's hard to have this image of yourself as a Top Student crumble. I hear that from many other students, and I think that if one doesn't realize that EVERYONE is feeling this, it may seem that everyone else has it all together and you're the only one struggling. Most people who come to law school have probably heard all their lives, from first grade onward, that they are "smarter." In college, scholarships get thrown your way, you win special fellowships or work for your professors on special projects. You have this feeling of being "good" at this school thing and feeling competent.

I think the Socratic Method (hearing someone give an answer that seems so much more intelligent than whatever you were thinking), and the evaluation method (not having feedback through assignments and midterm tests and what not) can really mess with you. I received an email from a fellow student. She's a student I think people assume "has it all together," and she said, "I feel like I'm hanging on by my fingernails." My personal metaphor for law school is one of a mouse running on a wheel. You've seen mice running too fast and the next thing, they're spinning around with the wheel. I feel that if I stumble, the wheel will fling me off.

I know this is turning into a long answer, but I'm trying to think of how to explain this feeling to someone who hasn't begun the experience (or who is in it and feels like they're drowning). We've all heard, "This isn't like being an undergrad ... This is going to be different from anything you've known ... The playing field is now leveled ..." which is true, but I think everyone lets it go in one ear and right back out again. Law school is different than simply continuing on to grad school or some other "tougher than college" environment. In the way that the military is a "different world," I think the law school experience has that element of complete and utter "forget your expectations; forget what you thought you knew."

While the student's comments may sound bleak, once again, take comfort in the fact that the feelings he expressed are nearly universal among first-year law students. In the meantime, while it sounds platitudinous, just be the best law student you can be. You will have no way of predicting what kind of a law student you will be grade-wise because, except in your legal writing course, you're unlikely to receive any performance feedback until the first semester is over. Trust that if you apply yourself Consistently, Rigorously, Efficiently, Diligently, and Organizedly (see the CREDO to live by in Chapter 10) from the very beginning, you will maximize your opportunity to succeed at your highest potential—the most that any person can do. Academic dismissal of students who follow a committed, sound approach to law school is uncommon.

Socratic Method/Getting Called On

Another commonly expressed fear, which I vividly recall experiencing as a beginning student, is being victimized by the Socratic teaching method, which emphasizes cold-calling on students to recite and analyze cases from the assigned reading. As one student articulated it:

> I was terrified of being called on—not of the act itself, but of the all-consuming silence that would follow the calling of my name, as eighty other people waited to see if I would sink or swim. Having a multitude of witnesses to a potential humiliation was a very unpleasant thought. Yet though my hands shook the first time I heard stentorian tones say "Ms. _____," and I felt sick with nervous apprehension with every question the professor posed—one after another after another—when he turned to someone else, I felt as if I had passed some test.

The student's reaction to the Socratic method mirrors those of many, both her initial fear and subsequent relief and satisfaction when she realized she could, in fact, "pass the test" of this unique rite of passage in American legal education. Chapters 7 and 8 are devoted to the Socratic method and class participation, so we'll postpone in-depth discussion of those matters. For now, just let me assure you that the horrors of the Socratic method are greatly exaggerated and that being terrorized by professors should be among the very least of your concerns.

Not Understanding the Material

A third frequently expressed fear is not understanding the material. While this anxiety could be seen merely as a variation of the failure theme, it falls into a discrete category. The *no comprende*-fear is more preliminary and primal in nature than failure. Students worry that they will arrive in this new academic world and find that the legal rules they're supposed to be learning are unintelligible ciphers and, worse, that they are the only ones without a decoding manual. The fear is reflected in answers to the "greatest fear" question such as "[t]hat I would be the only person to not understand the reading" and "[t]hat everyone will 'get it' and I won't."

I'm happy to report that this fear is also overblown. Coming into law school, the law naturally seems inaccessible and unfathomable because it's a complete unknown. I remember starting law school thinking, how could I, a former journalism student, possibly understand The Law? It seemed about as likely as learning to understand how to interpret ancient runes.

Some of the first cases students are required to read confirm their worst fears about not being able to grasp the law. Below is an excerpt from a famous Torts case decided in 1616 by the King's Bench in England that beginning students often are assigned in the first week of law school. The case, *Weaver v. Ward*,[8] is the earliest known decision expressly recognizing that a defendant might not be liable for damages for a purely accidental injury occurring without fault. But it's doubtful many students ever figure that out from the opinion itself, which reads like this:

> And upon demurrer by the plaintiff, judgment was given for him; for though it were agreed, that if men tilt or turney in the presence of the King, or if two masters of defence playing their prizes kill one another, that this shall be no felony; or if a lunatick kill a man, or the like, because felony must be done animo felonico; yet in trespass, which tends only to give damages according to hurt or loss, it is not so; and therefore if a lunatick hurt a man, he shall be answer-

8.   (1616) 80 Eng. Rep. 284 (K.B.).

able in trespass; and therefore no man shall be excused of a trespass (for this is in the nature of an excuse, and not of a justification, prout ei bene licuit), except it may be judged utterly without his fault.

Er, could you run that by us again? Why couldn't those old English judges speak ... well, English? Don't worry. Modern opinions aren't nearly as bad. Once you get past the moldy-oldies still included in casebooks because of their historical significance, the reading gets easier because most modern judges write lucidly and in plain English. Take a look, for example, at the judicial opinion in *Robinson v. Lindsay* reprinted in Chapter 11 as part of a case-briefing exercise. Compared to *Weaver v. Ward*, it reads like a *My First Reader*.

As with so many other challenges that seem overwhelming when we first encounter them, learning the law becomes less intimidating with each passing day as students begin to figure out basic legal terms and procedures. One of my favorite parts of teaching 1Ls is watching the satisfaction, even joy, as the light bulbs start to go on, as students start to realize, "Hey, I really can understand this stuff! I really can learn the law!"

Don't get me wrong. A lot of the material is difficult and not all students grasp the law equally well. Some legal topics (the law of "future interests" in Property comes to mind as a quintessential 1L example) do approach utter incomprehensibility, but even those riddles can be unraveled by most students if they're willing to put in the necessary effort.

Have faith that you've been carefully prescreened by the admissions committee of your law school, which has determined you possess the ability to understand law.

Damage to Non–Law School Life, Especially Relationships

A fourth oft-repeated fear is the toll that law school will take on a student's outside life, especially their relationships with friends, families, and significant others. This fear is well-grounded. Because the first year of law school is so all-consuming, students frequently fail to tend to the needs of their preexisting social and intimate relationships, with the result that those people feel neglected and even rejected. Although empirical evidence is lacking, divorce and other relationship breakups seem to be disproportionately high among law students, just as they are among lawyers.

The heavy workload isn't the only culprit. At the same time law students are neglecting their preexisting relationships, they're fostering new ones with peers with whom they have a lot in common, friends who can relate to, understand, and enjoy (even if only in a misery-loves-company sense) conversations about contingent equitable servitudes and *Marbury v. Madison*.

Keep in mind the feelings of the non-law students who love you. Remember that while the law may be fascinating to you, it's inaccessible and usually incredibly boring to them. Moderate your conversations about the law and law school. It's natural to want to share the new experiences you're enjoying/enduring, but do so in small doses.

Imagine if the shoe were on the other foot. Imagine that your significant other enrolled in a Ph.D program studying a subject completely foreign to you, say, genetics. Every night after school, he or she waxes rapturously for hours about mitochondrial DNA and hematopoietic stem cells. When you suggest dinner and a movie one night, the response is: "Are you kidding? Not with my paper on gene-mapping due at the end of the week!" When you go out with your partner's new friends, instead of sports, music or politics, the conversation turns immediately to homologous recombination and dishing about classmates and professors you don't know. How would you feel? Left out? Threatened? Unimportant?

You're going to need the support of your non-law school friends and other loved ones. Don't drive them away. Build time with them into your schedule. You can do it if you're organized (see Chapter 10). Make an effort to include them with your new law school friends and when you all get together, don't just talk about law school. When someone starts talking about law school, change the subject. Or be even more direct. Say something like: "Let's take a break and agree not to talk about law school tonight." (See Chapter 18 for more on how to lead a balanced life.)

Invite your loved ones to attend a class with you, or even a day of classes. Most professors let people bring visitors to their classes, although you should ask first. I always encourage my students to bring friends, family members, and partners to my Torts class. Sitting through a law school class will help your loved ones understand what you're experiencing and also make them feel more a part of the experience. Many law schools have student organizations for married students or students with families, which will give your partner a chance to meet similarly situated people. At gatherings, you'll be free to chat with your classmates about res ipsa loquitur while your partner chats with your classmates' partners about what a drag is it to be married to a law student.

The disputatiousness instilled in the personalities of students by the legal education system can also interfere with relationships outside of law school. The adversarial legal system and law school teaching methods program law students to question everything. Lawyers are literally trained to argue. Argumentation skills are among the most valued tools of a lawyer's trade, but do not rank highly on the list of traits considered essential by psychotherapists to successful intimate relationships. To a lawyer, the simplest assertion is an invitation to a challenging response. If a mate complains, "You don't give me enough attention," a law student might reply: "First, we must define the word 'attention.' Attention can reasonably mean different things to different people. And does one really 'give' attention? 'Give' suggests a conveyance and since attention isn't personal or real property, it can't be conveyed." At this point, the non-law student may give up and leave the room or perhaps change strategy and win the argument by burying a heavy lamp at high velocity into the cranium of the law student.

Questioning things will be your fate. You can't become a lawyer and avoid succumbing to this condition. We can blame the institution of legal education for ramping up our proclivity for arguing, which is an innate trait of many law students to begin with, but we're the ones responsible for managing it. Since we can't divorce ourselves from it, the most we can do is be aware of the issue, explain to our loved ones that we come by this trait honestly and don't mean anything personal by it, and invite them to point out to us when we get carried away with it.

In short, the fear that law school will take a toll on outside relationships is a real one, but it's something over which you have control. Not only does law school put your relationships at risk, stormy relationships put your law school success at risk. In one study of stress in law school, the number one "crisis" cited by students for falling behind in their studies was a relationship crisis.[9]

Not Being Able to Keep Up with the Workload

This last fear deserves, in real rather than imagined terms, the top ranking on all law student apprehension lists—by far. Students obsessing about getting called on in class or not understanding the material are worrying about the wrong things. In the 1992 presidential race, political consultant James Carville came up with Bill Clinton's election-winning campaign strategy. To keep the campaign simple and on message, Carville instructed campaign workers to remember: "It's the economy, stupid." Adapting Carville's slogan to law school, "It's the workload, stupid." Memorize this and repeat it to yourself.

In my experience, the vast majority of the people who do not succeed in law school or who succeed at levels below their potential do so because *they weren't prepared to handle the overwhelming workload.* They did not arrive at law school with either the mindset or an organized plan to carefully read (and reread) a minimum of 150 pages of dense legal analysis in casebooks each week, compose case briefs for twenty-five or more complicated judicial opinions each week, attend 14–16 intense class hours each week, prepare lengthy course outlines, learn an entirely new language, research and write (and then rewrite and rewrite) intricate legal memoranda and briefs in their legal research and writing courses, and still manage to juggle the other parts of their lives, including family and other relationships and, for part-time students, full-time employment. They get behind early ... and never catch up.

* * *

Overall, a healthy trepidation starting law school is not only a good motivator, but appropriate given the reality of what you're about to embark on. I'm not talking about counterproductive paralyzing fear, which inhibits learning and mental processes, but an informed apprehension that law school is going to challenge you in ways you've never been challenged before.

9. Marilyn Heins, Shirley Nickols Fahey & Roger C. Henderson, *Law Students and Medical Students: A Comparison of Perceived Stress*, 33 J. LEGAL EDUC. 511, 520 (1983).

To not have some anxiety about law school doesn't make one brave, but foolish. It means the person is clueless about what they're getting into. In every entering class, at least one student responds to my fear question with an answer such as "No fear" or "Nothing scares me." I've never done an empirical study, but to my knowledge not a single one of those students has ended up excelling in law school.

We'll talk more about the sources of 1L stress, including tips for reducing and managing it. In the meantime, if you're a worry-wart whose fears haven't been assuaged by this chapter, let me tell you that it is quite often the case, perhaps sadly so, that the students who worry the most perform the best.

CHAPTER 4

WHAT KIND OF STUDENT DO YOU WANT TO BE (AND BE KNOWN AS)?: TWENTY LAW STUDENT TYPES

Most students arrive at law school with at least some hope that they will become a great law student. Generally, their perception of "great" is quite limited, corresponding with a high GPA. But many attributes apart from grades work to define students, both to their peers and to the faculty and staff of the law school. And the good news is that, unlike grade performance, students have more control over most of these other defining qualities.

I came up with a list of twenty types of law students based on my experience. I feel fairly confident in the list, in part because it came to me so quickly and also because I ran it by several others profs and students. I can clearly picture specific students in each category. Of course, there's spillover among the categories, with students usually displaying traits from more than one type. Some of the types evoke positive associations, while some carry clear negative connotations. Several of the types, however, are two-sided coins, with both positives and negatives.

It's worth thinking in advance about the different types of law students and which type or types you would like to become. Just as important, it's worth thinking about which kind of law student you would like to become known as. Because 1Ls take the same classes from the same professors throughout the first year, everyone gets to know everyone else reasonably well. Perhaps more accurately, everyone *thinks* they know everyone else, with opinions often based on limited evidence derived from classroom performances, extra-curricular interaction, and rumor. From the moment you arrive at law school, people—students, faculty, and staff—will be forming opinions about you based on how you conduct yourself. Many of these opinions may be off-base, but one's perception is their reality. Thus, in perusing the list below, think not only about what type of student you desire to be, but how you want to be perceived by others. Here are twenty law student types:

1. The Frequent Participators. Every law school class has a few students who participate in class discussion with significantly greater frequency than other students. Interestingly, Frequent Participators are nearly always guys. As discussed in Chapter 7, studies show women voluntarily participate in class discussions at lower rates than men.

Most professors appreciate Frequent Participators. They sure beat the non-participators. There's nothing worse for a professor than trying to generate a class discussion and being greeted with silence. Unfortunately, too many students are deterred from participating on a frequent basis out of fear of being labeled a "gunner." Gunner is a pejorative label at-tached to *really* frequent participators, students who want to express an opinion on every topic. True gunners—the ones who engender dislike from their classmates—are students who not only volunteer frequently, but tend to do so with a misplaced air of superiority.

Recently, a 1L came to my office and said he was afraid to participate in class discussion on a regular basis because he didn't want to be labeled as a gunner. He explained that during orientation an upper-level student assigned to his group as a mentor warned them not to participate frequently in class because they would be marked as gunners whom no one would like or want to study with. A month or so later, another student from the same class came to see me and expressed concern that his classmates might perceive him to be a gunner. I told him he most definitely was NOT a gunner. Rather, he was a much-appreciated, reliable partic-ipator who helped me and his class by being willing to raise his hand when others wouldn't. Other students have ex-pressed the same fears to me. Most everyone, it seems, is afraid of being labeled a gunner, except, of course, for the true gunner.

Ideally, everyone in a class would participate at a roughly equal level, but that's just not the reality of group dynamics in law school classes. First-year classes are large at most law schools, averaging seventy-seven students per section according to data one of my research assistants analyzed from the 2006 *ABA-LSAC Official Guide to ABA–Approved Law Schools*. Many students never volunteer at all. Someone has to pick up the slack.

The worry about being labeled a gunner is exaggerated. Authentic gunners are extremely small in number and easily identified. Usually there is only one dyed-in-the-wool gunner per class and sometimes none at all. When in doubt, choose to participate. The benefits of regular class participation, as explained in Chapter 8, far outweigh the risk of being stamped as a gunner. Leave it to the professors to identify the gunners. They'll deal with them appropriately, generally by simply overlooking them when they raise their hands.

2. The Regular Participators and Occasional Participators. Between the extremes of the Frequent Participator and the Stealth Student (see below) are all the other students who make some effort to voluntarily participate in class discussions. Since the Regular Participators and Occasional Participators include a large percentage of the class, they're not really discrete types. Nevertheless, they're worth identifying because voluntary class participation of any type—since it involves a public display of your courage, preparation, and analytical ability—does help define you as a student. Even occasional voluntary participation will earn you most of the benefits that come from class participation.

3. The Stealth Student. The Stealth Student is a student who manages to blend into the surroundings so well that the student's very existence remains unknown, at least to the professors. Needless to say, Stealth Students don't voluntarily participate in class. They don't do *anything* in class that would draw attention to themselves. They don't arrive late, don't talk to their neighbors, don't shuffle their books or other belongings. For all I know, they may hold their breath and fail to blink for the entire class hour.

In professor-speak, Stealth Student sometimes has an added meaning as the student who manages to remain completely anonymous during the semester, only to blow everyone else out of the water come final exam time. Every class seems to have a curve-busting Stealth Student of this type. For reasons I've never figured out, the top-ranked student in a law school class, if not anonymous, is often a quiet type. Of course, you can't really choose to be a Stealth Student in this sense of the term. You can elect to seek anonymity (see Backburners below), although I recommend against it.

4.   The Backburner. In Chapter 6, I discuss the importance of sitting in the front of the classroom from an academic success standpoint, citing research showing that students who sit in the front perform better than those who sit in the back. Here, I merely list Backburners as a type of law student and explain how they may be perceived by professors.

By necessity, large first-year classes are held in large rooms. Depending on the design of the room, students who sit in the nose-bleed seats are sometimes so far away from the action that they barely seem to be a physical part of the class. They often camp behind their computer screens, sometimes wearing baseball caps that shield what little could otherwise be seen of their faces. Most students in the back voluntarily participate in class discussions infrequently or not at all. They're essentially invisible, which indeed may be their goal.

Fairly or not, professors may interpret the Backburners' seat choice and corresponding disengagement as part of a bad or bored attitude toward the course and learning the law. This isn't always an accurate or fair assessment, because good students also choose to sit in the back. But the physical arrangement by its nature creates a barricade even for those students. The Backburners don't necessarily generate bad reputations with professors. The bigger problem is they don't generate *any* reputation because they remain faceless and anonymous, unlike . . .

5.   The Front–Row Crowd. From an alternative universe, or at least the other side of the room, are students who routinely choose to sit toward the front of the room. Professors like the Front-Row Crowd because they are more engaged in discussions and also because professors *get to know* these students. Part of this connecting may be attributable to the personalities of people who choose to sit in front, but part of it is simply a matter of proximity. I usually arrive to class at least ten minutes early to get set up. With nothing else to do, I chat with the students in the front while I'm hanging out at the podium. Thus, every class, the Front–Row Crowd gets significant face time with the prof. See Chapter 9 on the importance of getting to know your professors.

6.   The Know–It–All. You can imagine what law professors think about students who believe they know more about the law and legal education than their professors. Know–It–Alls sincerely believe that within weeks or even days of starting law school, perhaps due to supernatural phenomena, they know the law and understand how to succeed in law school better than people who have devoted their lives to these endeavors. These students, usually one in every class, can be amusing, but are mostly irritating. I remember a student who, after three days of law school, sidled into my office, plopped down in a chair, and said: "Professor, you do a pretty good job, but I'd like to give you some suggestions on how to improve your teaching." Come exam time, the Know–It–Alls are routinely exposed as Turns–Out–They Didn't–Know–Much–At–Alls.

7.   The Chronically Late. Every first-year class has a couple of students who, left to their own devices, would arrive late for class much of the time. Because their arrival is disruptive in a very public way, it won't take you long to spot this type. Most professors will not tolerate the Chronically Late, seeking to deter them through a variety of measures ranging from stern looks to locking the door. See the section on classroom etiquette in Chapter 6 for more about the importance of being punctual.

8.   The Slacker. Regrettably, despite careful screening by admissions committees, every law school class includes its share of Slackers, students who do not read their assignments, brief their cases, attend class regularly, etc. No surprise: professors have a natural lack of regard for this type of student. As one would expect, Slackers flunk out of law school at disproportionate rates.

Even worse than the regular Slacker is the Bragging Slacker; i.e., a student who actually takes pride in boasting about how they don't read their assignments or brief the cases, as if there were something appealing about being lazy and irresponsible.

9.   The Overconfident Without Cause. Most first-year law students are scared or intimidated—with cause—by the Jupiter-size amount of foreign, dense material they're expected to master, but every entering class has a few students who approach law school from a "What, me worry?" perspective. They're marked by their casual attitude toward diligent studying. While other students are preparing case briefs or outlines, the Overconfident Without Cause shrug it off with "Briefs? Outlines? Who needs 'em?' " Overconfident students often are bright, and perhaps sailed through undergraduate school with minimal effort. They seem to be unaware of the fact that the same holds true for most of their classmates.

Overconfident students rarely achieve at high levels academically in law school because their cavalier attitude diminishes their motivation to study hard. No person has cause to be overly confident about succeeding in law school. As repeated throughout this book, law school is a completely different ballgame from undergraduate or other graduate programs. Students with chart-topping LSAT scores can and do flunk out of law school.

The Overconfident Without Cause are distinguishable from the Know–It–Alls. Unlike the KIAs, the OWC don't assume they know all the answers. Their laidback self-assurance keeps them from even thinking about the questions. One reason they're overconfident is because they haven't thought deeply enough to know what they don't know.

10.   The Insecure Contrary to Evidence. At the opposite end of the continuum from the Overconfident Without Cause are the Insecure Contrary to Evidence. These are students who worry themselves sick—sometimes literally so—because they're convinced that everyone around them is smarter than they are. They have a tendency to preface statements about the future with "If I don't flunk out ...." Their self-deprecation is sincere. They really doubt their ability, even when their credentials would suggest such extreme insecurity is unfounded.

Here's a confession I rarely share: I was a certified member of the Insecure Contrary to Evidence crowd as a first-year law student, to the point where I sought medical treatment in my first semester for stress-induced gastrointestinal issues. I even considered quitting law school. Despite entering law school with a high LSAT score and undergraduate GPA, I was convinced I was a total dolt as I sat in class listening to my brilliant classmates expound. "How did they think of that? Why couldn't I have come up with that? They're so much smarter than me!" I tormented myself with these thoughts.

When the first set of grades came out, I was pleasantly surprised to discover that my insecurities were misplaced. I landed in the top five percent of my class and stayed there throughout law school.

My experience is not unique. Many of the Insecure Contrary to Evidence end up as top students. One reason is that, because of their insecurity, they are motivated to work harder to overcome their perceived shortcomings. Another factor is that they see and worry about all the little details and complexities of the law—the same fine points that escape the notice of the Overconfident Without Cause and which are so important to performing well on law school exams.

11. Mr./Ms. Reliable. How professors love these students. It takes a while to figure out who they are, because they tend to volunteer infrequently (some of them no doubt overlap with the Insecure Contrary to Evidence). But once they become known to the professor, everyone else will know who they are because professors will call on them disproportionately. These are diligent students who are *always* well-prepared. They're life preservers when the class is wallowing in a mire of cluelessness or unpreparedness. When the going gets tough in terms of getting an answer to a question, the professor will turn instinctively to a Mr./Ms. Reliable. They're the "go to" guys and gals of the class.

No great shock, members of this group usually do well in law school. If you're already a law student and find yourself getting called on disproportionately for no apparent reason, maybe you've been identified by the prof as a Mr./Ms. Reliable. Of course, you might also have been identified as a Slacker whom the professor wants to make an example of, so don't start patting yourself on the back until you've figured it out. Because of their generally quiet demeanor, more Mr./Ms. Reliables exist than are identified by the professors, which is yet another good reason to contribute voluntarily in class. You want the professor to know if you're a Mr./Ms. Reliable.

12. The Nattering Nabob of Negativism. Borrowing a phrase that former Vice–President Spiro Agnew (under

Richard Nixon) used in 1970 to describe the media, in all social environments, we regularly encounter people who whine and complain about everything. Nothing is ever right for these folks. A disproportionate number of injustices seem to befall them. In law school, they complain about their professors, their books, their assignments, their classmates, their lunch. You name it, they're unhappy with it.

For some people, complaining is just a bad habit, but some individuals are bitter and unhappy by nature. Law school is going to be stressful enough as it is. Letting it consume you with negative energy is not only unhealthy, but an unattractive quality. If you're unable to develop a positive attitude, at least try to minimize your outward manifestations of negativity. Like our parents taught us, if you can't say something nice, you're better off saying nothing.

A tangible downside of bad-mouthing people is that just about everything one says about a classmate or professor will get passed along to others because of the marble-size world that is law school. Some comments find their way back to the object of the comment.

Be positive. Keep a sense of humor about everything, including yourself. People who can laugh at themselves are healthier people. Continual complaining about your petty trials and tribulations and constant bad-mouthing of others is just going to make you feel worse.

Avoid associating with Nattering Nabobs of Negativism. It's easy to get dragged into their drag of an existence.

13. Curious George/Georgette. Curious George was a children's book character created in 1941 by H.A. Rey and Margret Rey. A mischievous ape, Curious George's defining characteristic, as his name suggests, was his unquenchable curiosity. Curious George was a lovable character, as are most students who fit into this type. Whereas many students want to know the bare minimum they need to know to succeed in law school, Curious Georges/Georgettes always want to know *more* than they need to know. Their curiosity leads them, for example, to look up the note cases following the principal cases in their casebooks, track down the unabridged versions of the principal cases to learn more facts, or research the actors, places, and history surrounding the cases and case events.

A classic example is the Curious Georgette who, on reading an old case about the consent defense to intentional torts involving a woman who was vaccinated against her wishes on board a ship sailing "from Queenstown to Boston," decided she needed to know more about Queenstown. Because the plaintiff claimed not to understand the vaccination proceedings, the student was curious about what language the woman spoke. Her research turned up the interesting factoid that Queenstown was the final port of call for the Titanic on its doomed, maiden voyage. Her curiosity also led her to track down which casebook Dean William Prosser, the King of Torts, used when he first taught Torts back in the 1930s[10] before Prosser compiled his own most-famous-of-all law school casebooks. Interesting stuff, but not information that will be helpful come exam-time.

Professors appreciate CGs. With so many students uninterested in learning anything beyond "the rules," how could they not? On the other hand, while intellectual curiosity is a great quality, students need to be careful about how they allocate their scarce time.

A subcategory of the Curious Georges/Georgettes is the student obsessed with the great "What if?" These are students who, instead of focusing on the case facts or the hypothetical facts posed by the professor, insist on exploring their own extreme fact scenarios to test the application of legal principles. Within reasonable bounds, this is a valuable mental exercise, as a large part of learning to analyze law does indeed involve applying legal rules to changing fact patterns. Many what-if inquiries are excellent questions that lead to interesting and illuminating class discussion, so please don't be discouraged to pose such questions. It only becomes a problem when a student repeatedly flogs issues to death with what-ifs taken to absurd lengths. If a Civil Procedure professor discussing personal jurisdiction queries "What if the defendant was served with process in another county?", a What–If Curious George/Georgette will want to know "What if he was on another planet?"

14. The Party Animal. Despite the heavy workload, most law students seem to find plenty of time to socialize.

10. The book Prosser used was: 1930).
FRANCIS H. BOHLEN, CASES ON TORTS (3d ed.

This is healthy, of course, to a point. The bonding that occurs among first-year students is one of the great byproducts of the "trial by ordeal"-method of legal education. But some students quickly become known as partiers first and law students second, sometimes a very distant second. Since most law school socializing involves consuming alcohol, being known as the class Party Animal often carries other negative associations with it. Party Animals are rarely top-performing law students.

15.   The Star of Rumor Central. Because law schools are cloistered, competitive environments, everyone likes to know and talk about other people's business. Rumors, some of them fantastical, swirl with frequency. Sometimes they contain a kernel of truth, but like the old pass-it-along story we played in elementary school, the stories get more distorted each time they're retold. On reading this part of the book, one of my research assistants wrote in the margin: "Rumor passing in law school is worse than it was in high school!"

That seems to be a consistent theme. In response to a survey question asking students to identify their biggest surprise about law school, another student wrote:

> Honestly, my biggest surprise has to do with my fellow classmates and all the students in law school. I almost feel like I am back in high school again. There is so much drama between guys and girls as well as just between girls. I thought at this age, people would be over worrying about who likes who, etc., but that does not seem to be the case. I guess that's what happens when you are with the same seventy people every day all day!

With everyone watching everyone else, you need to be cautious in your behavior, both academically and socially, lest you end up the target of gossipmongers. Frequently, the wholly innocent get caught up in the gossip web. If you regularly hang out and study with a person of the opposite sex (or possibly even the same sex), do not be surprised if rumors begin circulating that the two of you are "sleeping together."

Not all law school rumors are unfounded. Often, gossip attaches itself to people who behave in ways that predictably lead to gossip. Be cautious about alcohol, drugs, and sexual activities. Very little remains private in law school. Avoid letting people take untoward pictures of you at social gatherings that could end up on someone's Facebook page. In a world where digital cameras are ubiquitous, embarrassing pictures are coming back to haunt more and more people. Law firms routinely search the internet for information about recruits when making hiring decisions. Law school honor code violations can also result from such behavior.

16. The Evaluator/Judger. These two closely related types are sometimes the same person, but not always. Both spend a disproportionate amount of time sizing up the competition, the Evaluator by keeping close tabs on everyone's progress and the Judger by overtly rating his classmates as smart or not smart, often based on their classroom comments. Evaluators are obsessed with knowing everyone's grades and comparing them to their own. At one school, we had to change the entire anonymous grade-number system because an Evaluator took the time to collect and chart the grades of every 1L by exam number when the first-semester grades were posted. After that incident, the school started assigning separate exam numbers for each course (rather than simply one number per student). As for the Judger, who may also qualify as a Know–It–All, it is presumptuous in the extreme for any 1L student to believe he is qualified to evaluate the knowledge and analytical abilities of his classmates. It probably goes without saying that Evaluators/Judgers are not well-liked by their classmates.

17. The Class Joker. As someone who appreciates humor and the value of it for bolstering the sense of community and energy level in law school classrooms, I love the Class Joker. Most first-year sections will have at least one real character. These are people who like attention and, importantly, actually enjoy being the subject of good-natured ribbing from the professor.

But be sure to distinguish between being an appropriate Class Joker and someone who makes misguided attempts to be funny by uttering sarcastic or offensive remarks or who tries to steal the show from the professor. Appropriate Class Jokers know their place in the hierarchy. Think of the appropriate Class Joker as the law school equivalent of a sidekick to a late-night talk show host (e.g., Kevin Eubanks to Jay Leno, Paul Shaffer to David Letterman). They can get away with some gentle teasing of the host, but remain cognizant of their primary role as the "straight man."

18. The Lightning Rod. As with the Class Joker, most law school classes have at least one Lightning Rod, a person willing to express strong and sometimes outrageous opinions about the issues being discussed in class. Often, these views can be associated with either the far left or right of the political spectrum. Sometimes their opinions are politically incorrect. Not all professors share my view, but I like having Lightning Rods as students, even when I disagree with their views, because their opinions often prompt other students who normally would not participate to jump into the fray. The surest identifier of a Lightning Rod is a person whose classroom comment ignites an immediate sea of waving hands. Some Lightning Rods offer their opinions with a wink and nod, knowing full well the role they're fulfilling and letting on to the prof that they're not necessarily wed to the opinions they express.

Be forewarned. Lightning Rods may open themselves to ridicule by their classmates. Unfortunately, as with the fear of being labeled a gunner, fear of derision deters many non-Lightning Rod students from offering honest opinions about charged issues, of which there are many in law.

A classic example from Torts is the famous Iowa "spring-gun case," *Katko v. Briney*,[11] which you are likely to study. Marvin Katko sued Edward and Bertha Briney after he broke into their unoccupied farmhouse intent on stealing their property and ended up losing a portion of his leg to a shotgun the Brineys had wired to the bedroom door. The jury awarded Katko substantial compensatory and punitive damages. The Brineys had to auction eighty acres of their farm to pay the judgment. Katko won on the principle that the law values life over property. From teaching this case for many years, I know that a large percentage of students in every class vehemently disagree with the result that a criminal can recover damages from a homeowner whose property he un-lawfully invades, but they're often afraid to express their disagreement until a Lightning Rod opens the door with an opinion like "The SOB got what he deserved!"

---

11.   183 N.W.2d 657 (Iowa 1971).

Even more unfortunate than students shying away from expressing their opinions about charged issues, many professors are so apprehensive of offending the overly delicate sensitivities of some students that they avoid even raising hot issues. That's a darn shame. Law school classes should be vital and exciting. If sensitive legal issues can't be discussed even in law school, we're in trouble as a society. But I digress.

19. The Cheater. From a professor's perspective, the only student type worse than the Slacker is the Cheater. People who cheat in law school are likely to cheat in the practice of law, hurting their clients and tarnishing a profession that is already held in low regard by many. The good news is that given the nature of law school exams, it's difficult to cheat effectively. The bad news is that this fact doesn't stop people from trying. At every law school where I have taught, incidents of alleged cheating have occurred. Sadly, several students at different law schools have reported to me that cheating not only occurs, but is common, although I can't vouch for the accuracy of such indictments.

Of course, whether you decide to be a Cheater isn't going to be influenced by any advice I give you. Nor do you need a book like this to apprise you of the potentially severe adverse consequences of cheating, which can include being suspended from law school or not being permitted to sit for the bar exam. You're the one who has to look in the mirror every day.

But here is some advice that may help honest souls. In some situations involving accusations of academic misconduct, I've come away convinced that the cheating was inadvertent or at least not motivated by a wicked intent. These incidents often involve students who, faced with a dilemma as to what is proper conduct, resolve the question in their favor without seeking guidance from the professor.

For example, cheating allegations arise disproportionately in first-year legal research and writing courses where gray areas may exist in the rules regarding matters such as collaboration and plagiarism. Instead of simply asking the professor for guidance when a question of right or wrong arises, the student makes a choice on his or her own—often unwisely giving him/herself the benefit of the doubt—that turns out to be the wrong choice. Even if the accused student is ultimately spared sanctions, the student endures the substantial emotional trauma of being investigated, put on trial, and suffering a tarnished reputation. In many cases involving alleged law school academic misconduct, the student could have avoided any problems simply by seeking clarification from the instructor. You cannot go wrong by following that course of action: when in doubt, ASK the professor.

20. The Earnest Hard Worker. Last, but certainly not least, is the Earnest Hard Worker. Don't be misled by the negative types listed above. While the negative types tend to stand out more than the positive types, they are a distinct minority overall. The Earnest Hard Workers, I'm happy to report, represent a majority of law students. Some of them achieve high grades, some don't. But even Earnest Hard Workers who don't come out at the top of their class earn the respect of those around them, both students and professors. I happily write strong recommendation letters on behalf of Earnest Hard Workers even if they received less-than-stellar grades in my courses.

* * *

There you have them. Twenty law student types. Make a list of the types that appeal to you, the types that don't, and the in-between types. Think about the list, then put it away. Revisit your list during the first semester to see whether you're living up (or down) to your aspirations.

CHAPTER 5

THE FIRST-YEAR CURRICULUM: WHAT TO EXPECT

Here's a list of the courses I took as a 1L in 1978:

Civil Procedure

Contracts

Criminal Law

Legal Research and Writing

Property

Torts

Here's a list of the courses you very well may take as a 1L more than thirty years later:

Civil Procedure

Contracts

Criminal Law

Legal Research and Writing

Property

Torts

Hmm, can we detect a pattern here? Nowhere is the resistance to change in American legal education more apparent than in the static nature of law school curricula. Several respected reports have criticized the traditional law school curriculum as outdated and in need of major reform. In particular, the status quo has been attacked for paying too much attention to teaching legal doctrine and legal analysis and too little attention to practical skills and ethics and professionalism.

The standard three-year law school curriculum is somewhat of an odd arrangement if one stops to ponder it for, say, two seconds. To prepare doctors to practice medicine, medical schools require, quite sensibly, years of clinical training involving hands-on patient care. Law schools traditionally have required nothing of that sort. At nearly all law schools, clinical courses and externships, in which students work with real clients, lawyers, and cases, are elective rather than required. I graduated law school without taking a single skills-related course other than my required first-year legal research and writing courses, a dubious feat that can be replicated today at most schools.

Some evolution is occurring, however slowly. A comprehensive survey conducted by the ABA Section of Legal Education and Admission to the Bar studied shifts in law school curricula between 1992 and 2002.[12] The survey found significant growth in the upper-division curriculum, principally in offering more skills and simulation courses and a wider selection of specialized electives. "No significant change," however, was detected in first-year course offerings. Specifically, the survey found that the following six courses—the same ones I listed above—are required in the vast majority of first-year programs, both full-time and part-time:

Civil Procedure: required in 95 percent of full-time programs and 84 percent of part-time programs.

Contracts: 95 percent of full-time programs and 92 percent of part-time programs.

Criminal Law: 87 percent of full-time programs and 88 percent of part-time programs.

Legal Research and Writing: 81 percent of full-time programs and 84 percent of part-time programs.

Property: 86 percent of full-time programs and 86 percent of part-time programs.

Torts: 89 percent of full-time programs and 93 percent of part-time programs.[13]

12. Catherine Carpenter, *A Survey of Law School Curricula 1992–2002*, 2004 A.B.A. Sec. Legal Educ. & Admissions to Bar Rep.

13. *Id.* at 25. These percentages were calculated based on the required curriculum for the first two semesters for full-time students and the first three semesters for part-time students.

Constitutional Law is also commonly featured in the first year, being required in 59 percent of full-time programs and 52 percent of part-time programs. It should also be noted that some schools have added new first-year courses since the 2002 ABA curriculum survey was completed, in areas such as lawyering skills, statutory analysis, and international and comparative law.

One significant change over the years is in how first-year credit hours (which average 15–16 per semester for full-time students and 10–11 for part-time students) are allocated. Most law schools have "semesterized" some or all of their first-year courses. Traditionally, most first-year courses were taught in two semesters, with three credit hours allotted to each semester (e.g., Contracts I and Contracts II, Torts I and Torts II). Within the last couple of decades, however, a majority of schools have combined at least some of the traditional two-semester, three-credit hour 1L courses into single-semester, four-hour courses.

One reason behind the change was to free up more hours for legal research and writing courses, a good goal given the importance of those courses and the fact that they tradition-ally have been under-credited (see Chapter 17). Another reason was to introduce more flexibility into the curriculum, freeing up hours for students to take more electives. In my opinion (an opinion with which many professors disagree), semesterization of first-year courses was a bad idea that caught on primarily because it was trendy at the time. First-year courses are the critical building blocks of learning funda-mental principles of law and the process of legal analysis. Moreover, when first-year courses get cut by one-third, im-portant material that is tested on the bar exam gets omitted with the result that most students are forced as a practical matter to take upper-level courses covering the deleted mate-rial, undermining the flexibility goal. Some schools have recently switched back from semesterization to the tradition-al model.

The purpose of this chapter is to give you a feel for the "Big Five" doctrinal courses that you'll be immersed in, if not submerged under, in your first year: Civil Procedure, Contracts, Criminal Law, Property, and Torts. "Doctrinal courses" are courses in which the primary purpose is to teach the body of substantive rules, or "doctrine," in the particular area of law. They're distinguishable from so-called "skills courses" such as Legal Research and Writing. Because Legal Research and Writing is such a different—and important— beast, it gets its own chapter (Chapter 17). Having a rudimentary sense of what each course involves will help you know what to expect, as well as give you a better context for processing the rest of this book. At a minimum, when you see your course list for the first time, it won't feel like reading a menu in a foreign language.

Your level of interest in and enjoyment of any particular course will depend partly on your personality type and learning preferences. Students who are more comfortable with concrete rules may love Property. Students who prefer abstractions may prefer Constitutional Law. Your enjoyment level for particular courses also will be heavily influenced by the professors teaching them. Good teachers can make any subject come alive, while ineffective teachers can make even the most interesting material coma-inducing. Similarly, organized, well-prepared teachers with good communication skills can make even the most complex material accessible and understandable, while disorganized, unprepared teachers can render even simple material obtuse.

Regarding the course content described below, law professors have a variety of casebooks to choose among for each first-year course. While casebooks for a subject generally cover the same basic material, some differences in coverage, and many more in organization, exist. Moreover, coverage may differ even between two professors using the same casebook because of the professors' individual preferences regarding what to emphasize.

Civil Procedure

All civil lawsuits are controlled by a set of procedural rules known, appropriately enough, as the Rules of Civil Procedure. Think of them as a kind of a rule book for the game of civil litigation, sort of like the rule book for Monopoly but a whole lot thicker and more difficult to interpret. The Rules of Civil Procedure tell the lawyers and the parties what they must do and may do in the pretrial and trial stages of a lawsuit, as well as how and when to do it. Criminal cases are controlled by a similar set of rules, but courses in criminal procedure usually are upper-level electives.

The Federal Rules of Civil Procedure, which are the focus of most 1L courses on the subject, govern lawsuits in the federal courts. Each state has its own set of civil procedure rules to govern civil lawsuits in their respective state court systems, but those rules track the federal rules pretty closely for the most part. The Federal Rules of Civil Procedure contain eighty-six rules, but you will closely study only a handful of them.

You'll spend a lot of time studying cases (many of which predate the adoption of the Federal Rules of Civil Procedure) that developed the key procedural concepts governing questions such as which court has jurisdiction to hear a particular case, whether a court has jurisdiction over the parties to a case, and which court system's rules of substantive law apply to a case.

Unlike your other first-year courses (except Constitutional Law), many of the cases in Civil Procedure are U.S. Supreme Court cases. You will quickly learn that Supreme Court cases are different from and more difficult to digest than other cases. They're usually longer, include more policy analysis, and often contain a maze of concurring and dissenting opinions that must be pieced together to discern the holding of the Court.

Principal among the topics covered in Civil Procedure are personal and subject matter jurisdiction. A court has the power to hear a lawsuit only if it has jurisdiction over both the parties (personal) and the type of case (subject matter). Sound simple? It's not. Personal jurisdiction is one of the most difficult, and most heavily tested, issues in Civil Procedure. (A good tip to remember across the board is that professors generally like to test on the most difficult material, not the easiest.) Depending on your professor, you might spend several grueling weeks studying the evolution of personal jurisdiction rules via a chronology of famous Supreme Court cases beginning with *Pennoyer v. Neff*.[14]

Each case modifies the one preceding it, leaving students wondering why they can't just study the last one, since it contains the most up-to-date treatment of the law. The

---

14. 95 U.S. 714 (1877).

answer is that a full understanding of complex legal doctrine sometimes can be achieved only by studying its historical evolution. It's probably a fair statement to say that in most Civil Procedure courses, students cannot excel without a thorough understanding of the law of personal jurisdiction.

Every 1L course has at least one classic case that all law students remember studying. For Civil Procedure, that case is *Pennoyer v. Neff*, a complicated artifact about personal jurisdiction with little modern relevance. Quoting Shakespeare's *Macbeth*, one law professor said about *Pennoyer*: "Confusion now hath made its masterpiece."[15] When I was a student, I'm not sure my understanding of *Pennoyer v. Neff* ever progressed beyond wondering why the case wasn't called *Mitchell v. Neff*, since the party who started the whole mess was not Pennoyer, but a colorful lawyer named J.H. Mitchell.

Another heavily covered area is known as the *Erie* doctrine, named after a famous Supreme Court case called *Erie Railroad Co. v. Tompkins*,[16] which concerns whether state or federal substantive law applies in a particular case being heard in federal court. Other topics commonly covered include rules regarding pleadings, motions, discovery, class actions, summary judgment (a mechanism for judges to dispose of a case without a trial), and the doctrines of res judicata and collateral estoppel (which determine whether a case or claim that has already been heard once can be relitigated).

As with all courses, student reactions toward Civil Procedure differ. One student consultant said it was one of her most "boring" courses, while another said it was "fun." Another student, who liked the course and loved the professor, said:

> This is not the most exciting class you will take. It is difficult to get excited about Rule 41, or 65, or any of the rules for that matter. They just aren't very "sexy." And honestly, I never heard any of my classmates come out of a Civil Procedure class and say, "Man, that was awesome. I can't wait to see how that Rule 18 issue is gonna turn out tomorrow!"

15. Wendy Collins Perdue, *Sin, Scandal and Substantive Due Process: Personal Jurisdiction and* Pennoyer Re-considered, 62 WASH. L. REV. 479, 479 (1987).

16. 304 U.S. 64 (1938).

On one issue, near unanimity of student opinion exists: Civil Procedure is one of the most difficult first-year courses. This is attributable in part to the fact that the subject matter is unfamiliar ("not even covered on TV!" wrote a student consultant) and also because the rules are technical and not intuitive. Moreover, civil procedure rules usually have to be interpreted in the context of litigation involving other areas of law (e.g., a contract, property or tort dispute), which you'll be trying to learn at the same time you're trying to learn civil procedure.

Contracts

Contracts focuses on the formation, performance, and breach of oral and written agreements. Much of the course focuses on the three essential ingredients to the formation of a binding contract: offer, acceptance, and consideration (the requirement that each party give something of value to the other as part of the bargain). Of course, infinite permutations exist regarding each of these requirements that make them much more complex than they might sound. One student advisor offered this capsule overview of the three requirements:

> This course is all about three words: offer, acceptance, and consideration. From the beginning of the course these three words are drilled into your head constantly. Chances are, if you're not paying attention in class one day and you end up getting called on, answering with one of the three "magic words" will at least get you in the ballpark of the correct answer. (Of course, I'm certainly not advocating drifting off in class.)

> This course began with a simple question, or at least what I thought was a simple question: What constitutes an offer? You will find that there are rarely any simple questions in law school. There's always something lurking under the surface of a seemingly simple question. We read and discussed LOTS of cases initially just trying to determine whether or not an offer was made. For me, this was interesting because as our professor correctly explained, we enter into contracts every day of our lives. From signing a credit card receipt to an apartment lease to accepting your

first job offer after law school—we all have experience dealing with contracts even though we may not think about it.

After addressing whether or not an offer was made, we examined what it means to accept an offer. Now, you might be thinking at this point, "Duh, I know what an offer is and how to accept it. Can they just go ahead and give me my law degree already?" That line of thinking would be a mistake. As you will learn, acceptance can be manifested in many ways, and one can be held to that manifestation even if they claim accepting the offer was not their intent. Be on the lookout for one of the most famous and interesting acceptance cases, *Lucy v. Zehmer*, which involved a negotiation between two intoxicated parties for a piece of farmland. One of the parties jokingly signed over his farmland on the back of a restaurant check thinking that the negotiation was done in jest. However, as he soon found out, this was considered a valid manifestation of acceptance and he had to sell his farm. (One moral of this case: don't drink and sell farmland. The two don't mix.)

The third piece of the Contracts puzzle is consideration. In my opinion, consideration was the most difficult of the three major concepts to understand. Whether or not a party gives consideration for an offer is a difficult question, and often court opinions will differ on seemingly similar cases with similar facts. Additionally, I found that most of our exam questions dealt with the issue of whether or not consideration was given to constitute a valid contract. [McClurg note: More support for what I told you about professors preferring to test on the most difficult material.] Don't feel too bad if you have no idea what I'm talking about now. Trust me, you will spend an inordinate amount of time discussing consideration during your Contracts class, and you'll likely be just as confused as I was afterwards. (Just kidding ... I hope.)

In addition to offer, acceptance, and consideration, you'll learn about the scope of contractual obligations, remedies for breaches of contracts, excuses for performance such as impossibility, and something called the parol evidence rule, which relates to what, if any, extraneous evidence outside the contract can be considered in interpreting the contract. No point trying to explain it here. As a student consultant who finished number one in her class wrote: "I still could not fully explain to you how the rule operates."

Like Property below, the facts in Contracts cases can be detailed and complex. It's critical to pay attention to the specific details. If the fact sections of your case briefs for Contracts seem longer than for Torts or Criminal Law, they probably should be.

Criminal Law

Criminal Law is the study of criminal offenses and defenses, primarily the former. Because criminal cases are intensely covered by the media and are a favorite subject of law-related television series and movies, students arrive at law school thinking the subject area will be heavily emphasized. But Criminal Law is the only first-year course that takes students out of the realm of civil litigation and into the darker world of crime and how the legal system responds to it.

Criminal Law is highly "element"-based. All criminal offenses are composed of elements that must be proved by the prosecution beyond a reasonable doubt. If any element is missing, a completed crime has not occurred. A great deal of class time is devoted to understanding the two most fundamental elements of a crime: actus reus (the criminal act itself) and mens rea (the mental state required to be convicted of a particular crime). You'll study the elements of core crimes such as homicide, theft, and burglary, as well as the elements of "inchoate crimes" such as attempt, conspiracy, and solicitation. Inchoate crimes, which can be tricky to understand, are offenses where the target crime is not actually completed. Defenses to crimes also have elements that must be proved.

Making matters more difficult, because modern criminal law is mostly statutory, you probably will have to study and compare the common law (judge-made law) to statutory law (laws passed by legislatures). Learning to read, interpret, and parse statutes is a different skill from learning to read and interpret cases. Confusing matters even more, it's possible you'll be required to study and compare both the English *and* U.S. common law *and* both the Model Penal Code (a uniform code of criminal law often used as a model for criminal statutes) *and* the criminal statutes actually adopted in your state. This could mean that for one criminal offense, such as homicide, you might be required to learn the distinct elements under English common law, U.S. common law, the Model Penal Code, and your state's criminal statutes. If your Criminal Law course is taught in this fashion, graphs and charts can be highly effective.

But it might be taught in a *completely* different fashion. In Chapter 9, I discuss the difference between professors who teach from a primarily practical perspective and those who teach from a primarily theoretical perspective. These divergent approaches can occur in any course, but Criminal Law is a prime candidate for theoretical teaching among 1L courses. Instead of focusing on all the detailed rules and elements, your Criminal Law professor might choose to concentrate (as mine did) on big-picture policy issues, such as the societal policies and theories underlying criminal punishment and sentencing. The difference in these teaching approaches is like night and day for students.

One pitfall to watch out for is that some important doctrines of criminal law—primarily the element of causation and defenses to crimes—parallel similar doctrines under tort law. Criminal Law usually is a one-semester course taught in the second semester, while Torts is usually taught in the first semester, or both the first and second semesters. As one student said, the overlap can be "both a blessing and a curse" because, while it's comforting to approach a topic with which you already are familiar, important differences exist in the details between criminal law and tort law. For example, "assault" under criminal law is a different concept from "assault" under tort law. Make a point to keep the two subject areas separate in your mind.

One upside of Criminal Law is that many of the cases have interesting, even juicy fact patterns, but the law itself can be less than scintillating because it often requires a lot of memorization of the different elements of different offenses.

Students coming out of Criminal Law often experience polar-opposite reactions to the subject. Some students go into the course thinking they won't like it and come out wanting to practice criminal law. Others complete the course swearing they will never have anything to do with a criminal case.

Property

In Property, students study the principles of law governing the ownership and transfer of personal property (stuff not attached to land) and real property (land or structures attached to land). This book, for example, is an item of personal property. The door you use it to prop open or the corner of the closet where it gathers dust are parts of real property. Most of Property—and most of what you will be tested on—will focus on the law of real property, in part because the rules applicable to personal property are fairly straightforward and easy to understand.

It is likely that your first assignments in Property will cover cases going back to the 1800s. Unlike the law of most other subjects, which evolves over time, many of the rules governing property rights were frozen in place centuries ago. Thus, historical context is more important to understanding Property than it is in some other 1L courses.

In approaching Property, keep in mind this big-picture point: a person does not "have" property, but rather has an "interest" in property. That interest can be acquired, lost, given away, or conveyed. That interest can be absolute or conditional. That interest can be partial or whole. Much of the study of property is simply how the law treats various interests in real property.

Well, "simply" may be a bad word choice. Property is filled with alien concepts such as adverse possession, easements, restrictive covenants, the fee system, marketable title to land, and, of course, future interests. I recall Property being my hardest first-year course and it was all because of future interests. The law of future interests is a maze-like set of rules regulating the ability of one to convey interests in land to someone in the future, such as by way of a will or trust.

One famous future interests rule—the Rule Against Perpetuities—is so ridiculously complicated that the distinguished California Supreme Court once suggested it's impossible for a lawyer to commit malpractice for misunderstanding the rule. You gotta love that, along with the fact that some of the satellite doctrines under the Rule Against Perpetuities have names that sound like old blues tunes. The "Bad as to One, Bad as to All" and "Unborn Widow" rules could have been classic hits for Muddy Waters. It's

all very confusing, so don't fret too much if your class
notes on the Rule Against Perpetuities end up looking
something like this:

> **Professor's lecture:** No contingent future interest in
> a transferee is good unless it must vest or fail to vest
> within twenty-one years of the death of some life in
> being at the time of the creation of the interest.
>
> **Student's notes:** No astringent foosball interest?? ...
> must vest OR FAIL TO VEST ... twenty-one years
> ... death ... life in bean ... creation? interest?
>
> **Professor:** The rationale for the rule is straightfor-
> ward. It's designed to limit efforts by grantors to
> restrict the free alienation of property by burdening it
> with contingent future interests.
>
> **Student:** Rationale for rule straightforward—designed
> to limit grant~~ees~~ ORS ... something, something,
> something—SLOW THE * * * * DOWN!—Alien Na-
> tion of Property? ... BUY STUDY AID!!!
>
> **Professor:** The simple way to understand the rule is
> to remember that it all has to do with the vesting or
> failure to vest of a contingent future interest within
> the lifetime of a measuring life or twenty-one years
> after that person's death.
>
> **Student:** Simple way to understand rule is to remem-
> ber that it all has to do with ... TWENTY–ONE
> YEARS, TWENTY–ONE YEARS, TWENTY–ONE
> YEARS ...

Fortunately, precisely because it is so convoluted, the Rule
Against Perpetuities usually isn't a major focus of a Property
exam. But the rest of the law pertaining to future interests
usually is. Why? Come and sing it with me one more time: *the
more difficult the material, the more likely it will be tested.*
While future interest rules are technical and tricky, once you
get a handle on them, they're easy to apply. That's part of
the good news about Property. Unlike the law in many
subjects, like Torts, where shades of gray dominate, the rules
in Property are more black and white. As a consequence,
more definite "correct answers" exist to property law questions. As one student advisor wrote, "many property problems operate exactly like math problems." Once you master
the rules, it's easier to apply them with confidence.

Torts

A tort is not a dessert. That's a torte. A tort is a civil wrong other than a breach of contract (which is also a civil wrong) for which the law allows the plaintiff a right of action for money damages. Torts is a subject with which entering students have at least superficial familiarity, whether they realize it or not.

Who, for example, hasn't heard about the infamous (albeit grossly distorted) McDonald's coffee spill lawsuit? That was a tort case. So are all the lawsuits for damages involving pharmaceutical products, asbestos, breast implants, and tobacco. Medical malpractice suits are tort cases. So are automobile accident suits. Basically, any time a person is physically (or sometimes, emotionally) injured through the conduct of another, whether in a plane crash or from slipping on a piece of lettuce at the supermarket, the potential for a tort suit arises. Tort law is also part of a controversial national political agenda known as the "tort reform movement" that receives a substantial amount of media attention.

Like Criminal Law, Torts is highly element-based. All torts consist of a set of elements, each of which must be proved by the plaintiff to make out a successful claim.

Most tort courses begin with a study of the seven basic intentional torts (i.e., claims arising from intentionally inflicted injuries): battery, assault, false imprisonment, intentional infliction of emotional distress, trespass to land, trespass to chattels, and conversion (the latter two relate to interferences with personal property). This is followed by a study of the basic privileges or defenses to the intentional torts: consent, self-defense, defense of others, defense of property, recovery of property, and necessity. The rules relating to intentional torts and privileges are fairly straightforward, which is one reason I built a lot of the examples in this book around them.

The bulk of every Torts course is the topic of negligence. I spend roughly 50 percent (fourteen of twenty-eight weeks) of my two-semester, six-credit Torts course covering negligence. Negligence law is essentially the study of liability for "accidents." People are liable for damages under negligence law when they fail to exercise reasonable care and that failure causes injury. Negligence principles are mostly intuitive but can be difficult to get a grasp on because they are so amorphous. What, for example, is "reasonable care"? And when can we say that an act is the responsible cause of an injury? If A makes and sells a violent video game to B, and B subsequently engages in violence against others after playing the game, did A fail to exercise reasonable care in making and selling the game? Was A a "cause" of the ensuing violence? These are the types of issues students grapple with in trying to solve the puzzles of negligence law.

Depending on the number of credit hours allotted to Torts, topics of study apart from the intentional torts and negligence may include strict liability (of which products liability is the largest component), wrongful death, tort damages, and defamation and privacy.

Torts is where students study one of the most famous and memorable cases in American jurisprudential history: *Palsgraf v. Long Island Railroad Co.*,[17] a wacky, confusing case, with opinions from two heavyweight judges, about an exploding package of fireworks that supposedly knocked a heavy scale on top of Helen Palsgraf at the Long Island train station in 1924. I always tell my students that *Palsgraf* may be the only law school case that *every* lawyer remembers. Several students have tested this assertion, always reporting back that the lawyers they ask about the case still remember it well.

Tort cases, like those in Criminal Law, can make for interesting reading because of the real-life drama involved when people injure each other, either intentionally or negligently. Sex, drugs, even rock and roll (e.g., lawsuits against Ozzy Osbourne on behalf of teenagers who committed suicide after listening to Ozzy's song, *Suicide Solution*)—Torts has a little of everything.

Students sometimes make the mistake of thinking Torts is easier than other first-year subjects and devote less time to studying it. It's true that many of the basic principles of tort law are not particularly intellectually difficult, but like all subjects, Torts is full of little twists and nuances that make it more complicated than it first appears. And like all subjects, it has its own unusually difficult topics, with "proximate cause"—one of the elements of negligence—being the signa-

17.   162 N.E. 99 (N.Y. 1928).

ture example. A student came to my office on the last day of Torts I and said:

> Professor McClurg, I wasn't having any problems with negligence. As we were going through it, I felt like a heavyweight boxing champ, knocking out every topic that came in front of me. Then we got to proximate cause and it was like I turned my head and got sucker-punched. It completely knocked me out.

Of course, one of the largest issues on the exam that semester was proximate cause.

Even if one were to accept the premise that Torts is "easier," it would be a mistake to treat it any differently in terms of the amount of studying and preparation one puts into it because Torts is usually worth the same credit hours as the other 1L doctrinal courses. As I always remind my students: "There are just as many low grades in Torts as in other subjects." The same holds true for every subject.

CHAPTER 6
THE FIRST DAYS: ORIENTATION, SEAT CHOICE, AND CLASSROOM ETIQUETTE

The first days of law school are exciting, memorable, and usually quite stressful. Everything is a blur because it's all so new: new people, new physical surroundings, a whole new language, and a mysterious new teaching methodology. It's enough to make anyone nervous. Even professors often start the semester a bit edgy.

The heartening news is that the comfort level in law school classrooms increases quickly. When I walk into Torts on the first day of class, even with eighty people in the room, it's so quiet one could hear a Xanax drop. But with each passing day, students get to know each other, their surroundings, and their professors a little better. They're relieved that the Socratic method appears to be not quite as torturous as rumored, that law professors are by and large decent folks who are good at and care about what they're doing, and that they can actually grasp the legal principles being taught. As in every other setting, familiarity breeds comfort and relaxes tension. Within just a couple of weeks, it sounds like I'm walking into a rowdy pub as I approach the classroom door. Instead of silence, I'm greeted with a cacophony of excited chatter and laughter.

You want to get off on the right foot in these first days. Missteps can result in embarrassment, risk branding you in a negative light, and create extra stress that can interfere with learning. The advice in this chapter is designed to help you come out of the blocks smoothly and cleanly as you begin the 1L race.

Getting the Most Out of Orientation

All law schools conduct an orientation for incoming students, usually in the week immediately preceding the commencement of classes. Orientations vary in length and scope, from two to as long as six days. Most orientation programs are two or three days, which is plenty long.

Students often find orientation frustrating and a waste of time. Who can blame them? Attending law school requires so much advance groundwork—from taking the LSAT to completing lengthy applications to arranging housing and financial aid to reading books like this one—that by the time law school actually rolls around, students walk through the doors champing at the bit to get going. But it doesn't work that way. First, it's orientation time.

A former student once drew an interesting analogy between law school orientation and having sex for the first time. These weren't the exact words, but they're close:

> You've waited all your life. You've dreamed about it, planned for it, obsessed over it, visualized it, practiced for it, and now the day finally arrives that you get to actually DO IT. You're totally psyched, when all of a sudden a bunch of people burst into the room and say: "Stop! You cannot have sex right now. Before you can have sex, you must to sit down and listen to us tell you for an entire week what it is *like* to have sex."

Students tend to take two diametrically opposite approaches to orientation: they either disregard it or immerse themselves in it with total devotion. Both approaches can be counterproductive. Blowing off orientation certainly is a poor way to get started on such a big new adventure in life. As discussed below, some orientation events will be of value to you. Equally important, not acting professionally during orientation reflects poorly on you.

The people responsible for organizing and running orientation are acutely tuned into negative attitudes, disparaging comments they overhear, and who doesn't attend required events. One of them is quite likely to pass the information on to one or more of your first-year professors, as in: "You have a student in your section—Mr./Ms. _____—who skipped out on orientation." Or: "You're not going to believe what I overheard this kid in your section—Mr./Ms. _____—say during the reception." Upper-level student orientation mentors and group leaders also sometimes relay information to faculty about the new students they encounter.

Here's a specific example of what I'm talking about. On the first day of a recent orientation, a colleague came into my office, clearly irritated. He said he had just met with the entering class to do a case-briefing exercise. The new students, approximately 150 of them, were supposed to have registered for the legal writing TWEN course site (see below) and downloaded a case for the exercise. From data available on TWEN, my colleague was able to determine before going into the orientation session that eight of the new students had failed to download the case. What did he do? First and foremost, he formed a bad impression of the eight students. Second, he purposely called on them during the exercise to expose their unpreparedness to the entire entering class. Third, he informed me and perhaps other first-year professors about their lack of preparation. This is not the way you want to begin your new career: with a bad reputation before the first class has even been held.

On the other hand, depending on the rigor of the orientation, completely immersing yourself in orientation as if your life depended on it is not a great idea either. I taught at one law school that had a six-day orientation, which included a lengthy session on the Saturday before school started when the students would have been better off at home preparing for their first week of classes. Just reading the schedule of events, many of which went well into the night, was exhausting. Some of the events required substantial reading to prepare for them.

It was all well-intended and each individual event had value, but it was simply too much packaged together. I watched the students arrive eager and bright-eyed on Monday morning of orientation week and leave Saturday afternoon looking like they had just finished first-semester exams. When classes began the following Monday, many of the students looked worn out already.

I suggest a middle-of-the-road attitude and approach to orientation in which your goal is to maximize the benefits while conserving your emotional and physical energy. Simply keeping in mind that orientation doesn't "count" for anything should help you keep your stress level in check and preserve some psychic energy. Take it seriously, but not gravely.

If the school assigns lengthy background reading material as part of orientation, by all means read it, but don't wear yourself out fretting over every line you don't understand. Pay particular attention to assignments pertaining to practical study skills, such as case-briefing or outlining. These crucial skills take time and practice to develop, so you want to take advantage of early opportunities to start learning about them. If the school holds a "sample class," which many schools do, make sure to prepare for it. They usually involve one assigned case to read. Personally, I've always thought these classes—which are intended to help "demystify" law school—are a waste of time. Because the students lack the background and context necessary to meaningfully process the case, they don't really resemble real classes. But since this is everyone's first group encounter with a professor and the Socratic method, you certainly don't want to be remembered as "that person" who showed up unprepared for the sample class.

Here are some things to focus on during orientation:

Get your assignments.

Be sure you get your assignments for your first classes if you haven't already done so. One distinguishing feature of law school from undergraduate school is that there are no free "Welcome to law school"-type classes. Most professors dive right into the material at the first class.

Your assignments for the first week of classes will be sent to you in the mail, distributed in hard copy form during orientation, posted on the law school website, posted on a bulletin board, or made available through some combination of these methods. The assignments may be available weeks in advance, so it's not a bad idea to check the law school website or visit the school even before orientation.

Buy required books and other materials.

If you haven't already done so, buy your required books and other required materials as early during orientation as possible. Not infrequently, for a variety of reasons, snafus occur in book orders that result in the bookstore running out of books. Stress reduction, not enhancement, is the order of the day. You do not want to be scrambling around trying to locate an alternative source for the first week's course assignments because the bookstore ran out of books. See Chapter 2 for more information about what books to buy and what not to buy.

If the bookstore does run out of books, borrow a classmate's book and make a photocopy of the assignments for the entire first week. Unless the bookstore can *assure* you the books are expected within a couple of days, find a copy elsewhere, such as through the publisher's website or via another online bookseller. Order it by express overnight shipping. It costs more, but this is not a luxury item. *If you get behind in law school at the beginning, you will never catch up.* If you live in a city with more than one law school, check out the bookstore serving the other law school. It may very well have the books you need.

Law schools have a responsibility to order sufficient numbers of required books for students, so don't hesitate to contact (politely, of course) the professor to inform her of the problem. She should provide you with a copy of the assignment, or might lend you an extra copy of the book. If many students are affected, the professor or law school administration should address the problem by express ordering the books or distributing copies of the assignments.

Register for your professors' TWEN sites.

If you haven't already done so, register with TWEN and for your professors' individual TWEN online course sites. TWEN is an acronym for The West Education Network, operated by West, a Thomson Reuters business, that is one of the world's largest legal publishers. Depending on the individual professor, TWEN sites can be used to access course materials (including syllabi, assignments, classroom policies, course calendars, etc.), participate in online discussions, receive and submit online assignments, work through quizzes, link to CALI (Computer–Assisted Legal Instruction) exercises, exchange email with your professors and classmates, and more.

TWEN sites have become extremely popular in recent years. Even the eighty-three-year-old emeritus professor in the office next to mine uses TWEN. The percentage of law professors using TWEN sites is unknown, but a West representative reported to me in 2007 that TWEN maintained 6000 law school course pages, which averages out to thirty-two courses per accredited law school. (A rival service, Lexis-Nexis Web Courses, also exists, but is not as widely used.) To participate in TWEN, you need a Westlaw password, which usually is issued during orientation. Register for TWEN as soon as you receive your password. Don't delay. Many professors use TWEN's email function to convey important course information to students. *A Student's Guide to TWEN*, including detailed information on how to register, can be found at: http://west.thomson.com/documentation/westlaw/wlawdoc/lawstu/twqrst06.pdf.

Get a locker.

Most law schools offer student lockers for a nominal fee. At the beginning of law school, you might not be sure whether you'll need or use a locker. But unless you absolutely can't afford it, you're better off getting one if the opportunity is presented, especially if you're at a school where there are not enough lockers to go around. Even if you end up not using it every day, having a place to securely stash some of those heavy books will come in handy from time to time.

Listen to advice, but sort it carefully.

Everyone will be giving you advice on how to succeed in law school, especially upper-level students. Upper-level students love to give advice to incoming students. Sometimes it's good advice. When I started law school, an upper-level student told me to buy the *Gilbert* study aid for Criminal Law. He explained that while our professor would talk almost exclusively about theory in class, come exam time he would expect us to apply and analyze black-letter law (i.e., the actual legal rules). Sure enough, class discussions were geared almost exclusively toward theory. My class notes were a garbled mess.

I followed his advice. I bought and studied the *Gilbert* for Criminal Law. The moment I started reading the final exam, which was my very first law school exam, I knew that study aid was the single best purchasing decision I had ever made.

The exam questions were classic issue-spotting/problem-solving essays requiring mastery of the black-letter rules we never learned in class. I received my first A in law school in Criminal Law.

But upper-level students also give some really bad advice, much of which involves ways to cut corners, so be wary of what they tell you. Although it will be socially awkward, if an upper-level student starts piling on the advice, I recommend asking the person for his or her GPA or class rank. The most vocal advice-givers are sometimes the weakest students. You could phrase it like this: "Wow, thanks for all the advice. Has it worked for you? Did you do well in that class? How did you come out in terms of GPA/class rank after the first year?"

Law professors also give advice to incoming students. Law professor advice is probably more reliable overall than student advice, but may not be as practical or realistic. For example, I can't picture my Criminal Law prof explaining to us: "I'm not really going to teach you much actual law in class, but I will expect you to know it all for the final exam, so I'd advise you to run, not walk, to the bookstore and get your hands on the *Gilbert* for Criminal Law."

Both learning and teaching styles are idiosyncratic. You're likely to receive conflicting advice even from professors. Don't be overwhelmed by it all. Process all advice before acting on it.

Visit all your classrooms.

A great trial lawyer taught me the value of always visiting a courtroom in advance of a hearing or trial to check out the lay of the land and get a feel for it. Familiarity with a place or situation prompts brain neurons known as "place cells" to fire, making us feel comfortable and at home. Studies show, for example, that if a person is shown a geometric shape for just one-thousandth of a second, far too quickly to register in the conscious mind, the person will like that shape better the next time they see it.

Visiting all your classrooms during orientation week will not only raise your comfort level, it will eliminate the added stress you'll suffer if you have to hunt them down for the first time in the rush between classes during those first days. Knowing where the rooms are also will help you avoid the embarrassing predicament of arriving late to class, something you want to avoid at all costs (see below). Moreover, an early visit will allow you to contemplate in advance the important decision of where you want to sit (see below).

Socialize.

Most orientations include one or more social events where students can meet and mingle with their classmates and some of the professors. Take advantage of these. Having a close network of supportive law school friends is invaluable to your success and well-being (see Chapter 18). Because everyone is in the same overcrowded lifeboat, most people jump at the chance to make friends in these early days.

If you spot someone at one of these events who you know is going to be one of your first-year professors (they'll usually be wearing name tags), go up and introduce yourself. This is hard for a lot of people to do, but as elaborated on in Chapter 9, there is value in getting to know your professors. The fact that they're attending the event (lots of profs don't) means that they're probably approachable people. Many law professors are shy, introverted types who are not good at "making the rounds," so don't wait for them to approach you. Don't worry. They're not going to ask you deep legal questions, but they may default to asking the classic introductory question, "What made you decide to come to law school?", which is the law professor socializing equivalent of "What's your sign?" or "What's your major?" So have an answer for that one.

Also make an effort to introduce yourself to the law school staff, such as librarians, faculty assistants, and employees in the registrar's office. These people can help you a lot. Treat them with respect, even deference. Some of them get treated shabbily by hierarchical professors and snotty students. They'll appreciate the courtesy.

Some law schools, although probably a diminishing number due in part to liability concerns, serve alcoholic beverages at these functions, usually wine and beer. Be careful about consuming alcohol as a way to calm your nerves. This is not a good time to get intoxicated.

Take a (Good) Seat

During the first week, maybe even on the first day, you will be expected to select a seat for each class that will be your permanent seat for the entire semester. The Socratic method requires that professors be able to call on students by name and to do that effectively, the profs need to know who is in which seat.

Seats usually are self-selected in law school. Your professors will pass around a seating chart configured to the particular room on which you will fill in your name in the box corresponding to the chair you are sitting in. Some professors will give advance notice as to when they intend to circulate the seating chart, but some will not. Some will distribute it on the very first day. Given the importance of seat selection, as discussed below, you want to arrive early enough for each class during the first week to be assured of getting a seat you prefer lest you become an accidental Backburner or member of the Front–Row Crowd (which would actually be a good thing, but you might not prefer it).

In the chapter on types of law students (Chapter 4), I differentiated the Backburners from the Front–Row Crowd in general terms. Now let's investigate in more detail why you should make a determined effort to select a front and center seat in all of your classes.

Non-law school educators have conducted a variety of studies on the relationship of seat choice to student personality-type and academic performance. While some of the results are inconclusive, they support one proposition quite clearly: students who choose to sit in the front of the room are generally better students. They have higher GPAs, participate more frequently in class, and receive better grades in the course. One study, for example, found that students sitting in the front received higher percentages of *A*s and students sitting in the back received higher percentages of *D*s and *F*s.[18]

Several studies have linked this better performance to personality differences between students who choose to sit in front and those who choose the back. In other words, with regard to the cause and effect relationship between seat selection and academic performance, research suggests that students who sit in front by choice do better because better students choose to sit in front. Correlatively, students who choose to sit in the back tend to have more negative attitudes

---

18. *See* Mary Ellen Benedict & John Hoag, *Seating Location in Large Lectures: Are Seating Preferences or Location Related to Course Performance?*, 35 J. ECON. EDUC. 215 (2004).

about school and about participating in class. Many of these students want to be disengaged.[19]

This research perhaps lends supports to the negative impression some law professors have of the Backburners. Thus, one reason to sit closer to the front, even if it goes against your preference, is to avoid being negatively stereotyped. Of course, like all stereotypes, this one is only right some of the time. I asked one very good student why she didn't sit closer to the front and she said, "I just don't feel comfortable with everyone behind me, looking at the back of my head." Moreover, because not everyone can sit near the front, some students may get stuck in the back against their wishes.

Practical reasons for sitting near the front.

Does sitting in back actually *cause* poorer performance? One interesting study found that it does. Conducted in a large physics course, the researchers randomly assigned seats to students and then measured their academic performance in the course. The study found that students in the back of the room "were nearly six times as likely to receive" *F*s in the course as students sitting in the front of the room.[20] While the overall research is inconclusive as to whether sitting in front by itself correlates with better test performance,[21] common sense suggests several reasons why seating could make a difference in law school:

• **Students in the front can hear better.** Most first-year law school classes are conducted by the Socratic method, meaning that much of the talking is done by students. While most law professors speak loudly enough for people in the back to hear them, most law students do not. Even when

19. *See* Herbert J. Walberg, *Physical and Psychological Distance in the Classroom*, 77 Sch. Rev. 64 (1969).

20. Katherine K. Perkins & Carl E. Wieman, *The Surprising Impact of Seat Location on Student Performance*, 43 Physics Tchr. 30 (2005). Interestingly, even when the professors flip-flopped the seating mid-semester, the students originally assigned to the front of the room continued to perform better than the group that started at the back.

21. A later study found that sitting in the back of the classroom did *not* adversely affect performance on exams. *See* Steven Kalinowksi & Mark L. Taper, *The Effect of Seat Location on Exam Grades and Student Perceptions in an Introductory Biology Class*, 36 J.C. Sci. Teaching 54 (2007). The authors noted differences that might explain the conflicting results with the Perkins–Wieman study, including that the Perkins–Wieman study involved a larger group of students and larger lecture hall. First-year law school classes, as noted, usually are quite large and, of course, are held in large rooms.

asked to speak louder, most students do not project their voices with the confidence and, hence, the volume of the professors. Moreover, students are facing the front when speaking, naturally detracting from the ability of students behind them to hear what they're saying. On several occasions, I've sat in the back of law school classrooms observing other professors' classes and always have been dismayed by how poorly the sound carries, even in well-designed classrooms. Many law school classrooms are not well designed. They're acoustical black holes.

• **Students in the front can see better.** Most law professors use some type of visual aid, whether it be Power-Point slides projected on a screen or old-fashioned handwriting scrawled on a chalkboard or dryboard. Naturally, you'll be able to see these visual aids better if you're closer. Generally, anything a law professor deems worthy of taking the time to write down or project on a screen during class is important.

• **Students in the front have fewer distractions.** As discussed in more detail later in this chapter, student misuse of notebook computers to instant message, watch videos, etc., can be very distracting to other students. The farther toward the front you are, the fewer of these and other student distractions you'll have to contend with.

• **Students in the front are more active learners.** It's well established by research that active learning is much more effective than passive learning. As already discussed, people in the front tend to be more actively engaged.

Finally, I'll share a closely guarded law professor secret with you. People in the very front get randomly called on less often than other students. Their physical closeness causes them to lower their voices even more than usual, as if they're engaged in private one-on-one conversations with the professor. Thus, professors don't call on them as often because they can't be heard by the other students. Also, in most classrooms the professor stands on a raised podium, causing the front-row students to drop below the professor's sight-line.

If it sounds like I have strong feelings about this issue, I do. I'll go so far as to say that making the decision at the beginning of law school to sit near the front in all your classes could alter your entire law school experience. Even assuming seating has no effect on exam performance, sitting in front will change the manner in which you experience law school. You'll be a participant in your class community, rather than simply an observer from a different zip code.

Classroom Etiquette

Law school classes are conducted more formally than most undergraduate classes, especially in the first year. Most first-year professors, for example, refer to students by their surnames, although younger profs are more likely to use first names. The expectations of student conduct and performance are substantially higher than in undergraduate programs, including the expectation that students conduct themselves like professionals. To avoid embarrassing yourself, offending your professors, and hurting your academic performance, follow these guidelines for classroom etiquette:

Be prepared.

As mentioned above, you will receive assignments *in advance* of the first class for each course and will be expected to be well versed in the material on the first day. Don't get caught being anything less than fully prepared, particularly in those first days. An ugly classroom incident could traumatize you for the semester and color your entire view of law school.

Many law professors follow the approach of being much sterner at the beginning of a course and then gradually becoming more laid-back as the semester progresses. The goal is to set a tone in line with the expectations of a professional school. It's always easier for a professor to move from being strict to less strict, whereas it's nearly impossible for a professor to move effectively in the other direction; that is, from being friendly to strict. This approach and mentality means that professors are more likely early on to "make examples" of students who commit classroom infractions.

No expectation is higher and no commitment is looked at as more important than being prepared for class. Successful application of the Socratic method depends on it. For most professors, there is no legitimate excuse for being unprepared on the first day of law school. Here are some sample explanations from law students for being unprepared on the first day and the likely reaction of the professor:

Student explanation: "I didn't know we had assignments for the first day."

Professor's thought process: "Everyone else figured it out. Therefore, you must either be lying or mentally defective."

Student explanation: "The bookstore ran out of books."

Professor's thought process: "You should have tracked down a book somewhere else, photocopied the assignment from a classmate's book, or come to me for help."

Student explanation: "I had a family emergency yesterday when I intended to prepare for class."

Professor's thought process: "You shouldn't have waited until yesterday."

"Being prepared" means being fully versed in the reading assignment. More specifically, as to each principal case assigned, you should know and have briefed: (1) the relevant facts of the case; (2) the procedural history that resulted in the case being heard by an appellate court (e.g., the trial court dismissed the complaint filed by the plaintiff and the plaintiff is appealing, or the trial court gave a legal instruction to the jury that the defendant asserts was incorrect and the defendant is appealing); (3) who won the case; (4) the substantive legal issue in the case; (5) the rule adopted by the court to resolve the substantive issue; and (6) why the court adopted the rule and resolved the case in the manner it did (i.e., the court's reasoning). We'll talk about these components in much more detail in the chapter on case-briefing (Chapter 11).

Be on time.

Don't arrive late to class. Most law professors expect students to be punctual. Nevertheless, even when this expectation is made clear to students during orientation and in course materials, the beginning of every new school year is marked by uncomfortable incidents in which one or more students stroll casually into the room after class has begun, only to be publicly called out for it by the professor.

This happened, for example, on the second day of a recent fall semester. I started class exactly on time, as always, and was just getting wound up when a young man ambled into the room and slowly made his way up the aisle to the back row where he sat. I stopped everything, as I always do, and gave him what my students, affectionately or not, call "the evil eye." The second his rear end touched the seat, I called on him and proceeded to interrogate him about the famous case of *Garratt v. Dailey.*[22]

Why did I do it? Not to be cruel. I hate classroom confrontations. I did it to let him and everyone else know that they had entered a new academic world, a world where learning is taken seriously and professional conduct is expected of all. To his great credit, the student recognized this, sending me an email near the end of the first semester that said:

> Thank you . . . for calling me out the second day of class when I walked in late. You have no idea how much that helped me get off to the right start in law school. I was and still am absolutely terrified of being called on in class. But after that experience, I felt like it could only get easier. I was still chewing my lunch when you gave me the stare and proceeded to ask me to discuss *Garratt v. Dailey.* I almost choked on my heart I was so scared, but managed to stutter through it somehow.

I did it because in the real legal world, lawyers are expected to be on time. My first job after law school was as a law clerk to U.S. District Court Judge Charles R. Scott, Middle District of Florida. Judge Scott taught me many valuable lessons about both life and law, including: don't ever show up late to court. Judge Scott was a kind man with a good sense of humor and mild judicial temperament, *except* when lawyers showed up late for hearings or trials. Each time this happened, I watched, wincing, as Judge Scott disdainfully scolded the lawyer—often in front of the lawyer's client and sometimes even in the presence of the jury—with comments like: "So, Mr. Smith, I suppose you think your time is more valuable than the court's time. More important than the time of these good jurors who came here to do their duty and serve their community. More important than the time of this court reporter who is being paid with taxpayer dollars." It's better to learn this lesson in law school than as

---

22. 279 P.2d 1091 (Wash. 1955).

a lawyer. Being reliable, including being on time, is part of becoming a professional.

I did it because it's distracting to everyone—professor and students alike—when people arrive late. That's why it's just as bad being one minute late as being ten minutes late. Students sometimes raise the weak defense that, "I was only a little bit late," but that can be even more disruptive because an interruption at the very beginning can throw things off track just as they're getting underway.

Of course, unexpected events arise that can cause even the most diligent students to arrive late. If that happens to you, try to send the prof an explanatory email before class or approach the prof after class and apologize. Most professors will be understanding if you have a good punctuality track record. Strict punctuality rules are aimed primarily at the Chronically Late (see Chapter 4), those students who, without some kind of deterrent, will regularly barge into class late.

Some professors are even more stringent than I am, locking the door to prevent late arrivals or instructing tardy students to turn around and exit when they walk in.

I'll share two inside secrets with you about punctuality in law school classes. First, while professors who enforce punctuality requirements sometimes take heat for being dictators, behind the scenes the vast majority of students are silently cheering them on. Your classmates may not tell you, but they don't appreciate late-arriving students either. I hear from these students all the time. They're paying good money to get the best education they can.

Second, even many professors who don't chew people out in class hate it when students arrive late. This is especially true for repeat offenders. I remember a colleague at one school who stormed into my office seething about a particular student who routinely arrived late. I recall the term "sonofabitch" being liberally sprinkled throughout the conversation. I asked the professor why he didn't simply lay down the law on punctuality and he said he didn't like conflict and that it didn't fit his personality. Carrying a deep-seated grudge against the tardy, however, apparently did.

Having said all that, you'll learn that not all professors are concerned about students being on time. You'll be able to spot them quickly based on their reaction, or lack thereof, to late-arriving students. A few profs even make a habit of arriving late themselves.

Turn off your phone ringer and mute your computer.

Yes, I know it's a no-brainer, but since it still happens, it needs mentioning. Everyone has experienced the annoying disruption of mobile phones ringing at inopportune times and in inappropriate settings. Most professors have written rules on the subject, but even if they don't, common sense dictates that you conscientiously turn off your phone before entering the classroom. Similarly, mute the volume on your computer to eliminate start-up and other sounds. One of my colleagues actually gives a "cell phone quiz" if a phone goes off—a real pop quiz that counts as part of the final grade.

Don't misuse your computer.

Don't use your computer in class to surf the internet or send or read email or instant messages or for any other purpose than taking notes. I know what you're thinking: "Well, of course, a professor would say that. They also told me not to chew gum in class when I was in elementary school, but I didn't see the harm in that either." I'm a realist. I know from experience that this is one of those pieces of advice that many people will ignore. That's why I'm going to engage in a bit of what may seem like overkill in discussing the issue in the hope that your rational self-interest will prevail in deciding whether to follow this advice.

Trust me. This is a much bigger issue among law professors than you could possibly imagine. Some profs already have banned computers from their classrooms and many more are considering doing the same. *Profs Kibosh Students' Laptops* blared a headline in the *American Bar Association Journal*. The *Washington Post* published an op-ed piece by a Georgetown law professor advocating a classroom computer ban. Just as I was about to submit this manuscript, the distinguished *Journal of Legal Education* published a lengthy article by a law professor documenting his computer prohibition and advocating that other profs follow suit. Every time I think the "great law school computer debate" is about to die down, some prof will stir it up again on the lawprof listserv, igniting yet another torrent of email on the subject.

So pay attention to these reasons why you should use your notebook computer only for note-taking while in class (and also pay attention to how to use it properly for note-taking as discussed in Chapter 12):

• **You can't listen and learn effectively if you're web browsing, instant messaging, etc.** The law is incredibly nuanced and complex. In most courses, a majority of what you will need to know for the exam will be derived from classroom elucidation of the reading assignments, not from the assignments themselves.

One response to the argument against extraneous computer use is that before computers, students played hangman, doodled, worked crossword puzzles or simply daydreamed in class. True, but that was never a good academic success plan either. Also, there's a qualitative difference in the ubiquitous and pervasive distraction of a computer compared to old-fashioned classroom distractions. Everyone probably has played tic-tac-toe in class at some point, but it's doubtful anyone ever spent a portion of *every* class playing it. Some experts argue that obsessive or compulsive internet use qualifies as an addiction, but I don't recall ever reading about folks struggling with doodling or crossword-puzzle addictions.

A more intriguing response is that today's law students are so skilled at multitasking that they really can learn law and check sports scores at the same time. Is it true? Research suggests the answer is "no," or at least "not as effectively." In general, studies regarding the ability of the brain to engage in simultaneous tasks show "almost without exception" that the performance of one or both tasks directly suffers.[23]

In the cited study, researchers tracked the wireless computer activity of students during class. Not surprisingly, the study showed students used their computers for a wide range of functions unrelated to the class, such as email and web browsing. The researchers then divided a class into two groups. Prior to a lecture, one group was told to use their computers as usual, while the other was asked to close their computers. Afterwards, the researchers gave the students a surprise test. The students who used their laptops during the

---

23. *See* Helene Hembrooke & Geri Gay, *The Laptop and the Lecture: The Effects of Multitasking in Learning En-* vironments, 15 J. COMPUTING HIGHER EDUC. 46, 49 (2003).

lecture performed significantly poorer on the test. Two months later the researchers replicated the test by switching the two groups of students, and got the same results.

Another study suggested that even if multitasking does not necessarily decrease the overall ability to learn, it negatively affects the kind of learning used to acquire new concepts and information and to engage in deep analysis—learning abilities that are critical to law students. Researchers did MRI brain imaging of fourteen twenty-somethings engaged in dual-task learning. The brain imaging showed that multitaskers engaged in "habit learning" rather than "declarative learning." Habit learning relies on a portion of the brain used for repetitive skills, whereas declarative learning involves a portion of the brain used for storing and recalling information. Basically, the researchers concluded that even though people can learn while multitasking, they can't learn the material as well or be able to adapt it to changing conditions.[24]

While some people are adept at doing several tasks simultaneously, the research suggests they can't do all the tasks well because of the brain's limited processing ability. So if your professor is defining the Rule Against Perpetuities at the same moment you're instant messaging your pal to see what time everyone is meeting up at the club, something has to give.

• **It's rude and disrespectful to nearby classmates, the professor, and to the class as a whole to abuse your computer privileges.** Law students frequently complain to me about the distraction factor when instant messages pop up on the computers of those sitting around them. Here's what one student said about it:

> The main distraction is instant messaging (IM). … IM is great for out of class to converse with friends or ask classmates questions about class material without actually having to find the person and audibly talk to them while in the library. In class though, it's just distracting. When someone is using it, their screen flashes, which is hard not to notice while sitting behind someone. Then you hear the keys typing when

---

24. *See* Karin Foerde, Barbara J. Knowlton & Russell A. Poldrack, *Modulation of Competing Memory Systems by* *Distraction*, 103 Proc. Nat'l Acad. Sci. 11778 (2006).

there are no notes to be taken, and every time someone signs on or off the IM network there is a little box that pops up notifying everyone of that occurrence. One IM sent during class has the possibility of distracting six people: two persons on each side of the recipient, the recipient, the sender, and perhaps two people behind the recipient. That's a lot of downtime in class for one little message.

In addition to avoiding distracting others, students have an obligation to the class community to stay engaged. Each time someone mentally checks out of a class, the class energy and dynamics suffer.

- **Most professors have explicit policies, often in writing, against using computers for any purpose other than note-taking.** Violating any explicit class policy can constitute academic misconduct. Occasionally, computer misuse crosses the boundary into the realm of overt cheating. Incidents have occurred where students instant message the answers to professors' questions to classmates being called on. Since classroom performance can affect grades, such conduct could be grounds for Honor Code prosecutions.

- **Everyone can see what you're doing.** Not only are you violating class policy and the professor's trust if you misuse your computer, you're doing it in front of a large group of eyewitnesses. Some students will lose respect for classmates who violate explicit law school or class rules. A few of them might even be willing to rat you out to the professor. It's happened with me. The professor, in turn, whether or not he ever addresses the issue with you, may never trust you again.

Moreover, the more frequently students violate professors' computer policies, the more justified professors will feel in banning computers altogether, to everyone's detriment. I'm a big supporter of computers and technology, but each time I learn of students violating my class policies regarding computer use, I move one step closer to banning them myself.

Don't talk to seatmates during class.

This is another obvious rule. Your colleagues are trying to concentrate on learning complex material. They don't want to hear your chattering, even if it's about the course material. I've had students ask to switch seats because of motor-mouth classmates. Also, talking draws attention to you. Some professors will see it as an invitation to call on you.

Keep in mind that your professors can see what's going on out there in the classroom. It always cracks me up that some students act as if they're protected by a Harry Potter-type cloak of invisibility just because they're sitting in a group of people. Professors notice when students smirk, sigh heavily, roll their eyes, and talk to their seat neighbors. Behave professionally in the classroom. One of the cardinal rules of courtroom etiquette for trial lawyers is never, ever do any of the above in response to remarks by other lawyers, witnesses or the judge.

* * *

Following the suggestions in this chapter will help you get off to a good start in law school in general and especially in your classes. Don't be intimidated by the admonishments. They're mostly common sense if you think about them. My guess is you'll be pleasantly surprised by how interesting and enjoyable law school classes can be.

CHAPTER 7

THE SOCRATIC AND CASE
METHODS: ORIGINS, PURPOSES,
FACTS, AND MYTHS

"Mr./Ms. _____, what's a tort?"

Often, these are the first words I utter at my initial Torts class of a new academic year. No introduction, no "let's get to know each other" chat, no overview of the class or review of class policies, not even a "Hi, I'm McClurg." I enter the classroom, set my book and notes on the podium, look at the class roster, pick a name, and ask the question. I'm expecting the textbook answer—literally. When a student gives the right answer (it's not a difficult question—the definition is in the second sentence of the initial reading assignment), I start leading the student through a series of hypothetical fact patterns designed to explore what conduct might or might not qualify as a tort under the definition. And, in the words of legendary comedian Jackie Gleason, *awaaaaay we go.*

Likely within minutes, perhaps even seconds, of beginning your first official law school classes, you will be introduced to the Socratic method. Despite continuing criticism, the Socratic method has been, is, and will likely remain law school's "signature pedagogy."[25] The Socratic method involves professors calling on students, typically without prior notice, to recite and analyze cases (i.e., written judicial opinions) and the legal principles raised therein. Most incoming law stu-

---

25. *See* WILLIAM M. SULLIVAN, ANNE COLBY, JUDITH WELCH WEGNER, LLOYD BOND & LEE S. SHULMAN, EDUCATING LAWYERS: PREPARATION FOR THE PROFESSION OF LAW 23–24 (2007) (report of the Carnegie Foundation for the Advancement of Teaching characterizing the Socratic method in these terms).

dents are at least somewhat familiar with the Socratic method, usually through having heard exaggerated horror stories about it from people who went to law school or from fictionalized accounts in movies such as *The Paper Chase* and *Legally Blonde* or in books such as Scott Turow's *One L.*

When I was a law student, my main question about the Socratic method was "why?" Why are the professors doing this to us? Why all the questions? Why no answers? Why don't they just tell us what the law is? Here's why:

How a Man Named Christopher Columbus Langdell Changed Your Life

The Socratic method is credited to and named after Socrates (470–399 BC), a Greek philosopher who engaged in continuous questioning of his students in a quest to discover moral and ethical truths. Along the way, he exposed their fallacies in reasoning, first, by getting the answerer to commit to certain assumptions and then asking questions designed to shine a light on the contradictions or other flaws in those assumptions. A hallmark of his method—one that continues to haunt law students more than two thousand years later—is that Socrates only asked questions. He rarely provided answers.

The origins of the Socratic method in law school teaching are traceable back to the 1870s and the inception of what is known as the "case method." To make any sense of the Socratic method, one must understand the case method. The two methods are inextricably intertwined. In the old days, law was taught in U.S. law schools principally through a lecture method. Much like in many of your undergraduate courses, students would read explanations of the law in textbooks, professors would expand on that law in lectures, and students would be tested principally on their ability for rote memorization. But in the 1870s along came Christopher Columbus Langdell, the man who is credited with (or blamed for) irrevocably changing the way U.S. law students learn law.

Langdell, a professor and later dean of Harvard Law School, believed that true mastery of the law could not be achieved by simply memorizing it. Rather, students had to develop a facility for *applying* legal principles to the varied fact patterns that lead to legal disputes, or what he called "the ever-tangled skein of human affairs."[26] By understanding how law is applied, Langdell believed students would be able to transfer what they learn in one context and apply it in other contexts. To implement his vision, he came up with the idea to replace explanatory textbooks with "casebooks" filled with appellate judicial opinions.

I still recall coming home from the bookstore before I started law school with my shiny new casebooks. I sat down and opened my Contracts book with excited anticipation. I was about to learn "law" for the first time! But I couldn't find any; well, not any I could make sense of. There was no explanation of contracts law, not even a definition of what constitutes a contract, just hundreds of pages of judicial opinions, many of them very old and opaquely written. I started reading the first case, but couldn't make heads or tails of it. I had no idea what the point was. If I had known then about Christopher Langdell, I probably would have cursed him. Casebooks haven't changed much. While most modern casebooks do contain some explanatory notes following the cases, the cases themselves remain the primary vehicle for learning law in U.S. law schools.

Under the case method, students do the heavy lifting. Instead of sitting passively listening to lectures, the case method requires students to think critically and discover the law on their own in response to questions posed by the professors.[27] The Socratic dialogue method of teaching developed as an instrument for implementing the case method. Think of it as the steering mechanism that guides the case-method vehicle.

How It Works

The classic portrayal of the Socratic method in law school came from the 1973 movie, *The Paper Chase*, based on John Jay Osborn's book of the same name. Actor John Housman won an Oscar for his portrayal of the curmudgeonly, imperious Professor Charles Kingsfield, a fictional Contracts professor at Harvard Law School, who torments first-year student

---

26. Peggy Cooper Davis & Elizabeth Ehrenfest Steinglass, *A Dialogue About Socratic Teaching*, 23 N.Y.U. REV. L. & SOC. CHANGE 249, 263 (1997) (quoting Langdell).

27. *See generally id.* (exploring the history and present use of the Socratic method); David D. Garner, *The Continuing Vitality of the Case Method in the Twenty–First Century*, 2000 BYU EDUC. & L.J. 307 (2000) (providing history and summary of the case method).

James T. Hart, played by Timothy Bottoms. The movie is a classic that all law students should watch, but too few do. It's fun. Rent it.

In the movie, Kingsfield is a terror, famously instructing his Contracts students, in that great John Housman voice: "You come in here with skulls full of mush and leave thinking like a lawyer." When poor Hart screws up in class, Kingsfield tells him: "Mr. Hart, here is a dime. Take it, call your mother, and tell her there is serious doubt about you ever becoming a lawyer."

Is this a dated portrayal of legal education? Of course it is. You can't make a phone call for a dime anymore. You can't even find a phone booth. In today's wireless law schools, Hart would simply close the screen to his Facebook page and zip out an instant message to his mom. Seriously, Housman's performance was exaggerated for dramatic effect, but it did capture the essentials of how the Socratic method operates. The traditional model incorporates these essential components:

- Cold-calling on a student from a seating chart.

- Asking the student to "state the case," which entails narrating the facts and other aspects about the case, such as its procedural history, issue, holding, and reasoning.

- Testing the student's understanding of the case with more questions, which usually include hypothetical fact patterns that require the student to interpret and apply the legal principle(s) from the case. This is the component of the Socratic method most closely connected with the oft-stated goal of the method to teach students to "think like a lawyer."

- Failing to offer concrete answers to the questions asked based on the assumption that the students, through the dialogue, should be able to figure out the answers on their own.

Depending on the skill and technique of the professor, for students, the whole thing can come off as resembling a bizarre treasure hunt in which neither the professor nor the casebook provides the answers, at least not directly. In fact, most of the answers are contained in or inferable from the judicial opinions in the casebooks, but they're often hidden between the lines.

The Current State of the Socratic Method

For decades, the Socratic method has been under attack from within legal academia.[28] What is the current state of the Socratic method? It depends whom you ask. Some have proclaimed its demise. One professor, an advocate of the method, wrote that "[p]opular myth has it that the Socratic method is pervasive in American law schools," adding that "nothing could be further from the truth."[29] But a different writer says "[t]he Socratic Method remains the primary method of law teaching today."[30]

Who's right? Both. The disagreement stems from problems in defining the Socratic method. In its original form as a dialectical "flight of the imagination through a world of allegories, parables and myths,"[31] the method is not only dead, it probably never lived in legal education in the first place because most law professors and students simply do not possess the skills and knowledge to carry it out. In its modern law school image as a teaching method where the professor "hides the ball" and then humiliates students who can't find it, that too is clearly on the wane.

But broadly defined as a style of teaching in which professors call on students, usually without warning, expecting informed, intelligent answers as part of a back and forth exchange (as opposed to simply lecturing), the Socratic style does indeed remain the dominant teaching methodology in U.S. law schools, particularly in the first year.[32]

28. *See, e.g.,* STUCKEY ET AL., *supra,* at 132–41 (calling for reduced reliance on the Socratic method).

29. Donald G. Marshall, Socratic Method and the Irreducible core of Legal education, Presentation at Law Alumni Distinguished Teacher Inauguration (January 19, 1994), *in* 90 MINN. L. REV. 1, 2 (2005).

30. Cynthia G. Hawkins–Leon, *The Socratic Method–Problem Method Dichotomy: The Debate Over Teaching Method Continues,* 1998 BYU EDUC. & L.J. 1, 5 (1998).

31. Paul N. Savoy, *Toward A New Politics of Legal Education,* 79 YALE L.J. 444, 468 (1970).

32. Professor Stephen I. Friedland surveyed law professors back in the mid–1990s to determine how they teach. He sent out approximately 2,000 questionnaires, to which he received 574 completed responses. Ninety-seven percent of the respondents said they use the Socratic method as least some of the time in first-year courses, with 31 percent reporting they use it most of the time, and 41 percent reporting they use it often. Comparatively, only 31 percent of the professors surveyed reported that they use a lecture method "some of the time" in first-year courses (a percentage that soared to 94 percent in upper-level courses). *See* Stephen I. Friedland, *How We Teach: A Survey of Teaching Tech-*

With so Much Criticism, Why do Professors Keep Using the Socratic and Case Methods?

The Socratic and case methods have faced resistance since their inception. After 140 years of criticism, why do most first-year professors continue to use them? Because we genuinely believe that the combination of the Socratic and case methods is the most effective way to train new law students to develop the critical-thinking skills they will need as lawyers.[33] Like all students, I hated the Socratic method back in law school. As a professor, however, I came to appreciate the great usefulness of dialectical questioning as a tool for teaching students to discover knowledge on their own. Plus, it's fun scaring the hell out of people.

Seriously, the Socratic and case methods, in the right hands, can be excellent tools for guiding students to "think like a lawyer," which simply means learning to reason well. As Langdell recognized, you could memorize all the legal rules in the world, but still be a lousy lawyer. Good lawyering is about problem-solving and the Socratic and case methods are intended to force students to learn by doing rather than simply by being told how it is done.

The difference in the way 1Ls think about legal problems at the beginning and end of the first year is dramatically apparent. Even the Socratic-haters would be hard-pressed to deny that they really did arrive at law school with "skulls full of mush," yet exited the Socratic arena as facile thinkers and astute legal problem-solvers. Look at this comment from a 1L two weeks away from finishing his first year:

> Just the other week I was eating lunch with some of my section friends and reading through a case for class. Without thinking, I said something like, "Don't you all think that we are so much better at reading cases now?" They looked at me like I just stated the most obvious thing in the world. I had just never really thought of it like that. When you stop and think about the evolution of your abilities from the beginning of the year to the end, it is really astonishing.

niques in American Law Schools, 20 SE-ATTLE U. L. REV. 1 (1996).

33. After visiting sixteen law schools across the country, the authors of the 2007 Carnegie Foundation report on legal education concluded that "nearly all the law faculty" with whom they spoke endorsed the case-dialogue method as the best way to train 1Ls in "the craft of legal reasoning." *See* SULLIVAN ET AL., *supra*, at 66.

The Socratic method has benefits in addition to fostering the development of legal reasoning skills. It helps train students to think on their feet and articulate their reasoning, vital abilities for any lawyer. It provides a strong incentive for students to be prepared, substantially enhancing the quality of the classroom experience for all involved. What percentage of students in your undergraduate courses would you estimate spent hours preparing for *every* class? In first-year law school courses, the figure is close to 100 percent. While the level of preparation varies among students, only rarely do 1L students come to class completely unprepared. One big reason is that they don't want to be publicly embarrassed in front of their peers and professors if called on. The Socratic method also facilitates a much more interesting exploration of legal issues than pure lecturing, the principal realistic option in large classes.

Is it a perfect methodology? Far from it. First, the success of the method is heavily dependent on the skill of the professor. As one colleague commented in reading this chapter, "Some professors do it well, but I'm not sure that's the norm."

Also, the large size of law school classes renders most students passive bystanders in the process at any given time. The true Socratic method envisions one-on-one instruction or small group tutorials—which can't be accomplished in most 1L classes. Both the Socratic and case methods work better in small classes, but a lack of resources prevents most law schools from considering them for first-year courses. But even students who aren't directly participating learn from watching and listening to Socratic dialoging. The Carnegie Foundation report on legal education observed that one way in which the Socratic method enhances student intellectual development is through *modeling*; that is, the students learn by watching and modeling the cognitive skills of the professor displayed during case-dialoging.[34]

34. The Carnegie Foundation report on legal education classified law school case-dialoging as a type of "cognitive apprenticeship" in which student intellectual development occurs through faculty-student interaction. Observing professor-student Socratic exchanges at sixteen law schools, the report's authors observed professors employing four basic apprenticeship teaching methods identified by cognitive theorists: *modeling*, by demonstrating in class the type of cognitive skills the professor seeks to instill in the students; *coaching*, by providing guidance and feedback; *scaffolding*, by providing support for students who haven't yet mastered critical-thinking skills; and

Other shortcomings of the Socratic method are discussed in the facts and myths section below, but when all is said and done, I remain convinced that the Socratic method, while flawed, beats the viable alternatives for training 1Ls to conduct legal analysis.

Sample Socratic Dialogue

With that introduction, let's see what the Socratic method looks like in action. Back in 2002, at the University of Arkansas at Little Rock, I asked a research assistant to videotape several Torts classes in preparation for a teaching presentation at the Institute for Law School Teaching. The following excerpted transcript, from a class on April 22, 2002, will give you an idea of how the Socratic method works.[35] Note the date. This class occurred near the end of the first year, when students had already mastered case-dialoging.

The issue under discussion is defamation law (i.e., libel and slander), which is part of tort law. Specifically, we were exploring the famous 1964 U.S. Supreme Court case of *New York Times v. Sullivan*,[36] in which the Court held that the First Amendment limits the ability of states to award tort damages for defamation against public officials.

Without being overly specific, the Court imposed a high hurdle known as the "actual malice" test that public officials (later extended to include any public figure) have to meet to recover damages for defamation. The test requires a public official to prove that the defendant knew the defamatory statement was false or published the statement in reckless disregard of whether it was true or false, which the Court later interpreted to mean that the plaintiff must prove the defendant subjectively (i.e., internally in his own mind) entertained serious doubts as to the truth of the statement. Ever wonder why you don't read about more defamation suits brought by public officials or public figures? *New York Times v. Sullivan* is the reason.

On the videotape, the back and forth exchange set forth below, which explores the application of the *New York Times* test to a hypothetical, was lively, rapid-fire action. The tone

fading, by encouraging students to go it alone when they've shown themselves prepared to do so. *See id.* at 60–61.

35. The transcript is not perfectly verbatim from the original videotape, but it is reasonably close.

36. 376 U.S. 254 (1964).

of some of my questions, not apparent from the cold text, was
sarcastic. But by this point, the students knew how to play
the Socratic game. They didn't take my questioning personally, nor should they have. The discussion involves three students, whom I'll call Mr. Forbes, Ms. Davidson, and Ms.
Carvel and label as S1, S2, and S3 in the transcript.

The excerpt begins after a good deal of lecture and dialoging about the case itself. We pick up just after, in good
Socratic fashion, I got Mr. Forbes to commit himself to the
desirability of the actual malice test as a means for protecting
free speech:

Me: Mr. Forbes, let me give you a hypothetical. Suppose we have a
candidate running for public office. He's running for governor
of the state. He's a man who has led an exemplary life. As far
as we know, there are no blemishes on his record of any
significance. An anonymous source calls the state's largest
newspaper and says "I have inside information that this
person is a child molester." The reporter tries to ask questions, but the caller hangs up. The newspaper publishes the
allegation that the person running for governor is a child
molester. It's false—completely false. Can he win? Can he
prove actual malice under *New York Times v. Sullivan*?

S1: Did the newspaper know that it was false?

Me: All they knew is what I've told you. It was a tip from an
anonymous source. They didn't check it out. They didn't
investigate it.

S1: I don't think the plaintiff can prove actual malice. He can
show negligence. They obviously should have investigated. But
that's not enough.

Me: Why can't he prove actual malice?

S1: It doesn't satisfy the test.

Me: Should they be able to get away with that? This person's life
has been ruined. He lost the governorship. Would you vote for
somebody if there are allegations out there that they were a
child molester?

S1: I don't know. I think probably not.

Me: We can certainly imagine a lot of people thinking that, "Even
if it's *possibly* true, I don't think I want that person as
governor."

S1: Public officials have to put up with a lot of things that are said
about them that I think we know as a society, often times, are
questionable whether they're true or not.

Me: Is that a fair price to expect a person seeking government office to pay? Should they have to put up with that? Ms. Davidson? [Raised hand to volunteer.]

S2: I'd just say that's an oversimplified hypothetical because people in the news business just aren't going to take one anonymous tip and publish something like that, something that's so defamatory and inappropriate. So they're going to follow up and—

Me: Let's suppose in this case they didn't follow up.

S2: But they are not going to do that because they know they're going to get sued and lose.

Me: But that's my question, are they going to lose? Mr. Forbes said they're not going to lose.

S2: Under the actual malice test? Well, I guess they wouldn't lose unless what the newspaper did was reckless disregard for the truth.

Me: Based on the facts I gave you, do we have any evidence that they knew it was false?

S2: No.

Me: Do we have any evidence that they in fact, and can we prove, that they entertained—in their heads—serious doubts as to whether it was true or false?

S2: No, I guess not.

Me: So that would mean that under the actual malice test, the newspaper would win.

S2: But I think that those instances are so rare that we need to protect it just as much as we need to protect the times when it's true.

Me: So you're a fan of the actual malice test?

S2: I think, well, I don't know, I'm not sure I really like the actual malice test, but I like protecting free speech at all costs.

Me: Well, then you love the actual malice test because that's basically what it does. It protects speech at almost all costs. Here, the cost is that an innocent person who has led an unblemished life has had his life completely ruined by a false, unsupported allegation and has no remedy.

S2: I think the court said in *New York Times v. Sullivan* that the value of free speech to society is worth more than one person's reputation. We have a greater good that we're concerned with and that's the public's right to free speech. It's a utilitarian view.

Me: That is what they did, but, of course, it's not going to be just one individual. It's going to be some number of individuals. The question is, where do we strike the balance between free speech and the states' interest in protecting the reputational rights of its citizens? Did the court strike the balance in the right place? In this case, you feel comfortable that this person's life has been ruined by a false allegation and he has no remedy whatsoever? He's just "one individual." One very sad individual.

S2: I think he'll have a remedy.

Me: What remedy?

S2: They have spin-doctors who work for them. They'll fix it somehow.

Me: Oh yeah, it's easy to get around an allegation of being a child molester. It's no big deal, just spin it a little. "Oh well, I wasn't a child *molester*, I was a . . . "—how are we going to spin that one?

S2: If they can spin oral sex in the White House [referring the President Bill Clinton–Monica Lewinsky incident], I think you can spin being a child molester.

Me: They didn't spin it all that well. [Laughter] But beyond that, it's still an allegation of—

S2: It's a shame, but it's the price we pay to protect free speech. So yeah, it's too bad, but I don't have a high opinion of public officials anyway.

Me: Ms. Carvel? [Raised hand to volunteer.]

S3: I was just going to say because they are public officials, they have an opportunity to speak to the public and defend themselves.

Me: Okay, that's true.

S3: Also, because they are unprotected, I think people will look at those statements and not take them as seriously because they are commonly done.

Me: Ms. Carvel, I've heard some of the most audacious stories about people right here at the law school. Have you heard any? About the students, the faculty. I'm thinking surely people couldn't possibly believe that. But then talking to students, I realize people do believe them—just because someone says it, people believe it. If you print it in the newspaper, don't you think a lot of people are going to believe it, even if it's completely preposterous?

S3: Yeah, but I go back to the person is probably going to be able to defend themselves. I agree there are a lot of negative aspects to it, but they are in a position to defend themselves compared to a person who is not a public figure.

Me: That's a very good point, and what we're going to see at the next class in *Gertz v. Welch* is that the Supreme Court has constructed different, more protective rules for private figure defamation plaintiffs. One of the main rationales they give is that public figures have greater avenues for self-help. Okay, so the guy comes out and says to a room full of cameras, "I am not a child molester," and that's just going to make it all go away?

S3: No, it's not.

Me: No. He's still going to probably lose the election, isn't he?

S3: I don't know. I hear so many different things in politics, and so many of them are false. Maybe in Brazil where I'm from, it's worse. I don't know. We just hear all kinds of things about politicians, and I don't believe them.

Me: You don't?

S3: I don't.

Me: So if you were going to vote for this person for governor, and it came out in the state's largest newspaper that he's a child molester, it wouldn't affect your decision? You'd just dismiss that.

S3: I don't know if I'd dismiss it.

Me: You'd still vote for him?

S3: Maybe.

So there you have it: your first real Socratic dialogue. It wasn't so bad, was it? If you could watch the videotape, you'd see that students seemed to be enjoying it. Of course, they were veteran 1Ls who had left their fears of the Socratic method behind. They'd been through almost an entire year of Socratic-dialoging and had learned that the tales of terrorizing they heard about it prior to coming to law school were myths.

Let's explore those and other myths, as well as some facts, about the present-day Socratic method and its intimate companion, the case method:

Ten Facts and Myths about the Socratic Method

1. The Socratic method strikes fear in the hearts and minds of 1Ls. FACT. There's nothing quite like being called on without prior notice in front of a large group of peers and expected to speak articulately and intelligently about a question you've never thought about before. It's enough to make anyone anxious. Imagine you're sitting there in class minding your own business. The professor is talking at a hundred miles an hour when all of a sudden your name rings out:

> *Mr. Smith!* A shoots at B, but misses and hits C, who loses control of her car and crashes into D, driving a school bus full of children—H, I, J, K, L, M, N, O and P—down a winding mountain road. The school bus careens into a gas pump at the exact second lightning hits the pump. In the explosion, E, a piece of glass, hits F, walking his dog, G, nearby. G gets loose and viciously attacks Q, a law student, carrying an armload of casebooks up a staircase. The books fall on R, causing massive head injuries. R is rushed to the ER by EMTs, gets CPR from an RN and an IV from an MD, but he's DOA. To make matters worse, his HMO refuses to pay for his MRI. Who wins? [Three second pause.] Quick, quick, Mr. Smith! We don't have all day.

There's no way around it. Even when wielded in a humane manner, the process is inherently intimidating. One of my favorite law school stories involved literally the very first person I ever called on as a Torts professor, way back in 1987. I asked a student to state the facts of a case. In a nervous, timid voice, she stated the facts quite suitably. Trying to give her affirmation, I said, "Yes, those are the facts in a nutshell." The student became visibly distraught. I later learned she thought I was accusing her of having not read the case and simply swiping the facts from the West *Nutshell Series* study aid for Torts. Those crazy law students.

One common fear students have about the Socratic method is that they will blank out in a panic attack when called on. Although rare, it does happen. In fact, it happened to me. My Constitutional Law professor was a Socratic traditionalist in the truest sense. I arrived at every class anxious about being called on. One day the professor called on me in that smug, challenging way we professors enjoy. I don't remember the question or even the subject matter. I only remember a cloud of anxiety enveloping my brain to the point where it stopped functioning. I heard the professor repeat "Mr. McClurg?" No response. After the passage of some time, probably just seconds but it seemed much longer, he moved on to another student. I never uttered a word. I share this story with my first-year students and they seem to find it comforting.

2. Professors use the Socratic method to intimidate and break down students. MYTH. In writing this book, I came across several articles by law professors talking about the degrading, alienating, and hostile wielding of the Socratic method, and wondered whom they were talking about. When I finished the manuscript, I thumbed through a law school prep book that compared the Socratic method to Darwin's theory of natural selection, warning that "only the strong will survive."

Trust me. While surviving the entirety of the first year is difficult, surviving the Socratic method is not. I've taught at several law schools and am acquainted with many law professors. While I'm sure some ruthless and sadistic law professors exist, I personally don't know a single professor who uses the Socratic method to *intentionally* bully or break down students. My experience is consistent with Professor Paul Brest's that "[t]he terrorist version of the Socratic method has almost disappeared."[37] Asked in a survey to name the biggest surprise about law school, one of my 1Ls wrote: "What is the big deal about the Socratic method? It is written about like it's some kind of torture. I have yet to see anyone really crucified."

Professors use the Socratic method for the reasons described above—not for the purpose of intimidating students.

3. The Socratic method is an inefficient way to convey information. FACT. One of the major complaints students have about how law school classes are conducted is that the Socratic method and accompanying class discussion waste too much time with questions and student comments, time that could be used more efficiently if the professor would simply explain the material in a lecture format. It's true that the Socratic and case methods are not an efficient

37. Paul Brest, *Plus Ca Change*, 91 MICH. L. REV. 1945, 1948 (1993).

way to convey information. What students overlook, however, is that conveying information is only one goal of teaching law in the first year, albeit an important one. As discussed above, training students to reason well and solve legal problems are the principal aspirations of both the Socratic and case methods.

As a student, it's hard to appreciate these goals because mastering legal reasoning is a gradual process and we live in an instant-gratification society. Compare studying law to working out at the gym to build and tone muscles. Many people who join health clubs give up too quickly because they don't see immediate results. But those who stay with it for a few months will be standing in front of a mirror one day saying, "Wow, check out those Calvin Klein abs!" It's sort of the same thing with law. After a few months, you can stand in front of the mirror and say, "Wow, check out those flabby abs, but at least I know how to apply the Model Penal Code to decide whether conduct constitutes a conspiracy!"

4. Under the Socratic method, law professors only ask, not answer, questions. MYTH in modern practice. This may have been accurate in the past, but it is no longer true of most professors. Even most Socratic traditionalists lecture at least some of the time. Recently, Elizabeth Mertz conducted a study of first-year Contracts classes at eight law schools and found that the percentage of class time devoted to lecture ranged from 21 percent to 95 percent.[38]

In addition to doing at least some explaining via lecture, most professors will attempt to give concrete answers to student questions that have concrete answers (many questions don't), although it is common for law professors to try to get students to figure out the answers to some questions first. "What do *you* think?" is a classic, frustration-inducing law professor response to student questions. Professors don't do this to embarrass students or because they're too lazy to answer a question. Remember, the goal of the Socratic method is to force students to learn by doing. Accordingly, questions that relate to problem-solving are often met with the "What do you think?"-response. For example, if we were discussing the defense to negligence known as "implied assumption of risk" and a student asked me to explain a point of law involving the defense, I'd happily do it. But if the

---

38. *See* SULLIVAN ET. AL., *supra*, at 51–52 (discussing Mertz study).

student asked, "Would it be implied assumption of risk for the plaintiff to get into a car with a drunk driver, knowing the driver is drunk?", I might reply, "What do you think?" because I'd want the student to reason through the puzzle applying the rules we learned.

5. In law, there are no right answers, only good arguments. MYTH. Some sources are fond of espousing this view to students, but it's simply not true. Many legal questions have clearly right or wrong answers. Not everything in the law is gray. If the professor asks whether the plaintiff prevailed in a particular case and you say "yes," that's a right answer if the plaintiff in fact prevailed but a wrong answer if the defendant won. If the professor asks you to state the elements of the tort of battery, you either know them and can state them (right answer) or you don't know them and can't state them (wrong answer). If the professor asks for the court's holding in a case where the court made the holding clear, again, you'll be giving a right answer if you can state the holding accurately and a wrong answer if you can't (although there is often room for interpretation as to what exactly was the holding of a case). In general, many of the questions posed in connection with Socratic case *recitation* are likely to have right and wrong answers.

On the other hand, much more so than in scientific disciplines, it is true that in law many questions do not have objectively right or wrong answers. Many legal standards are vague, purposely so because they must be applied to an infinite variety of factual permutations (that "tangled skein of human affairs" of which Langdell spoke). In Torts, for example, you'll see that much of the law of negligence, the principal topic covered in the course, depends on whether a person acted "reasonably under the circumstances." Since the answer depends both on one's own conception of reasonable behavior and also the particular circumstances of the case, certainty remains elusive in determining whether a party was negligent.

Note also that questions soliciting your opinion or other subjective assessment of a result, rule or policy—and there will be many such questions—lack objectively right answers. Or stated another way, such questions can have many right answers. This doesn't mean professors will not challenge your answers to such questions. They very well might, even if they agree with them.

Back in the beginning, I advised you to "embrace uncertainty" precisely because the law is so indeterminate. But don't buy into the ridiculous notion that there are no right or wrong answers in law school.

6. Professors penalize students who don't know the answer or who are unprepared for class. MYTH as to the first part and, depending on the professor, FACT as to the second part. Most professors show patience for prepared students who simply don't know the answer and empathy for prepared, but obviously nervous students, who fumble with their answers. Note the caveat *prepared*. While some professors allow students to simply take a "pass" when called on (sometimes limited to a certain number of passes per semester), most first-year professors expect students to be prepared for each class. Professor responses to unprepared students vary widely, but can include: no response, a scowl, placing a mark by the student's name on the seating chart, ranting at the student or the class as a whole, walking out of the room if several students are unprepared, and lowering the student's grade.

7. The Socratic method entails cold-calling on students without prior notice. FACT, but undergoing change. Traditionally, this was a fact, and probably still is in most first-year classes. Part of what makes the Socratic method anxiety-provoking is the element of surprise. Most professors just call on students randomly from the seating chart, with no particular rhyme or reason to their selection process. Often I'll look at the seating chart before class, and jot down four or five names on a Post–It note based on my recollection of not having heard from those students much or recently. Some professors use a more scientific method, such as keeping track of how many times they've called on students by making check-marks on the seating chart. Some professors randomly draw names from a stack of cards, as if they were awarding door prizes instead of interrogation. Some professors rely primarily on volunteers, usually more so as the year progresses.

Increasingly, professors are turning to what is called a "panel" or "designated hitter" system of selecting students to be called on. Even many Socratic traditionalists use this method in upper-level courses, but until a few years ago, the panel system was uncommon in first-year courses. The panel system entails the professor identifying a group of students in advance (usually from four to six) to be in the Socratic hot seat on a particular day. The advantage of this method for the professor and the class is that, because the students know in advance they are going to be called on, they are better prepared, raising the level of classroom discussion and reducing the time-waste that can result from engaging less than fully prepared students. The advantage for students is that they can relax on the days when they are not "on panel," knowing they won't be called on.

The downside of the panel system for legal education is that many students take advantage of it, using it as a license to not prepare on the days they are not on panel. Many students have confided this to me. Often the confessors are diligent students indignant that so many of their classmates are getting away with not preparing for class. Of course, in the end, students who don't prepare for class only hurt themselves.

8. Because the chances of getting randomly called on in a large first-year class are small, it's a worthwhile cost-benefit trade-off to not prepare and take your chances. MYTH. The first part is basically true. In a large first-year class, the odds of getting called on in any particular class on any particular day are relatively small—but not lottery-odds small. Typically, a Socratic professor will cold-call on two to five people per class hour (although I know one professor who calls on as many as twenty students per class, asking only one question per student).

In an average-size class of seventy-seven students, this means that your odds of getting called on in any particular class range from one in thirty-three to one in fifteen. This is setting aside subjective factors that may increase your chance of getting called on, such as: the professor thinks you're unprepared, the professor knows you're reliable, you're wearing a bright yellow shirt, you came up to talk to the prof before class and are fresh in his mind's eye, you arrived late to class, etc. Fifteen to one odds or even thirty-three to one odds get beaten all the time. Gamblers spend billions annually betting on odds worse than that.

I can turn the low-odds argument around as a reason why you should *always* be prepared. Precisely because you *won't* get called on randomly very often in a large class, it's important that you don't screw up what may be your only opportunity to look good when you do get called on. A single incident of unpreparedness can define you in the eyes of your peers and professors. Unless you volunteer, you might not have an opportunity to redeem yourself.

9.   If you make a mistake during Socratic questioning, you'll be humiliated in front of the professor and all of your classmates. MYTH. No one likes to be publicly embarrassed. A central component of the angst generated by the Socratic method is the fear of "looking stupid" in front of the professor and one's peers. This is a needless worry, however, for several reasons. First, and regrettably, most students simply aren't listening that closely to what other students say in class, particularly as the year wears on. Those in the back can't hear a lot of student comments and many students who can hear aren't paying attention because they're interested only in what the professor has to say. I know this from years of experiencing situations where a student gives a correct answer, and I say, "Yes, that's it. Did everyone get that?", only to be greeted by a sea of shaking heads and bewildered looks.

Second, if it's a hard question, most of the rest of the class won't know the right answer either. Thus, many students won't even recognize a wrong answer unless and until the professor points it out, at which point they'll be concentrating not on the wrong answer you gave, but on trying to get the right answer down in their notes and hoping the professor doesn't call on them in the meantime.

As for the professor, she's up there trying to orchestrate a large class and doesn't have time, even if she had the inclination, to stop and focus on wrong answers. Additionally, wrong answers don't trouble most professors unless the professor believes the student is unprepared. When students approach me after a class profusely apologizing for giving a "stupid" answer during class, I often don't remember what they're talking about.

Coincidentally, the very day I was editing these paragraphs, I came out of Torts and found a student waiting for me at the bottom of the stairs. She said she wanted to apologize for her classroom performance. I had no idea what she was talking about. I remembered calling on her, but didn't notice any shortcomings. I told her so. She proceeded to reel off three perceived failings: "I said 'I don't know' to one question, but I did know. I had it in my notes. I just wasn't thinking right about it. Then I said 'I'm not sure' to another question. Finally, I was going to give the right answer on one question but you corrected me before I had time to finish." Bless her heart. I said I thought she did fine.

We all tend to be our own harshest critics. If you make a mistake during Socratic questioning, in most instances, you're likely to be the only one who notices or remembers it. Now, it's true that if a student says something that is way off-base, some students may snicker and even talk about it after class. But you just have to ignore those kinds of people and trust in karma. Their time will come.

Here's a little secret about the Socratic method that may also ease your mind about giving a wrong answer in class. In truth, at least for questions involving hypotheticals, the very last thing the professor wants to hear in many situations is a quick correct answer because it ruins the Socratic treasure hunt the professor was looking forward to engaging in. Often, when professors pose hypothetical fact situations, what they prefer is an answer that's just wrong enough to allow the professor to artfully nudge the student down the Socratic path toward insight, but not so wrong that the only path is directly to another student. An immediate correct answer can ruin everything. So take heart—some wrong answers are actually welcomed by the prof!

10. The Socratic method has a negative impact on women and minority students. Partly FACT as to practical effect. A substantial body of academic literature discusses the barriers women and minority students traditionally have faced in law school.[39] One area where I see continued

---

39. If you're interested in learning more about these important issues, track down some of these sources: LINDA F. WIGHTMAN, WOMEN IN LEGAL EDUCATION: A COMPARISON OF THE LAW SCHOOL PERFORMANCE AND LAW SCHOOL EXPERIENCES OF WOMEN AND MEN (1996); Carole J. Buckner, *Realizing* Grutter v. Bollinger's *"Compelling Educational Benefits of Diversity"—Transforming Aspirational Rhetoric into Experience*, 72 UMKC L. REV. 877 (2004); Celestial S.D. Cassman & Lisa R. Pruitt, *A Kinder, Gentler Law School? Race, Ethnicity, Gender, and Legal Education at King Hall*, 38 U.C. DAVIS L. REV. 1209 (2005); Sandra R. Farber & Monica Rickenberg, *Under-Confident Women and Over-Confident Men: Gender and Sense of Competence in a Simulated Negotiation*, 11 YALE J.L.

disparity—and I'm not suggesting it's the only area—is in classroom participation.

Several surveys show that female students voluntarily participate much less frequently in law school classes than male students. For example, a survey of students at the University of California at Berkeley found that a majority of women and persons of color *never* asked questions or otherwise voluntarily participated in class, while almost two-thirds of white male students reported doing both.[40] While the survey is dated, the results are consistent with my current experience even though women now make up roughly half of all law students.

Reasons offered by scholars as to why the Socratic method negatively impacts women include increased feelings of alienation and fear, the adversarial and competitive nature of the method, sexist conduct by certain male professors, an interest in protecting the sanctity and integrity of one's beliefs, less willingness to engage in grandstanding, a lower interest in dominating class discussion, and—I love this one because it's so true—better recognition by women than men of the limits of one's knowledge. In short, male students, as a group, are more willing to engage in the adversarial, competitive "sport" of the Socratic method than women.

As suggested by the UC Berkeley study, as well as other studies, minority students also generally volunteer in law school classes at lower rates. The obstacles to participating may loom even larger for minority students because of the under-representation of persons of color at most law schools. Experience has shown me that the smaller the number of any group in a class, the less likely it is that individual members of the group are willing to inject themselves into class discus-

& FEMINISM 271 (1999); Paula Gaber, *"Just Trying to be Human in this Place": The Legal Education of Twenty Women,* 10 YALE J.L. & FEMINISM 165 (1998); David D. Garner, *Socratic Misogyny?—Analyzing Feminist Criticisms of Socratic Teaching in Legal Education,* 2000 BYU L. REV. 1597 (2000); Donald K. Hill, *Law School, Legal Education, and the Black Law Student,* 12 T. MARSHALL L. REV. 457 (1987); Elizabeth Mertz, Wamucii Njogu & Susan Gooding, *What Difference Does Difference Make? The Challenge for Legal Education,* 48 J. LEGAL EDUC. 1 (1998); Jenni-

fer L. Rosato, *The Socratic Method and Women Law Students: Humanize, Don't Feminize,* 7 S. CAL. REV. L. & WOMEN'S STUD. 37 (1997); Janet Taber et al., *Gender, Legal Education, and the Legal Profession: An Empirical Study of Stanford Law Students and Graduates,* 40 STAN. L. REV. 1209 (1988).

40. Suzanne Homer & Lois Schwartz, *Admitted but Not Accepted: Outsiders Take an Inside Look at Law School,* 5 BERKELEY WOMEN'S L.J. 1, 29 (1990).

sions. Minority students currently comprise 22 percent of law students nationwide, a substantial improvement from the past, but the percentage at many schools is significantly smaller.

Because class participation carries several advantages (discussed in Chapter 8), the relative lack of classroom participation by women and minority students can have an adverse impact on them. We can't hope to reorder society here. The best I can do is offer my candid, practical advice to women and minority students, which is that an immediate solution lies solely in your power. To the extent men or non-minority students participate more in class, it's because they voluntarily ask more questions and offer comments in class discussions, undoubtedly for many of the reasons listed above.

Professors want to hear from all of their students. More important, your classmates need to hear from you. If you are a woman or minority student reading this, make a vow to raise your hand and contribute to class discussion. *Professors will call on people who raise their hands, regardless of gender, race or other identity traits.* Band together with like students and commit to join the fray. There's strength in numbers. Even a small group of students can unify to build a stronger, mutually supportive whole.

* * *

Before moving on, it should be noted that professors do use teaching approaches other than the Socratic and case methods in the first year. As mentioned, most professors do at least some lecturing. Some do a large amount of it. Some professors use a "problem method" in which students read cases and apply them to solve written problems, but the problem method usually entails Socratic-style questioning. A few doctrinal professors assign drafting or other exercises and some professors occasionally use small-group breakout discussions. But ask any former or current law student what first-year law school classes are like and you won't be hearing much about the other methods. You'll hear about the Socratic method.

CHAPTER 8
REASONS TO PARTICIPATE IN CLASS AND A DOZEN TIPS FOR DOING IT WELL

A law school class can and should be a vital and exciting learning environment. Many of the issues discussed in law school have enormous implications for society. Indeed, the most controversial issues of our time are rooted in the law: abortion, affirmative action, civil liberties, environmental policy, gun control, presidential power, the rights of children, workers, and the disabled ... the list could go on and on.

If every student committed to being a participant in classroom discussion, even if only occasionally, law schools would be much more interesting places. When Socratic dialoguing and discussion are firing on all cylinders, the atmosphere in law school classrooms can be electric. The professor, however, is only one cylinder. No matter how much energy and effort he or she puts forth, stimulating classroom experiences cannot happen without the help of prepared, engaged students.

Unfortunately, too many 1Ls choose not to voluntarily participate in class, often because they're intimidated. Some students no doubt perform a cost-benefit analysis and decide it's easier and safer to just stay on the sidelines. I understand that decision. The problem is that students undervalue the return on participating in class, while, as we saw in the previous chapter, exaggerating the potential risks and costs. This chapter explains the upside of being a class participator and offers a dozen tips for doing it successfully.

The Benefits of Class Participation

Class participation carries several benefits with it, some tangible and some intangible. First, active student participation in class discussions adds to the energy level and sense of community in the classroom, making for a more lively and memorable experience for everyone. Class hours in courses where students actively participate in the discussion fly by compared to those in courses where lecture predominates. Lecturing may be less intimidating than active dialogue and discussion, but it's also approximately five million times more likely to induce drowsiness.

Second, you will better remember the classes in which you participate and feel more satisfaction about your law school experience. I sat through my first trimester in silence, except when I got called on. Part of me wanted to participate, but I was afraid. The second trimester I started to open up a bit, raising my hand here and there, and immediately felt better about myself and my law school career. Instead of sitting in class thinking, "I wish I could be one of those brave people who volunteer," I thought, "Hey, now *I'm* one of those brave people."

Third, participating will help sharpen your oral communication and group speaking skills, essential abilities for lawyers of any stripe.

Fourth, your professors want to get to know you, but with so many students, we can't realistically accomplish that unless you speak up from time to time. As discussed in Chapter 9, getting to know and getting known by your professors carries its own potentially substantial benefits. Volunteering in class is one of the best ways to become known by your professors.

Fifth, it is an established fact of legal education that if you volunteer even once in a while, you will get called on less often when you are *not* volunteering. In fact, there's an inverse correlation between how often students raise their hands to speak and how often they get called on randomly, because professors want to hear from as many students as possible. Would you rather speak up at a time when you already have something to say or wait until the professor cold-calls on you?

Finally, class participation brings the possibility of the very tangible benefit of a grade raise, although this should be at the bottom of your list of reasons to participate. Many professors raise grades for class participation. In a typical first-year Torts class of seventy to eighty people, I usually raise between ten and twenty grades by one step (e.g., from a *B-* to a *B*) for consistent, quality class participation. In a system where class ranks can shift depending on minute differences in GPAs, sometimes differences of only hundredths of a point, even modest grade raises can have an effect.

Law school can be a scary place, but I encourage you to go to classes willing to discuss the material. Your thoughts and opinions are valuable and your contributions to class discussion will help make law school a more enjoyable, meaningful, and memorable experience for everyone.

A Dozen Tips for Shining in Class

Whether we're talking about voluntary class participation or involuntary participation (i.e., getting called on), *any* student can shine in class by following these tips and reminders, which are aimed both at bolstering your performance and preventing you from making a bad impression:

1. Come to every class prepared. This is the threshold requirement for any successful participation. If you're prepared, you have nothing to fear from the Socratic method or other participation. Conversely, if you're not prepared, you're a sitting duck.

2. Commit to being a participator. Many students actually do want to participate, but leave their participation to the professor's decision to call on them. In other words, they don't volunteer. But given the large number of students and the small number who get called on randomly in a typical class, that's not a good plan.

Commit yourself to being a participant in class discussion. You don't have to participate every day to make a lasting, good impression in class. Just make a good faith effort to do it on a semi-regular basis. Here's my challenge to you: make a vow (and keep track of it) that at a minimum you will voluntarily participate at least *one time each week* during your first semester of law school. I'm not even talking about once a week in each class, although that would be great. Just once a week total, ideally mixing up your participation among different courses. The typical semester is fourteen weeks long, which means that following this vow will commit you to speak in class voluntarily only fourteen times during the entire semester. Even this modest level of participation will be sufficient to bring you many of the benefits of class participation.

Participation can assume three forms:

Ask a question. Asking questions is an easy way to participate. As mentioned in Chapter 7, it's possible the professor might turn it around on you and ask, "What do you think?", but more often than not the professor will just answer the question. Thus, question-asking can be a painless form of class participation. Even if the professor turns the question back at you, chances are you'll do fine since it's something you've thought about at least a little bit or you wouldn't have asked the question.

Volunteer an answer. If a professor asks a question to which you think you know the answer, raise your hand! Professors ask some really hard questions, but they also ask a lot of easy ones (easy, that is, if you're prepared). I was disturbed when one of my research assistants told me that many students won't volunteer to answer easy questions because they don't want to be seen as someone who only tries to answer easy questions. That's silly. The professor wants someone to answer them, or she wouldn't be asking them. Moreover, what may seem simple to you probably isn't simple to everyone. You'll get just as much credit for volunteering to answer an easy question as a hard one, with better odds of giving a right answer.

Offer an opinion. The Socratic method often functions in two parts, beginning with one-on-one case-dialoguing and progressing into generalized, inclusive class discussions of the issues. At this stage, professors often seek answers about what students think the law should be, rather than simply what it is as espoused in the case. Since opinions cannot, by definition, be demonstrably right or wrong, you have little to lose by joining in such discussions. Of course, the professor may very well want to explore the basis for your opinion (since gut feelings don't cut it as legal analysis), so be ready for follow-up questions that might require you to defend your opinion with reasons.

3. Approach the Socratic method as a game or sport. A common criticism of the Socratic method is that it takes on the appearance of a game or sporting event. But so what? Most people enjoy games and sports. That should make it more, rather than less palatable. Instead of approaching the Socratic method with dread or terror, look at it as a potentially fun type of "brain game." Keep your wits about you. Free your brain from the shackles of fear. Listen carefully to the professor's questions and let your brain work for you. And remember, the goal of the game is not to win. The goal is the game itself.

Many professors still execute the Socratic method in the style, albeit not the brilliance, of its creator: they seek to get the answerer to commit to a position, then, through questioning, attempt to expose the contradictions or fallacies in that position. They sometimes do this by leading students down a garden path, then cutting their legs off at the end of the path. Your goal is to make it to the end of the path with your limbs intact. Cues that you're on your way down the garden path can take the form of statements by the professor such as, "Well, let's change the facts just a little," or "Suppose instead of what happened in the actual case, the plaintiff . . . ."

The purpose is not to inflict cruelty, but to sharpen critical-thinking skills. Untrained legal minds think too narrowly about the consequences of adopting particular legal positions. One way to teach them to think beyond the immediate case is, once a student has committed to a position, alter the facts, have her apply her position to the new facts, and test whether she agrees with the results. (See the Socratic dialogue excerpt in the preceding chapter for an example.)

If a professor is leading you down the path, you'll be confronted with a recurring choice: (a) stick with your original position, which may now appear absurd in light of the altered application; (b) modify your position; or (c) distinguish the professor's new factual situation from your position.

If you believe in your position, don't feel compelled to change it simply by the nature of the questioning. Defend it. As often as not, the professor will agree with you and will simply be playing devil's advocate. On the other hand, as Emerson said, "A foolish consistency is the hobgoblin of little minds." If the new result would be clearly ludicrous and cannot be distinguished from the original facts and position, there's nothing wrong with conceding your original view may need revising. Frequently, however, the best course is to try to distinguish the new situations posed by the professor from your original position. Again, trust your brain and your reasoning instincts.

4. Listen! You need to pay attention during a law school class. Listen carefully to what the professor is saying, especially if he or she starts out on a hypothetical. Sometimes the hypotheticals are elaborate and complicated. It's annoying and a waste of time when a professor relates a complicated hypothetical, calls on a student to analyze it, and the student responds, "Um, could you repeat the question?"

5. Give yourself permission to fail. Many students who are well-prepared and perfectly capable of discussing the issues in law school reading assignments freeze up in class because they put too much pressure on themselves to succeed. They have a hard time answering questions about a case even though they know the answers. If a friend came up to them before class to discuss the same case, they'd be able to do it with no problem. Why? Because they wouldn't be thinking, "Ohmigosh, everyone's watching me. I don't want to look stupid."

By giving yourself permission to fail, you'll stop trying so hard and actually perform better. This advice is commonly given to public performers. I first encountered it taking acting lessons. It works. I follow it when teaching. Law students aren't the only ones who feel exposed when talking in front of eighty or so people. Law professors get nervous too. One veteran colleague commented on reading a draft of this chapter: "I still can't eat before class!" Even after twenty years of teaching and several teaching awards, I still feel stress in class to "not screw up." Sometimes, while speaking in class, I'll find myself concentrating so hard on not making a mistake that my mind becomes clouded and my thoughts and speech less facile. When this happens, I've trained myself to—right there on the spot—give myself permission to fail. An internal voice says, "So what if you make a mistake? It just shows you're human. It's no big deal!"

As discussed in the previous chapter, law students are their own worst critics when it comes to their classroom performance. Don't worry about making a mistake in class. It really is no big deal. Give yourself permission to fail so you can stop trying so hard.

6. Don't be afraid to disagree with professors. A major point of the Socratic method is to stimulate a true dialogue—a back and forth colloquy between the professor and the student. But this can only work if the student is willing to partake in the back and forth. Most professors welcome and appreciate students who challenge them with contrasting legal arguments and policy positions. The problem is that most students are reluctant to offer dissenting opinions to those of their professors, first, because students tend to believe it's impossible they could be right and the professor wrong and, second, because they don't want to risk antagonizing the professor.

Regarding the first point, viable arguments exist on both sides of many legal issues. If legal issues were clear-cut, they wouldn't be "issues." The *New York Times v. Sullivan* Socratic dialogue sample in Chapter 7 illustrates this point well. Reasonable minds can disagree as to where to strike the balance between protecting free speech and allowing states to compensate citizens who have been injured by defamation. It's a perfectly legitimate position, for example, to argue, as have some U.S. Supreme Court justices, that First Amendment freedom of speech should be absolute, precluding any tort actions for defamation.

As to the second point, it's true that some law professors are convinced they are right about everything, but most of us are in this business in part because we enjoy the stimulation of intelligent debate. My best classroom moments occur when students are willing to "mix it up" a bit. Looking back at the Socratic dialogue excerpt you can see that those students definitely were not afraid to disagree with me. Of course, you want to disagree in a respectful fashion.

Generally, you want to limit outright disagreement with the professor in class to policy-based or other open-ended issues, rather than the fine points of black-letter law. Most experienced law teachers know their subjects well, so there's a greater likelihood that you will indeed be "wrong" in contending with the professor on a point of pure law. Moreover, even if you're right—which certainly can happen because professors do make mistakes—it's a bad idea to show up the professor in class.

A colleague at another school told me of a brazen incident in which a prof made a legal point in class, and a student took it on himself to email the author of the casebook *during* class questioning the professor's interpretation of the law. The author apparently wrote back saying the student had it right and the professor was wrong. The student then used the email to call out the professor in class! Now, there's a case for banning computers. Don't get any ideas from this incident—especially if you're one of my students.

If you think the professor is wrong on the law, approach the professor after class and raise your point in the form of a question, as in: "Professor, I wrote down that you said a, b, c, but this note in the casebook seems to say the law is x, y, z. I'm having a hard time reconciling them."

7. Don't take it personally if a professor or another student challenges your position. Students come to law school with varying degrees of skin thickness. Some sensitive students will fall apart if you look at them the wrong way, while others would hardly notice if you Tasered them. Professors frequently challenge students to explain or defend their positions even when they agree with the position. This is part of the Socratic process. Don't take it personally. Don't get your feelings hurt.

A student recently told me a tale about a classmate who volunteered to answer a question in class during his first semester. According to the student reporting the event, the professor replied in a condescending tone, "Why would you think that?" Later, the student swore he'd never volunteer in class again. All I can say about this one is gimme a break! Lawyers have to be able to defend and explain their positions. If you make an argument to a judge and she says, "Why would you think that?", you can't fall apart and swear never to go to court again.

I once represented a pro bono divorce client. We were in the judge's chambers for what I thought would be a simple five-minute motion hearing. The room was packed with other lawyers sitting in chairs lining the walls waiting for their cases to come up. To my shock and dismay, the judge decided to transform the mundane hearing into a debacle. He called my client "garbage" and refused to sign an order I prepared because it contained the phrase "among the parties." "As my eighth-grade English teacher taught me, Mr. McClurg," he said sarcastically, "when you're dealing with only two people, it should say *'between* the parties,' not *'among* the parties.'" He berated me for what seemed like an eternity. A week later, a newspaper article reported that the judge's spouse had sued him for divorce alleging physical abuse, which my pro bono client had also alleged against her husband. Maybe that explained his behavior, but at the time I felt humiliated.

Folks, it ain't pretty out there in the real world of practicing law. It makes law school look like summer camp. I'm sympathetic to the sensitivities of students, and certainly don't condone professors treating students rudely, but at some point you just have to suck it up and realize that responding to questions, even sarcastic ones, asking for clarification or explanation of your positions, is simply part of being a lawyer.

Other students also may challenge your position in class discussions. I love it when this occurs and results in a good back and forth exchange. Hearty debate is what great law school class experiences are built upon. Unfortunately, it happens too rarely these days, attributable perhaps to some kind of unwritten code that one shouldn't challenge one's classmates. As with challenging questions from professors, many students apparently fail to distinguish between pointed legal debate and personal attacks. If a friend vigorously challenged you on a legal point outside of class, you'd partake in the debate without any hurt or hard feelings. You'd probably enjoy it. Ideally, that's the way you should feel in a law school class environment, although I recognize it's easier said than done.

8. If you're unprepared, have the good sense to keep your mouth shut. Not infrequently, students ask questions that are directly answered in the reading material, leading to the sound inference that they haven't studied the assignment. I can tell you from many conversations that this is a particular pet peeve of law professors. If you're not prepared, lie low and pray you don't get called on. Don't take it on yourself to announce to the class: "I'm not prepared and I'm going to prove it to everyone."

In the same vein, don't come to class early to read the material for the first time. Professors get irritated when they arrive early and see students skimming the reading assignment in their unmarked books for what appears to be the first time. It's another case of announcing to the professor that you're not prepared. Sometimes professors will purposely call on such students to expose them. I don't, because I know it will be a waste of everyone's time. But I do form negative opinions of such students.

9. Redeem yourself. If you get called on and come across as unprepared, whether you are or not, redeem yourself by volunteering at a later point. Most professors are forgiving souls who will respect your effort to redeem yourself. If you're prepared and the professor asks you a question to which you don't know the answer, simply say "I don't know," but then add something to show you're prepared.

On a related note, if you should happen to blank out in a panic attack when called on (à la my Con Law episode), approach the professor after class and explain what happened to avoid having the professor think you were unprepared. I once called on a woman who gave no answer at all. I concluded she was unprepared. Fortunately, two of her classmates came up after class and told me she was prepared but simply freaked out.

10. If at first you don't get called on, try, try again. Some students are discouraged from participating after they raise their hands once or twice and the professor doesn't call on them. Either they think the professor is intentionally ignoring them or they just can't muster the courage for repeat attempts.

Don't take it personally if you raise your hand and the professor doesn't call on you. Managing discussion in a large class isn't as easy as it may look. The professor's mind is racing to stay ahead of the discussion at the same time he or she is asking or answering questions, many of which come from left field. In an active discussion, twenty hands may be raised at the same time.

Choosing which person to call on among several students with raised hands is often dictated simply by the physical proximity of the person volunteering to either the professor or a student who is already engaged in the dialogue. Alternatively, the professor may ignore raised hands to return to a student who has already spoken on the issue to see what that person has to say in reply to a new idea that has been injected. If you volunteer regularly, the professor may pass you over just to get some other players into the game. Also, to keep from falling behind, the point comes in all class discussions, even the most stimulating of them, where the prof has to make the decision to cut things off and move on. So don't give up. No professor I know would intentionally ignore a volunteering student on a repeated basis except in the case of the notorious gunner who always wants to dominate the class discussion.

When you do raise your hand, make sure you really raise it. Some students think they are raising their hands when, in fact, they're just making tentative, half-hearted waves a few inches above the table. I've had students ask me why I didn't call on them and the answer is because I never noticed them raising their hands.

11. Don't be smug or arrogant. Don't mutter comments, smirk, snicker or otherwise act smugly if one of your classmates gives a "dumb" answer. Next time it could be you. Similarly, if you do challenge a classmate's opinion (which I've already encouraged you to do), articulate your position reasonably and professionally, as a lawyer would do. Avoid using a tone or language that makes it sound like a personal attack.

12. Know your professors' preparation expectations. Law professors are unique individuals. Much of the advice in this book needs to be construed and applied within the context of your particular professors, including class preparation expectations.

Some professors, for example, simply ask a student to state the facts of the case as a springboard for a broader class discussion, while others will stay with a student and expect him/her to be able to recite the case backwards and forward. Some professors will routinely ask about the procedural history of the case, while others will rarely or never ask about it. Figuring these things out will make it easier for you to prepare for class.

Here's a student-provided example of how knowing your professors can alter your approach to class prep. Asked to compare the second semester to the first, the student said that in some ways the second semester was easier because she and her classmates knew what to expect in terms of class preparation from each professor. She wrote:

We know that certain teachers will not call on you if they have called on you in a recent class, at least not usually twice in one week. For example, if I am called on to participate in class on Monday, I am usually safe for the rest of the week in that course. So I might not re-read the assignments right before class as I usually would to make sure I am extra-prepared. On the other side, some teachers really do call on people at random and therefore students know they always have to be ready because the teacher is unpredictable. This is just one example of how to learn and "work" the system.

As the semester progresses and you become more comfortable with your professors, you'll know better what each of them expects and is looking for in terms of class preparation.

CHAPTER 9

LAW PROFESSORS

When I was a kid, I loved the television show, *Leave it to Beaver*. Through reruns, most young people probably are at least somewhat familiar with the misadventures of young Theodore Cleaver ("the Beav"). Beaver had a teacher named Miss Landers who began every class with a sunny, "Good morning, class." The class always responded in unison, "Good morning, Miss Landers."

In one episode, the Cleavers invited Miss Landers to their home for dinner. They dined on the back patio. Meanwhile, unknown to Beaver, his pal, Larry Mondello, had charged Gilbert and Whitey, two other regulars in the Beav's posse, twenty-five cents each to perch in a backyard tree to witness the event. When Miss Landers stood from the dinner table, the revelation that she wore sandals was met with shock and amazement:

Gilbert: Look! She's got toes!

Whitey: Where?!

Larry: There! Coming right out of her shoes!

Busted for spying by Miss Landers, Larry explained why they did it: "Gee, Miss Landers, none of us ever saw a teacher eat before."[41]

New law students share a similar fascination about their professors. In part because the 1L universe is so small, your first-year professors will become the center of it, at least early on. Like the Beaver and his buddies, you and your

---

41. *Leave it to Beaver: Teacher Comes to Dinner* (ABC television broadcast Nov. 28, 1959).

122

classmates are likely to pay attention to and talk about not only your professors' teaching styles, but their physical appearances and mannerisms.

While it diminishes fairly quickly, at the beginning law students often view their professors with something approaching veneration. At a social gathering during orientation many years ago, I was standing in the restroom at a urinal when a young man next to me exclaimed, "I can't believe it! I'm peeing next to Professor McClurg." I'm pretty sure he was serious.

So pervasive is the extent to which professors permeate the psyches of new law students that students commonly have dreams about them. A Torts student once reported a grisly nightmare in which I had him tied to a stake while peppering him with questions about the tort of battery. Each time he answered, I shouted, "Wrong!" and lopped off one of his limbs with an ax, saying "Is that a battery? Is that a battery?" Obviously, the dream was farfetched. I never would have asked such an easy question.

Who are These People?

Whether cast in terms of "know your boss" or, as some students might say it, "know your enemy," it's worth knowing a little about who becomes law profs and what makes them tick. Who are these people you can't escape even in your sleep, these maestros who will stand before you and dictate so much of your existence: your schedule, available leisure time, success or failure, your very sense of self-worth?

Well, as it turns out, they're just that: just people, like Miss Landers. In the very first days of my career as a law professor, way back in the summer of 1986, the dean invited me to his house with a group of other professors to watch a football game on television. It was my first ever social encounter with a group of law professors. Except for the law professor interviewing process, my only brushes with law profs had been as a student. I was nervous—intimidated I might not be able to keep up with their deep thoughts and brilliant discourse.

When I arrived, I planted myself on the sofa in front of the television next to a dapperly dressed, gray-haired eminence who had been teaching law for decades. That's when something happened that forever changed my perspective of

law professors. On the television screen, Alabama was playing an SEC rival, I forget which. Alabama had the ball. The
quarterback took the snap and handed the ball off to a
running back, who slipped through the middle of the line for
a modest gain. The play prompted the oracle seated next to
me to plunge his index finger into his cupped, orifice-imitat-
ing opposite hand and cackle, "The old Ex–Lax play—right
up the hole!" (Ex–Lax is a chewable laxative.) Hmm, a joke I
might have made in the sixth grade. I relaxed and enjoyed
the game. Just regular people.

Not much empirical information exists about the characteristics of law professors. We research just about everything
except ourselves. Nevertheless, some general observations
can be made:

• Most of the nation's 7,000 full-time law professors are
white males, although the number of women and minority
professors has increased substantially in recent years. In the
early 1970s, women and minorities together constituted only
8 percent of all law school faculty members. Today, roughly
36 percent of all law professors are women and 16 percent
are minorities (with some overlap between those two
groups).[42] Given that most women and minority professors
have entered the profession recently, they're more likely to
be younger and untenured.

• Legal research and writing professors are disproportionately women. Due to the fact that these jobs traditionally
have not been tenure-track positions (and pay lower salaries
as a result), this subset of law faculty jobs is often referred to
by law professors as the "pink ghetto." More than 70 percent
of full-time legal writing instructors are women. Women
directors of legal writing programs outnumber men by more
than 2:1.[43]

• Nearly 40 percent of law professors hold Juris Doctor or
advanced law degrees from just eleven "elite" law schools,
with 21 percent coming from Harvard and Yale. (My alma

42. *See* Ass'n of Am. Law Sch., Statistical Report on Law School Faculty and
Candidates for Law Faculty Positions:
Preliminary Tables 2005–2006, tbl.1A
(2006), http://www.aals.org/documents/
statistics/20052006statisticson
lawfaculty.pdf.

43. Ass'n of Legal Writing Dirs.,
ALWD/LWI 2007 Survey Results, viii
(2007),   http://www.alwd.org/surveys/
survey_results/2007_Survey_Results.pdf.

mater, the University of Florida, has generated about 1 percent of the total. Go Gators!)[44]

• Law review membership and other academic honors, such as Order of the Coif (top 10 percent of the class), are common credentials for law professors.[45]

• Many law professors hold advanced law degrees (i.e., an LL.M or S.J.D.) and a growing number have Ph.Ds in other disciplines.

• Disproportionate numbers of professors have held one or more federal judicial clerkships, a prestigious kind of internship working for a judge.

• A majority of law professors have had some practical experience in either corporate, government or private practice prior to becoming professors, although the preference to hire professors with practical experience is most pronounced in lower-ranked law schools.[46]

• Politically, more law professors probably lean left than right, although no recent data exists to support this assertion. As a general proposition (with many exceptions both institutionally and individually), law faculties at schools on either coast tend to be more liberal, while law faculties in the heartland tend to be more conservative.

I'm happy to report to you that the overall caliber of law faculties is extremely high, probably much higher than you encountered in undergraduate school. This is true at all law schools, because far more qualified candidates exist than available positions. Perhaps you've heard the adage, "Those who can *do*, those who can't *teach*." With regard to law profs, a more accurate statement of the second part would be, "those who are incredibly well-credentialed and extremely lucky teach."

44. *See* Ass'n of Am. Law Sch., *supra*, at tbl.9A. As of 2005–06, the following number of professors held Juris Doctor or advanced law degrees from these eleven schools: Columbia University (352), Georgetown University (220), Harvard University (1138), New York University (284), Stanford University (239), University of California–Berkeley (236), University of Chicago (340), University of Michigan (356), University of Pennsylvania (191), University of Virginia (194), and Yale University (781).

45. The two most powerful predictors of a law professor's first teaching appointment are the status of the law school from which the professor graduated and the professor's academic achievements while in law school. James R.P. Ogloff, David R. Lyon, Kevin S. Douglas & V. Gordon Rose, *More Than "Learning to Think Like a Lawyer:" The Empirical Research on Legal Education*, 34 Creighton L. Rev. 73, 130–31 (2000).

46. *Id.* at 131–32.

Beginning law profs do lack one important credential: they generally have no classroom experience or training. To teach first-graders to spell "cat" or add 2 + 2, teachers are required to take courses in educational theory and do internships working in classrooms. Not so for law profs teaching complex material and analytical skills to adults. The only training new law professors receive is an optional two-day new teacher workshop sponsored by the Association of American Law Schools. It's a "learn while you earn" affair.

When I was first hired as a law professor, the school assigned me to teach Family Law. Not only did I know little about Family Law, I knew nothing about how to teach it or any other subject. I defaulted to trying to imitate the professor who taught me Family Law back in law school. Big mistake. At my first class, after ten minutes of brain-death inducing lecture on the ecclesiastical history of domestic relations law dating from the twelfth century, I saw a woman in the back of the room roll her eyes and nudge the person next to her. That image burned in my brain for the rest of my scintillating lecture. Fortunately, because I was so nervous, the students' pain was short-lived. Orating like Socrates on speed, I covered twenty pages of notes in about thirty-five minutes and ended twenty minutes early (nowadays, I cover about seven pages of notes in fifty-five minutes). Starting at the next class I reverted to just being myself. That worked much better, although I still recall a comment on my initial set of student evaluations that said: "Is there a fund to send this guy back to Florida?"

A Kinder, Gentler Law School Nation

Perhaps the biggest surprise of the first year will be that most of your professors will not be the sadistic ogres portrayed in print and screen accounts of law school. In asking a group of new students to name their biggest surprise about law school, the most common answer related to professors defying this stereotype. Here's a sampling of the responses:

- The biggest surprise has been the attitude of the professors. After reading Turow's *One L*, which was recommended by many friends as an accurate depiction of first-year life, I expected professors to create a clear barrier between themselves and the students. I anticipated a class environment based heavily in fear, with an undertone of student humiliation. I may have just been lucky in my draw of sections, but I have found that the professors actually enjoy what they do (or are great actors). In all classes, there is a relaxed feeling in the dialogue and discussion. This certainly has not taken away from the fear—but for me it has shifted the fear from a fear of public humiliation to a fear of disappointing. In discussions with my classmates, everyone seems to share the same view—that the desire to be prepared and understand the material is not to avoid being humiliated in class, but to live up to the expectations that we place on ourselves and that the professors place on us.

- The surprise would go back to a misguided belief in professors who are emotionally detached from their students. The professors seem to be genuinely concerned about the students understanding the material, raising their own opinions, asking questions, and not getting overwhelmed in the whole process. I think I would find it hard as a professor to remember names in a class of seventy to eighty students; however, I have already noticed that occurring in most of my classes.

- I was pleasantly surprised by my instructors. They've all turned out to be human! Seriously, though, the stereotype of a law school professor is a bitter old man who never cracks a smile and sleeps hugging *Black's Law Dictionary*. In general, my instructors have been quite charming and funny.

- My biggest surprise has been the personality of the professors. While they have all made it very clear that we are to be prepared before class, I never felt as though they were trying to embarrass or belittle us. That being said, the professors are still quite intimidating.

- The biggest surprise I've had is the level to which the professors have gone out of their way to stress that they're not here to scare us or chase us away, but rather to shape us into what we need to be in order to succeed in a career in law. I've really appreciated that. That might not be quite as evident at other schools—perhaps it's just a reflection of the faculty at my school.

Of course, as noted in the last comment, this sampling of comments comes from only one entering class at one law school. But while I never surveyed my students before, I believe similar responses would have been evoked at every law school where I have taught. Certainly, not every professor at every law school is kind and caring. To the contrary, every school has some professors who do not exhibit those qualities. But in general, law professors are not mean-spirited people who are out to "get" students.

If anything, many professors, particularly older ones, would complain that the pendulum has swung too far the other way, with too many professors going out of their way to be friendly to or even friends with students. Part of this attitudinal drift is motivated by the desire to get good student evaluations, which both feed the ego and play a role in promotion and salary decisions. Also, with students paying high dollars for tuition, particularly at private schools, and with so many law schools competing for the same pool of talented students, law school administrations feel pressure, which they pass on to the professors, to achieve customer satisfaction. In law school-speak, it's called being "student-centered." Some law schools have even resorted to advertising that their professors are nice.[47]

A larger explanation for the shift toward "feel good" legal education is attributable to the fact that the old school Socratic traditionalists are retiring or getting close thereto and are being replaced by a new breed of Gen–X and Gen–Y professors who grew up in a world environment emphasizing affirmation and self-esteem building. That young law professors have a different view of the Socratic method than their predecessors was dramatically driven home to me at a recent annual Faculty Recruitment Conference. Most people become law professors by registering for and attending this conference, at which they can interview with several schools in one place.

At this particular conference, we interviewed twenty-five prospective law professors. One of our stock interview ques-

---

47. *See* Michael Vitiello, *Professor Kingsfield: The Most Misunderstood Character in Literature*, 33 HOFSTRA L. REV. 955, 973 (2005) (quoting law school ads touting the schools' kinder, gentler atmosphere).

tions is: "What kind of teaching style do you see yourself adopting?" The answer from nearly every candidate was "soft Socratic" or "modified Socratic," uniformly followed by a clarifier to the effect that while the candidates would call on students, they wouldn't "put them on the spot," "embarrass them," or "intimidate them." Some of the candidates mentioned they wanted to rely on volunteers, rather than cold-call on students. One candidate summed up the feel-good movement by saying: "Hey, let's all leave the classroom feeling good about ourselves!" That is an exact quotation I captured in my notes.

In one sense, I suppose this is good news for law students, but in another sense not so good. Tossing out softball questions to volunteers or letting unprepared students "pass" on questions is certainly less stress-provoking for students, but it's also much less intellectually rigorous, and, ultimately, more boring. The classes you will remember best will be those where your professors challenge you to figure out legal problems and defend your positions. Moreover, as mentioned in the previous chapter, the real world of practicing law is anything but kind and gentle. As Professor Michael Vitiello observed: "Treating our students gently is not kind. Instead, by abandoning the demanding form of the Socratic method, we fail to prepare our students for the rigors of practice."[48] But then, Vitiello is an old guy like me.

The Quirkiness Quotient

At their best, law professors are highly skilled, hardworking, creative intellectuals dedicated to perfecting their craft and concerned for the welfare of their students. At their worst, they can be arrogant, bitter, insecure, narcissistic, spoiled prima donnas who sometimes forget they have one of the best jobs in the world. In between those extremes, we're all a bit quirky. Not necessarily quirky in a bad way: we just tend to move to the beat of a different drummer, like maybe Keith Moon or John Bonham (deceased wild and crazy drummers from The Who and Led Zeppelin, respectively). This grand tradition started early on. Jurisprudential scholar Jerome Frank once described Christopher Langdell, the father of the case method, as "a brilliant neurotic."[49]

48. *Id.* at 959.

49. Jerome Frank, *A Plea for Lawyer–Schools*, 56 YALE L.J. 1303, 1303 (1947).

Why do so many law professors tend to be a bit ... er, unusual? In part, it's because academia overall attracts highly intelligent people who don't fit comfortably into normal corporate or other business environments. It's not a matter of whether they *can* do it. They just don't want to. But the nature of the job also encourages people to let out what might otherwise remain hidden eccentricities in other settings. Most beginning law professors arrive at their first jobs behaving and appearing as pretty normal people. But unlike the rest of the working world, law professors are subject to very few workplace rules or restrictions.

There's the oft-repeated tale of the new law professor who arrived for the fall semester fresh from a corporate law firm wearing a navy-blue suit, starched white shirt, silk rep tie, and shiny wingtips. By the time spring rolled around, he was walking around in a Speedo and a cape, head shaved, a tattoo of the great Judge Learned Hand covering his scalp, sticks of smoking incense in his ears, and insisting he be called Klaatu. Now here I am writing books about law school. Who would have ever thought?

Seriously, law professors can dress as they wish, say what they want to whomever they want, and come and go pretty much as they please. They enjoy more or less complete autonomy over their lives, a luxury enjoyed by few other workers. Once a law professor achieves tenure, he or she is virtually untouchable. Small wonder they let their inner-selves show through more than most other workers.

My legal humor website, lawhaha.com, collects funny memories of law school. One category of stories is "Those lovable, quirky law professors." It includes tales about a bald, white professor who raps in class, a professor who acts like nothing unusual has occurred when a tooth flies out of his mouth and bounces off a table during a lecture, a professor who begins teaching the wrong class from the wrong book, a legendary professor who walks smack into the door on the way in and proceeds to teach the entire class with blood streaming down his face, and a distinguished professor who stalks the classroom for an entire hour with toilet paper hanging out the back of his pants.[50]

---

50. You can read about these and other interesting law professors at http://www.lawhaha.com/ funnycategories.asp?cat=professors.

As with all people, their uniqueness is part of what makes law professors interesting cats.

Theoretical vs. Practical Professors

Which would you find more appealing? Learning "rules of law" or studying the history, policies, and jurisprudential theories that shape those rules?

One difference among law teachers that affects students is whether they teach primarily from a practical or theoretical standpoint. Law can be taught from a variety of theoretical perspectives. Among the more popular are economic theory, feminist theory, and critical race theory. The difference between a subject taught through a theoretical or policy-oriented lens compared with a practical approach is so dramatic that it can seem like a completely different course.

As an inexact rule of thumb, the higher a law school's ranking, the more likely the professors will lean toward theoretical classroom teaching. Conversely, law professors at lower-ranked schools tend to be more practically oriented, focusing on teaching the substance and application of law. The perceived missions of law schools play a role in forging this rough dichotomy. Schools perceived to be "elite" see it as part of their mission to develop students into future legal scholars, policy-makers, and others who will shape the law. Lower-ranked schools, many of which are regional schools, are more likely to see their primary mission as training students to become competent practitioners. Of course, you'll get a mix of theoretical and practical teaching at all law schools and from most individual professors.

In my experience, most students, although certainly not all, prefer practically oriented teaching.[51] Black-letter law and

51. An interesting study identified three general types of law professor: the "Socratic Trainer," the "Caring Teacher," and the "Anti–Socratic Practitioner." The Anti–Socratic Practitioner was described as a teacher who "recognizes that the purpose of law school is to prepare students for the practice of law" and who emphasizes practical skills and "[h]ow-to knowledge." A group of seventy-seven law students at a midwestern law school was asked to rank their image of an ideal professor. First-year students ranked all three personae relatively equally. Third-year students, however, had a much different notion of the ideal professor, ranking the Anti–Socratic Practitioner a clear first. Fifty percent of third-year students chose the Anti–Socratic Practitioner as their ideal professor, 40 percent the Caring Teacher, and only 5 percent the Socratic Trainer. While the study is dated and limited by the fact that it involved only one group of students at one law school, I think it fairly reflects the relative interest most students have in learning the practical aspects of law. *See* Douglas D. McFarland, *Students and Practicing Lawyers Identify the Ideal Law Professor*, 36 J. Legal Educ. 93 (1986).

exposure to the "real world" of practicing law seem more meaningful and relevant to what they're trying to accomplish than legal theory. I felt similarly as a law student. Most of my professors were very theory-oriented. In some courses, my class notes for the entire term were less than ten pages. My classmates and I all appreciated the few professors who taught us actual law. One reason adjunct law professors—practitioners hired to teach particular courses—tend to be popular among students, in addition to being notoriously easy graders, is that they approach their classes from a real world perspective, supplementing class presentations with large doses of "war stories."

In hindsight, however, I came to appreciate my theoretical professors. For most lawyers, law school will be the only time in their professional lives when they will be afforded the luxury of being able to think *about* the law. Practicing lawyers spend every day of their careers immersed in the practical application of law. For many, the real world they craved to learn about as law students gets old very quickly. Enjoy your law school opportunities to explore the origins, philosophies, and policies of law.

Overall, legal education is gradually becoming more practically oriented. In 1992, a committee of the American Bar Association published what became known as the "MacCrate Report" calling for more emphasis on teaching practical skills in law school. While many in the legal education community initially resisted the report, most law schools have since made at least some progress in implementing more skills-based training. Recently, the *Best Practices for Legal Education* and Carnegie Foundation *Educating Lawyers* reports reached similar conclusions and made similar recommendations.

Important tip: Think back to my story in Chapter 6 about the *Gilbert* study aid that saved me in Criminal Law. If you have a professor who teaches principally from a theory standpoint, find out from the professor or upper-level students how the professor usually tests. Some professors will teach theory, but expect students to know and apply black-letter law on the exam.

Is It Important What Your Professors Think of You?

Here's something you need to know about law professors: they watch you, notice things about you, form opinions about you, and in many cases share those opinions with others. In other words, law professors behave about the same way toward students as students behave toward them. If there were a ratemylawstudents.com website similar to the popular ratemyprofessors.com, it might be heavily trafficked. (As it turns out, an anonymous undergraduate professor does run a site called rateyourstudents.blogspot.com, which, although it doesn't involve law students, offers an interesting window into how professors think.)

I suppose it would be nice if law professors, being professionals, could rise above forming opinions of their charges, but that's too much to ask. We're human beings. Just like professors make impressions on students, both good and bad, students make impressions on professors, again both good and bad. Does it matter what your professors think of you? Well, yes and no.

Why it isn't important: anonymous grading.

Suppose you're convinced a professor does not like you. Maybe he happened to stroll by one day while you were indicting him in the hallway to your classmates as the worst professor in the history of legal education. (These things do happen, so be wary of what you broadcast within the small confines of a law school.) As if your stress level wasn't high enough, now you're saddled with the worry that the professor will take out his dislike for you in calculating your grade. Relax.

The main reason why it's *not* important what your professors think of you is that law school grading is anonymous. All law schools require students to use anonymous exam numbers, rather than names, on exams. The numbers are issued each semester by the registrar's office. I remember being suspicious as a law student as to whether professors had some way of matching exams with particular students, but they don't. The system really is anonymous.

What students don't realize is that professors don't want to know the identity of exam-writers. Students look at anonymous grading as protecting students, whereas professors look at it as protecting professors (against claims of favoritism, dislike, discrimination, etc.). In truth, anonymous grading probably works more to the detriment of students than to their benefit. It's much easier to assign a low grade to a cold anonymous exam number than to a living, breathing person, particularly if it's a student the professor has come to like and respect. Human nature is such that professors would be inclined to give such students the benefit of the doubt when grading their exams. To the contrary, I can hardly imagine a professor intentionally grading an exam more harshly because the professor didn't like the student.

Two exceptions to anonymous grading exist that affect 1Ls: legal research and writing courses and grade bumps. According to a 2007 survey of directors of legal research and writing programs, 40 percent of law school programs do not grade writing assignments anonymously. Approximately 37 percent grade all major writing assignments anonymously, while the remaining 23 percent of programs grade *some* major writing assignments anonymously.[52] Maintaining anonymity in legal research and writing classes is difficult because students are sectioned into smaller groups than other first-year classes, submit more than one draft of the same writing assignment, and often meet with their professors individually to discuss those drafts.

The other exception has to do with grade bumps. Many professors raise or "bump" grades based on classroom participation/preparation/attendance. Some profs also lower grades for the same reasons. In most cases, such changes are limited to one grade step (e.g., from a B to a $B+$). Because evaluating the quality and consistency of class participation and preparation is a subjective undertaking, there is room for a professor's impressions of students to enter into the calculus, consciously or unconsciously.

Why it is important: references, research assistant positions, and other helping hands.

While your grade likely will not be affected by your professor's opinion of you, professors can impact your life in other ways, often without you knowing it.

• **References.** In my second year of law school, I decided I wanted to become a law clerk to a federal judge on graduation. It became my single-minded goal. Federal clerkships, in which recent graduates work closely with a federal judge

52. Ass'n of Legal Writing Dirs., *supra*, at 9. The percentages were calculated from raw data provided in the report.

doing tasks such as researching and drafting court orders and opinions, are prestigious, highly sought-after positions. I got lucky and landed a clerkship with U.S. District Judge Charles R. Scott.

Federal judges receive tons of applications from qualified people. My law school credentials were good, but no better than many other applicants. How did I get the job? According to Judge Scott, a strong letter of recommendation written by Professor W.D. MacDonald, whom I worked for as a research assistant, tipped the balance in my favor. Four short paragraphs, just 110 words, literally changed my life. The letter opened the door to the clerkship and the clerkship opened the door to becoming a law professor.

Like all experienced professors, I've had the opportunity to change many students' lives through my own recommendations. I don't know how many letters I've written in my career, but in a recent Spring semester, I counted about fifteen. Whom do professors recommend? Any student they believe in. You don't have to be a straight-*A* student to get a strong recommendation. To the contrary, even students without high grades can obtain glowing recommendations if the professor likes and respects them and their work habits. I recently wrote a strong letter for a student who received a *D* in Torts that helped her land a summer job. Why? Because she impressed me with her work ethic and attitude.

Students don't realize how often professors' opinions of them are solicited without their knowledge. Professors commonly receive inquiries about students from judges, lawyers, and other professors who are considering hiring the student, even when the student didn't list the professor as a reference. Law review editorial boards and scholarship award committees sometimes seek input from professors when considering applicants. As I was writing this, the admissions director asked me to look at a list of students who had applied to be fall orientation leaders and make recommendations. Bar examiners send forms to professors seeking their evaluation of former students. I've even had FBI agents show up in my office to interview me about students who have applied for jobs with the Bureau or other government agencies. Accordingly, the impressions you make on your professors can impact your life without you even realizing it.

• **Research assistant positions.** Most law professors hire research assistants, which are good gigs. The jobs pay, albeit less than most law firm clerking jobs. They're flexible, allowing students to work on their own time. The assignments help sharpen research and writing skills. Research assistants receive one-on-one mentoring from experts. Sometimes the assignments they receive involve interesting, cutting-edge legal issues.

And if you do a good job, you could end up with one of those killer recommendation letters like I got from Professor MacDonald. The best, most meaningful recommendations come from people who are closely familiar with a person's abilities and work habits. In law school, the professor-research assistant relationship is one of the primary avenues for a professor to gain that kind of insight about a student.

The actual work assignments vary widely depending on the professor and the professor's confidence in the particular research assistant. They usually involve assisting the professor in preparing articles and books for publication (e.g., researching, drafting, cite-checking, proofreading). Several research assistants, for example, assisted me in writing this book.

Unfortunately, like many other privileges in law school, research assistant positions usually go to students with high GPAs and class ranks, although this is not always true. If you're interested in working as a research assistant for a professor, be a proactive early bird. Approach professors around the midpoint of the second semester and ask whether they anticipate hiring any research assistants for the summer or the next year and, if so, whether you could apply.

• **Other helping hands.** Beyond references and research assistant positions, you never know when you might need a helping hand from a professor. Students frequently need law school advice, of course, but that's only the beginning. Sometimes they need legal advice. Sometimes they need life advice. Sometimes they just need a sympathetic ear. Many professors, used to playing dual roles as teacher and therapist, keep a box of tissue handy in a desk drawer.

Personal issues on which law students seek guidance and advice run the gamut. A few years ago, a third-year student I'll call Terrence asked to meet with me. When he came into my office and asked to close the door, I knew something was wrong. He sat down and unloaded a heavy burden he had been carrying around for three years. The bar application deadline was the following week. Everyone in his graduating class had completed and submitted their applications except him. He was terrified that an incident in his past would lead, at best, to a full-blown fitness hearing and, at worst, to the bar refusing him admittance. He even contemplated moving to another state before realizing he'd run into the same obstacle.

Terrence had impressed me more than once as being not only a good student but a good person. He received excellent grades and was a member of the law review. Most important, way back as a 1L, he demonstrated his integrity and good heart when he approached me after Torts class more than once troubled by legal doctrines that led to unjust results. I offered to help Terrence draft an explanation of the incident to submit with his bar application. I thought that, framed properly, the incident could be explained away. It worked. His bar application sailed through.

Would I do the same thing for every student? No. I did it for Terrence because I believed in him. This is just one of dozens of examples of lending a helping hand to students that I could cite. Other profs could do the same.

The overarching point of this section is that your professors can be an important link in your legal education and development and future as a lawyer. Apart from tangible assistance, getting to know some of your professors will make you feel more a part of your law school community, which could make law school a more enjoyable and fulfilling experience overall. Indeed, this might be the best reason of all to get to know your profs. It's a good, comforting feeling simply to walk down the hall and have a professor greet you by name. As discussed in Chapter 18, researchers have suggested that the high student-teacher ratios in law school and the consequent disconnectedness between professors and students is a significant cause of distress and discontent in law students.

Five Easy Ways to Get to Know Your Professors

I was able to write the recommendation letter for the student who received the *D* in Torts and help draft the bar application for Terrence because I had come to: (1) know

them; (2) like them; and (3) respect them. Most fundamental-
ly, a professor can't help you if he or she doesn't know you.
Professors often have to decline requests by students for
letters of recommendation, for example, simply because they
don't know the student. Students can't remain completely
anonymous—never participating in class, never asking questions after or out of class, etc.—and then expect profs to come
up with glowing endorsements of them. What's to recommend? That their breathing never created a disturbance in
class? That they appeared to be conscious when the professor
looked in their direction? Many such students may actually
deserve good recommendations, but professors can only go by
what they know.

When I was in law school, I was too shy to get to know
any of my professors except the one I worked for as a
research assistant. I always envied my classmates who did get
to know them. I'd see a group of them sitting with a prof at
an outdoor picnic table at lunch and hear them in the profs'
offices when I walked down the hall. At law school parties
and other social events, they'd hang around the profs, chat-
ting with them and yukking it up. If I re-did law school
knowing what I know now, I would make it a point to get to
know my profs.

Not all professors are easily accessible or approachable by
students. Some professors, truth be told, want little to do
with law students. Teaching as a visiting professor at one
top-tier law school, I had lunch with another visiting professor. He made a comment that stuck with me: "Being a law
professor would be the greatest job in the world if it wasn't
for all the damn students." But most profs don't think that
way.

Here are five easy ways to get to know your professors:

1. Introduce yourself as early as possible. Due to a
psychological phenomenon known as "primacy effect," people
tend to best remember the first things they see or hear in a
list or series of events. Trial lawyers are well-acquainted with
primacy effect and the corollary principle of "recency effect"
(people also tend to better remember the last items in a
series), and carefully structure their presentation of trial
evidence based on these phenomena.

At the beginning of a school year, the profs don't know
any of the students yet. If you make it a point to introduce

yourself to your first-year professors at that time, they'll be more likely to remember you once school starts, when you will become just one of the madding crowd. Mixers during law school orientation provide a good opportunity to introduce yourself early. If you can't catch up with a prof during such an event, stop by the professor's office during the week before classes begin.

Here's an example of the primacy effect in action. I've mentioned I distribute a questionnaire to my 1Ls. A couple of weeks before classes begin, I post instructions for the students to pick up the questionnaires from a box outside my office, complete them, and return them to me. The vast majority of students wait until just before classes start to pick up the questionnaires and don't return them until the first week of school. In one recent class, however, a student I'll call Sarah showed up at my office with the carefully completed questionnaire the day after I made them available, long before most students have ever darkened the doorways of the law school. A minor act, but one that showed both diligence and earnestness. Midway through the first semester, I received a call from a campus administrator asking if I knew any of the 1Ls who had applied for a part-time job in her office. She read through a list of names and when she mentioned Sarah, I gave her an endorsement, relating the questionnaire story. Hers was one of the only names I recognized at that point. She got the job.

2. Volunteer in class. Professors take note of and appreciate the students who volunteer in class. As I've said already, we need your help to make the whole Socratic thing work. Being known as a class participator also gives professors something concrete to say about a student in a recommendation letter. See Chapter 8 for more discussion of the benefits of class participation.

3. Stop by your professors' offices to ask questions. Stop by your professors' offices from time to time with a question about the material being covered in class or any other question about law school.

Most professors post office hours during which they are available to meet with students, but surprisingly few students take advantage of them. If a professor hasn't posted office hours, don't hesitate to inquire about them. Many professors have an open-door policy, meaning that students are free to stop by any time the professor is in the office. If you feel intimidated about volunteering in class or going to visit professors in their offices, approach the podium after class and ask a question about the day's discussion. Particularly in first-year classes, it's common for a few students to gather around the podium after class to ask clarifying questions or continue discussion about the topic of the day.

Another way to ask questions and interact with your professors is through TWEN course sites, which, as discussed in Chapter 6, most professors maintain. TWEN sites feature a discussion forum in which students can post and answer questions about cases and other course content. Some professors participate in these online discussions, while others leave them for student use. But even most professors who don't participate in the forum discussions check in on them from time to time to see what's being discussed. Since usually only a small number of students use the forums, they're a good way to get your name in front of the professor and demonstrate your interest in and engagement with the course material.

4. Email the professor a topical news article pertaining to the course material. One easy, low-stress way to initiate contact with a professor, while also demonstrating that you have your eye on the ball, is to email the prof a topical news article relevant to a subject covered in class. You can send the article with a simple note such as, "I don't know if you saw this, but it reminded me of what we were discussing in class today."

5. Give the professor a compliment if it's sincere and deserved. Professors find it rewarding to be appreciated by their students. If your professor is doing a great job, let him or her know. Don't worry about being seen as a brownnoser. Profs can tell the difference between sincere appreciation and phony-baloney attempts to kiss up. If you're too shy to do it in person, send an email.

Five Easy Ways to Make Your Professors Wish You Had Chosen a Different Career Path

Whereas it can take a bit of extra effort to get your professors to know you, it doesn't take any special effort to get them to like and respect you. It does, however, take a lot of regular effort. Professors like and respect good students.

It's that simple. By good students, I don't mean students at the top of the class, although they usually will be included. I mean students who are diligent, hard workers. Good students come to class regularly, well-prepared, on time, and act like the professionals they are on the road to becoming. Referring back to Chapter 4, good students are best defined by the student types of Mr./Ms. Reliable and The Earnest, Hard Worker. If you're already in law school and suspect your professors of showing favoritism to some students, it might be true. But take an honest, objective look at those students. My guess is most of them will be "good students" as defined above.

But what about getting your professors *not* to like and respect you? Here are five common ways students can get on professors' nerves:

1. Coming to class late or unprepared. Yes, I know it sounds obvious. Of course professors don't like it when students show up late or unprepared. But what students don't realize is that some professors *take it personally* when students routinely show up late or unprepared or otherwise demonstrate a lack of commitment to the task at hand. Caught up in their claustrophobically small, ivory-tower worlds, professors' courses occupy positions of supreme importance in their lives. Disrespect shown by a student toward a professor's course is sometimes internalized as disrespect for the professor, even if not intended that way.

2. Acting with a sense of entitlement. No quicker way exists to turn off a law professor than by approaching him or her about a law school issue displaying an air of entitlement or belligerence. Anti-authoritarianism is, I believe, one of our most widely shared traits. Hard-nosed approaches will backfire faster than you can say res ipsa loquitur, if indeed you can say it at all.

You can't successfully bully a law professor. Usually, this is true even if the professor is out of bounds or dead wrong on the issue. As I've explained, law professors, especially tenured professors, operate with near-complete job autonomy. Even deans—their ostensible bosses—have a hard time *making* professors do something they don't want to do.

"You can catch more flies with honey than vinegar" are words to live by when dealing with law professors. You can influence people more effectively by acting respectfully and nicely than by being confrontational. The classic situation demonstrating the accuracy of this idiom as applied in law school involves approaching professors about exam or writing assignment grades. Students who visit a professor to discuss a grade fall into one of four categories:

• Students who sincerely want to learn where they went wrong and how to do better next time.

• Desperate students who arrive with the hope they can somehow cajole the professor into changing their grades.

• Students who performed well on the exam or assignment, but want to bask in their glory and make sure that the professor knows they did well.

• Angry students who come to express their outrage at the grave injustice that has been dealt them and to demand redress.

Of these four groups, professors have a genuine interest in talking only with the first group. Most professors are more than happy to try to help students who want to help themselves and the more sincere and nicer the student acts, the greater their willingness to lend a hand. Students in Group 2 are easily identified by the fact that they quickly lose interest in actually reviewing the exam or assignment once it's made clear there is no chance of a grade change. Assuming they don't press the issue, Group 2 students don't kindle bad feelings in their profs. As for Group 3, professors are always happy to run into the students who did well, but don't really want to waste time engaging in unnecessary exam/assignment reviews with them. If you did well, just be happy and move on.

Then there's Group 4, whose methodology wins the award for "Most Likely to Cause a Law Professor to Shout 'Get the Hell Out of My Office!' " Approaching a professor with a mindset of entitlement, especially if tinged with belligerence, about an exam or any other law school issue is the worst approach one could take. It will practically guarantee your not getting what you want.

3. Whining and complaining. Somewhat related to number 3 is whining and complaining. When professors give assignments or issue class policies about attendance, punctuality, etc., most students just do the assignments and follow the policies. But a few—some of whom qualify as Nattering

Nabobs of Negativism (see Chapter 4)—prefer to waste time whining and complaining about them. Most just whine or complain in the hallways, but the worst offenders insist on taking up valuable class time discussing, debating or challenging the assignments or policies. In the words of the old Nike slogan, when a professor gives you an assignment or tells you to follow a particular rule, "Just do it!"

4. Being overly familiar. Being professional schools, law schools are more formal environments than most undergraduate programs. Don't act overly familiar with your professors, even the friendly ones. Don't call professors by their first names (even if they call you by yours) unless they've expressly invited you to do so. I'll never forget the smug 1L fresh out of college who, a week before law school even started, sauntered into my office, sat down, put his feet on my desk and said, "So, Andrew, how do you see this year shaping up?" I stared at him like he was from Mars.

Younger faculty, especially women and minority professors, may face extra hurdles in being taken seriously by and gaining the respect of students. Students say things to them they would never consider saying to older professors. One young professor told me about a student who approached him after class and said, "With your last name, you could have been a great porn star." Sorry, I can't tell you the last name.

5. Being a smart-a** in class. Originally, because this is a book for the whole family, I wrote "smart aleck," but that just doesn't quite capture the same meaning. If a professor asks a question in class, do not reply with a flippant or jokey answer even if you're convinced it's hilarious. Especially avoid comments that poke fun at or otherwise embarrass the professor in front of the class. The ability to laugh at one's self is a sign of a healthy ego. Unfortunately, not all professors have healthy egos. In asking fellow professors to name the dominant traits of law professors, "insecure" was a common response. Even secure professors, however, don't appreciate being made the butt of a student's joke in class.

Perhaps unfairly, professors do not always abide by the same guideline. Professors often make humorous remarks at the expense of students. Most of these are intended and received as good-natured fun, although students may not always perceive them that way.

This doesn't mean students can't ever say funny things in the classroom. Quite the contrary is true. Countless are the memorable classroom moments defined by a funny student comment. Context is everything. The point here is that students should not *try* to be funny in the classroom.

Learn Your Professors' Individual Styles and Expectations and Adapt to Them

In writing this book, I sent an email to my colleagues asking for input about the top traits of successful law students. Here's what one wrote back:

> Truth be told, my first reaction to [your] query was that the top trait of successful law students is that they do not waste their time or money on books telling them how to succeed in law school. I literally beg first-years to stay away from all manner of outside advice, and instead to follow what their teachers tell them to do in each of their courses.

Hmm, that can't be good for book sales, but she makes good points. I don't agree with the first part or I wouldn't be writing this book, but I couldn't agree more with the second part. While most good law school advice applies across the board, the fact is that law professors, like students, are individuals. They have different teaching styles, different preferences, and different expectations.

Ultimately, you want to do what your individual professors tell you to do in their courses, even if it conflicts with other advice. Why? Because your professors are the ones who will be evaluating you—not the external advice-givers. So, for example, if your Civil Procedure professor instructs you to tell her everything you know about a subject area if it comes up on the exam, do it, even though it runs contrary to the standard exam advice to NOT engage in a general brain-dump (see Chapter 15 discussing common essay exam mistakes).

The above is a real example. At one law school where I taught, a number of students came to me questioning my advice to stay focused on the issues in writing answers to essay questions and not to discuss law that is irrelevant to the specific issues raised. "Professor X," they said, "told us she wants us to write down everything we know about the subject." I told them that couldn't possibly be what she meant. Professors often say one thing, but students hear another. But when I asked Professor X about it, she said they were right. She wants her students to tell her everything they know about a subject. Who's right? Well, she is for her exams because she's the one grading them. It doesn't matter what others think.

In addition to following the specific advice of professors in their particular courses, learn their expectations by observation and adhere to them even if they're different from the expectations of other professors. If one professor does not tolerate latecomers to class, don't be late for that class, even if other professors don't seem to care. If one professor expects students to recite the detailed procedural history of every case when called on in class, be sure to capture the procedural history for every case in that course in your briefs and review it before you get to class, even if your other professors only rarely ask about the procedural history. In short, tailor all law school advice to your individual professors as necessary.

CHAPTER 10

THE TOP FIVE HABITS OF SUCCESSFUL STUDENTS: A C.R.E.D.O.

Assuming you're on the road to being a *successful* law student, you'll be spending a majority of your non-sleep, non-classroom hours during the first year studying and doing study-related activities. Accordingly, we'll spend a substantial portion of the book learning how to study and prepare for exams successfully. The mass of complex material, unique teaching methodologies, and unusual manner of student assessment (just one exam at the end of the semester) impose different and far more intense study demands than students are used to from previous educational experiences.

Later pages are packed with specific study and exam advice, with chapters devoted to case-briefing, note-taking, outlining, exam preparation, essay exam mistakes, and tips for tackling law school multiple-choice questions. This chapter approaches academic success from a wide-angle view. Every student begins law school at the same starting line. As the first year unfolds, some students pull ahead while others fall behind. By the end of the year, at law schools all across America, the class is divided into GPA and class rank strata that include a top, middle, and bottom. What factors determine which group students end up in?

Your LSAT Score Does Not Predetermine Your Fate

One obvious answer is innate ability. I'd be less than candid if I told you that everyone entered law school with the exact same chance of landing in the top of the class. Empiri-

146

cal studies show a positive correlation between LSAT scores and first-year grades, between undergraduate GPAs and first-year grades, between a combination of LSAT scores and undergraduate GPAs and first-year grades, and even between Scholastic Aptitude Test (SAT) scores and first-year grades.

On the other hand, these correlations are not nearly as strong as most law students and law professors have been led to believe. As you perhaps know, the predictor of success in law school receiving the most weight in the admissions process is an applicant's LSAT score. While validity studies do show a positive correlation between LSAT scores and first-year grade performance, the correlation is fairly small. Correlation is measured by a coefficient for which 1.00 represents a perfect correlation and zero shows no correlation beyond one attributable to random chance. In 2005, the Law School Admission Council (LSAC), the folks that administer the LSAT, conducted a validity study using data from 181 law schools.

The median correlation between LSAT scores and first-year grades was only .34. The correlation varied wildly among schools, from a high of .56 (reasonably strong correlation) to a low of .04 (virtually no correlation). The correlation was higher when LSAT scores were considered together with undergraduate GPAs, ranging from .24 to .65, with a median correlation of .46.[53] The LSAC measures but did not include in the validity study the correlation between undergraduate GPA alone and first-year grades. Wouldn't that be interesting to know?

While the LSAT correlates with success for many students, it does not reliably predict the success level of any individual student. Do not start law school thinking that your fate has been preordained by your LSAT score. I've witnessed students with extremely high LSAT scores flunk out of law school and I've known students with below-average LSAT scores (two students with 148 LSAT scores come to mind) who graduated in the top ten percent of their classes and were editors of the law review. When I asked a class of 1Ls who were close to finishing their first year what advice they would give to a close loved one starting law school, I received this reply from a fellow who wrote the top exam in Torts:

53. Law Sch. Admissions Council, 2007–2008 LSAT & LSDAS Information Book 97 (2007).

Do not let below-average undergraduate GPA or LSAT scores discourage you from attending law school if you get accepted. Admittedly, I fell somewhere slightly below average in both, and I nearly decided that I shouldn't come to law school for fear that I wouldn't be able to pass. I spent the first month of law school in constant worry of not being able to compete with classmates who had great LSAT scores. I ended up in the top five of my class after the first semester. My friends love to give me a hard time about how worried I was. My advice would be that if you want to go to law school, use below-average entrance numbers as MOTIVATION in proving your scores wrong, not as reasons you won't pass!

The LSAT measures a limited range of skills, primarily the abilities to read, comprehend, manage, and analyze complex text. While these abilities are critically important to succeeding in law school, other important ingredients to academic success in law school exist that are not measured by the LSAT.

The cheery news is that students have a large degree of control over these other ingredients. Innate cognitive abilities and mental processing skills developed over a lifetime (e.g., reading comprehension skills) are what they are at the time a student begins law school. Over time, law school helps students advance these abilities and skills, but students who want to succeed at their highest level don't have time to waste in that regard.

A C.R.E.D.O.

Keeping with the essential goal of this book to offer practical advice that can be implemented by any student on day one, I thought long and hard about the habits (as opposed to innate traits) that successful law students have in common. I observed the behaviors of my current top students. I considered outstanding students from years past whom I had come to know, particularly my many excellent research assistants. I thought back to my own law school experience. I consulted other law professors. From all that, I came up with a list of five habits that most successful law students share. Top law students almost invariably are: (1) Consistent; (2) Rigorous; (3) Efficient; (4) Diligent; and (5)

Organized. Put these habits together as an acronym and you have a CREDO to live by.

It's true that the CREDO habits are part of the intrinsic personality of some people, but unlike mental processing ability, you have the power, with effort, to adopt and adhere to the CREDO habits even if they're not part of your default personality. *I urge you to do so.* Make a conscious decision at the beginning of law school to follow them and stick with it. Write the CREDO on Post–It notes and stick them on your refrigerator and study carrel.

As you read the descriptions of each habit below, consider whether the attribute is a natural part of who you are. Be honest with yourself. Your law school fate may depend on it. Identify your CREDO strengths and weaknesses. Take note that the habits overlap to a large extent. For example, students who are consistent are more likely to be organized. Those who are organized are more likely to be diligent, etc.

Consistent.

Time for a pop reading-comprehension quiz. Identify the recurring theme in the below list.

The most successful law students:

1. Read *every* assignment.

2. Attend *every* class.

3. Take good notes in *every* class and fill in gaps as soon as possible.

4. Brief *every* case.

5. Outline *every* course.

If you answered "consistency," congratulations! You can now brag to people that you nailed your first law school test. Successful law students are consistent and steady from beginning to end. They don't skip a reading assignment because they were out late the night before. They don't miss a class unless they're on their deathbeds, and even then will ask their caretakers to wheel them in on a stretcher. If they do miss a class, they still read the assignment and make sure to get good notes from classmates. If the professor allows it, they arrange for the class to be audio or videotaped. They don't stop briefing their cases when they hit "The Wall" of the first semester, which occurs somewhere between the seventh and tenth weeks. They recognize that the material covered at the end of the semester is just as important and as likely to be tested as the material at the beginning of the semester. They don't give up after the first semester because they're disappointed by their grades (which most students are—more on that in Chapter 19). They understand that law school is a marathon, not a sprint. Their consistency gives them a definite edge over their classmates who are less consistent, even classmates who are more gifted intellectually.

Of all the mistakes new law students make, being inconsistent in reading assignments, briefing cases, attending class, outlining, periodically reviewing the material, and conducting other study activities is one of the most fatal. Why? Because a law school exam—remember, there's only one per course—is only three or fours hours long, yet covers an entire semester of material. For a three-credit class, that's forty-two class hours. For a four-credit class, it's fifty-six class hours. Do the math. How do professors work forty-two to fifty-six hours of material into a three- or four-hour exam? They don't. They can't.

Instead, they usually pick out a handful of issues—issues covered in just a handful of classes—and package them into the essay questions on which your outcome in that course will depend. It's true that many law professors also use multiple-choice questions, in part precisely because it allows them to spread the exam coverage more thoroughly and fairly, but multiple-choice questions, if included at all, usually make up only a portion of the exam.

Here are two concrete examples to consider. I went back and studied my Torts I and Torts II exams from a recent year. I always split my exams between essay questions and multiple-choice questions, with each section weighted to count for 50 percent of the exam. In Torts I, the essay section was one lengthy, brain-busting mega-question—yet it only addressed four major issues. I perused my class notes and calculated that the four issues covered in the question were directly covered in portions of only seven out of forty-two class hours. Thus, any student who missed one or more of those seven classes and didn't compensate for the gap was at risk of blowing a substantial portion of the exam.

In Torts II, I gave my students four shorter essay questions instead of one large one. I calculated that the material addressed in those questions was directly covered in only eight of forty-two class hours. Of course, with respect to both exams, background material necessary to comprehend the issues covered on the exams consumed more class hours, but that background material by itself would not enable students to perform well if they missed any of the classes covering the specific issues.

This is the way it always works. While some professors may be able to eke out somewhat broader coverage by using a larger number of short essay questions or by dividing longer questions into multiple parts, the bottom line is that missing law school classes or assignments is the legal education equivalent of playing Russian Roulette. You could get lucky. In my courses, it's statistically possible that a student could miss several classes and still be present at every class where a major issue was covered that wound up on the essay portion of the exam. Even then, the student's performance would suffer for missing the preliminary coverage necessary to fully understand and analyze the issues. But it's also statistically possible that a student could prepare for and attend 80 percent of the classes in the semester, learning all of the material in those classes, yet still miss the direct coverage of *every single issue* tested on the essay portion of the exam. Of course, the most likely result is somewhere in the middle.

Here's an interesting factoid. Out of curiosity, I went and dug out the grade and attendance records from a recent Torts class. I added up the absences of the students who received the top seven grades in the class (all *A* or *A-* grades) and those of the students who received the lowest seven grades in the class (all *C-* or *D+* grades), roughly the top and bottom 10 percent of the class. The results didn't surprise me. The top seven students had only one absence among them; that is, six had perfect attendance and one student missed one class. The lowest seven students had twenty-three absences among them.

The inclusion of multiple-choice questions can broaden the course coverage of an exam, ameliorating somewhat the impact of missing a few classes, but students who miss classes or skip assignments still suffer comparatively because their *consistent* classmates will not miss *any* classes or coverage. Also, not all professors use multiple-choice questions.

In short, to have a chance to succeed at the highest level, you must be consistent in your studying and preparation from day one.

Rigorous.

Rigorous is a word with several definitions. Here, it's used to mean "scrupulously right" or "exacting." Legal language is precise. Loose language or vague definitions of legal tests don't cut it. Similarly, partial or incomplete statements of rules won't suffice. If you fail to get the law rigorously right in your notes and outlines, you'll have no chance to accurately state and apply it on the final exams.

Part of being able to apply law effectively on exams comes from a natural analytical gift that some folks are fortunate to possess, but if you can train and police yourself to capture the law accurately and precisely in your notes and outlines, you'll gain ground on many other students, even those with superior analytical skills. Note-taking is addressed in Chapter 12 and outlining in Chapter 13.

It's difficult to offer meaningful comparative illustrations of rigorously right and amorphously wrong statements of the law since many readers may not yet have started law school and, thus, lack a foundation to recognize the difference. But let's give it the old college try. Suppose the professor is defining the tort of assault in class. She explains that "an assault is a volitional act intended to cause imminent apprehension of a harmful or offensive bodily contact to another person, and such apprehension results, directly or indirectly." This one short statement contains several important words and phrases constituting what we call "operative language." They include the elements of a "volitional act" (as opposed to an involuntary act), "intent" (specifically an intent to cause an imminent apprehension of a harmful or offensive bodily contact), and the requisite consequence (i.e., that imminent apprehension of a harmful or offensive bodily contact results, directly or indirectly). Within these elements, all of the following words have distinct legal significance: "imminent," "apprehension," "harmful," "offensive," and "directly or indirectly."

If one were attempting to state the definition of an assault on an exam, leaving out or mischaracterizing any of the above terminology would result in a non-rigorous—i.e., wrong—statement of the law. For example, students often mistake "apprehension" for "fear," but technically they are not the same thing. A person can apprehend a bodily contact from another without being in fear of it, in which case an assault would still occur. Suppose a 98–pound weakling came up to basketball player Shaquille O'Neal on the street, shook his fist and said, "I'm going to sock you Shaq!" Shaq is more than seven feet tall and weighs more than 300 pounds. It is unlikely he would be afraid of the 98–pound weakling, yet he could still apprehend that a harmful or offensive bodily contact was imminent. Thus, the elements of the tort of assault would be satisfied.

Here's another example, involving a non-rigorous *incomplete* statement of the law. When you take Torts, you'll learn that, as a general rule, landowners owe no duty to protect trespassers from dangerous conditions on their property. A major exception exists, however, with respect to child trespassers, to whom landowners owe higher duties. The dominant test nationwide for when a duty is owed to a child trespasser comes from section 339 of an influential treatise known as the *Restatement (Second) of Torts*, with which you will become very familiar in your Torts course. Section 339 provides:

§ 339. Artificial Conditions Highly Dangerous To Trespassing Children

A possessor of land is subject to liability for physical harm to children trespassing thereon caused by an artificial condition upon the land if

(a) the place where the condition exists is one upon which the possessor knows or has reason to know that children are likely to trespass, and

(b) the condition is one of which the possessor knows or has reason to know and which he realizes or should realize will involve an unreasonable risk of death or serious bodily harm to such children, and

(c) the children because of their youth do not discover the condition or realize the risk involved in intermeddling with it or in coming within the area made dangerous by it, and

(d) the utility to the possessor of maintaining the condition and the burden of eliminating the danger are slight as compared with the risk to children involved, and

(e) the possessor fails to exercise reasonable care to eliminate the danger or otherwise to protect the children.

Suppose you had a Torts essay exam question involving a child who was injured trespassing on the site of a chemical factory located three blocks from an elementary school when she went swimming in an unguarded and unfenced pool of sulfuric acid that looked like clear water. Which of the five factors from section 339 would you need to apply on the exam to analyze the problem fully and correctly? *All of them.*

Section 339 is what is known as a "multifactor legal test," which are common in the law. The five factors—(a) through (e)—are *all* part of the test. The determination of whether an occupier of land owes a duty to a child trespasser can be reached only by considering all five factors (note that they're joined by the conjunctive *and*, not the disjunctive *or* as is the case with many legal tests). Not just two or three factors, or even four. Why? *Because it's a five-factor test.* And the only way a student could possibly apply all five factors accurately would be if he or she had written them all down in her notes and/or outline and studied the complete test prior to the exam.

Sounds simple enough, you say. Well, yes and no. Even though section 339 appears in full in our casebook and even though we go over the test thoroughly—factor by factor—during a Torts class and even though I tell my students to make sure they get the complete test in their notes, and even though I let students bring in a "cheat sheet" to the exam on which they can write down all the legal rules and tests we covered, whenever I include a child trespasser issue on an exam, I'd estimate as many as 50 percent of the students fail to accurately set forth and discuss the entire five-factor test. Some discuss section 339 in general terms. Others discuss some but not all of the factors. Some students fail to mention section 339 at all. Because the individual factors are not terribly difficult to apply, the students who are able to state the test rigorously right in their exam answer can usually address the issue reasonably well.

Note that it is unlikely all of the factors of section 339 or any other multifactor legal test will be *in issue* in an exam question or require equal discussion. In the hypothetical given, for example, factor (b) would not require extensive discussion because it's fairly obvious that an unguarded and unfenced pool of sulfuric acid that looks like clear water is a condition that a landowner should realize involves an unreasonable risk of death or serious bodily harm to trespassing children. Factor (b) could be addressed and dispensed with in perhaps a single sentence, but it *would* have to be addressed because it's part of the test.

Another way to describe the quality of being rigorous is to say that good students recognize the importance of *paying attention to detail* in capturing the law. They're not just in the ballpark. Not just close enough for rock and roll. They get it precisely right.

Some law professors use partial or complete open-book exams. Depending on the professor, this may include allowing students to bring in their casebooks, relevant rule books (such as the Federal Rules of Civil Procedure in Civil Procedure), notes, and outlines. Other professors allow students to bring in one or more sheets of paper which they can fill with whatever material they wish. Thus, it may not be necessary to memorize all of the rules with precision, but one would still have to be able to readily access them. For example, if a Torts prof gave an open-book exam and the book contained section 339 of the *Restatement (Second) of Torts*, a student wouldn't necessarily have had to copy the section into her notes or outline, but she would have to know where to quickly find the section in the book, through page tabbing or some other means. As you might imagine, it's too late to begin figuring out the law or even figuring out where to find it during an exam.

Efficient.

So much to do, so little time in which to get it all done. Such is the nature of law school. With a typical load of four doctrinal courses and a time-consuming legal research and writing course, the plates of full-time students quickly fill up and begin overflowing. Part-time evening division students have it even harder. They take fewer courses, but have to juggle full-time careers and often families along with law school.

As a consequence, it should come as no surprise that all successful law students possess or develop efficient time-management skills. They establish schedules for getting things done and adhere to them. They do all the things they need to do, but don't waste time on things they don't need to do. Being efficient can enable students to succeed at a higher level than inefficient students who labor harder and longer. Think of efficiency as the ultimate and only approved "corner-cutting" method for law school success.

Efficiency in law school is a skill that takes some time to develop. At the beginning, everything is so new and confounding that students can't help being inefficient. The learning curve, however, is climbed fairly quickly. Within a few weeks, you'll find yourself becoming much more adept at, for example, reading and briefing cases.

The *E* in CREDO is tied quite closely to the *O*. People who are more organized tend to be more efficient in how they allocate and apply their time. More on organizational skills below. Let's concentrate on some tips for improving your efficiency:

• **Don't waste time during the day.** Given that time is such a precious commodity, it's unfortunate that many students waste so much of it during the school day. First-year law students frequently complain that class schedules are not designed efficiently in that too many lengthy gaps exist between classes. They don't realize schedules are set up this way intentionally as a way to encourage (perhaps "compel" would be a better word) students to stay on campus during the day, rather than just attend their classes and flee the building. As a result, you're likely to have several free hours available each weekday. Use them productively rather than fritter them away.

Study habits and preferences vary by personality. I hated studying late into the night. I realized this at the very beginning of law school. When I studied late at night, I'd end up dreaming about law and working in my sleep all night. I awoke feeling tired and un-rested. After a few weeks of law school, I began developing an awareness of how many hours I wasted during the day. My friends and I began each morning playing ping pong in the student lounge. We'd shoot the breeze between classes, even when there were lengthy gaps between the end of one class and the start of another. At

lunch, we'd hang out and talk some more. I don't recall the
specifics, but I have no doubt that, in the grand tradition of
all 1Ls, many of our lengthy discussions were wasted gossip
and gripe sessions about courses, professors, and classmates.
One day it occurred to me that if I became more efficient
during the day, I'd have more free time at night.

So I changed course. I began using every spare minute of
the day productively. Within a couple of weeks, I had refined
my system to the point where, by the time I left to go home
(i.e., when many of my classmates were just getting ready to
begin their studying), I usually had every assignment for the
next day read and briefed. I missed spending more time with
my friends at school, but the payoff came each night. I found
myself with plenty of time to work on my legal research and
writing projects and still have time to just hang out and
relax. Those long nights of working out legal problems in my
sleep ended. I had found a time-management plan that fit me
perfectly.

The point of this story isn't to persuade you to adopt my
plan. It worked for me, but it might not work for others.
Some people are "night people" who prefer to work and work
better at night than during the day. My purpose is to encourage you to think about how to organize your days so as to be
able to use your time more effectively. Each hour wasted
during the day is one more hour that must be put in at night.

• **Don't let diligence work against you by taking on
unnecessary tasks.** It's hard for a professor to tell enter-
prising students to stop "wasting" time in the pursuit of
extra legal knowledge, but sometimes I do. Some super-
studious and/or inquisitive types (see entry for Curious
George/Georgettes in Chapter 4) go above and beyond the call
of duty in ways which, while admirable, can actually be
detrimental because time is such a limited resource.

A classic example is students who look up the note cases
in their casebooks. Most casebooks have main cases called
"principal cases," which are followed by notes that reference
additional cases, sometimes dozens of them. After all these
years, I'm still impressed when a student comes up after class
and begins discussing details of one of the note cases that he
or she has taken the time to look up and read in its full
version. Impressed, but troubled. If the professor hasn't
instructed you to look up a note case, he's not going to expect

you to know its content. Thus, although you might gain a bit of extra knowledge, it's essentially wasted knowledge. Or more apropos to the discussion, wasted time. It could even be harmful knowledge if your extra reading gets you looking at the legal problem in a way different from how the professor and principal cases covered it. Truth be told, I've used the same Torts casebook for nearly twenty years and still haven't looked up some of the cases in the notes.

• **Read and follow instructions on assignments.** Efficient law students read and follow the instructions for their assignments. Like the brick-house-building pig in *The Three Little Pigs*, they spend a little more time up front and benefit from that investment later. Students who don't exercise the care to carefully read and follow instructions from their professors can end up squandering enormous amounts of time redoing assignments. Worse, often they won't even be granted the opportunity to correct their mistakes.

Legal research and writing courses offer the most opportunities during the semester for students to follow or not follow instructions, so I turned to a director of a legal writing program for help on this one. I emailed him the above paragraph and asked if he knew of any specific examples to demonstrate my point. Here are two attention-getters he sent back:

1. In the spring semester of the course, students must research and write an appellate brief. Students work on their brief for most of the semester, spending dozens of hours on it. The brief assignment covers two issues. I divide the class into two groups. One group works on Issue 1, the other on Issue 2. Students are told their issue and the issue list is posted on the TWEN course site. Despite this, one student a year on average researches and writes about the *wrong* issue. If they're "lucky" enough to figure this out before they turn in the final draft, all of their work will have been wasted. They have to start over and redo the entire brief. If they don't figure out the mistake before turning in the final draft, they get an *F* for the assignment no matter how good the brief is.

2. Each year, a student uses the wrong ID number on his or her assignments. Students are assigned ID numbers at the beginning of the year and told to use the

numbers in lieu of their names. Some simply make up their own number or use an incorrect number. Later, when I'm assigning final grades and can't find a grade for a pre-assigned ID, I simply mark it as an *F*. When grades are posted, offending students must then go through all the hoops to get the grade changed. They could have avoided all the distress and headaches associated with this time-consuming process simply by following the instructions.

• **Prepare for every class, but don't over prepare for any class.** As discussed throughout this book, class preparation is essential in law school, particularly in light of the Socratic teaching method. But some well-intentioned, diligent students actually spend too much time preparing for class, especially in briefing cases. Students who focus obsessively on case briefs not only take away time that could be better spent, they sometimes lose sight of the big picture. They end up lost in a forest where they can only see the trees around them (i.e., unnecessary details of the case) rather than the forest itself.

It always saddens me when failing students bring me their thick packages of case briefs, as if to prove to me how hard they worked. I page through the stack, saying sincerely, "Wow, you really a put a lot of work into these," but also thinking, "Wow, you really wasted a lot of time on these overly long and excessively detailed briefs, time that you probably could have used more profitably."

As discussed in Chapter 11, case briefs are essential for 1Ls, but the law of diminishing returns applies to them. A brief that takes an hour to write may not be significantly more helpful than one that takes twenty or thirty minutes. It may be *less* helpful if it contains too much irrelevant detail. Because cases vary in complexity, it's impossible to offer a specific time estimate as to how long you should spend writing a brief for any one case. As a general guideline, however, a case brief should not exceed one single-spaced typed page, and even that would be on the long side. Most cases can be adequately briefed in half a page.

Don't misconstrue the above advice: class preparation and case-briefing are necessary to first-year success. But so are lots of other tasks we perform in our daily lives that can be done more efficiently and, hence, effectively. It all comes back to the fact that time is a scarce, fixed resource that needs to be allocated and used wisely. One reason some students give up on case-briefing is because they never learn to do it efficiently. So instead of compromising, they go from spending an hour per brief to not doing them at all. Brief all your cases, but don't spend disproportionate time on any one brief. Let this be your mantra: be prepared for *every* class, but don't over prepare for *any* class.

● **Limit your study aids. Some students go overboard in trying to read too many study aids.** Study aids can be extremely helpful, but one per course is about all most students need or can realistically handle time-wise. In addition to draining precious hours from your day, using more than one study aid for the same course can result in confusion since different study aids will present the material differently from one another, and all of them are likely to present it differently from how the professor presents it. The key to using study aids efficiently and effectively is to identify the best study aid for each course in the first instance. Quite often, a "gold standard" study aid—one that is widely recognized as the best—exists for each course. As recommended in Chapter 2, find out either from the professor or upper-level students which one that is, buy it, and stick with it.

● **Limit your extracurricular activities.** Law schools offer many opportunities for students to participate in law-related extracurricular activities, such as student organizations, which are discussed in Chapter 20. Participation in these activities can be both enjoyable and rewarding. Grades aren't and shouldn't be the be-all and end-all measure of achievement in law school. While I encourage you to join a student organization if you find one that appeals to you, don't bite off more than you can chew during the first year in terms of extracurricular activities.

A 1L came to me recently and said she wanted to start a new law school organization. She wanted my advice as to whether her idea for the new organization was a good one and whether she should pursue it. "Yes," I said as to the idea. "No," I said as to whether I thought she should pursue it as a 1L. I applauded her for her initiative, but advised that from a purely academic success standpoint, it was unwise to take on such a time-consuming commitment. Wait until next year, I recommended.

Diligent.

I use "diligent" in the sense of hardworking and staying on task from day one. The most frequently expressed reason I've heard from dismissed law students as to why they were unsuccessful is:

I didn't understand [choose one: how much work was involved/what I was up against/the demands of law school] until it was too late.

For any of the advice in this book to help—but particularly the study advice in the ensuing chapters—*you need to follow it from the very beginning*. The material is simply too vast in amount and too complex in content to try to play catch-up.

To be successful, commit yourself to being diligent before you ever cross the threshold of the law school front door. (More overlap: diligence overlaps with consistency, as well as rigorousness and efficiency.) While the first semester of law school may seem like an eternity when you're in the midst of it, you'll be shocked at how quickly it passes. You cannot afford to get even one class behind.

As mentioned at several points in this book, many 1Ls are cursed by their previous educational successes. They arrive at law school having performed well in high school and undergraduate school without having had to expend tremendous energy. They may have managed a *B* average with only a modicum of effort. When first-semester grades are distributed, many are shocked to find they are hanging on to their status as students in good standing by the barest of decimal point margins or, worse, that they're already on academic probation and headed toward the door. How could this be, they ask? In my experience, the answer in nearly every instance is: they weren't diligent enough.

It's not foolproof, but it's a fair generalization to say that nearly all top law students work extremely hard and most students who flunk out of law school didn't work hard enough. I love this comment from a student asked to list one thing she wished she knew when she started law school: "You don't have to come from a family of legal scholars to do well in law school. Hard work is truly the great equalizer."

Organized.

On the second day of law school in a recent fall semester, a student came to me after Torts and said she missed class because she forgot it met on Wednesday. I smiled and said, "Make sure you get someone's notes because the stuff we covered was important." She assured me she had it covered, thanked me, and left. I wanted to tell her that I doubted very much that she had it covered because the material was complex, especially for a beginning law student. I wanted to tell her that her Torts grade might already be in jeopardy because she missed the critical class at which we delved into the fundamental element of "intent" that underlies all of the intentional torts, a subject we would be studying for the next five weeks and which is invariably tested on the exam. I didn't say any of it because it was already too late. She had already missed the class. She missed it because she wasn't organized enough to keep track of her class schedule.

Last but certainly not least in the CREDO of successful law student habits is "Organized." Being organized is a fitting habit with which to conclude the CREDO because it's intertwined with so many of the other habits of successful law students. Being organized makes it easier to be consistent, rigorous, efficient, and diligent because successful application of those habits depends on having an organized approach and plan. Being organized is an asset in the pursuit of any endeavor, whether it's planning a vacation or preparing your tax return. It's an especially critical trait in law school because of the volume of material that needs to be managed and ordered.

Other things being equal, law school is one place where being a bit "anal retentive" or "obsessive" can be a benefit, at least assuming students are obsessing about the right things. In Chapter 2, I mentioned the Myers–Briggs Type Indicator (MBTI), a personality inventory grounded in Jungian psychological type theory that measures preferences for different personality indicia, specifically: Extraversion vs. Introversion, Sensing vs. Intuitive, Thinking vs. Feeling, and Judging vs. Perceiving. I explained that your "type" is a combination of four letters, one from each pairing. I suggested you take the MBTI and buy Martha and Don Peters' book, *Juris Types*, explaining how the MBTI applies to law student learning styles. If you followed my advice or you've taken the

MBTI in a different context, track down your result sheet. Look at the last of the four letters in your personality type and see if you're a "J" or a "P."

While Ps possess some advantages over Js in law school (Js need to work harder at accepting ambiguity, delaying decisions until all the evidence is in, and listening in class for more than "the answer"), Js have the advantage with regard to this critical trait of being organized. The natural preference of Js is to organize, plan, and order the world around them. In general, they are more methodical. To the contrary, Ps prefer flexibility and open-endedness to planning and deadlines. They often find themselves scrambling at the last minute to finish tasks.

These preferences frequently carry over to education and work environments, where Js benefit from their organizational and planning skills and attention to detail. If you are the type of person who often forgets or loses things, is frequently late, and is always finishing tasks at the last minute, the chances are excellent that you're a P. Be conscious of this preference and recognize that, while a P-preference carries other benefits in educational settings, you'll have to work harder on organization, planning, and scheduling than your colleagues with a J-preference.

Alright, enough with the psychoanalysis, especially since you're going to need a whole lot more of it after the first year. Kidding. Let's turn to two concrete organizational suggestions. I'll give you others related to study techniques and exam preparation in later chapters. These are big picture organizational tips that are easy to follow if you commit yourself to doing so consistently. They not only will improve your chances of success in law school, but save you time, headaches, and unnecessary emotional trauma in the long run.

• **Keep track of your schedule with a day planner.** To even begin resembling an organized person, you need to keep track of what's going on in your life. Your law school life will be much busier than your prior life. Added to all your existing family, social, and (for part-time students) employment obligations, will be: class times (regular, rearranged, and make-up classes), reading assignments, room assignments, study group sessions, deadlines for legal research and writing assignments, speaker luncheons, review sessions, extracurricular meetings for law student organizations, professors' office hours, computer research training sessions, days you're "on panel" to be called on in class if your professor uses that method of class participation (see Chapter 7), application deadlines for scholarships and clerkships, academic support and writing workshops, and, of course, your exam schedule. (I've actually had students show up late for exams because they got the time wrong.)

Beyond these specific events, it's helpful to manage your schedule by blocking out times for study activities (e.g., "work on Contracts outline," "read Property hornbook on future interests") and even recreational activities and errand-running (e.g., "lunch with Matt and Lisa," "go grocery shopping").

I never owned a day planner until I attended law school, but used one religiously once I got there, starting at the very beginning. For some reason (it possibly has something to do with the Obsessive–Compulsive Action Figure in my office given to me by a former colleague), I've kept every day planner for each year of my life since I started law school. I located my moldy day planner from my first year of law school in a box in the attic while writing this book. For my first three weeks of law school at the University of Florida I found, along with all of my reading assignments and regular class times, dated entries like these:

5 pm library tour

Buy Bluebook (Uniform System of Citation)

Buy supplement and highlighters

Study group meets at carrels 2 pm

Legal research lecture Rm 190, 4:10 pm

Get photos taken and fingers printed for FL bar application

Study group meets 7 pm

10:20 Lexis instruction

Dicky Betts concert 2 pm

9:00 pm poolside party at Viscaya

Torts–Contracts class switch

Exercise 1 due in legal research

Fla. Bar exec. dir. 1–3 pm auditorium

Torts meets for two hours—12:40 in Aud. 1:50 in 190C

No study group tonight. Call to confirm cancellation.

Poker game tonight

Extra K [Contracts] class 1:50 in 190A

Later in the trimester, I found entries blocking off time for things like: "Study Property," "work on brief," "Finish reading *Legalines*," "Review Civ Pro notes," and "Make case index for Con Law."

Maybe these calendar entries will cheer you up. I laughed out loud at the fact that I apparently was able to work in a pool party, rock concert, and poker game in those first three weeks of law school. So much for my stories about trudging twenty miles through the snow—in Florida!—to get to law school. But, hey, that's part of the beauty of being organized: it frees up more recreational time.

It's comforting to know that some things never change. In response to a request for organizational tips, here's what one of my research assistants, a top student, wrote back. Notice the similarities in her approach to the one I adopted nearly thirty years earlier:

My helpful hint for being organized with so much going on is to write everything down and block off time periods. My calendar breaks down each day of the week into hours so that I can block off class times and then also I'll block off each hour or so for a certain purpose (example: "update Civ. Pro. Outline" or "read *Glannon's* on res ipsa loquitur"). I even have workout time blocked off a few days a week. I realized I might be somewhat OCD after looking back at this. I found that having a plan of what I was going to study and when I was going to do it helped me get it done with much less stress. I did this especially on the weekends because I'm the kind of student who will sit down and work all day, but you have to take a break sometimes or you will quickly go insane. So with my list I would, on Saturday mornings and/or afternoons, do what I had planned, and then I would have the rest of the day to do something non-school related.

Being old school, I prefer old-fashioned day planners, but it doesn't matter how you keep track of your schedule, just as long as you do it. If you prefer to use a PDA or calendar on your cell phone, that's fine. Whatever method you choose, just make sure you keep it with you at all times and keep it current.

• **Organize the materials you accumulate for each course.** Your course materials are the lifeblood of your survival and success. For each course, you'll have a mass of material to organize. For doctrinal courses, in addition to your casebook and other required books (e.g., statutory supplement books), course materials will include your syllabus, case briefs, class notes, outline, and extra materials distributed by the professor via handout, bookstore purchase and/or online through the professor's TWEN site.

These extra materials can add up. They may include additional cases, statutes, problems, law review articles, and treatise excerpts. For your legal research and writing course, you'll have assignments, research (e.g., cases, statutes, law review articles), and drafts of your papers.

You need to keep these things organized, so you can put your hands on them when you need them. And, importantly, you need to bring all necessary materials to each class. At least once a week, I experience a moment in Torts that provides me with enough information, if I stopped to gather it, to divide the class into two groups I could label *Most Likely to Succeed* and *Less Likely to Succeed*.

How is that possible? Like many professors, I distribute additional materials to supplement the casebook. Mine are in the form of a package of photocopies. They're called, not very creatively, the *Supplemental Materials for Torts I* (or Torts II), and consist of about fifty pages of state-specific tort statutes, key sections from the *Restatements* of the law of torts (influential treatises), extra cases, and a hodge-podge of other stuff.

At the beginning of the course, I tell students both orally and in writing to bring the *Supplemental Materials* to *every class* because they won't know in advance when we'll be referring to them. I also caution them that everything contained in the *Supplemental Materials* is important and fair game for the exam. Every few days, we'll come to a point during a class where I say, "Now get out your *Supplemental*

Materials and turn to page *x*." The *organized* students—the students who are more likely to succeed—promptly pull their *Supplemental Materials* out of their backpacks or flip to them in their course notebooks. The *unorganized* students—those who are less likely to succeed—sit there looking around for the nearest organized student whose shoulder they can glance over—because they forgot to bring the *Supplemental Materials* to class.

They're not bad people or even bad students. It's predictable that a separate item not used in every class will be inadvertently left behind in a locker, car or at home. Regardless of whether their actions are foreseeable or understandable, students who forget to bring essential materials to class are hurting themselves. When we're going over, for example, a complex statute in class that is contained only in the *Supplemental Materials*, there's simply no way for students who don't have the statute in front of them to follow the lecture.

Similarly, like most other profs, from time to time I'll distribute additional handouts in class with the instructions to read them and bring them to the next class. You'd be amazed how many students show up at that next class empty-handed.

Avoiding these omissions is a fairly simple matter: keep all of your course materials together in one place so that they go wherever you go. One efficient (ahh, see that overlap again) way to do it is by putting all your materials for each course into a separate three-ring binder notebook. In this one notebook, you can insert everything you could possibly need for the course, where it will be accessible at a moment's notice. Put the course syllabus and class policies at the front, followed by your case briefs, class notes, outline-in-progress, and extra "handout" materials such as those described above. Use tabbed dividers between the different materials. Keep the notebook current. If the prof distributes a handout, punch holes in it and insert it that day. Buy a heavy-duty three-hole punch to make it easier. In terms of size, a three-inch binder is probably about right for most courses. It will seem too wide and unwieldy at the beginning of the semester, but will fill up by the end, particularly if your professor distributes a lot of photocopied materials.

Of course, many modern students keep items such as class notes, case briefs, and outlines on their computers. An increasing number use computer note-taking programs to manage their data (see Chapter 12). But even those students need to keep track of paper materials, such as my *Supplemental Materials*.

I wrote to three top-ranked students to ask how they manage their course materials—whether the old-fashioned notebook way or via computer—and got mixed answers. The first student said:

> I have a binder for each class with a syllabus tab, handouts/statutes tab, and then a notes section with class notes and briefs. I imagine I am a bit old-fashioned and that most of my classmates keep it all on the computer.

The second student also endorsed the notebook approach, saying:

> I buy a three-ring binder for all my classes. I have done so since the fall of my 1L year and it helps me tremendously to stay organized. I make tabs for all subparts of the subject. My notes section includes my case briefs and class notes.

The third student endorsed the computer approach:

> I definitely keep everything on computer. If I get something in paper form only, I usually keep up with it at my house, but it has to be digested and integrated into my notes to be of much use. There are a few people who keep the binder notebooks, but they are mainly the people who don't have a laptop.

One advantage of having everything in hard-copy form in a notebook is that the material is easier to retrieve when needed. In class I sometimes ask students to flip back to a case or to a topic in their notes that ties in with the current discussion. The students with hard copies of their class notes and briefs in an organized notebook are right there with me. The students with everything buried in computer files have more difficulty locating what they're looking for, and often don't even bother to look. Regardless of whether you keep your course materials in electronic or hard-copy form, the important points are to do it in an organized fashion and to bring all necessary course materials with you to class so you'll have them when you need them.

If you start out organized, it's a snap to stay that way. On the other hand, if you start out disorganized (e.g., briefs are in your locker, outline is in the back of your car, handouts are ... hmm, not sure ... maybe propping up the leg of that bar stool you were sitting on the night before), it will take considerable effort to collect everything when you need it. You might never be able to pull it all together and your performance will suffer accordingly.

* * *

As we prepare to launch into several chapters relating to study, exam-preparation, and exam-taking strategies, pause and take stock of the CREDO habits. Keep them in mind as you read the forthcoming specific advice for enhancing academic performance. Note how much of the advice ties in with the CREDO habits.

CHAPTER 11
CASE-BRIEFING

A "case brief" is a synopsis of a judicial opinion that captures the key elements. Most first-year professors will expect you to come to class having not only carefully studied the assigned cases, but having prepared a written case brief for each of them. Some first-year professors demand that students prepare briefs. When a student is badly fumbling the ball during a Socratic encounter, it's not uncommon for a professor to ask, "Did you read the case? Do you have a brief?" Briefs constitute a kind of prima facie evidence that a student is prepared, even if the student's oral performance seems to belie that fact.

Case-briefing is a tedious, unglamorous aspect of being a good law student. Because case-briefing is time-consuming and carries mostly intangible benefits that are hard for students to see, many students give up on case-briefing too soon. Nearly all new students begin their law school careers as diligent case-brief writers. As the first semester draws on, some students stop briefing their cases. In the second semester, the number of students briefing all their cases dwindles further. The trend accelerates in upper-level courses.

Students who stop preparing case briefs try to compensate by "book-briefing," a technique in which students use underlining, highlighting, and marginal notes in the casebook to track the case in a brief-like form. I confess that I resorted to book-briefing cases in some upper-level courses when I was a student, but I prepared a written brief for every case in every course in my first year. You need to do the same. Here's why:

Why Case-Briefing is Necessary

Learning to read and analyze a case is crucial to understanding law and legal method. Indeed, it is the principal goal of the case method. By reading, I don't just mean decoding the words. That will be hard enough at the beginning given that law has a language of its own. In addition to all the new terminology you'll encounter, like "enfeoffment" and "summary judgment," you'll come upon familiar words that have different meanings in law than in their everyday usage. A new student reading a property law case might think "legal issue" means the procedural or substantive issue of law in the case, when, in fact, the term is legalese for "children."

But far more challenging than learning the meaning of legalese is *comprehending* what the case actually says: sentence by sentence, paragraph by paragraph, and, finally, as a whole. As you'll learn, one reason preparing for law school classes takes a long time is because cases require careful reading *and* rereading. But even reading a case five times is not by itself going to enable you, the novice legal reader, to fully comprehend it.

In evaluating the utility of case-briefing, students tend to focus on the usefulness of the final product—the briefs themselves, but the *process* of composing case briefs is as important if not more so. Case-briefing forces you to identify what's important, separate it from what's not important, extract it from the opinion, and assemble it into an organized framework. It requires you, as one writer on legal reading put it, to "talk back" to the opinion; that is, to go beyond simply underlining or highlighting the court's words and figure out what the case is really about. Additionally, the physical process of extracting this knowledge and writing it down in your own words will help you remember what you read.

You will not accomplish either of these goals as well through book-briefing. This is no time to overestimate yourself. No matter how smart you are or think you are, beginning 1Ls simply are not capable of reading, deconstructing, and digesting complex law without composing case briefs. Even law professors, who, unlike you, are expert legal readers, essentially brief all the cases they assign to students in their own class notes. They don't just read the cases, mosey into class and start talking about them. They extract all the essential ingredients from the case and put them into writing in their own words.

The end-results, the briefs, are also useful. Briefs are helpful in class, especially if you get called on. They aren't a foolproof security blanket because your professors often will ask about parts of the opinion you didn't understand or didn't think were important enough to write down, but in most instances good briefs will allow you to get through the basics of Socratic questioning unscathed.

Briefs also are helpful in composing course outlines, although don't make the common mistake of simply incorporating your briefs as part of your outlines. Outlining is covered in Chapter 13.

Finally, briefs can be useful in exam preparation as a refresher for what was covered throughout the semester. Because briefs are prepared before you attend the classes in which the cases are covered, you don't want to rely too heavily on them as an exam study aid because your professors invariably will emphasize different aspects of the case and/or present the material differently in class than the way you first conceptualized it. An exception is if you edit your briefs, as many students do, either during or after class to make corrections and incorporations based on the class presentation.

Like most other skills in life, case-briefing is a skill that takes practice to develop. Your early briefs will be terrible. Expect it and don't let it alarm you. Your first briefs are likely to be too long, filled with unnecessary detritus while still omitting important elements of the case. I still remember the first case brief I composed in law school. It was for Contracts. Our casebook contained no topic headings (which is unusual), so I was clueless even as to the general subject matter I was supposed to be looking for in the case. I studied the opinion carefully, then began writing longhand in a spiral notebook. My final product was anything but "brief," consisting of more than two single-spaced pages of rambling, unrelated fragments copied directly from the case. I knew it was junk, but had no idea how to improve it.

Within a few weeks, my case briefs began undergoing dramatic transformation. They became more compact and accurate. Without realizing it at the time, I was learning how to analyze law. The case and Socratic methods were working. This will happen to you. Have faith.

Casebook Structure and Organization

Before we get into how to prepare a brief, let's look at how casebooks are structured since they are the source of all the raw material for your case briefs. Most casebooks are divided by topic, with broad topics divided further into more refined subsections. Thus, for example, most Torts casebooks will begin with a section on "Intentional Torts." That section, in turn, may be broken down as follows:

1. A beginning subsection addressing "intent," the critical element common to all of the intentional torts;

2. Separate subsections for each of the seven basic intentional torts (battery, assault, false imprisonment, intentional infliction of emotional distress, trespass to land, trespass to chattels, and conversion); and

3. Separate subsections covering the main "privileges" or defenses to the intentional torts (consent, self-defense, defense of others, defense of property, recovery of property, and necessity).

Within each subsection heading, the casebook will offer one or more judicial opinions that stand for and elucidate fundamental rules or principles regarding the topic. These opinions will have been heavily edited and redacted by the casebook authors. An appeal may require the court to resolve numerous legal issues in its opinion, but in law school casebooks the court's opinion generally is being considered only with regard to a single issue. Thus, portions of the opinion relating to extraneous issues will have been excised. Other extraneous content also may be trimmed or summarized, including case citations, analysis of case precedent, immaterial factual and procedural background, and dissenting and concurring opinions.

This is all good news for law students. It means that instead of having to read a fifty-page opinion, you may only have to read a five-page opinion. The extent of the editing depends both on the editing skill and philosophy of the casebook authors, as well as the nature of the course. U.S. Supreme Court cases, for example, are usually longer, even after extensive editing, than other cases, in part because it's often necessary to include portions of concurring or dissenting opinions. Thus, in 1L courses where Supreme Court cases play a large role, such as Civil Procedure and Constitutional Law, the opinions in your casebook will tend to be longer.

Principal (or "main") cases usually are followed by notes, many of which discuss additional cases. Unless they tell you otherwise, it's safe to assume your professors do not expect you to brief or even look up the full versions of the note cases (also called "squib cases"), although you certainly will want to study any assigned notes carefully. Professors may devote significant class time to discussing selected notes. Also, the notes often contain clearer, more comprehensive explanation of the law than the principal case itself.

How to Read and Brief a Case

I can't give you a concrete formula for how to read a case. The ability to read and synthesize judicial opinions is developed through repetition and by modeling the case analysis conducted by your professors in class. I can give you some good tips though:

Place the case in context.

Before you begin reading a case, place it in the proper spot on your big-picture canvas of the course by paying attention to where the case falls within the casebook's table of contents and section headings. Every case is put in a casebook at a particular place for a reason. A tort case that falls under the broad table of contents heading of "Intentional Torts" and the subheading of "Intent" is inserted at that spot to teach you something about the crucial element of intent that is common to all intentional torts. Even if the case involves the tort of battery, it's not there to teach you about battery. Nor is it there to teach you about tort damages or negligence law or any other topic. How do we know? Because cases intended to teach you about those topics will be grouped under their own relevant headings and subheadings. Casebook authors place cases under particular topical subheadings because they want to use the case to teach you something important about *that particular topic.*

This tip may sound simple and obvious, but many students miss it completely. By failing to contextualize the case—i.e., figure out where it fits in the context of the particular reading assignment as well as the broader topics being covered—they are unable to make discriminating choices when reading the case about what is important and what isn't. Even a judicial opinion that has been substantially edited for a casebook can touch on several points. Contextualizing the case within the framework of the book will help you get your bearings before you begin reading, which in turn will make it easier for you to identify the correct issue when you come upon it. It also will help you tailor your briefs more efficiently.

Don't skim.

Judicial opinions can't be skimmed by novices. The material is too complicated. You need to read every word. As Legal Writing Professor Leslie Burton wrote me in an email:

> [W]hen you read, you can't just *read*. You have to read every word. You have to read every sentence. Then you have to reread and analyze to make sure you understand. I once had a class of students who clearly hadn't understood the statute that they had read for homework. When I explained in class how to interpret the statutory language, one student complained: "But that would mean that we would need to read every word." Yes, that's right.

The devil is in the details in law, so you need to pay attention to them. One problem for new students is they're not sure what details to focus on. While all details must be read, not all of them are important. Getting a feel for distinguishing which details are important (e.g., what was the court's holding?) and which ones aren't (e.g., what was the Court of Azzize and why did it have three Zs in its name?) takes practice.

Realistically, as you progress through law school, you'll learn that some portions of some judicial opinions in some courses can, in fact, be skimmed. Sometimes it depends on the length of the opinion and the manner in which it has (or hasn't) been edited. Sometimes it depends on the professor. You'll learn that some professors focus on the details of every assigned case, while some rely on the cases only to get the basic legal principles out of them. I still recall spending hours reading a sixty-page opinion in Corporations only to come to class and learn that the professor was interested only in the one-sentence holding that corporate officers owe a fiduciary duty to shareholders.

Some professors never even mention the cases they assign. My Secured Transactions professor assigned tons of reading from the casebook each class, but never breathed a word about any of the cases in class. After a couple of weeks, my mates and I decided it was pointless to continue reading the casebook assignments. Instead, we took furious notes, memorized Article 9 of the Uniform Commercial Code (which is the subject of Secured Transactions), and bought a good study aid. But don't get your hopes up. It's unlikely you'll run into either that type of professor or course in the first year. Secured Transactions is what is known as a "code course," meaning the bulk of the law in the area is derived from a code, or book of statutes, rather than from cases. Most first-year doctrinal courses are heavily dependent on case law.

In any event, you won't be in a position to skim *any* portion of *any* case until *after* you've mastered the art of case-reading.

Resolve confusion as you encounter it.

Research by Professor Leah Christensen on how law students read cases shows that higher performing students stop and clarify their confusion about portions of a case as they read it before moving on. To the contrary, lower performing students are more likely to just plow ahead, leaving their questions unanswered.[54] If you read a paragraph that doesn't make sense to you, go back and reread it before moving to the next one. As Christensen found in her study, students who don't stop and clear up their confusion when reading a case may make an incorrect assumption about the case that taints their entire view and comprehension of it.

Highlight.

Highlighting with markers is a helpful tool for law students. I highlighted my books extensively as a law student and still do it as a professor. I find that the process of highlighting helps me absorb and retain material better. Highlighting also facilitates quick review of the material, as

54. *See* Leah M. Christensen, *Legal Reading and Success in Law School: An* *Empirical Study*, 30 SEATTLE U.L. REV. 603, 640 (2007).

when you're refreshing your memory of the reading right before class. If you're called on in class, highlighting makes it easier to track down the relevant excerpt of the case to answer the question.

Many students develop systems using different colored highlighters for different components of the case. For example: green for facts, yellow for procedure, purple for reasoning, and pink for the case holding. I stuck with basic yellow, but a multi-colored system is worthy of consideration.

Not long ago, I had a student who made no marks of any kind in her casebooks. When I asked why, she said she wanted to be able to recoup more money for the books when she resold them after the semester. Bad cost-benefit analysis. She was academically dismissed at the end of the first year. Your success, in which you're already investing thousands of dollars, not to mention your blood, sweat, and tears, is worth far more than a few extra bucks come book resale time. Mark those books up!

Of course, highlighting is not a panacea. I'm not suggesting the academic difficulties of the student referred to above were attributable solely to a lack of highlighting. Some students think if they apply heavy-handed highlighting and underlining to a case, they've done an excellent job of studying the case, but that is not necessarily true. You can highlight every line of a case in a color pastiche worthy of being hung in a gallery, yet still come away without a real understanding of it.

Abbreviate.

With respect to both case briefs and outlines, developing a shorthand of abbreviations for oft-repeated words and terms will increase your efficiency. Traditionally, for example, law profs and students abbreviated "plaintiff" with a pi symbol (π) and "defendant" with a delta symbol (Δ). Why didn't we just use P and D? Because we didn't have computers and those two letters can end up looking like each other when handwritten. I still use π and Δ when writing by hand, but P and D are fine if you're using a computer. "Contract" is abbreviated "K," while "contracted" can be shortened to "K-ed." Similarly, "reasonable" can be shortened to "R" and "reasonably" to "R-ably." Terms can also be abbreviated.

"Fee simple absolute" can be "FSA," "intentional infliction of emotion distress" can be "IIED," etc.

The Essential Components of a Case Brief

Different advice-givers offer different formats for case briefs, which can be confusing to law students. But don't worry. There is no single correct format to use for case-briefing. If you peruse different recommended templates for case-briefing, you'll see that while they may use different section headings or put them in a different order, they all seek to capture the same main points about a case. When you get to the case-briefing exercise below, for example, you'll see that three top-ranked law students all used slightly different formats in briefing the sample case and I use a different one still in my sample brief.

Regardless of the specific format, when reading a case, you want to identify and include in your brief these points about it:

The relevant facts.

Law means little except in relation to facts. A change in a single fact can change the outcome of the case. Thus, the facts of a case are critical.

The trick is separating the relevant facts from the irrelevant ones. Well-written judicial opinions will do much of the work for you in this regard. A skilled judge will focus on the relevant facts in setting forth the case in the written opinion. Further aid will come from the casebook authors, who may edit out unnecessary facts or even summarize the key facts for you.

Nevertheless, the cases in your casebooks (as well as questions on your exams) often will contain both material and immaterial facts. In compiling a case brief, a critical analytical challenge facing you will be to distinguish them and include only the material facts in your brief. This challenge, which is part of the broader challenge of learning to conduct legal analysis, will be especially difficult at the beginning of law school because you will lack any foundation for making the distinction. This is one reason case briefs usually are longer at the beginning of law school and get shorter as students progress. At the beginning you'll be more likely to include non-material facts in your briefs.

The number of relevant facts to include in a brief will vary by the course and individual case. For example, the relevant facts of many cases in Torts and Criminal Law may be simpler and fewer in number than the relevant facts of Contracts and Property cases, which often involve complex business transactions. In tort cases, for example, the dates of events usually are not important, whereas they often are in contract cases. Of course, these are just general propositions. Everything depends on the particular case. In some tort cases the dates are crucial and in some contract cases they're not.

The procedural history/posture of the case.

The procedural history and posture of a case is the portion of the opinion explaining how the case ended up before the appellate court that wrote the opinion in the casebook. Under U.S. law, a party who desires to appeal an adverse ruling in a trial court must identify a particular error alleged to have occurred during the trial or pretrial proceedings. It's not a ground for appeal simply that the party lost the case and wants a second bite at the apple.

Understanding the procedural posture of a case is extremely difficult at the beginning of law school because students lack knowledge of the procedural mechanisms of the U.S. litigation system. The problem is exacerbated by the fact that the course designed to impart much of that knowledge— Civil Procedure—often is not included as part of the first-semester curriculum and even when it is, the course is taken contemporaneously with the other first-year courses.

To give you a head start, below are the *Top Five Most Commonly Alleged Errors on Appeal* you will encounter in reading appellate court opinions in civil cases (as opposed to criminal cases), which will make up most of your first-year reading. Understanding these five errors will put you ahead of your classmates in the early weeks of law school.

PRODUCT WARNING: If you have not started law school yet, studying the five errors may cause drowsiness. In extreme cases, eye-glazing can occur. If you experience these symptoms, stop reading, tab this page, and return to the five errors when you begin reading your initial casebook assignments.

Top Five Most Commonly Alleged Errors on Appeal

1. *The trial court erred in granting a motion to dismiss (sometimes called a demurrer).* All lawsuits are commenced with the filing of a complaint by the plaintiff. The complaint outlines the grounds for the lawsuit and essential facts supporting those grounds. The rules of civil procedure provide that if a complaint is defective on its face, the defendant can file a motion to dismiss the complaint (and, hence, the lawsuit). A variety of grounds exist for dismissing a complaint. One of the most common is a generic assertion that the complaint fails to state a valid claim. If the defendant moves to dismiss the complaint and the court agrees that the complaint is deficient, the court can dismiss the complaint without the necessity of holding a trial. Frequently, plaintiffs who have had their complaints dismissed will appeal on the basis that the trial judge committed error in granting the motion to dismiss (or demurrer).

2. *The trial court erred in granting a motion for summary judgment.* Somewhat similar to a motion to dismiss, a motion for summary judgment is a mechanism for disposing of a case without a trial. The motion can only be granted when no major factual disputes exist and the moving party is entitled to judgment under the law. If material facts are in dispute, the case must go to trial so that the fact-finder (either the judge in a bench trial or the jury in a jury trial) can resolve the disputed facts based on all the evidence. Unlike a motion to dismiss, which is based only on the content of the complaint, a motion for summary judgment can be supplemented by external facts established by documents, affidavits, depositions, and answers to written questions called interrogatories. But again, those facts can't be in dispute. Alleged error in granting summary judgment is a common basis for an appeal.

3. *The trial court committed an error during a trial that led to an adverse jury verdict.* When the jury returns a verdict for one party, the losing party may appeal if the party can point to an error in the trial. While a variety of errors conceivably can occur during a trial, two of the most common trial errors asserted as grounds for appeal are, first, that the evidence was insufficient to support the verdict, and, second, that the trial court erred in giving or failing to give a particular jury instruction.

The first ground—that the evidence was insufficient to support the verdict—is self-explanatory. The argument often arises in conjunction with the more specific assertion that the trial court erred in denying the losing side's motion for directed verdict made during the trial, which is discussed separately below.

The second ground—that the trial court erred in giving or failing to give a particular jury instruction—requires some elaboration. As it is often said, in a jury trial the "jury is the judge of the facts and the judge is the judge of the law." This means that the jury determines what actually happened based on the evidence it hears and the judge determines the appropriate law to govern the case. When all the evidence has been received, the judge instructs the jurors as to that law by reading them written "jury instructions." These instructions are often contentiously fought over by the parties. If the judge gives a jury instruction that a party believes is wrong under the law or refuses to give an instruction that a party believes is required by the law and that party loses, the party may assert that alleged error in an appeal.

4. *The trial court erred in granting or denying a motion for a directed verdict.* A motion for a directed verdict is a motion made during a trial by either the plaintiff or defendant (usually the defendant) in which the moving party argues that, even viewing the evidence in the light most favorable to the other side, no reasonable jury could find in the non-moving party's favor. If the judge agrees, the judge will grant the motion, directing a verdict in favor of the moving party, hence, "taking away" the case from the jury. The party against whom the directed verdict was issued may appeal arguing that the granting of the motion was in error. Conversely, if the judge denies the motion and the jury returns a verdict adverse to the moving party, the moving party may appeal arguing error in refusing to grant the directed verdict.

5. *The trial court erred in granting or denying a motion for new trial or judgment notwithstanding the verdict.* After a verdict has been rendered, it is common for the losing party to file a motion for a new trial or, less commonly, for a judgment notwithstanding the verdict (called "motions for j.n.o.v."). Such motions argue that the verdict was contrary to the evidence or that some other error occurred rendering

the jury's decision defective. If the judge orders a new trial or enters a j.n.o.v., the losing party may appeal alleging error in that decision. Conversely, if the judge denies the motion, the moving party may appeal the denial as error.

Students face a dilemma in deciding how much procedural history to include in their case briefs. In some instances, the procedural history of a case may be complex, requiring an entire paragraph to explain it accurately. I recommend that you begin law school by including an accurate procedural posture for each case in your briefs, both to protect yourself in class in case the prof calls on you asking for such information and also to start you on your way toward understanding litigation procedure. This can be time-consuming, however, and often unnecessary because many professors skip over the procedural posture of cases in class. After you progress several weeks into the course, be more discriminating about how much procedural information you include in your briefs. If you have professors who rarely ask about the procedural history of a case, you can start trimming that section of your briefs in those courses.

The issue(s) in the case.

To have any chance of learning to analyze law properly, you will have to learn to "spot issues": in cases, on exams, and in the practice of law. Identifying the key issue in the case is the essential foundation on which any quality case brief is built. Some folks have an analytical knack for issue-spotting from the moment they start law school. Most others develop the skill over time. Regrettably, some students never master it.

"The issue" of a case generally is *the point* of the case, as in "What's the point?" For each case, ask yourself: Why is this case in this book in this section under this subsection? What are the casebook authors trying to teach me by including it? Thinking about these questions can help you pinpoint the issues.

Students frequently confuse the *procedural issue* in the case, such as those listed above, with the *issue of substantive law* they're supposed to be focusing on. Such mistakes are perfectly understandable and in one sense technically aren't even mistakes since courts often explicitly state the issue in procedural terms, as in: "The issue in this case is whether the trial court erred in granting the defendant's motion for directed verdict."

But that's not why the authors put the case in the book. That will be the technical procedural issue in a hundred cases you will read. The issue you're looking for is the underlying issue of *substantive law* that the court is taking time to explain and offer rules and reasoning regarding. It may be that your professor also will want you to know the procedural issue, but come exam time, you'll be tested on the substantive law.

How do you spot the issue of substantive law? Sometimes you'll be lucky and the court will say: "The issue in this case is ..." followed by the substantive legal issue. Usually, however, the court will not expressly identify the issue, leaving it up to you to infer the issue from the court's discussion of the holding, rules, and reasoning.

Often you'll have to think beyond the narrow issue raised by the case facts and infer a larger issue from the holding. For example, in studying the tort of intentional infliction of emotional distress, you might read *Slocum v. Food Fair Stores of Florida, Inc.*,[55] in which a stock clerk told an elderly woman who asked for the price of an item, "If you want to know the price, you'll have to find out the best way you can ... you stink to me." The woman allegedly suffered great emotional distress and a heart attack because of the statement.

You will learn that to make out a claim of intentional infliction of emotional distress, the plaintiff must prove "extreme and outrageous conduct" by the defendant as one of the elements of the tort. The broad issue in *Slocum* was whether mere insults constitute extreme and outrageous conduct (the answer is that they generally do not), not the narrow question of whether it's okay to tell an elderly person she smells bad. But, unfortunately, the *Slocum* court never came right out and said that was the issue, leaving it to students to infer the broader issue from the narrow facts.

Here's a great tip for issue-spotting. In addition to placing the case in the context of the subject headings as already suggested, study the notes following the case. Often these notes will identify the issue more clearly than the case itself.

---

55.   100 So. 2d 396 (Fla. 1958).

For example, the first note following the *Slocum* opinion as it appears in the famous Prosser, Wade and Schwartz torts casebook asks: "Why is the intentional infliction of mental disturbance by the *insult* not a tort in itself?"[56] This note question essentially identifies the issue for students.

The rule(s) adopted by the court regarding the issue(s).

Ultimately, you usually will be looking to find one or more legal rules in a case. These are the rules that you will be expected to know and apply on the exam. The rules are intimately tied to the issue. One way to think about it is that the issue is the *question* of the case and the rule as applied is the *answer* to the question.

Generally, each case in a casebook will stand for one particular rule or an exception to a rule. If the case stands for an exception to a broader rule and you haven't already studied the broader rule in another case, be sure to capture both the broad rule *and* the exception in your brief. The case-briefing exercise below provides an example elucidating this point.

As with issue-spotting, sometimes identifying the rule is simple while other times the rule can be elusive. The rule of the case is often bound up with the court's "holding" in the case; and, indeed, many people label the rule section of their briefs as the holding section. The holding is the court's resolution of the issue, which often incorporates the rule. Thus, one tip for rule-spotting (as well as issue-spotting) is to look for sentences that begin with "We hold . . . ."

Note, however, that not all casebook cases will stand for specific rules. With some frequency, cases are included in casebooks to give general background about a particular subject area. These cases are harder to brief. In fact, some of them will not be brief-able under the traditional format.

The court's reasoning.

Life would be much easier for law students if courts labeled the different sections of their opinions like law students are advised to do in their case briefs. Certainly, this is true with regard to the court's reasoning, the last essential

---

56. Victor E. Schwartz, Kathryn Kelly & David F. Partlett, Prosser, Wade and Schwartz's Torts: Cases and Materials 56 (11th ed. 2005) (emphasis added).

component of a good case brief. Identifying the court's reasoning can be particularly difficult because it may be scattered all over the opinion. Moreover, a lot of what could pass as reasoning is superfluous or nonessential. Because you're writing a brief and not a dissertation, you're looking for those nuggets of reasoning that *directly* support the court's resolution of the case. *Why* did the court take the position it did in resolving the issue the way it did? Answer that question before you begin trying to write down the court's reasoning. Don't just copy from the opinion. Think about it first and then put it in your own words. As one of my research assistants, a top student, commented on reading this section:

> I would give more emphasis to the importance of *first* identifying and *second* putting in your own words the court's reasoning. The "why" of the case is what helped me the most in applying the law to different hypotheticals, both in class and on exams. Once I became effective at figuring out the "why" for the holding and/or rule of law, I found that briefing and understanding cases was easier.

A Case-Briefing Exercise

If you haven't started law school yet, here's an exciting chance to write your very first case brief using a real law school case: *Robinson v. Lindsay*, an opinion from the Supreme Court of Washington involving a lawsuit for negligence by a minor injured in a snowmobile accident against the driver of the snowmobile. The case is included in the popular Prosser, Wade and Schwartz Torts casebook, used at 124 law schools, including in my Torts course. Here are the components of the exercise that you'll find below:

> ***The case.*** The opinion issued by the Supreme Court of Washington, with a brief prefatory explanation of the legal doctrine on which the case rests.
>
> ***A case-briefing form.*** A template for writing your own brief of the case.
>
> ***Sample briefs from real law students.*** Three sample briefs of *Robinson* written by three top law students in a recent Torts course, along with comparative analysis.

My brief of the case. A brief I composed, with explanatory notes.

The case: *Robinson v. Lindsay.*

To make the exercise meaningful, you'll need a tiny bit of
background in the applicable legal doctrine. As explained
back in Chapter 5, a tort is basically any civil wrong, other
than a breach of contract, for which the law allows the
recovery of money damages. Negligence law is the largest
slice of the tort-law pie. Under negligence law, an actor is
liable for injuries caused to another if the actor owed a duty
of care to the injured person, breached that duty, and such
breach caused injury to the plaintiff. When a duty of care is
owed under negligence law, it is usually a duty to use the
degree of care that a hypothetical "reasonable person" would
have used under the same or similar circumstances. Most
adults are held to this same "standard of care," as it is
known.

As with everything in the law, exceptions exist. Thus,
people with physical disabilities are expected to exercise the
degree of care that a reasonable person with the same disability would exercise. Professionals, such as doctors and lawyers,
are expected to act with the same degree of care as other
professionals. Children, as we learn below, also get their own
standard of care, but with an exception (so we basically have
an exception to an exception at work). *Robinson v. Lindsay*
appears in the Prosser, Wade and Schwartz casebook under
the broad heading of "Negligence" and the subheading "The
Standard of Care." Prior to reading the case, students know
nothing about how children are treated under negligence law.
Keep that in mind as you read the case and consider what the
casebook authors and professor would expect a student to get
out of the case.

So here we go, beginning with the court's opinion:

ROBINSON v. LINDSAY

598 P.2d 392 (Wash. 1979)

UTTER, Chief Justice.

An action seeking damages for personal injuries was
brought on behalf of Kelly Robinson who lost full use of a
thumb in a snowmobile accident when she was 11 years of

age. The petitioner, Billy Anderson, 13 years of age at the time of the accident, was the driver of the snowmobile. After a jury verdict in favor of Anderson, the trial court ordered a new trial.

The single issue on appeal is whether a minor operating a snowmobile is to be held to an adult standard of care. The trial court failed to instruct the jury as to that standard and ordered a new trial because it believed the jury should have been so instructed. We agree and affirm the order granting a new trial.

The trial court instructed the jury under WPI 10.05 that:

In considering the claimed negligence of a child, you are instructed that it is the duty of a child to exercise the same care that a reasonably careful child of the same age, intelligence, maturity, training and experience would exercise under the same or similar circumstances.

Respondent properly excepted to the giving of this instruction and to the court's failure to give an adult standard of care.

The question of what standard of care should apply to acts of children has a long historical background. Traditionally, a flexible standard of care has been used to determine if children's actions were negligent. Under some circumstances, however, courts have developed a rationale for applying an adult standard.

In the courts' search for a uniform standard of behavior to use in determining whether or not a person's conduct has fallen below minimal acceptable standards, the law has developed a fictitious person, the "reasonable man of ordinary prudence." That term was first used in Vaughan v. Menlove, 132 Eng.Rep. 490 (1837).

Exceptions to the reasonable person standard developed when the individual whose conduct was alleged to have been negligent suffered from some physical impairment, such as blindness, deafness, or lameness. Courts also found it necessary, as a practical matter, to depart considerably from the objective standard when dealing with children's behavior. Children are traditionally encouraged to pursue childhood activities without the same burdens and responsibilities with which adults must contend. (citation omitted) As a result, courts evolved a special standard of care to measure a child's negligence in a particular situation.

In Roth v. Union Depot Co., 13 Wash. 525, 43 P. 641 (1896), Washington joined "the overwhelming weight of authority" in distinguishing between the capacity of a child and that of an adult. As the court then stated (citation omitted):

> [I]t would be a monstrous doctrine to hold that a child of inexperience—and experience can come only with years—should be held to the same degree of care in avoiding danger as a person of mature years and accumulated experience.

The court went on to hold (citation omitted):

> The care or caution required is according to the capacity of the child, and this is to be determined, ordinarily, by the age of the child.... [A] child is held ... only to the exercise of such degree of care and discretion as is reasonably to be expected from children of his age.

The current law in this state is fairly reflected in WPI 10.05, given in this case. In the past we have always compared a child's conduct to that expected of a reasonably careful child of the same age, intelligence, maturity, training and experience. This case is the first to consider the question of a child's liability for injuries sustained as a result of his or her operation of a motorized vehicle or participation in an inherently dangerous activity.

Courts in other jurisdictions have created an exception to the special child standard because of the apparent injustice that would occur if a child who caused injury while engaged in certain dangerous activities were permitted to defend himself by saying that other children similarly situated would not have exercised a degree of care higher than his, and he is, therefore, not liable for his tort. Some courts have couched the exception in terms of children engaging in an activity which is normally one for adults only. *See, e.g.,* Dellwo v. Pearson, 259 Minn. 452, 107 N.W.2d 859 (1961) (operation of a motorboat). We believe a better rationale is that when the activity a child engages in is inherently dangerous, as is the operation of powerful mechanized vehicles, the child should be held to an adult standard of care.

Such a rule protects the need of children to be children but at the same time discourages immature individuals from engaging in inherently dangerous activities. Children will still be free to enjoy traditional childhood activities without being held to an adult standard of care. Although accidents sometimes occur as the result of such activities, they are not activities generally considered capable of resulting in "grave danger to others and to the minor himself if the care used in the course of the activity drops below that care which the reasonable and prudent adult would use . . . . " (citation omitted)

Other courts adopting the adult standard of care for children engaged in adult activities have emphasized the hazards to the public if the rule is otherwise. We agree with the Minnesota Supreme Court's language in its decision in Dellwo v. Pearson (citation omitted):

> Certainly in the circumstances of modern life, where vehicles moved by powerful motors are readily available and frequently operated by immature individuals, we should be skeptical of a rule that would allow motor vehicles to be operated to the hazard of the public with less than the normal minimum degree of care and competence.

Dellwo applied the adult standard to a 12-year-old defendant operating a motorboat. Other jurisdictions have applied the adult standard to minors engaged in analogous activities. Goodfellow v. Coggburn, 98 Idaho 202, 203–04, 560 P.2d 873 (1977) (minor operating tractor); Williams v. Esaw, 214 Kan. 658, 668, 522 P.2d 950 (1974) (minor operating motorcycle); Perricone v. DiBartolo, 14 Ill.App.3d 514, 520, 302 N.E.2d 637 (1973) (minor operating gasoline-powered minibike); Krahn v. LaMeres, 483 P.2d 522, 525–26 (Wyo.1971) (minor operating automobile). The holding of minors to an adult standard of care when they operate motorized vehicles is gaining approval from an increasing number of courts and commentators. (citations omitted)

The operation of a snowmobile likewise requires adult care and competence. Currently 2.2 million snowmobiles are in operation in the United States. (citation omitted) Studies show that collisions and other snowmobile accidents claim hundreds of casualties each year and that the incidence of accidents is particularly high among inexperienced operators. (citation omitted)

At the time of the accident, the 13-year-old petitioner had operated snowmobiles for about 2 years. When the injury occurred, petitioner was operating a 30-horsepower snowmobile at speeds of 10-20 miles per hour. The record indicates that the machine itself was capable of 65 miles per hour. Because petitioner was operating a powerful motorized vehicle, he should be held to the standard of care and conduct expected of an adult.

The order granting a new trial is affirmed.

Brief the case yourself.

Before you look ahead, take some time and brief the case yourself. Here's a form you can use. This template tracks the one I use below in my brief:

Robinson v. Lindsay (Wash. 1979)

Facts:

Procedural History:

Who won?:

Issue:

Holding/rule(s):

Reasoning:

Sample briefs from three top law students.

To add authenticity to this case-briefing exercise, I solicited help from three top students. At the end of their first year, these students ranked number one, two, and three in an entering class of approximately 150 students. I asked the students to track down their case briefs for *Robinson*, which we had covered in the eighth week of their first semester.

Not surprisingly, being outstanding students (although they didn't know they would be at the time), they had each briefed the case. This fact should teach you something perhaps even more important than the content of their briefs. Students who brief every case are demonstrating those essential CREDO qualities of Consistency and Diligence. By the eighth week of law school, I'm sure some students had stopped briefing all their cases. One of the students whose brief I asked to use responded to my email request as follows:

> I think one reason that I did so well was that I briefed EVERY case that I read in Torts I and II. Case-briefing is so important, both to be prepared for class on a daily basis and also to study for exams. Case-briefing also helped me with being able to analyze legal rules and material facts.

The three students located their briefs, submitted them without alteration as requested, and gave me permission to share them with you. Their briefs illustrate the point I made earlier that case-brief formats can vary and still accomplish the same goals. The formats they used are all somewhat different, yet each brief captured the essential elements of the case.

Student Brief No. 1

Facts. Billy Anderson (13 years old) was driving a snowmobile owned by Lindsay. Anderson had driven snowmobiles for about 2 years prior to the accident. He was pulling Kelly Robinson (11 years old) on an inner tube attached to the snowmobile. Robinson's thumb got caught in the tow rope and was severed. It was reattached but was not fully functional.

Procedural History. Trial produced a jury verdict for Anderson. A new trial was ordered because jury was not instructed to hold Anderson to the adult standard of care.

Issue. Whether a minor operating a snowmobile is to be held to the adult standard of care.

Holding. Yes.

Reasoning. Courts usually don't hold children to the adult standard of care. The standard is usually what is reasonably expected of children of the same age—a reasonably careful child of the same age, intelligence, maturity, training, and experience. But if the activity the child engages in is inherently dangerous (as it is here), the child should be held to the adult standard of care. This discourages immature individuals from engaging in such conduct/activities where the risk of harm is great.

Rule. When a child engages in an activity which is normally undertaken only by adults and requires adult qualifications, the child is held to the adult standard of care.

Student Brief No. 2

Facts. Snowmobile accident where plaintiff of 11 years of age was injured by a 13-year-old boy driving. The 13-year-old boy was driving a snowmobile, pulling the 11-year-old girl on an inner tube which was attached to the snowmobile with a tow rope. The girl's thumb got caught in the tow rope and was severed.

Alleged Error. The trial court instructed the jury to judge the 13-year-old boy's conduct against that of a reasonably careful child under the same or similar circumstances.

Legal Issue. What standard of care should the court use to judge the child's conduct?

Holding. Court overturns the trial court and holds that the 13-year-old boy should be held to the standard of care of an adult because he was partaking in an adult activity that was inherently dangerous (another chip in the "fault principle")—public policy must protect the general public over the interest of the children.

Rule. General standard of care applicable to children is that of a child their own age, experience, intelligence, maturity, training and experience would exercise under the same or similar circumstances. (Ultimately an objective standard, but not purely objective ... based on certain similar attributes of the reasonable child.)

Rule. "Adult Activity Exception"—When children partake in inherently dangerous activities, normally undertaken by adults, children should be held to the standard of care of an adult.

Reasoning. The "adult activity exception" protects the need of children to be children but at the same time discourages immature individuals from engaging in inherently dangerous activities. There would be great hazards to the general public if children were not held to adult standards when undertaking in adult activities that are inherently dangerous.

Student Brief No. 3

Facts. Billy Anderson, 13, was driving a snowmobile, belonging to D, pulling P. P's thumb was severed when it was caught in tow rope.

Procedural History. Jury verdict in favor of Anderson, trial court ordered a new trial.

Legal Issue. Whether a minor operating a snowmobile can be held to an adult standard of care.

Alleged Error. Jury instruction to hold to adult standard.

Holding. Children involved in dangerous activities, usually reserved for adults, must be held to an adult standard of care.

Reasoning. Exception to the reasonable person standard when dealing with children's behavior. It would be a monstrous doctrine to hold a child to the same standard of an adult. The caution should be judged based on the capacity of the child. Held only to a standard of care of a reasonable child his age. However, when a child is engaged in an inherently dangerous activity, such as driving a motor vehicle, he should be held to an adult standard of care.

Rules.

Disposition. Affirm

Dissents/Concurrences.

Notes.

Comparing the student briefs.

All three sample briefs are of good quality, no surprise since they came from three top law students. Are they exquisite works of art? No, but case briefs don't have to be. In fact, the more perfect the case-brief composition, the more likely the student spent too much time on it. All three students got the job done.

Note one important quality they all have in common: they're *brief* as case briefs should be. *Robinson* is a fairly simple case with simple facts. Not all briefs would be this short, but it bears reemphasizing that effective law students brief every case, but do so efficiently. It's also worth mentioning that brief 2 (as the writer told me) benefited from the fact that the student edits his briefs during class as part of his note-taking, as many students do. So, for example, when I made the point in class that the normal child standard of care is an *objective* standard (i.e., it compares the conduct of the child actor to how other similar "reasonable children" would have acted) even though it looks like a *subjective* standard (in that we tailor it to take into account the child's personal traits such as age and intelligence), the writer of brief 2 inserted the point in his brief either during or after class. Amending your briefs to fit the lecture is a good strategy because it enhances their accuracy and completeness, making the briefs more useful as an exam prep tool.

Let's compare the student briefs, using my brief-formatting template:

Facts. The facts of this case, as is true of many tort cases, are fairly simple and straightforward. Brief 1 contains the most complete statement of the facts, but the two key facts— that the alleged negligent actor was a minor and was driving a motorized snowmobile—are set forth in all three briefs.

Procedural History. The procedural history of the case is stated most accurately in brief 1. The procedural history in brief 2 (designated as "Alleged Error") is incomplete and in brief 3, even when the "Procedural History" and "Alleged

Error" sections are combined, the result is both incomplete and too vague.

Who won? While not included in most case-brief templates or in any of the student briefs, it's a good idea to insert a separate section stating which party ultimately prevailed because it helps students see the forest through the trees. Very often in class, I'll ask "Who won?" during case-recitation dialoging. You'd be amazed at the number of puzzled responses this question generates from even exceptionally well-prepared students with full briefs.

Issue. All three of the students nailed the issue. Briefs 1 and 3 stated the narrow issue accurately and nearly identically; i.e., whether the minor snowmobile operator should be held to an adult standard of care. Brief 2 stated the issue more broadly in terms of what standard of care should be applied to children.

Holding/rule(s). Because the students had not yet learned the general standard of care applicable to children, it was important for them to get out of this case not only the exception that the court ended up applying, but the standard of care normally applicable to children. Notably, all three briefs did include the general standard of care applicable to children even though it wasn't directly an issue in the case. Brief 2 put it in the rule section, while briefs 1 and 3 placed it in their reasoning sections. Where they inserted it isn't that important. The important thing is that they all captured the general child standard of care, although brief 3 did not state it with sufficient precision. Significantly, all three briefs accurately stated the court's holding/rule adoption that when a child engages in an inherently dangerous activity the child will be held to an adult standard of care.

Reasoning. Only brief 2 captured the two essential reasons given by the court for its holding, which are that the exception is needed to protect the public and to discourage immature individuals from pursuing dangerous activities. Brief 1 got one of the reasons. Brief 3 omitted both.

My brief, with comments.

Here's my brief of *Robinson*, based on years of reading and teaching it. My brief contains only the information I want my students to get out of the case. Explanatory comments are included in brackets.

Facts. P was an 11-yr-old girl who lost her thumb in a snowmobile accident in which she was being pulled by a rope on an inner tube. Suing 13-yr-old D driver for negligence.

[**Comments:** Again, note how short and simple the relevant facts were in this case. The only truly material facts were that the defendant was a child and that the plaintiff's injury resulted from the defendant's alleged carelessness in driving a powerful motorized snowmobile.]

Procedural history. Trial judge instructed jury as to child standard of care. Jury verdict for D. P moved for new trial on basis that judge erred in not instructing jury regarding the adult standard of care. D appeals granting of that motion.

[**Comments:** My procedural history is a tad longer and more precise than that of the students. I don't spend a lot of class time on the procedural history of most cases in Torts. By the eighth week, these bright students no doubt had figured that out and perhaps made a cost-benefit decision to scrimp a bit on the procedural history in their Torts case briefs. This goes back to my tip in Chapter 9 that you want to learn and adapt to the expectations and preferences of your individual professors .]

Who won? Plaintiff.

Issue. What standard of care are children generally held to under negligence law and what standard are they held to when engaged in inherently dangerous activities such as driving a snowmobile?

[**Comments:** Note that I framed the issue to address both the general rule *and* the exception, both of which are important to take from the case.]

Holding/rule(s). Children are held to a different standard of care from adults. A child must "exercise the same care that a reasonably careful child of the same age, intelligence, maturity, training and experience would exercise under the same or similar circumstances." An exception exists when children engage in inherently dangerous activities, such as driving a motorized vehicle. In such cases, they will be held to an adult standard of care.

[**Comments:** Note first that in stating the normal standard of care applicable to children, I quoted rather than paraphrased the court's test. Precision is crucial to accurately stating law. To ensure accuracy, when a court states a test, you're often better off quoting it than paraphrasing it too succinctly, at least when the test is reasonably short. Compare my quotation of the rule to student brief 3, where the student stated the general standard of care applicable to children as "caution should be judged based on the capacity of the child." That's too broad because, first, it makes it sound like a subjective rather than an objective standard of care, and, second, it fails to include the specific traits (age, intelligence, training, etc.) that judges and juries are to look at in evaluating how a similarly situated reasonable child would have acted.

With regard to the exception, as I mentioned above in discussing the *Slocum* case, your goal is to draw rules of general application from the case (which I and all three students did), not rules limited narrowly to the facts. If the court's exception to the child standard of care applied only to snowmobiles, it wouldn't have much of an impact. But it's broader than that. It applies to any circumstances in which a child engages in an inherently dangerous adult-like activity. At a minimum, the court made it clear that the exception (i.e., the adult standard of care) applies any time a child operates any type of powerful motorized vehicle.]

Reasoning. Court offered two basic reasons for adopting the exception to the child standard of care. First, court said it would discourage children from engaging in activities normally reserved for adults. Second, court said the rule is necessary to protect the public.

[**Comments**: Note how I compressed the reasoning section to include only the reasons *directly supporting* the court's adoption of the exception. The court included additional discussion expanding on the two justifications set forth above, but since this is a brief, you're only aiming to capture the most vital elements of the reasoning. Additionally, the opinion includes other discussion that could be considered reasoning in a broad sense, but it doesn't relate directly to why the court adopted the rule it did. The fact offered by the court, for example, regarding the number of snowmobiles in use was not essential to the court's adoption of the exception. One way to be more efficient in writing briefs is to not spend inordinate amounts of time restating all of the court's discussion as reasoning.]

Sizing up your brief.

How does your brief stack up to the examples? Did it contain the essential components of the case as reflected in the sample briefs? Go through this checklist, looking at whether you:

1.   Included the two most relevant facts (that the defendant was a child and the accident occurred because of the defendant's carelessness in driving a powerful motorized vehicle).

2.   Included the procedural history (if you haven't started law school yet, you wouldn't have much background to go on in getting this portion correct; but note that the alleged trial court error—granting a motion for new trial—is included in my *Top Five Most Commonly Alleged Errors on Appeal* list).

3.   Stated the issue correctly (either broadly in terms of what standard of care should apply to children or narrowly in terms of whether children should be subject to an adult standard of care when they engage in inherently dangerous activities).

4.   Included the general rule regarding the standard of care applicable to children.

5.   Included the exception to that rule for situations when children engage in inherently dangerous activities.

6.   Identified the court's two principal reasons for the holding (deterrence of children from engaging in dangerous activities and the need to protect the public when they do).

Also pay attention to anything you included in your brief that *doesn't* appear in the student briefs or my brief. Think about why you included the information. In retrospect, does it still seem important to you? If you got all or most of the points listed above, congratulations! If you missed some, don't fret. Like I said, case-briefing is a skill that takes time to develop. Consider this exercise your first baby step on the road to becoming an expert case analyzer.

CHAPTER 12
NOTE-TAKING

When students ask me to reveal the deep dark secrets of successful study strategies for law school, they're always surprised by the simplicity of my answer: read every assignment, brief every case, attend every class, *take good notes in every class*, and prepare course outlines. The CREDO chapter (Chapter 10) covered the importance of consistency in reading assignments and attending class. The last chapter addressed case-briefing and the next one tackles outlining. Here we take up note-taking.

As shown by dozens of studies, taking notes furthers two important goals: encoding and storage of information. With regard to encoding, the process of taking notes enhances attention, idea-processing, organization, and retention of classroom material. In other words, writing down lecture content leads to better learning of the content than simply listening to it, even if one never reviews the notes. Thus, while students think it's a blessing when professors give them copies of their PowerPoint slides or notes, which some law professors do, they're missing out on one of the primary benefits of note-taking: the encoding function.

Numerous studies also support the storage function of note-taking. Students who take notes and review them before tests perform better than those who don't. Who would have thought? Certainly, given the volume and complexity of material presented in a law school course and the long time lapse between its delivery and the exam—fifteen weeks from the first week's material until the exam—"storing" key classroom content is essential to success in law school. Using a computer analogy, your brain could be seen as the computer's temporary memory and your notes as the hard drive on which you're able to store the information permanently. Without good class notes, you'll have no hope of remembering what you will need to know to perform well on a law school exam.

As said earlier, casebooks are not designed to teach or explain the law per se. While cases selected for inclusion in casebooks stand for particular rules or principles, the rules won't necessarily be clearly identified or articulated, nor will the case cover all the satellite doctrines or exceptions to the rule or show how the rule is or should be applied to fact patterns different from the one involved in the case. These are areas that will be, or at least should be, fleshed out in class.

Study aids can help fill these gaps, but are not sufficient standing alone. The same case can be viewed and interpreted through different lenses. Professor A might approach a case from an historical perspective, while Professor B may approach the same case from a law and economics standpoint. Even professors who approach the case from a plain vanilla, black-letter law approach will emphasize, define, and organize rules differently than the study aids.

The only approach that matters to you is the one taken by the professor who will be grading your exam. And that professor's approach can only come from one source: class presentations. Accordingly, it's critical to be a good listener in class and to work diligently at capturing with precision the law and its application as they emerge during class presentations. Unfortunately, carrying out this mission will be much easier to do in some courses than others as professors and their teaching styles vary greatly. The amount of effective notes a student is able to take in a course depends greatly on the particular professor.

Most law professors will attempt to present the material in a clear ("clear" being a relative term when it comes to law), organized fashion designed to facilitate student understanding and effective note-taking of the material. Some professors, however, look down on what they see as "spoon-feeding" the law to students, based on a belief that developing analytical skills requires students to bear more of the burden to figure out the law on their own. Recall that a hallmark of the traditional Socratic method was to ask questions without providing answers. Other professors may spend more time discussing the policies and policy implications behind rules than the rules themselves. Attempting to take meaningful notes in courses taught by these professors can be frustrating.

And then there are those professors who are simply unclear or poor communicators. They deliver jumbled lectures and engage in confusing questioning and question-answering not for pedagogical reasons, but because they are inexperienced, unorganized, unprepared or simply have brains that work that way. Needless to say, effective note-taking in classes taught by these professors also will be difficult. Students will be forced to fill in the blanks on their own through other means, primarily study aids.

Let's assume you're in a class conducive to effective note-taking. How do you become a successful note-taker? Effective note-taking consists of more than just trying to write things down. It's a four-step process that includes: (1) attentive listening; (2) capturing the key material, while omitting unimportant material; (3) filling in gaps after class; and (4) conducting subsequent periodic review.

Be a Good Listener

Your first challenge is to be a good listener. Obviously, you can't take effective notes if you're not listening carefully. This is easier said than done for a generation that has grown up with many more distractions than previous generations, including wireless internet service in the classroom. I've already admonished you in Chapter 6 to avoid the temptations of wireless technology while in class. But even if you don't succumb to that temptation, listening carefully to a fifty-minute or longer legal discussion can be a challenge. You have to train your mind to pay attention. When you find it straying, force it back on track.

You must listen to your classmates as well as your professors. Unlike other educational disciplines, in law school, due to the Socratic method, notes-worthy comments often will come from your fellow students. If a professor asks a question and a student gives an answer to which the prof gives thumbs-up approval, that's essentially the same thing as the professor saying it. Some professors will stop to highlight correct student answers, but others will simply move on to the next point.

Capture the Key Material and Leave Out the Rest

What do you write down? This, of course, is the million dollar question with regard to effective note-taking. Due to the Socratic method, law school note-taking is hard to get a handle on at first. Instead of straight-forward lecture, most of your classes will be filled with back and forth colloquies between the professors and students. Which parts of them are important? As one student wrote in reply to the survey question asking about the biggest surprise of law school:

> The biggest surprise is the note-taking. It is not your usual note-taking, and I doubt that there is any real way to prepare for it. Law school classes are just not your usual lecture-based discussions, so you are left wondering whether you should write down the banter between teacher and student or just the hypotheticals, etc. People who are used to undergraduate lectures and things written on the board or shown on Power-Point are in for a rude awakening.

Some law students write down too little, while some students write down too much. It's easy to understand how capturing too little of the material could be a problem. If you don't record what you need to know in your notes, you'll forget it and won't have it available to study for the exam (see below).

Students have a harder time understanding how they can write down too much. Isn't more always better? No. Students who try to write everything down in class spend too little time actually processing the information. You're not training to be a stenographer. You're trying to learn and understand law. You can't learn it without thinking about it. Note-taking research shows that when the presentation pace is quick and the informational density high, fast and furious note-taking competes with the mental resources needed to process the information.[57]

As noted, I started my legal career as a law clerk to a federal district court judge. In that role, I sat through many

---

57. *See* Gilles O. Einstein, Joy Morris & Susan Smith, *Note-Taking, Individual Differences, and Memory for Lec-* *ture Information*, 77 J. EDUC. PSYCHOL. 522, 522–23 (1985).

trials and got to know the court reporters who transcribed them. During one jury trial, I asked the court reporter what she thought about the testimony of a key witness. She said she didn't remember anything about it. Surprised, I said something like, "How could you not remember any of it? You took down every word verbatim!" She said she never thinks about what's being said because it would interfere with her recording it accurately.

Too many computer-equipped law students do the same thing in trying to transcribe every word spoken by the professor. This is one of the big drawbacks of using a computer to take notes, and a principal reason why some professors object to computers in the classroom. Not only does attempting to transcribe the class interfere with your actually *hearing* and processing the material, it results in you writing down tons of stuff that you don't need in your notes. This clutter, in turn, often gets transferred to course outlines (see next chapter), reducing their effectiveness.

Having said that, there's greater danger in writing down too little than too much. Note-taking research shows that college students take down fewer than 50 percent of principal lecture points.[58] Studies also show a correlation between the quantity of notes taken and better test performance. When in doubt, err on the side of recording a point rather than omitting it.

In terms of *how* you write it down, some non-law school research suggests that reframing the professor's words in one's own words can result in greater depth of information-processing.[59] This makes sense as a general proposition. The law, however, is a precise business where every word can have significance. "Shall" is not the same as "should." "And" is much different from "or." Usually, you're better off trying to replicate the rules as stated by the professor or case as closely as possible. If a legal test discussed in class is derived directly from a case, statute, rule book or *Restatement* treatise, get the operative language in your notes verbatim, unless it's already in your briefs. But do it after class. Don't

58. *See* Alan C. Eggert & Robert L. Williams, *Notetaking in College Classes: Student Patterns and Instructional Strategies*, 51 J. GEN. EDUC. 173, 195 (2002).

59. *See id.* at 175 (discussing studies).

waste your mental processing ability copying it into your notes during class.

With that introduction, let's look more specifically at what you should be looking to record in your notes. Generalizing is always fraught with danger when it comes to law school professors, but for most first-year courses *your primary goal* will be to record anything resembling a legal rule, test, principle, or doctrine, including sub-rules, exceptions to rules and sub-rules, and exceptions to exceptions. Whenever a professor begins a sentence with "The rule is ..." or "The test is ..." or any words to that effect, write it down.

It's not sufficient to capture the general principles, which nearly all students will do successfully. The most successful students are those who capture—and understand—the more specific subordinate rules. A group of note-taking researchers categorized lecture points on four levels, with level-1 ideas being the most general and levels 2-4 representing subordinate ideas clarifying, defining, and describing the general ideas. They found that 91 percent of students listening to the lecture captured the level-1 ideas in their notes, but the percentages declined with each level of increased specificity. The students recorded only 60 percent of level-2 ideas, 35 percent of level-3 ideas, and 11 percent of level-4 ideas.[60]

Law school exams emphasize and reward specific analysis over general analysis. For example, if a Torts essay question involving intentional torts presents a fact pattern in which A shoots B, 100 percent of the class is going to recognize that act as a potential tortious battery. To give you some idea how much recognition and understanding of general issues and principles counts as compared to specific issues and rules, when I give an intentional torts essay question worth 100 points, mere recognition of a simple battery in the question facts usually counts for only three points. More specific identification and analysis of subordinate issues, such as whether the tortfeasor had the requisite intent to commit a battery or a legal privilege to do so, count much more, usually in the neighborhood of 15-20 points. So don't just write down the "big rules." Record the small ones too: the distinctions, the exceptions, etc.

60. *See* Kenneth A. Kiewra, Stephen L. Benton & Lance B. Lewis, *Qualitative Aspects of Notetaking and Their Rela-* *tionship with Information–Processing Ability and Academic Achievement*, 14 J. INSTRUCTIONAL PSYCHOL. 110, 113 (1987).

To enhance understanding of rules, include in your notes the *core reasoning* underlying them. Understanding the "why" of a rule will make it much easier to apply it. As an example, you'll learn in Torts that a tortious battery can result from an intentional *offensive* touching of a person even if it doesn't cause physical harm. From one of our cases, my students learn, and we discuss in class, that the reason the law allows recovery for merely offensive batteries is to protect human dignity. In fact, offensive batteries are what we call a "dignitary tort." Understanding this reasoning allows students to solve legal problems they might otherwise not be able to resolve. In class I pose a hypothetical in which Student A kisses Student B after she falls asleep while studying for an exam. Student B finds out about the kiss later and is extremely offended. Does she have a valid claim for battery even though she was asleep when the kiss occurred or would she have to be awake and contemporaneously aware of the kiss? Students who understand the reasoning behind allowing recovery for offensive batteries can correctly answer that she would have a valid claim even though she was asleep because a person's dignity can be just as offended if they find out about an offensive bodily contact after the fact.

You should also strive to capture in your notes (either during or after class) the essence of the professor's hypothetical fact patterns posed in class. Remember that your goal is to learn to analyze and apply law, not simply memorize it. Moreover, professors often base exam questions on hypotheticals they used in class or which are closely related to hypotheticals they used in class.

Finally, unless it's obviously immaterial, write down anything the professor takes the time to write on the board or project on a screen. The professor wouldn't go through that trouble unless he or she believes the material is important.

What can you safely leave out of your notes? Frequently, in Socratic case-dialoging a turning point occurs where the dialogue shifts from fleshing out the assigned case and corresponding rules to a more generalized policy discussion of the issues marked by "What do you think?"-type questions. At this point, you usually can relax and participate in and enjoy the discussion without worrying about having to write anything down. Most professors expect 1Ls to analyze and solve legal problems on the exam, which usually does not require extensive policy discussion. But 1L profs do use policy questions, so, again, generalizing is always risky. In addition to extended policy discussions, you're usually safe in omitting discussion of off-topic tangents, anecdotes by the professor, statistics offered by the prof to back up points, and cases and statutes the professor mentions offhandedly (meaning does not invest any substantial time in discussing) which are not part of the assigned reading.

Student Notes Comparison

Before we move on to other note-related tips, let's take time out for a real example to highlight what we've covered so far. Below is a comparison of class notes taken in a Torts class by two students we'll call Jane and Roger regarding the privilege of self-defense to the tort of battery. I chose this example because self-defense is one of the few areas that I cover by lecture—accompanied as always by hypotheticals—rather than through case-dialoging, making it easier for readers to follow. The privilege of self-defense, where applicable, operates to negate what would otherwise be an actionable tortious battery (i.e., an intentional harmful or offensive bodily contact on a person).

I'll spare you further legal explanation because the class notes below, particularly Jane's, do a good job of explaining the doctrine. Jane's class notes are on the left and Roger's on the right. Jane did a good job capturing the salient information. Roger did an okay job. I'm sure some other students took far worse notes, but Roger's notes suffer from omissions and errors. Jane finished second in her class of approximately 150 students after her first year, whereas Roger finished somewhere in the middle. In other words, the comparison below is between the notes of a "top student" and an "average student." My comments are bracketed and in bold on Roger's side of the ledger. I inserted spacing as necessary to make the same basic points line up side-by-side.

Jane's notes	Roger's notes
Self-defense	**Self-defense**

Test of the Privilege of Self–Defense (another objective test):
    Were the circumstances such that a
    reasonable person would believe
	Reasonable Belief—If a reasonable person would believe that they were threatened with a battery or false imprisonment, they have a privilege re-

that they were threatened by a battery?

Was the amount of force reasonable under the circumstances? Was it proportionate to the threat against you?

Hypo: A, a person who has martial arts training, is walking alone at night in a dangerous part of town. B comes up behind A and grabs A's shoulders from behind. A throws an elbow and shatters B's face. Turns out B is A's best friend playing a practical joke. B sues for battery. A claims self-defense.

> What makes A's belief reasonable according to the facts? Under those circumstances—WHY?
>> Dangerous neighborhood
>> At night
>> Alone
>> B came up behind

Reasonable Belief: if a reasonable person under these particular circumstances would believe that they were threatened by a battery, they have the privilege of self-defense to protect themselves.

> * Mistake: Self-defense is a privilege to prevent threatened battery and allows for a reasonable mistake.
>> Why? Self-preservation is the first law of nature
>> Why not make him wait and turn around? B/c it might be too late!
> * You don't have to wait and determine that the force is absolutely necessary.

Hypo: suppose that A turns around and unloads a gun into B.

> Unloading a gun into a person who grabs your shoulder would not be considered reasonable force.

Reasonable Force: if a reasonable person under the particular circumstances would believe that the amount of force used was proportional to the amount of force threatened.

> You are allowed to use the amount of force proportionate to the force that is threatened against you.
> Note: You might be privileged to threaten more force than is propor-

gardless of a mistake. This is because the court believes in the "first law of nature is self-preservation."

[Roger got the basic rule down, but missed the entire "set-up" hypothetical (see Jane's notes on left) that formed the basis for most of the discussion. Getting the professor's hypotheticals down in your notes helps one understand how legal rules are *applied*. Note how the hypothetical that Jane captured involving A and B fleshes out the meaning of objective reasonableness (i.e., how would a reasonable person have acted under the same circumstances?), which is the test for a valid assertion of self-defense. The circumstances are what dictate whether conduct is reasonable, yet Roger—because he didn't take down the hypothetical—may have missed this crucial aspect, as we'll see below.]

[Critically, self-defense allows room for reasonable mistakes in the decision to use force against another. Roger mentioned "mistake" in his basic statement of the rule at the beginning, but did not explain what it meant. Jane, as we see on the left, elaborated on the mistake concept and the policies behind it.]

Reasonable amount of force—You are allowed to use the amount of force reasonably necessary to prevent the battery. You can use proportional amount of force to prevent the battery. You can however threaten to use more force than you are actually allowed to use.

[Again, we see that Roger got the basic rule down that not only must the *decision* to use force in self-defense be reasonable, the *amount* of force must also be reasonable. But we also see that Roger again omitted the hypothetical showing how this principle would be applied.]

tionate against you. You can threaten more force than you can actually use.

A turns around and threatens B with a gun would be reasonable force.

Deadly Force—Force that threatens death OR serious bodily injury
The only reason you can use deadly force is when a reasonable person would believe in your circumstances that you are threatened with deadly force.
Because we want to restrict it, there is the old rule "the Retreat Rule." Now it's a minority rule. Doesn't have the relevance that it once did because of the modern use of guns.

Deadly force—threatens death or serious bodily injury. You must prove that he believed that he was threatened with deadly force.

[Oops. Roger misstated the rule regarding when it is premissible to use "deadly force" in self-defense in a manner that could prove fatal to his understanding of the entire doctrine. Note that he says that the actor must prove "he believed" he was threatened with deadly force. Because the privilege of self-defense is an objective rather than a subjective test, it's not enough for the actor to prove he personally believed deadly force was necessary. The test is whether a *reasonable person under the same circumstances* would have believed the use of deadly force was necessary. Since this same rule of objective reasonableness under the circumstances applies to the use of any force in self-defense, Roger's misstatement calls into question his understanding of the basic rule, even though he wrote it down correctly at the beginning of his notes. In other words, Roger's failure to capture the earlier hypothetical and explanation involving objectively reasonable mistakes may have led to this later error. Moreover, the absence of the earlier explanation in his notes would make it less likely that Roger would detect the contradiction and error when later reviewing his notes.]

Retreat Rule—if a person can safely retreat from the use of deadly force, they are required to do so to avoid defending with deadly force.
Never from a dwelling
Never if the retreat would be unsafe (and if you are threatened with a gun, you really can't retreat safely)
Only applies to the use of deadly force

Traditionally we had the retreat rule, a person must retreat if they can before using deadly force. It is now seen as the minority rule. You are not required to retreat from your home ever.

[At common law, before a person could use deadly force in self-defense (except in his dwelling), he had to retreat *if he could do so safely*. Roger got the basic rule down,

but left off the italicized qualifier.
What would Roger do if the exam
involved a person confronted on the
street by an assailant with a gun?
Would he know the actor had no
duty to retreat, even in a jurisdiction following the retreat rule, before responding with deadly force?
Jane would because she got the entire rule down.]

From this example, we see the difference between good
notes and average notes. Jane went beyond the general rules
and got many of the subordinate rules. Roger tended to stop
after he got the general rules. Jane captured the hypotheticals. Roger didn't. Jane stated the rules more rigorously right
than Roger. Jane also got more of the core reasoning behind
the rules than Roger.

Fill in Gaps Quickly

Note-taking is a two-part endeavor: taking initial notes in
class and filling in the gaps shortly thereafter. For a variety
of reasons—the density of the material, professors who talk
too fast, daydreaming—you're likely to miss accurately capturing all important points in your notes during class. It's
critical that you clarify any confusion and plug any holes in
your notes shortly thereafter, preferably the same day.

Dr. R.L. Kaplan, a neurologist, has written an ebook
offering study strategies to students of all ages. He points out
that most college students mistakenly think that after learning new information, they gradually forget a little bit of it
with each day that passes. Not so. Memory curves developed
by psychologists more than 150 years ago show that the
greatest memory loss occurs within hours—not weeks or even
days—after learning the material. By the second day, people
forget 40-70 percent of what they learned. For law students,
this means that the material you learned in Property class on
Monday is already being flushed from your memory by Tuesday. According to the memory curves, within thirty days after
taking notes, students will have forgotten 95 percent of the
material.

Thus, to the extent possible, you should update your notes
daily. Make sure that any legal rules you took down were
recorded completely and accurately. Fill in the professor's
hypothetical fact patterns that you remember from class but
weren't able to write down.

Resolve any points on which you were confused. Not only will it be easier to do this while the material is fresh in your mind, it's essential to do it because learning law is like building a brick house, with each brick being laid on top of the ones that precede it. The bricks on top are only as strong as the foundation below. As an example, most Torts courses begin with a study of the intentional torts. Intentional torts coverage usually starts with the crucial element of intent (the fault standard applicable to all of the intentional torts), followed by study of the individual intentional torts (e.g., battery, assault, false imprisonment). If you don't fully comprehend intent (which many students don't) before the professor moves on, you won't be able to fully comprehend the individual intentional torts. Moreover, if you leave points of confusion unresolved, there won't be time at the end of the semester to go back and begin clearing them up.

Means by which to clear up confusion include: (1) reading study aids; (2) working through CALI (Computer–Assisted Legal Instruction) exercises, which are accessible to law students through the TWEN network; (3) asking classmates for clarification, whether individually or through a study group (see below); and (4) if confusion still persists, seeking help from the professor. Most professors are happy to help students who are struggling to understand material *provided* the students have already tried to help themselves.

If you have to miss class, make sure you get that material covered in your notes by borrowing a classmate's notes or arranging to tape the class if you know in advance you're going to be absent (check with the professor about his or her taping policies). As discussed in Chapter 10, you cannot afford *any* gaps in coverage.

Conduct Regular Periodic Review

Assuming you have managed to listen well, record good notes during class, and fill in any holes afterwards, you should sleep well at night, knowing that you're doing a good job of laying the major groundwork in your exam preparation. The final step in the note-taking process is periodic review. With only a few days between the end of classes and your first exams, you can't wait until the end of the semester to start reviewing the material. The importance of periodic review cannot be overstated.

At the beginning of their second semester, shortly after they had completed their first set of law school exams, I asked a first-year class: "What, if anything, do you intend to do differently in the second semester than in the first semester?" The responses were astonishingly consistent. A majority of the students stated that they intended to do much more frequent periodic review of their notes and, closely intertwined, to start working earlier on their outlines and do a better job of updating them regularly. Several student comments on these points are excerpted in the next chapter.

Consider Forming or Joining a Study Group

Student "study groups," in which a small number of students (usually from three to five) work collaboratively, are a popular law school study model. I include them in this chapter because one common study group strategy is for group members to get together and literally "compare notes." Regularly comparing and discussing class notes with others allows group members to reorganize, add to, and correct mistakes in their own notes, while also fulfilling the goal of periodic review. Study groups also work collaboratively on outlines, exam preparation (such as working through old exams together), and function as social and emotional support networks.

Some students find study groups invaluable, while some don't. Whether you will benefit from a study group depends on two principal factors: your individual learning style and the "fit" among the group members. Extraverts, for example, may take to group study better than introverts. I joined a study group early in my first semester of law school because I thought it was the thing to do. I might have been influenced by the fact that study groups were featured so prominently in the movie, *The Paper Chase*, which we were all very much into at the time.

The group was made up of me, my friend Mac, and a woman named Lynn. Three weeks in, Lynn had the good judgment to quit. I don't recall her exact words, but the gist of her gripe was something like: "All you two ever do is debate everything. We never get anywhere." She was right. Mac, who remains my good friend today, and I wasted hours of precious time debating every point, in part just for the sake of the debate. In retrospect, my only surprise was that it took Lynn three weeks to jump off that train wreck. After that, I rarely participated in group study. It just didn't work for me. Perhaps it's because I'm a bit introverted by nature, but I work more effectively and efficiently on my own.

But other students give study groups an enthusiastic two thumbs-up. Look at this message from a student in response to the year-end question asking what advice students would give to a close loved one who was beginning law school:

> Group study is key! I formed a study group (leading to great friendships) with two other classmates, and we surrounded ourselves with class discussion throughout the day. To our surprise, all of our ranks after the first semester were inside the top ten. The odds of it being purely coincidental seem pretty minimal.

I have a feeling these particular students would have been successful even without group study, but the point is that whereas I found study groups to be of little use, she found her study group to be vital to both her success and well-being. So join a study group if it feels right to you, but don't feel compelled to join one, and don't hesitate to jump ship if it's not working out for you.

Before forming or joining a study group, think hard about the people with whom you'll be collaborating. If it doesn't feel like a good match, it probably isn't. If you do form a study group, discuss your objectives and strategies in advance. Make sure they are clearly articulated and that everyone in the group buys into them. When you meet, stay with the program. Keep socializing separate from study sessions. Socializing is an add-on benefit of a study group, but business should be business when you gather to study. Plan separate social events for the group.

Consider Using a Computer Note-Taking Tool

Most law students take class notes on computers. To oldsters like me, that by itself seems "high-tech." But more and more law students are going beyond using basic word-processing programs and capitalizing on specially designed computer note-taking programs. One of my research assistants—a top-ranked student—swears by these programs. The differences between ordinary note-taking on computer and using one of these programs, she says, are analogous to the differences between an address book and a PDA or a basic cell phone and an iPhone.

I'm not recommending the note-taking programs described below, but thought you should be aware of their existence. Your own learning style and familiarity with a particular way of note-taking—which may involve only pen and paper—should dictate how you take notes in class. But if you're proficient with computers, I can see how these programs could be helpful in enhancing both efficiency and organization in managing the vast amount of information you'll be absorbing and trying to keep track of. As we saw in the CREDO chapter, being "efficient" and "organized" are two of the top five habits of successful law students.

Computer note-taking programs give law students the ability to easily manage in one place all the information they will be collecting in their courses. Think of a note-taking program as one big digital three-ring binder notebook. Instead of using separate notebooks for each course, you can use only one. Instead of paper dividers and tabs, you can set up computer tabs to organize your information. Instead of inserting pages of notes into your notebook after a class, you can insert notes directly into your digital notebook during class.

"Wizzy-wig" programs.

The most popular genre of note-taking programs is known as a WYSIWYG (pronounced "wizzy-wig") or "what-you-see-is-what-you-get." Microsoft OneNote is the industry standard in this genre and the most popular computer note-taking program overall. The same research assistant mentioned above estimated that one-third of her classmates take notes using OneNote. OneNote works as a personal information collector, organizer, and manager, incorporating familiar Microsoft programs with familiar icons, keyboard shortcuts, formatting tools, and quick-find functions.

OneNote works a lot like Microsoft Word with the big difference that OneNote allows users to view and access all of their notes and folders from any screen. Once a student labels a particular note or brief with a heading, the labels appear table of contents-style along the right side of the page where their content can be accessed with a click. So, for example, when your Property professor asks you to recite the facts of Case X, your brief for that case is one click away. No need to fumble around scrolling through virtual pages or flipping through papyrus pages in search of the brief.

In addition, by opening a new window, you can view your case briefs and class notes side by side. Another advantage of OneNote and similar programs is the facility to quickly move and reorganize text (think of a fast computer equivalent to opening your three-ring notebook, removing a page, and inserting it in a different place).

In addition to OneNote, WYSIWYG programs exist that are designed specifically for law students. Some of these programs contain a feature allowing students to integrate digitized law school study aids directly into the program to customize the content, and also provide law-related templates to use in creating case briefs and outlines.

Other programs.

Other, more advanced computer programs that could be used to take and manage notes also exist, such as programs that allow users to store their materials online. Google and Yahoo, for example, both offer free online database and document management systems in which all your information is stored on a server. Because the data is stored on a server rather than on individual computers, online databases give users the ability to access notes from any computer at any time, avoiding the disastrous consequences of a computer crash if you haven't backed up all your notes (which you should ALWAYS do—see below). On the other hand, online storage is also a drawback of this type of program. If you can't access the internet—say because of wireless connectivity problems in a particular classroom—you won't be able to access your notes.

The most advanced category of computer information management programs that could be used for note-taking are wiki systems. Wiki is the programming platform that drives the familiar Wikipedia online encyclopedia. Like Wikipedia, wiki databases allow users to collaborate on a document or set of documents. These programs could prove useful for study groups. Members of the group could share and comment on each other's class notes or ideas, edit misstatements in their buddies' work, and get help while studying alone by accessing the others' online notes. It is likely that wiki programs will eventually have the most advanced tagging, linking, and filtering features available. Obstacles to using them include a steep learning curve and the fact that most of them are online databases, raising the same potential problems with internet connectivity as other online database programs.

WYSIWYG programs are the here and now. The future of other computer information management programs and their popularity with law students remains to be seen. Who knows? It might not be long before digitized professors will be teaching virtual students and we can all stay home.

Before you invest time or money in any computer note-taking program, familiarize yourself with your professors' computer-use policies. As mentioned, some law professors have banned computers from classrooms. If you have an interest in one of these programs, you should become intimately familiar with the program *prior* to starting law school. You don't want to be trying to figure out a new computer program at the same time you're struggling to understand the concept of personal jurisdiction.

Whatever computer information management system you use, make sure you *regularly back everything up*, including your case briefs, class notes, outlines, drafts of assignments for your legal research and writing courses, etc. This rule is so basic, yet every year I hear sad stories from students who lost all of their computerized notes, outlines, legal research papers, and other data when their computers crashed or were stolen. Buy a USB flash drive and back up all your computer work each day. Three different manuscript readers, all of whom have witnessed the terrible consequences of students losing all their work, urged me to emphasize this point more strongly, so let me repeat: **REGULARLY BACK UP ALL YOUR COMPUTER WORK**! Is that enough emphasis?

CHAPTER 13
OUTLINING

One major factor distinguishing legal education from other disciplines is the sheer amount of material covered. Professors usually start out slowly, knowing that students need to become acclimated to the nomenclature and basic procedures of the law. The snail's pace at the beginning lulls some students into a false sense of security, prompting thinking along the lines of, "Hey, this isn't so bad. We're only covering one case per hour in each class!"

One week into a recent fall semester, a new 1L came to my office and said, "Professor, everyone kept telling me I'll be working day and night in law school, but this Saturday I was sitting there looking for something else to do. Am I missing something?" I told her to enjoy it while she could because the pace would start quickening soon.

Within a few weeks, the reading assignments get longer. The concepts get harder. Professors begin covering more material in class. The demands of Legal Research and Writing kick in with a vengeance. It all comes at students relentlessly, without a break. Before they know it, students are mired up to their ankles, then knees, and finally necks in a thick quicksand of dense material.

Must I Really Make Outlines?—Yes!

Only one answer exists for administering this huge inventory of knowledge: preparing an outline for each course. Most law students do prepare course outlines. Certainly most successful students do. While I've known successful law students who did not prepare course outlines, they are few and far between. Many students prepare two outlines for each course, a comprehensive main outline and a secondary capsule outline that they use for review immediately before exams.

Some students attempt to rely solely on outlines prepared by students who took the course in earlier years. These are abundantly available. Some can even be downloaded from the internet. It sounds like a good plan on the surface. Why go through all the work to prepare an outline for a course if someone else has already done it for the exact same course taught by the same professor? Especially if you can lay your hands on a really great outline composed by a top student, it seems like a no-brainer. And, in fact, you probably can obtain great outlines composed by top students. Every law school has its share of famous, ridiculously thorough student outlines for particular courses that get passed down from class to class year after year. Back at the University of Arkansas at Little Rock, for example, every 1L coveted a copy of "Bob's Bible," a student outline for the late legendary Professor Robert R. Wright's Property course that was so complete it even included Professor Wright's jokes.

But it's *not* a good plan to rely on outlines prepared by others. The reason the students who made the great outlines came out on top was because they *made* the great outlines, not because they *had* the great outlines. As with case-briefing, the *process* of constructing outlines is at least as important as the final product. Making the outlines is what forces you to organize, synthesize, and, hence, really learn the material. Composing an outline and updating it throughout the semester also requires the periodic review of the material so essential to success. An empirical study of note-taking showed that students who took and reviewed their own notes on a lecture performed better on a test than students who were given a copy of the *lecturer's* notes to review.[61] Moreover, because people have different learning styles and process information differently, even well-done outlines prepared by someone else are not likely to present the material in the manner or form in which *you* learned it.

Similarly, resist the temptation to rely exclusively on commercial outlines, even those keyed to particular casebooks. Commercial outlines are not adequate by themselves because they will not capture all of the material the professor

61. Judith L. Fisher & Mary B. Harris, *Effect of Note Taking and Review on Recall*, 65 J. EDUC. PSYCHOL. 321, 323 (1973).

emphasized and, just as importantly, will not present it in the same way—either substantively or structurally—the professor presented it and expects to hear it back on the exam. I can't tell you how easy it is, when reading exams, to spot the students who relied on external outlines. They cite cases that weren't covered in the course and state legal doctrines in formulations foreign to the professor. Professors do not like this and grade accordingly.

Having said all that, let me emphasize that both previously prepared student outlines and commercial outlines or other study aids can be extremely helpful supplements in filling in gaps in your own outlines. But that's what they should be used for: as supplements only.

If you're going to invest the time in doing outlines—and they take a lot of time—you might as well do them right. I've known several academically dismissed law students who produced prodigious outlines. I've seen 150–page outlines for my courses that were a waste of paper. Without the right content and schema, outlines are not only unhelpful, they can be a trap because students often mistakenly assume they're doing a good job if they're pouring tons of time into making long outlines.

Below are ten sound outlining suggestions. Effective outlining goes hand-in-hand with effective note-taking. Thus, several of the outlining tips overlap with suggestions given in the previous chapter on note-taking, and vice versa.

Ten Tips for Preparing Outlines

1. Collect the raw material by briefing all your cases and taking good notes in class. A good outline can't be constructed without the raw material to put in it. For most courses, your outlines essentially will be an organized version of your class notes and portions of your case briefs (not the whole things—see below), beefed up in some places and streamlined in others. Think of outlines as the third step in exam preparation, with case-briefing and class notes being steps one and two. It's not possible to skip or slack off on the first two steps and produce effective outlines. Use study aids and previous student outlines to help you fill in gaps.

2. Never try to outline a topic before you attend the class where the topic is covered. Usually, diligence pays dividends, but sometimes being overly diligent can work to your detriment. Some eager students make the mistake of trying to outline a topic before attending the class where it will be covered. This cannot be done successfully. In outlining, pay attention to what the professor emphasizes in class about the reading material, not what you thought was important when you read it. A fellow Torts professor and I used to joke that we'd probably get *C*s if we took each other's exams because we emphasize different doctrines in class and present some of them differently.

3. Begin your outline around the fourth week of the semester. You can't wait until the end of the semester to start an outline. There won't be enough time. The beauty of gradually assembling good outlines week by week is that by the time you get to the end of the semester, you've already done most of your studying for the exam. At the same time, however, 1Ls can't effectively begin an outline at the very beginning of a semester because they lack an understanding of both the material itself and the course framework within which it fits. I recommend commencing your outlines somewhere around the fourth week of classes.

At the beginning of their second semester, shortly after they had completed their first set of law school exams, I asked a class of Torts II students: "What, if anything, do you intend to do differently in the second semester than in the first semester?" The most common answer *by far* involved starting outlining earlier and engaging in more periodic review. Here's just a small sampling of a much larger number of replies:

- Outlining as the classes progress! While I did not wait until the last minute for this, I felt that I did wait longer than I should have. The outlining process was very helpful for exams, but was very overwhelming when left for too long.

- Outline earlier in order to gain a more united rather than divided understanding of the material. It will also alleviate some stress.

- Now that (I think) I know how to prepare outlines better for this type material, I'll start earlier on that and review it more often during the semester.

- I intend to change the way I outline. Instead of outlining towards the ending third of the semester

220 OF A RIDE

as I did previously, I plan to spend time each week putting my class notes into outline format. I think this will help me become more prepared for finals.

- I intend to use Fridays and Saturday to compile, clarify, organize, and consolidate the previous week's notes into a working outline. Waiting until six weeks before exams last semester to outline was a grave and very stressful mistake.

4. Keep your outline updated on a weekly basis. Some of the above comments touch directly on this point. You want to input material in your outline while it's fresh in your mind. As discussed in the previous chapter on note-taking, memory fades quickly. You also don't want to fall behind and leave yourself with too much ground to make up. If you follow the recommendation in the note-taking chapter to update your notes daily, you'll be in good shape to update your outlines on weekends.

5. Organize outlines by tracking the headings and subheadings in your casebooks or course syllabi. The organization of an outline is nearly as important as the content. Rules can only be understood in the proper context and framework. You could memorize every rule in an entire course area and still perform miserably on the exam if you don't know where they properly fit in the analysis.

Organize your outline by *topics* (not cases) in the same chronological order as they are covered in the course. If your professor moves straight through the book starting at the beginning, simply track the table of contents and section headings in your casebook. Some casebooks are more clearly organized and include more helpful and detailed headings than others. If your casebook includes only broad topical headings, it will be up to you to develop more specific subheadings within them.

Some professors prefer to skip around in the book, which can make outline organization more difficult. If a professor does that, you're usually better off outlining the topics in the order the professor covers them, rather than in the order the book covers them.

Many professors will provide a course syllabus with subject headings. Assuming the syllabus subject headings are reasonably specific (and that the professor does, in fact, follow the syllabus), you can use them as an organizational guide in structuring your outline.

Topic areas should be organized as an inverted pyramid beginning with the broadest topics on top and moving down toward increasingly narrower topics. Similarly, within topics, the broad rules go on top, moving down to narrower sub-rules and exceptions.

Whatever you do, don't try to reinvent or redesign the law in your own organizational schema. Just about every year a student comes along who decides that he can reconceptualize the law in ways better than legal scholars (including his professors) have ever done before. I once had a student, for example, who decided that the entire course in Torts could be reduced to a flow chart. When he showed it to me, I didn't know whether to burst out laughing or refer him to psychological counseling. It looked like the schematic for the space shuttle, with hundreds of lines and arrows and circles and boxes going in every direction. The student flunked the course.

6. Emphasize rules, sub-rules, exceptions to rules and sub-rules, and exceptions to exceptions. Most law school exams will test your knowledge of specific legal rules and doctrines and ability to apply that knowledge. While some professors include policy-type essay questions on first-year exams, they do not usually count as much as questions testing your understanding of and ability to apply black-letter law. As such, your outlines should focus on incorporating "the law" of the course with accuracy and precision in a sound organizational framework. This includes all rules, sub-rules, exceptions to rules and sub-rules, and exceptions to exceptions, as well as the core reasoning and policies behind them (i.e., the "why" of the rules).

7. Include case references, but not full case briefs in your outlines. Do not make the common mistake of simply incorporating your case briefs into your outlines. Extensive recitations of case facts and procedure not only are unnecessary, they'll clutter up your outline and distract you from the doctrine and rules on which you need to be concentrating. Lead with the rules in your outlines, not the cases.

Students frequently ask if they need to know the names of cases for the exam. With typical law school ambiguity, I tell them, "It depends." You definitely should know the names of the "big cases" that stand for big principles. To the extent legal doctrines are closely associated with famous cases, integrate coverage of those cases into your outlines. Even then, however, your primary focus should be on the law emanating from the cases rather than the cases themselves.

It also can be helpful, but usually is not essential (unless your professor tells you otherwise), to know the names of the non-famous cases you covered in the course. Tying specific rules to specific cases in your essay exam answers can bolster the credibility of your answers and boost you above close competition. For example, if a fact pattern in an essay question resembles a case covered in class and you're able to write, "These facts are reminiscent of *Smith v. Jones*, where the court held x," that's more impressive than simply saying, "The rule is x." To facilitate recall of case names and also to remind you of the context in which particular rules were covered, I recommend including in your outlines the names and very short descriptions of cases *following* the statement of the rules emanating from the cases.

Let's use *Robinson v. Lindsay*, the case used for the case-briefing exercise in Chapter 11, as an example of how to outline a discrete subtopic. You'll recall that *Robinson* addressed the standard of care under negligence law for children, both the general standard and the exception to that standard when children engage in inherently dangerous activities. These rules would fit in a Torts outline under the following topic headings:

Negligence >

    Breach of Duty >

        Standards of Care >

            Exceptions to Normal Standard of Care >

            Children>

Note how the topics move downward from general to specific. Under the subheading for children, we should find something like this:

Children—

General rule: Children are held to a different standard of care from adults. A child must "exercise the same care that a reasonably careful child of the same age, intelligence, maturity, training and experience would exercise under the same or similar circumstances."

Exception for inherently dangerous activities: An exception exists where the child is engaged in an inherently dangerous activity normally undertaken by adults. In such cases, the child will be held to an adult standard of care to protect society and discourage children from engaging in such activities.

(*Robinson v. Lindsay*—13-year-old defendant driving snowmobile.)

Note how I led with the rules and tacked on the case only at the end, rather than, as many students mistakenly do, lead with the case and bury the rules within the case discussion. Come test time, most professors aren't going to give a whit about the specifics of *Robinson*. To test the rules from *Robinson* in an essay question, the professor most likely would use a fact pattern involving a child actor engaged in a dangerous activity.

8. Incorporate the professor's hypothetical fact patterns in your outlines. In Chapter 12, I recommended attempting to record in your class notes the hypothetical fact patterns your professors use in class. These hypotheticals should also be incorporated into your outlines alongside the pertinent rules. Exams are all about applying law, not simply reciting it. It is not uncommon for these same hypotheticals, or something very close to them, to show up on exams.

9. Err on the side of including too much, rather than too little, material. How long should a good outline be? No precise answer exists as many variables are involved, including the particular course, the way it is taught, and outline formatting choices such as line spacing, margins, and font sizes. One of my research assistants, a top student, said that when she started law school, she inherited a large batch of student outlines that ranged from 18 to 127 pages long. She said her own outlines average about seventy pages per course.

Outlines that are too short will lack essential details. A few years ago, I presented a workshop on course outlines with Professor Lillian Aponte Miranda, a colleague at the Florida International University College of Law. Professor Miranda had the good idea to use her law school outline from

Constitutional Law as a sample for the students to look at.
When she projected a page from the outline onto a screen, the
students' jaws fell open. They couldn't believe how detailed it
was. Good outlines are detailed because the law is detailed.

Of course, outlines that are too long cease to be useful
outlines and become unwieldy treatises. But if you're not
sure whether to include something in an outline, go ahead
and stick it in there. Material can be deleted with ease. It's
much more difficult to go back and try to find and add what
you left out.

10. State rules completely and precisely. One reason good outlines tend to be quite lengthy is because they set
forth legal doctrine completely and with precision. When
you're taking notes or writing your outline, you might think
a shorthand statement of a rule will suffice because the
detailed version of the rule is still fresh in your memory. By
the end of the semester, however, you're not going to remember the details you omitted.

Here's a comparative example involving the definition of
the two types of tortious intent, an essential element of all of
the intentional torts and a concept most law students encounter at the beginning of the first semester. Compare these
two outline approaches to defining the terms, one complete
and precise and the other incomplete and imprecise:

Complete and Precise Definition of Tortious Intent

Two kinds of intent. Two kinds of intent are recognized under tort law: "desire intent" and "belief intent."

Desire intent is where the person acts with the desire
or purpose to inflict the requisite consequence of the
tort (e.g., for a battery, a harmful or offensive bodily
contact).

Belief intent is satisfied when the person acts believing to a "substantial certainty" that the consequence
will follow, even if he doesn't desire the result to occur.
(Hypo: throwing a rock into a crowd of people, but
"not wanting to hit anyone.") It's not sufficient to
constitute belief intent that the result was foreseeable
or even probable. The actor must subjectively believe
that the result is substantially certain to follow.

Incomplete and Imprecise Definition
of Tortious Intent

Two kinds of intent: desire and belief.

Don't laugh. I've seen lots of outlines resembling this second example. Students who compose short and sweet outlines of this type may very well understand the two kinds of intent at the time they keyboard in the words. The problem, as stated, is that come exam time—many weeks and hundreds of rules later—they're not likely to remember the important details they need to know to apply the concepts.

* * *

Like so many skills in law school, composing effective course outlines is a technique perfected through practice. Don't just assume you're doing your outlines right. Get some input from your classmates or professors. I see nothing wrong with, after a couple of weeks working on the beginnings of an outline, asking your professors if they would be willing to take a look at your work to see if you're on the right track. Make it clear that you are not expecting the professor to do a line-by-line review to see if you have the law right. Rather, explain that you just want to make sure your overall format and approach are in the ballpark. Not all professors are willing to look at outlines, but many will do so if asked. Doing this early could save you hundreds of hours of wasted time if you're going down the wrong road.

CHAPTER 14
EXAM PREPARATION

How fearful it is to go through the first semester with only one shot to make the grade. I just didn't realize how much that would freak me out.

1L's "biggest surprise" about law school

This chapter offers tips on exam preparation, while the next two chapters address strategies for maximizing performance on essay and multiple-choice questions, respectively. Why is the chapter on exam preparation one of the shortest in the book when it seems like it should be one of the longest? Because—great news!—if you follow the advice in the preceding chapters, you already will have completed 90 percent of your exam prep by the time exams roll around. Indeed, Chapters 11 (case-briefing), 12 (note-taking), and 13 (outlining) could all accurately be denoted as "exam preparation" chapters. This chapter is limited to the final stretch: how to get ready for exams in the days immediately preceding and during exam week. But first let's deal with that inconvenient truth about law school reflected in the student's comment above.

Why Only One Exam?

New law students express both surprise and dismay when they learn that, except in their legal research and writing courses, their entire academic fate in a course usually rests on a single in-class examination at the end of the semester. Of all the alleged deficiencies in legal education, this is the one I have the hardest time defending. Particularly because so much rides on GPA and class rank in law school, it seems unsound to evaluate a student's knowledge and understanding of fourteen intensive weeks' worth of complex law based on a single exam.

The authors of the 2007 *Best Practices for Legal Education* report noted that effective student assessment tools must be *valid*, *reliable*, and *fair*, and concluded that the single-exam format fails all three of these criteria.[62] Flaws in the existing evaluation regime include the time-crunch factor (the system favors students who can read, think, and write quickly), lack of comprehensive course coverage (professors can't cover 42-56 class hours of material in a three- or four-hour exam), and the absence of feedback to students during the semester (students have no way to gauge their progress until after the final examination, when it's too late).

While a few schools require or at least encourage multiple testing instruments during a semester (such as a midterm exam in addition to the final exam) and some admirable first-year professors voluntarily supplement the final exam with graded midterm exams, papers or quizzes, the vast majority of law schools and professors continue to adhere to the make-it-or-break-it, single-exam tradition.

Why do law schools test this way? What are the justifications for not giving students more bites at the apple, including different size bites from different angles, during the semester?

We've discussed in other contexts how legal education, rooted as it is in tradition, is slow to change and this is another good example. Part of the explanation for the "one exam at the end of the term"-format is historical. In the earliest days of American legal education, exams were administered weekly and even daily (so be careful what you wish for in terms of wanting more feedback).

The transition to the modern format came as a response to Christopher Langdell's case method back in the 1870s. As we've discussed, the goal of the case method is to train students to analyze and apply, rather than simply memorize, law. To test these abilities, law professors developed the modern issue-spotting/problem-solving essay question. One explanation for the single-exam format is that solving the complex legal problems posed by this type of question requires an accumulated body of knowledge and training in

---

62. STUCKEY ET AL., *supra*, at 239.

legal analysis that can be acquired only over time. Believe it or not, the situation used to be even more onerous, with exams typically given only annually or as students approached graduation.

More modern justifications include a legitimate concern that incorporating other exams (such as midterms) into the semester distracts students from their ongoing course work. It's true. When teaching with first-year professors who give midterms, I notice dramatic declines in both attendance and preparation in Torts around mid-semester as students shift all their energies to preparing for the midterm in the other course.

A practical explanation for why most law professors don't give exams during the semester, one that professors might be reluctant to concede, is that they simply don't want to take on the job of grading them. This is one more drawback of the large student-faculty ratio in first-year law classes. Grading law school exams, if done diligently, is a substantial burden. It takes several weeks to grade final examinations in a large first-year class. A three-hour law school essay exam generates answers ranging from 3000 to 5000 words, or ten to seventeen double-spaced type-written pages. Multiply those page numbers by the seventy-seven students in the average-size first-year class section and we're talking roughly 800 to 1300 pages of often painful (disorganized, ungrammatical, misspelled, point-missing, and flatly incorrect) reading for the professor.

Unlike in other educational disciplines, law professors do not rely on teaching assistants or graduate students to grade papers. And contrary to popular perception, most law professors (albeit not all) work hard. They put in long hours preparing for classes, doing administrative work such as serving on law school committees, and, especially, researching and writing. At most schools, tremendous pressure exists to "publish or perish."

I know, go ahead and get out the world's smallest violin. Poor oppressed law professors. I'm not trying to justify the practice, just explain it. The bottom line is that it takes an unusual professor who is willing to take two or three weeks out of the middle of a busy semester and devote them to grading a midterm exam or paper. If you have professors who do this, take the time to express your appreciation to them.

Countdown to Exams

In the meantime, no point griping about what should be. Let's get you ready to play the hand that will be dealt to you. Here are some tips for final exam prep:

Plot an organized study schedule and follow it.

Nowhere are effective time-management skills more important than during exam prep. You need to map out a schedule that allows you to arrive at each and every exam fully prepared. Usually (but not always), you'll be afforded at least a few days to study prior to the commencement of exams. This breathing space is called "reading week" or "dead week" ("dead" as in no classes), although it's not always a full week. Some schools don't afford any break between the end of classes and the start of exams. If you're at such a school, you'll need to begin your final exam preparation while classes are still in session.

Don't make the mistake—which many students do—of using all your free days during the reading week studying for the first exam. You need to spread your pre-exam study days among your different courses to account for the fact that some of your exams will be stacked back to back, with perhaps only one free day between them. One benefit of being a 1L is that law schools intentionally schedule first-year exams with at least one free day between exams. In your second and third years, you might have exams on consecutive days or even on the same day.

Begin by plotting all of your reading week and exam period days on a calendar grid so you'll be able to assess your available time from a big-picture point of view. You'll probably find that you need to begin studying for some of your later exams first. Below is a sample prep grid for a twelve-day combined reading week and exam period:

Day 1	Day 2	Day 3	Day 4	Day 5	Day 6
Study Civ. Pro.	Study Contracts	Study Torts	Study Torts	**Torts Exam 9:00 am** Study Civ. Pro.	Study Civ. Pro.

Day 7	Day 8	Day 9	Day 10	Day 11	Day 12
Civ. Pro Exam 9:00 am	Study Property	Study Property	**Property Exam 9:00 am**	Study Contracts	**Contracts Exam 9:00 am**
Break			Study Contracts		

Note how I front-loaded the studying for the Civil Procedure and Contracts exams because of the one-day gap between those exams and the immediately preceding exams. This allowed me to allot a minimum of two full days to each exam. I built in a break after the Civil Procedure exam to take the afternoon and evening off to relax and recharge brain cells. Because of the gap in the preparation for Civil Procedure and Contracts, I included an extra half-day of study for those exams on the same day of the previous exams, but if you feel adequately prepared, you might want to consider taking breaks on all exam days. That's what I did back in law school.

Divide your study time relatively equally among courses that weigh equally in credit hours. Sure, Property may seem harder than Torts, but if both courses are worth four credit hours, it makes sense to devote roughly equal study time to them. You're not competing against the course. You're only competing against your classmates. A *B* in Torts is worth the same as a *B* in Property. You also have no way of knowing how tough the exam or the grading will be in a particular course. Torts might seem easier than Property, but the exam could be harder. Similarly, your Torts prof might be a more rigorous grader than your Property prof.

Seeing the above grid should help drive home my point about most exam preparation being accomplished during the semester through consistent class preparation, note-taking, outlining, and periodic review. Two days per exam is barely enough time to review and absorb your notes and outlines. It definitely is not enough time to begin learning the material for the first time.

Within each study day on your grid, break your tasks down more specifically. For example, a "Study Torts" day might be broken down more specifically as follows:

Study Torts
1. Read case briefs once.
2. Read outline twice.
3. Review Torts flashcards with study group.

4. Work through one practice intentional torts and one negligence essay question.

There is no single correct way to allot your study time. I asked one of my research assistants, ranked number one in her class, to summarize her exam prep schedule from the first semester. Here's what she wrote:

I started about a month before the first exam and made a study schedule very similar to the one you included. I alternated one subject per day and studied anywhere from fifteen minutes to two hours depending on how much time I had. My studying consisted of reading over my class notes, rereading cases and other reading assignments, and doing practice questions. I looked at old exams, did problems in the textbooks, and did CALI exercises online. About a week before finals I increased my studying to two subjects per day (still alternating to give each equal weight). When dead week and exams started I upped my study time to about three hours per subject a day.

I continued to study two subjects per day except for the day before an exam, when I studied only the subject that was tested the next day. I always took the evening of an exam off and did something else (like go out with non-law school friends or watch a movie). Starting so early really helped to decrease my stress level when exams rolled around. Since I had so much of my exam prep already done, I had a lot more free time and was able to stay rested.

While there are differences in the details, notice the common thread in our approaches: *thoughtful advance organization and time distribution*.

Work through practice exams.

One of the best exam preparation strategies is working through practice exams. If you were training to be a motorcycle mechanic, you wouldn't just study books on how to do it. You'd get your hands dirty disassembling and reassembling motorcycle engines. It's like that with every skill in life. People training to be pilots don't just read books about it before climbing into the cockpit of a Boeing 747. They study, practice with flight simulators, and start with smaller aircraft. Since most law school courses don't offer this kind of practice, you have to do it on your own.

Students spend so much time memorizing the law and too little time studying and practicing the *process* of law school exam-taking. Many students know all the law there is to know, but still don't perform well on exams because they never learned how to take a law school exam. The best way to get a handle on that process is through practice exams.

Working through practice exams advances several goals. First and perhaps foremost, it helps you know what to expect, increasing your comfort zone. You don't want to show up for your first law school exams not having any clue what they're going to look like. Doing practice exams also helps train you to spot issues, the all-critical threshold step to good exam performance. If you can't spot the issues, you obviously have no chance of analyzing them. Third, if you're working through old exams from your professors, you will get a feel for what to expect from that particular professor, since professors usually are consistent in their approach to fashioning exams.

You might even get lucky enough to stumble on a question that turns up on the real exam. Many professors recycle exams over the years. While most don't release exams they have any intention of recycling, a few do. I remember getting together with a group of classmates to go over old exams in preparation for my Civil Procedure exam the following day. We started later than I wanted and I've already told you I wasn't much of a group studier, so I barely glanced at the exams before calling it a night and going home to bed. As soon as the exam was distributed the next day, I wished I had stayed longer. The essay question was the *exact same question* I laid eyes on the night before.

Many of the law school study aids listed in Appendix A contain practice essay questions. These can be very helpful, but the best approach is to work with original source material: exams prepared by your professors. It's true that substantial similarity exists in law school exam structure and content. A typical law school essay question consists of a narrative in which various actors engage in conduct that raises issues relevant to the subject matter. Nevertheless, despite marked similarity in approach, professors have their own styles for writing exams. Returning to the analogy above, if you were training to be a Kawasaki motorcycle mechanic, you'd be better off practicing on Kawasakis than on Suzukis even though substantial similarities exist between the two brands.

Most law professors make copies of old exams available to students, usually by placing them on reserve in the library. Don't hesitate to ask about their availability at the library reserve desk or to ask your professors directly. Unfortunately, unlike the study aids, most of these sample exams will not include answers, although some might.

Especially in your first semester, it's wise to actually "take" at least a couple of practice exams in a mock-testing situation. Treat it like the real deal. If possible, use the same rooms where the real exams will be held. Time yourself. Try to replicate the entire experience. Remember: familiarity reduces stress. I don't recommend writing lengthy answers to *every* old exam because such a time-demanding approach will detract from your other exam preparation, *but do read* all sample exams made available by your professors to practice your issue-spotting skills. Each first-year course raises a limited number of issues suitable for essay testing, so you're likely to come across some of the same issues that will appear on the real exam even if they're packaged in different fact patterns.

If you're working through old exams from the same professors, consider asking the professors if they would be willing to review or at least discuss your answers with you. Many professors will decline such requests because going over practice exam answers with individual students is both time-consuming and somewhat unfair to other students. But some profs are willing to do it if asked.

If you're into group studying at all, reviewing practice exams can be a productive study group activity. A group of students is more likely to spot all the issues on a question than any individual student. Reviewing exams with a group can help you learn from your oversights. If someone points out an issue you missed, ask what portion of the question flagged the issue for him or her.

By all means, if your professors afford you opportunities to take one or more practice exams during the semester, which many professors do, take full advantage of them even if the exams are not graded. I distribute two practice essay questions in Torts, one addressing intentional torts and one addressing the tort of negligence, along with a full model answer to each question. I've witnessed students go from writing *F* or *D* answers on the practice exams to *B* or *A* answers on the real exam because they learned from their mistakes. I've also watched way too many students unwisely squander the best opportunity they will have to learn how to take my exam by blowing off the practice exams because they're "too busy"—a classic case of penny-wise, pound-foolish. If a professor gives you a practice exam and answer, he's essentially telling you: "This is exactly how I want you to do it."

Get exam supplies in advance.

Acquire whatever supplies you might need for your exams well in advance. It will reduce your stress and allow you to avoid distractions from your exam focus. I vividly recall an adventure back in law school in which my law school pal, Terry Perkins, and I were driving frantically around Gainesville, Florida trying to find some exam bluebooks an hour before an exam started. The situation got so desperate we literally ended up driving on the sidewalk at one point to get around traffic. We made it to the exam on time, but just barely.

These days, most law schools provide essential exam-taking materials to students at the exam, such as bluebooks, pencils for filling out multiple-choice score sheets, and even scratch paper. But find out in advance to make sure. If you intend to write your exam by hand, buy non-fine point black pens, which will make your writing easier on the eyes. Don't use pencils or pens with weird-colored ink. Some things may look pretty in pink, but law school essay-exam answers are not one of them. (Yes, I've really had students write exams in pink ink.)

Other supplies you might want to consider bringing to the exam are: a watch for keeping track of time, an eraser, correction liquid (e.g., Wite–Out) or tape if you plan on writing by hand, appropriate snacks and drinks (not loud, crunchy ones), pain-reliever such as Ibuprofen (in case your stress causes a headache), and soft-foam earplugs. I used the latter in every law school exam and also for the bar exam. Available at any drug store, they're inexpensive, comfortable, and do a good job filtering background noise. They helped me concentrate. As for drinks, be careful about consuming too many fluids during an exam because restroom breaks will cut into your exam time.

If you're using a computer, register for and download the required security software in advance.

Most law schools allow students to take their exams on computers and a vast majority of students do so. The benefits of using a computer on exams were discussed in Chapter 2. To prevent cheating, law schools subscribe to one of a variety of exam-security software applications, such as ExamSoft. Students taking their exams on computer are required to register for, download, and use the software during the exam. The software blocks access to computer files during the exam.

If you intend to use a computer, don't wait until the last minute to register for and download the software. Glitches can and do occur. If they do, you don't want to be worrying about having to resolve them right before an exam. This happened just recently. A student came to my office about forty-five minutes before her first law school exam was to begin. From our previous conversations, I knew she was already prone to stress and stress-related physical reactions. Flustered, she explained that she had just tried to download the exam security software, which had been available to students for at least a couple of weeks, and got an error message. Fixing it required a phone call from the law school's Information Technology (IT) guy to the president of the software company. They finally got it working—she hoped— as she raced off to the exam.

Install the software as soon as it becomes available and give it a practice run-through. At most schools, the IT staff will hold training sessions on the use of the software or otherwise make themselves available for technical assistance.

Rest and relax.

Even during exams, you need to allot yourself time to relax and recoup. This includes getting normal sleep every night (recommended eight hours) and also scheduling breaks during the exam period for relaxation. With regard to sleep, studies show that sleep-deprived students perform worse than those with adequate sleep. (See Chapter 18 for more about maintaining health and well-being.) These same studies show that "pulling an all-nighter" not only is ineffective at bolstering exam performance, it can impair performance. Lack of sleep negatively affects attention, concentration, and memory. Cramming is a particularly bad strategy for law school success because of the huge amount of material. If you're at the point where you feel the need to desperately cram all night for an exam, it may already be too late.

The flipside is that if you've worked consistently and diligently throughout the semester, you shouldn't have to cram all night. With the vast majority of your preparation completed before the exam period arrives, you should have time to study for your exams in an organized fashion that allows you to hit the sack at a normal time. Again, that is the critical point to appreciate: the bulk of exam preparation occurs long before exams begin, starting with the first week of class. Your best overall strategy for arriving at exams fully prepared is to follow the CREDO habits (Consistent, Rigorous, Efficient, Diligent, Organized) in Chapter 10 from the beginning of the semester until the end. If you read every assignment, brief every case, attend and take good notes in every class, compose outlines for every course, and engage in periodic review, you'll be rounding third base headed for home when exam week arrives.

CHAPTER 15
LAW SCHOOL ESSAY EXAMS: FIFTEEN COMMON MISTAKES

Alright! Finally, the good stuff: the secrets to succeeding on law school exams. Well, kind of, sort of. Hate to be a buzz-kill, but the truth is that no secret formula or system for acing law school exams exists. If anyone offers to share such a formula or system with you, tell them thanks, but no thanks. My best advice for excelling on law school exams is to apply the CREDO habits (Chapter 10) to all of the other advice I've already given you. If you fail to consistently, rigorously, efficiently, and diligently pursue your studies in an organized fashion, no amount of exam advice in the world is going to put you on top.

But even following all that advice isn't sufficient to ensure your best performance. Lots of—no, make that *most*—dili-gent, hard-working students fail to maximize their potential on their first rounds of exams simply because they lack experience and understanding about what to do and what not to do. In this chapter and the next one, we'll see what we can do to rectify that problem.

Most law school exam questions come in one of two basic forms: essay questions and multiple-choice questions. While other types of questions are sometimes used (e.g., true-false, short answer), essay and multiple-choice questions predomi-nate. This chapter addresses essay exam strategies, while Chapter 16 zeroes in on multiple-choice questions.

Types of Law School Essay Questions

Law school essay questions can assume several shapes and forms:

Issue-spotting/problem-solving questions.

The classic format for law school exams, and the focus of this chapter, is the issue-spotting/problem-solving essay question. These notoriously complicated and convoluted questions are comprised of hypothetical fact patterns in which various actors interact in ways that raise legal issues among them. Students are expected to identify those issues and solve them through thorough, organized analysis. A sample issue-spotting/problem-solving essay question and model answer are included as Appendix B. You might want to flip to it and look it over just to get a picture of what we'll be talking about.

Short essay problem-solving questions.

Also common are short essay problem-solving questions. As the label suggests, such questions are literally shorter in length than issue-spotting/problem-solving questions. They're also narrower in scope, usually focusing on one or two issues. As a result, short essay questions are less daunting than issue-spotting/problem-solving questions. Often, short essay questions will expressly identify the issue for students, eliminating altogether the challenge of issue-spotting. Even if the question doesn't expressly identify the issue, the issues are easier to recognize because fewer actors and fewer activities are involved in the question. For the same reason, answers to short essay questions present fewer organizational problems than questions raising multiple issues among multiple parties. A sample short essay question and model answer are included as Appendix C.

Policy questions.

Another oft-used type of essay question is known as a "policy question." Policy questions don't test students' ability to apply law to facts and solve legal problems. Depending on the question, they don't necessarily even test one's knowledge or understanding of specific principles of law. Rather, they focus on a student's ability to construct a thoughtful argument or analysis regarding a policy issue relevant to the course material. Here's a sample policy question that could be used in a Torts course:

The U.S. rule regarding payment of attorneys' fees and litigation costs is that each side must bear its own fees and major costs (such as expert witness fees). Most other nations follow the "loser pays" rule, in which the losing party must pay the winning party's attorneys' fees and costs. Compare the two approaches as applied in personal injury cases and discuss their relative advantages and drawbacks to a legal system.

Be forewarned: Some professors will intentionally ask policy questions addressing issues never discussed in the course because they want to see how students apply what they learned to new situations. The story might be apocryphal, but I once heard of a policy question that asked simply: "What is law?" Most policy questions aren't that broad, but by their nature, grading policy questions is subjective in the extreme. Will the professor reward you for thinking like he does about the policies? Punish you for thinking differently? Boost or lower your grade for taking an outlandish position? No way to know. Policy questions tend to benefit creative thinkers who are good writers over the students who worked the hardest and learned the most in the course.

Don't get me wrong. Policy questions have undeniable value. Lawyers often are at the forefront as lawmakers and legislative advocates, and the abilities to think beyond the rules and analyze, critique, and advance the policies behind law are vital to all lawyers. My issues with policy questions are that they don't measure acquired knowledge as well and are not as susceptible to objective grading as non-policy essays—which themselves entail a high degree of subjective interpretation. If your professor uses policy questions, it's perfectly appropriate to ask the professor what the grading criteria will be for them and for a sample question and answer to review.

If this section has you worried about policy questions, relax. Although many law profs use them, they usually count for only a small portion of the exam.

Other types of essay questions.

Between the traditional "apply law to facts"-type essay questions and pure policy questions are a host of other essay questions—which can be long or short—limited in their content and format only by the ability of law professors to think creatively (in other words, there are no limits). A professor could ask you, for example, to draft a statute or answer a list of questions about a given fact pattern or put yourself in the role of the client, or just about anything else. Such questions may be hybrids that combine policy discussion with legal problem-solving.

The Fifteen Most Common Law School Essay Exam Mistakes

The traditional issue-spotting/problem-solving essay question remains the dominant vehicle for testing legal analysis in first-year courses, so we'll focus on that format in this chapter. Most of what is discussed below also applies to short essay problem-solving questions and much of it applies to any type of essay question.

I've graded thousands of law school essay exams. Year after year, at law school after law school, students make the *exact same mistakes*. Accordingly, I decided the best way to explain how to do things right in answering essay questions was to explain what students commonly do wrong. I'm sure other professors could come up with additional mistakes or reframe entries on my list, but here are what I believe to be *The Fifteen Most Common Law School Essay Exam Mistakes*:

1. Failing to carefully read and follow instructions.

2. Starting to write before analyzing the question and organizing your answer.

3. Not managing time properly and efficiently.

4. Writing about issues that don't exist or failing to write about issues that do exist because the facts indicate they ultimately would fail on the merits.

5. Not attaching significance to or misreading key facts.

6. Failing to be precise in stating legal rules and analysis.

7. Failing to structure exam answers in a rough IRAC (Issue, Rule, Application, Conclusion) framework.

8. Leaving out the *relevant* rules of law.

9. Giving a general dissertation on the law rather than answering the question asked.

10. Omitting or skimping on the analysis.

11. Doing the "Monster [Issue] Mash."

12. Overlooking and, hence, wrongly addressing "givens."

13. Making factual assumptions without saying so or making unreasonable factual assumptions.

14. Being sloppy.

15. Writing too little.

If some of the mistakes seem to fall under the "Well, duh, that's obvious"-category, trust me when I say that law students regularly do themselves in by committing even the most bald-faced of these errors. I'll give you several examples along the way.

1. Failing to carefully read and follow instructions. After more than twenty years teaching law students, I continue to be astonished at the number of students who self-destruct simply by not reading and following the exam instructions. On law school exams, instructions show up in different places: (1) most exams begin with a set of instructions applicable to the exam as a whole; (2) each essay question will have its own instructions applicable to that question, usually at the end of the question; and (3) a multiple-choice (or other objective) section is likely to have its own specific instructions at the beginning of the section.

Knowing it's impossible to be too clear when dealing with stressed-out law students who are overly anxious to begin writing, I go out of my way to include very clear instructions. Nevertheless, year after year, a substantial number of students fail to follow parts of them. Here are some examples of ways students have committed academic suicide-by-misreading in my Torts course:

• The two basic divisions of tort law are the intentional torts and negligence law. Each fall semester, I give one big essay question on *either* the intentional torts *or* negligence law. The instructions at the end of the essay question state: "This is an intentional tort question. Do not discuss negligence." Or vice versa: "This is a negligence question. Do not discuss intentional torts." (See Appendix B for example.) Would you believe that students have missed that instruction and spent their time writing, in whole or in part, about the wrong subject? Believe it. It happens.

• Although I cover some state-specific law in Torts, I don't test it on essay questions. The instruction page of my exam always contains the statement: "Do not discuss [name of state] law unless the question specifically instructs you to do so." Despite this unequivocal directive, some students invariably turn to discussing state law on essay questions.

• To assist students in focusing on and addressing the issues I want them to discuss, I usually include explicit instructions not to discuss potential claims between certain parties and/or not to discuss particular issues. Students frequently overlook these instructions and analyze claims or issues specifically excluded. Here's a recent example. In Torts, you'll learn that violating a statute, such as a traffic law, can, in effect, automatically stamp the offender's conduct as negligent. It's called the doctrine of negligence per se. In a recent essay question, I included the specific instruction: "The question does not mention any statutes or ordinances, so you should not discuss any." I only made it through three of seventy-four exams before coming to one that rocketed into a lengthy discussion of how a principal actor in the question most likely violated some traffic statutes and, therefore, was negligent per se. Other students committed the same error.

Oversights like these are killers on several levels. First, time is a precious commodity when taking law school exams. Every minute spent writing about the wrong or non-issues is one less minute students have for writing about the issues that matter. Second, students receive zero credit for content addressing wrong or non-issues, no matter how brilliant their analysis. Law professors don't even read irrelevant analysis. We just flip pages searching for the point where the student (hopefully) gets back on track. Some professors mark down for incorrect analysis.

Finally, blunders from not carefully reading the instructions cast both the exam and exam-writer in a negative light. Picture your professor as a kind of forensic pathologist. Exam-writers are anonymous, but at every step of the way in reading an exam, the professor is picking up clues and drawing inferences about the writer, both positive and negative. Silly errors from misreading or not following instructions generate negative impressions that affect the grade the exam receives.

Consider a recent exam question that, after reciting the facts, cast students in the role of a defense lawyer, asking them to draft a law office memorandum regarding the relevant issues. The instructions began: "The case has now progressed to the point of trial. *You work for the defense lawyer who will serve as main trial counsel.* She wants you to draft a memorandum explaining and evaluating . . . (italics added)." About 10 percent of the class somehow misread this clear instruction and wrote their memorandum as if they were representing the *plaintiff*. While the error didn't directly alter the substance of the analysis, you can see how such a blatant misreading would taint the professor's view of the exam and its author.

Don't think these mistakes couldn't happen to you. Students, even very intelligent ones, frequently get careless in the stress and rush of the moment.

2.   Starting to write before analyzing the question and organizing your answer. Poor law students. Law professors give them incredibly difficult exams and, too often, not enough time to complete them adequately. It's no wonder students feel the urge to begin writing answers before giving sufficient thought to what they're writing about. The temptation is understandable, but you must resist it. Failing to digest the question and organize your answer before you begin writing leads to a jumbled mess. It also substantially increases the likelihood of your overlooking key instructions (see above) and facts and issues (see below).

Take adequate time to carefully read and do a rough outline of the question before you begin writing. Don't skim the question. Pay attention to every word. Use a highlighter to mark key facts and issues as you read. On a piece of scratch paper, compose a rough outline as you go. Not a formal outline with Roman numerals, etc. Just jot down issues (including claims and defenses) as you spot them. Then take a few minutes to organize them. Unless instructed otherwise, address issues in the order they are raised by the question. It's always jarring when students take the issues up in reverse order.

In addition to improving the organization of your answer, outlining the issues will prevent you from forgetting about them. Many have been the students who, on reviewing their exams alongside my model answer, say, "Doh! I spotted that issue when I read the question, but then completely forgot about it."

If the question raises issues involving multiple parties, organize your answer under subheadings listing the parties, as in "A v. B." In addition to making your exam easier and more appealing to read, using subheadings will help force you to address all claims, defenses or other issues between A and B before moving on to other parties (as opposed to, for example, discussing A v. B, then moving on to C v. D, then going back to A v. B, then adding a tad more about C v. D, then remembering one more point about A v. B, etc.). Using separate issue subheadings also enhances clarity and organization, as in "Res Ipsa Loquitur" or "Concurrent Cause." See the model answers to the sample essay questions in Appendices B and C for examples. Compartmentalize all issue discussions (see "Monster [Issue] Mash" below). Don't blend them together.

How much time should you spend reading the question and outlining the answer before you start writing? It's impossible to say with exactitude because it depends on how much time has been allotted for the question and on the nature of the question itself. As a general guideline, I recommend devoting *at least* 20 percent of the time allotted for the particular question to reading the question and thinking about your answer before you begin writing (e.g., twelve minutes for a sixty-minute question; eighteen minutes for a ninety-minute question).

3. Not managing time properly and efficiently. Because time is scarce on most law school exams, it's crucial that you efficiently allocate your time among the different exam components and monitor it as you progress through the exam.

Not infrequently, students will get so wrapped up in answering one question (or addressing one issue in a multi-issue question) that they run out of time before getting to the others. This is a mistake that can have disastrous consequences. My Torts exams are weighted equally between essay questions and multiple-choice questions. One time a student was in the process of handing in her exam when she suddenly turned ashen. "I forgot to answer the multiple choice section!" she said. I felt sorry for her, but there was nothing I could do. Time was up. It wouldn't have been fair to the other students to give her more time. She lost 50 percent of the possible points on the exam by not monitoring and apportioning her time. While hers is an extreme example, it is common to be reading an exam answer that suddenly cuts off in the middle of a question with a note such as "Time called!"

When students run out of time, it's usually not because they spent their time profitably writing an exquisite answer to one question or one issue at the expense of others, but because they squandered their time engaging in one of the:

Top Five Law School Essay Exam Time-Wasters

1. Engaging in a generalized brain-dump that doesn't answer the question asked.

2. Going off on wayward tangents analyzing non-issues.

3. Writing lengthy introductions that simply restate the facts of the question or lengthy conclusions restating what has already been said.

4. Restating legal rules that have already been stated once.

5. Spending disproportionate time on the first issue simply because it's first.

Numbers 1 and 2 are parts of larger mistakes discussed below. With regard to number 3, cut to the chase when writing answers to essay exams. You don't need an introduction to your answer other than one sentence such as: "This question raises several issues that I will address in the order of their appearance." While you definitely want to discuss relevant facts as part of your legal analysis (see below), don't begin your answer by restating or summarizing the facts of the question, as some students do. You'll be taught to do that for the law office memoranda you'll be assigned to write in your legal writing course, but it doesn't carry over to exams. Similarly, while most professors will want you to offer your predictive conclusions as to the resolution of each issue raised in the exam, you do not need a concluding paragraph that summarizes or restates the conclusions you already articulated in the body of the analysis.

Number 4 is similar to number 3 in that it involves avoiding repetition. Once you've stated a legal rule or test in an essay question, you do not need to restate it. Suppose you have an intentional torts essay question in which A commits a battery against B and later in the same question C commits a battery against D. In discussing B's battery claim against A, it would be proper to state the elements of the tort of battery. But when you get to D's battery claim against C, it's not necessary to restate them. Simply refer back to the previous statement of the elements. You might say, for example: "The elements of battery have already been stated above in connection with B's claim against A, so I won't repeat them." Then proceed to identify and analyze any specific issues regarding those elements raised by the facts as to D's battery claim against C.

Similarly, if you have a question requiring you to apply a multifactor legal analysis, don't bother listing all the factors at the beginning of the analysis and then restating them in your analysis. Here's a concrete example from a recent Torts exam. The exam contained a products liability essay question that required students to analyze whether a piece of factory machinery was defective in its design. To show a design defect, the plaintiff has to show the existence of a "reasonable alternative design" or "RAD." The RAD analysis we learned in class requires the consideration of six factors. A fairly large number of students wasted time listing the six factors at the beginning of the question and then repeating each factor as they went through the analysis, a waste of at least five minutes.

As for number 5, it seems to be a phenomenon of human nature to devote a disproportionate amount of time and attention to the first item in a list of items. I see this happen in faculty meetings all the time. No matter how insignificant the first item on the agenda, the faculty will discuss it to death at the expense of items that appear later on the agenda, even if the latter items are far more important. Thus, the law school's inclement weather policy (first item on the agenda) may get fifty-five minutes of discussion in a one-hour meeting, while a proposal to abolish grading (last item) gets five. Law students often do the same thing on exams. They'll spend far too much time belaboring the first issue at the expense of other important issues that come later.

Size up and apportion your time at the beginning of the exam. Many students smartly calculate and write down the specific starting and ending times next to each question before they begin. Place a watch set to the classroom clock in front of you and keep tabs on it. Some professors will include suggested time limits for essay questions and other components of the exam, but some will leave it to you to calculate on your own.

You want to allocate your time in accordance with the points assigned to the question. Assuming it's a three-hour essay exam and you have three equally weighted questions, you'd want to spend approximately one hour on each question. If one question is worth 200 points and the other two are worth fifty points each, you'd want to spend two hours on the 200-point question and thirty minutes each on the two 50-point questions.

If you do find yourself running out of time before you've had a chance to tackle a question or to address all the issues in a question, use your remaining time to hit the high points. Jot down as many issues as you can. Simply mentioning an issue, even without analysis, can get you some points. Some professors, particularly inexperienced ones, will load up a question with too many issues, making it impossible to analyze them all adequately. You're better off addressing all the questions and all issues within a question adequately than trying to address one question or one issue superbly.

Finally, use all your available time on the exam. It kills me when I see people leaving exams early. Students devote hundreds of hours over a fourteen-week period learning the subject matter of a course well enough to give themselves a fighting chance on a single three-hour exam. Why, why, why, I ask myself—as I fight off the urge to smash my head into the wall—would anyone not take advantage of every single available second? What, are they in a hurry to grab lunch, take in a movie, start studying for the next exam?

Falling on their knees and begging for another hour—that I could understand. Leaving early? It befuddles me (even though I did it as a law student). I make it a point to try to give students adequate time to complete the exam, but I also know that it takes me longer to write my model answer to the essay questions than I give students to write their answers—and I already know the answers before I start writing!

If you finish early, it's almost always because you: (a) did not spot all the issues; or (b) did not fully consider them. If you *think* you've finished early, use your leftover time to reread the questions and your answers. Maybe you'll spot an issue you overlooked. I remember walking out of a law school exam early and immediately realizing I missed a huge issue. If I had sat there a few more minutes, it might have come to me. Or maybe you'll notice on rereading that you forgot to state the applicable rules in a question or that your analysis on a particular point needs beefing up. At a minimum, you'll be likely to notice missing punctuation, misspelled words, and other typos you can correct.

But let's go ahead and assume the "worst-case scenario." Let's assume you stick around and read over your exam and not a single potential improvement comes to mind. What have you lost? Thirty minutes of your life? Stay the entire time. Stare at the ceiling. Contemplate your navel. But stay.

4. Writing about issues that don't exist or failing to write about issues that do exist because the facts indicate they ultimately would fail on the merits. Students often come into exams hell-bent on finding particular issues in essay questions whether they exist or not. I think this occurs because every course has major issues to which the professors devote disproportionate class time. It's smart to be alert to such issues. If the professor is fair, it stands to reason that issues receiving substantial coverage will be more likely to show up on the exam than issues receiving less coverage. But it's a mistake to attempt to convert class time spent on an issue into a predictive formula for whether the issue will be on the exam.

Once when I was teaching as a visiting professor at a West Coast law school, I discovered a student was operating a gambling ring in which he set odds and accepted bets from other students as to which issues would be tested on their forthcoming exams, including Torts. I recall, for example, learning that the odds of the negligence defense known as "assumption of risk" turning up as a major issue on my Torts exam were 4–1 in favor of it appearing. Presumably, these odds were tied to the fact that we had spent two full classes on the doctrine. I bet heavily against the odds, omitted the issue, and cleaned up. Ha! That'll show 'em. Kidding, but I do think I intentionally left the issue out of the exam.

Again, it's wise to be on the lookout for issues on which the professor spent a lot of class time, but it's not smart to *insist* that those issues will be in the exam.

A well-written exam will contain facts that fairly raise certain issues. If those facts aren't there, the issues aren't there, even if you think they should be there. On the other hand, if you're unsure whether a question is intending to raise a particular issue, err on the side of discussing it rather than leaving it out. The principal harm from discussing a non-issue is wasted time. Most professors don't deduct credit for off-point analysis. The harm from not discussing something intended by the professor to be an issue is much more severe: no credit.

Which brings us to the next point. Many students make a kind of opposite mistake to writing about issues that don't exist: they fail to write about issues that do exist based on their conclusion that, under the facts, the issue ultimately lacks merit. If the professor includes facts that raise an issue, but also includes facts that appear to kill it as a legitimate issue, discuss the issue. Don't think, "Ahh, the professor's trying to trick me into thinking that's an issue, but I'm not falling for it." Don't confuse "exam issue" with "successful outcome on the merits." If the professor includes facts both raising and dismissing an issue, that's precisely what the professor wants you to discuss.

I regularly give my first-semester students a practice midterm exam in which a series of potential intentional torts unfold at a holiday office party. I'll use several examples from the practice exam in this chapter. One issue involves the tort of assault. Contrary to the popular understanding of the word, in tort law, an assault occurs when a person acts intending to create in another an *imminent apprehension* of a harmful or offensive bodily contact. No actual bodily contact is required (if a contact does occur, it's a battery). In the exam question, an employee named Dick pulls a knife and threatens his boss with it from behind. The boss, however, has a hearing impairment and doesn't hear the threat. Because his back is turned, he also doesn't see the knife. Thus, because the boss was not in imminent apprehension of a harmful contact, no assault actually occurred. Many students read these facts and think, "Ahh, McClurg's trying to trick me into thinking this is an assault, but I'm not falling for it," and omit discussing the assault claim. But I *am* looking for students to discuss it. That's why I put the facts in there. Assault is an issue in the question, even though the claim would ultimately fail on the merits because an essential element—imminent apprehension of a bodily contact—is missing.

5. Not attaching significance to or misreading key facts. Failing to spot issues obviously is a crucial misstep in analyzing an essay question, but identifying "failure to spot issues" as a common mistake would be too broad and unhelpful. Instead, I'll focus on a couple of narrower points that commonly result in a failure to spot issues: overlooking key facts designed to raise issues or simply misreading those facts.

Each fact in an essay exam question should be scrutinized from the perspective of, "Hmm, why would the professor insert that fact? It must be there for a reason." Reading the question in this manner will help you spot more issues. Most facts are included either to raise issues, narrow issues, or exclude them.

But not all facts. Just as part of learning to properly read and digest a case requires an ability to separate material from immaterial facts, successful law students are able to discriminate between material and immaterial facts on exams. Professors sometimes include introductory narrative simply to set the scene; that is, to set up the question for the legally significant events that follow. In those situations, facts in introductory paragraphs may be immaterial to answering the question.

But there are no reliable rules here. The very first sentence of a question might be critically important and legally irrelevant facts might be sprinkled throughout the question (sometimes with the pedagogical intent of challenging students to distinguish relevant from irrelevant facts, but often simply to facilitate the story-telling aspect of the question). Again, ponder every fact and ask: why would the professor have inserted this fact?

Just as bad as overlooking the *significance* of key facts is overlooking the facts themselves. When grading exams, I commonly scribble in the margin: "Read the question!" This comment is born of frustration in reading student analyses that are off-base simply because the student did not carefully read and take note of the clearly stated facts.

A recent example occurred in answers to a Torts negligence question in which a neighbor intentionally and maliciously set fire to a puddle of highly flammable solvent negligently left by construction workers in the basin of an in-ground swimming pool being installed in the backyard of the house next door. The issue was one of "intervening causes." Specifically, the issue was whether the neighbor's act in intentionally setting fire to the solvent was sufficient to relieve the pool contractor of liability for its negligence in leaving the flammable solvent in the pool. You don't need to know anything about the law to understand this example other than that the most important factor dictating the path of analysis was whether the intervening actor (the neighbor, in this case) acted intentionally or only carelessly in starting the fire.

The question facts explained that the neighbor, a guy named Hitchcock, was a "curmudgeonly old coot" who was unhappy about the pool being built next door and wanted to prevent it from being completed. This excerpt followed:

> After the construction workers left on the afternoon during which they applied the solvent, and when no one else was home at the Froid house, Hitchcock snuck over to survey the pool. Access was easy because of the back fence having been removed by the construction workers. "Dang," he muttered. "I can hear them now, howling and hooting like banshees all summer long. There goes the quiet enjoyment of my home. I've got to stop them, but how?" As he pondered this question, he sniffed. "What is that smell? Whew, its strong." He sniffed again and realized the smell was coming from the pool. That's when he noticed the puddle of solvent accumulated at the bottom of the pool.
>
> "Well, well, well, what have we here? Wonder if it burns? One way to find out." He lit a match, chuckled maliciously, and tossed the match into the pool. The solvent burst into flames with an intensity that surprised and frightened Hitchcock. He immediately rushed back home, hoping no one had seen him.

Toward the end, the question stated: "Hitchcock admitted in a deposition to starting the fire."

Thus, the question makes it pretty darn clear that Hitchcock acted intentionally and also that everyone knew he was the culprit. I don't see how it could have been much clearer. Nevertheless, I graded several exams in which the students' analyses got bogged down and went off course in speculating as to whether the fire was set intentionally or accidentally and also whether anyone would ever be able to identify Hitchcock as the arsonist. Each time, I responded with "Read the question!" This issue was the largest point-getter on the entire exam. The students who didn't read the question with sufficient care hurt their grades.

6. Failing to be precise in stating legal rules and analysis. Many students understand the law, but lose ground on their exams by expressing legal rules and analysis in general, conclusory or layperson terms, rather than in specific, precise legal terminology, which is what professors are looking for. Specific always trumps general on law school exams.

A couple of examples will bolster the point. Tort law recognizes as a defense to a battery a legal privilege to use reasonable force to protect other people. The privilege is known as the "defense of others." "Defense of others" is a term of art. It's the legal name attached to the privilege. In the same practice exam mentioned above (see mistake no. 4), Dick harassingly pinches a co-worker, Jane, at the office party. Jane cries out and a chivalrous co-worker named Moe comes to her aid. Moe punches Dick in the face, breaking his nose, to repel his advances toward Jane. Every student who takes this practice exam recognizes Dick's potential battery claim against Moe and almost all students successfully identify Moe's potential privilege to use force in defense of others. But compare the following two statements of the privilege issue:

> **Student 1:** Moe will raise the privilege of defense of others, asserting he had a privilege to use reasonable force to protect Jane from Dick's advances.

> **Student 2:** Moe will argue that he is not liable because he was helping Jane.

Both students identified the issue, but notice the difference—and it's a BIG difference—in how they framed it. Student 1 did it correctly, using the precise legal language "privilege of defense of others." Student 2 did it incorrectly, framing the issue in the vague, layperson language "because he was helping Jane." "Helping Jane" is not a cognizable legal privilege. Thus, even though both students spotted the issue, Student 1 would out-point Student 2 by paying attention to the language used.

Here's another example from the same practice exam, involving the assault scene previously mentioned above. In response to Moe's attack on him, Dick pulls a knife, points it at his boss, and says, "Nobody move an inch or the boss gets it." The boss, however, is unaware of the threat because his back is turned and he has a hearing impairment. Thus, as already discussed, no assault occurred because the boss was not in "imminent apprehension of a harmful or offensive bodily contact"—an essential element of the tort of assault. That's the correct, precise legal language. But many students, though recognizing and understanding the issue and correct resolution, botch the analysis by using loose language. Instead of saying "the boss has no valid assault claim because he was not in imminent apprehension of a harmful or offensive bodily contact," they'll say something like "the boss will lose because he was unaware of what was happening," which is a true statement, but is not legal analysis. Use specific, precise legal language when analyzing legal problems.

7. Failing to structure exam answers in a rough IRAC (Issue, Rule, Application, Conclusion) framework. In law school, you will (or should) learn about what's called the "IRAC" method for analyzing legal issues. IRAC is a mnemonic that stands for:

ISSUE

RULE

APPLICATION

CONCLUSION

IRAC is not a mechanical formula, but simply a common sense approach to identifying and fully analyzing a legal issue. Before one can begin to analyze a legal issue, of course, one has to know what the issue is. Thus, quite logically, step one in the IRAC methodology is to identify the specific legal issue. Step two is to identify and state the relevant rule(s) of law that will apply in resolving the issue. Step three is to apply those rules to the facts of the question—that is, to "analyze" the issue. Step four is to offer a conclusion as to the most likely result. Exam answers to issue-spotting/problem-solving questions should be constructed keeping in mind a *rough* IRAC framework.

Here's a very simple example, continuing with the same fact pattern from the practice exam we've been discussing. Recall that Dick pinched co-worker Jane at the office party. Moe came to her assistance by punching Dick in the face and breaking his nose. Dick would sue Moe for battery (one issue) and Moe would assert as a defense the privilege of defense of others (another issue). Here's how the defense of others issue could be addressed in an IRAC format:

> **[ISSUE]** Moe will assert the privilege of "defense of others" in response to Dick's battery claim, arguing that he was acting to defend Jane from Dick's offensive battery. **[RULES]** The privilege of defense of others allows one to use reasonable force to protect another from a threatened battery. Reasonable force is measured by a proportionality standard. The force used in defense must be proportionate to the force being defended against. **[APPLICATION]** Moe may have been privileged to use some mild force in defending Jane from a physically harmless pinch, such as pushing Dick away. But smashing Dick in the face and breaking his nose to ward off a pinch at an office party was disproportionate, unreasonable force. **[CONCLU-SION]** Because he used excessive, unreasonable force, the privilege will fail and Moe will be liable to Dick for battery.

Some students misconstrue the IRAC methodology as an inflexible formula, which it most definitely is not. Some even go so far as to set their answers up in the form of an outline with headings like "ISSUE: ...," "RULE: ...," etc. Don't do that! I inserted those words above only as a guide. An answer to an essay question should read like, well, an essay. IRAC is simply a structural way of thinking about legal analysis in the context of issue-spotting/problem-solving essay questions. It has no application to some types of essay questions, such as policy questions, and limited application to questions that, say, identify the issue for you (such as in the sample short essay question included as Appendix C).

Moreover, even for issue-spotting/problem-solving questions, IRAC cannot be applied with mechanical rigidity. It worked that way for the above issue because the issue was extremely simple. The more complicated the issue, the less likely you'll be able to fit your answer within a precise IRAC framework. The issue may require more than one level of analysis. It may be necessary, for example, to first state the issue broadly, discuss principles and rules relevant to the broad issue, then move on to a narrower aspect of the issue raised in the question. Rules often must be intermingled with the application, rather than neatly separated from it. Sometimes it will be more effective to offer conclusions before you give the analysis. Nevertheless, IRAC is useful because it identifies the essential components of a sound, complete legal analysis and suggests a rough framework for addressing them. Even when the answer structure does not track a precise I, R, A, C ordering, all of the IRAC components will be included in a good answer.

You'll probably encounter IRAC early and often in law school, especially in your legal writing courses (where you also might learn other mnemonics for structural legal analysis with names like CREAC, TREAC, and CRRPAP). My goal here is to introduce you to IRAC and also to highlight below the two most common failings in executing it on essay exams: which are to omit the two middle parts: Rules and Application. Far too many students "IC" the exam, causing the professor to go "Ick!" when reading it; that is, they successfully identify the issue and offer a conclusion about how it should be resolved, but leave out both the relevant legal rules and any substantial application/analysis. Mistakes 8 and 9 address the R portion of IRAC and mistake 10 addresses the A portion.

8. Leaving out the *relevant* rules of law. It's unfortunate how many students, after spending a grueling semester learning hundreds of rules of law, neglect to include those rules in writing answers to essay questions on their final exams. A student can't successfully perform legal analysis—applying law to facts—without stating the relevant law they are applying. What makes this omission so surprising, as well as a crying shame, is that so many students who fail to state the rules know them inside out. They simply don't write them down. Frequently, when I point out to students during exam review sessions that they failed to include the relevant rules of law in their answers, the response is along the lines of: "Well, I assumed you knew the law, so I didn't think I needed to include it."

Usually, I believe them, but professors can only go by what students actually write down. Giving students the benefit of the doubt wouldn't be fair to the other students who did it right and included the law, but more important, a complete analysis requires a statement of the relevant legal rules as a precursor to applying them.

The cure for this deficiency, assuming the student does, in fact, know the rules, is simple. Even average students can bolster the quality of their answers just by remembering to perform the essential step of inserting the relevant rule after identifying the issue and before proceeding to the analysis (or depending on the nature and complexity of the question, weaving rule statements into the analysis). Give yourself a memory prompt by making a note at the top your exam: "Don't forget the R in IRAC."

9. Giving a general dissertation on the law rather than answering the question asked. Note the repeated emphasis above on *relevant* rules. The R in IRAC refers to the specific rule or rules that will govern resolution of the particular issue. It does not envision a treatise-like brain dump of everything one knows that is somehow related to the general subject matter. This is an extremely common mistake. Professor Joseph Glannon estimates that 20 percent of his students fall prey to this error, which he labels "abstract expressionism."[63] That figure may be low.

The only law (i.e., rules) that should be mentioned in answering an essay question is the law that addresses the specific issues raised in the question. This will rarely include broad-based discussion of a large subject area. If a negligence question, for example, raises an issue about causation-in-fact (an essential element of a cause of action for negligence requiring facts showing that but for the defendant's alleged negligent act, the injury would not have occurred), there's no

63. JOSEPH W. GLANNON, THE LAW OF TORTS: EXAMPLES AND EXPLANATIONS 598–600 (3d ed. 2005).

reason to discuss rules pertaining to the other elements of a claim for negligence *because they don't answer the question.* Indeed, there's no reason to discuss all of the rules related to causation-in-fact. The only rules that warrant mentioning are those necessary to resolve the specific causation-in-fact issue actually raised by the question. Once again, specific always trumps general. Generalized discussions of the law that don't answer the question asked are a waste of time. Most professors won't even read them.

10. Omitting or skimping on the application/analysis. Some students include the issue, relevant rule, and conclusion, but leave out the application, thereby "IRC'ing" their exams and irking the professors forced to read them. The application part of IRAC is what most professors refer to as the "analysis" portion, so we'll use that term here. It's difficult to explain in a vacuum how to analyze legal problems. Studying the sample exam questions and answers included in Appendices B and C will give you an idea of what legal analysis looks like. Consider the samples in conjunction with these tips regarding analysis:

If you're not talking about the facts, you're doing it wrong. As stated above, analysis is applying law to facts. Highlight the relevant facts in the question and make sure to weave them into your analysis. Facts dictate results. Change one fact and you'll often get a different result. Chances are good that if you're writing a lengthy block of text without discussing any of the facts in the question, you've substituted brain-dumping in place of legal analysis.

But you can't just *state* the facts. You need to tie them to the legal point you're relying on them to make. Recently, a student emailed me his analysis of a practice exam issue and asked me to comment on it. The question involved intentional torts and the issue he wrote about was battery. He correctly stated the issue and correctly listed the elements of battery (i.e., the rules). Then he set forth the relevant facts. The problem was he simply *listed* them, and then concluded the elements of a battery were met. No good. He needed to tie the facts to the specific elements of battery he was asserting were satisfied.

Explain your reasoning process. A simple way to think of legal analysis is as an "explanation." You're trying to explain to someone what the issue is and how it should be legally resolved. The more complete the explanation, the better it will be. Too many students keep their reasoning to themselves. Your professors can't read your mind. They can only evaluate what you actually explain.

Related to this point, many students mistake conclusions for analysis. They're not the same thing. Analogize analyzing a legal issue with working through a mathematical formula, such as: $2 \times 2 + 4 - 8 = 0$. Some students, presented with a fact pattern on a law school essay question, will begin and end their analysis with: "The answer is zero." But the professor needs to know what formula they used to get to zero, which includes both the rules and explanation of how the rules were applied. Other students will include some analysis, but leave out major portions, resulting in something resembling: $2 \times 2 = 0$. Because their analysis is incomplete, their work product is defective even when they reach the correct conclusion.

Avoid "he argues/she argues" analysis. Too many students, having been told it can be important to argue both sides of an issue, fall into he argues/she argues mode, which is not really analysis at all. He argues/she argues answers track this format: "A will argue x. B will argue y. A will argue z. B will argue ...." As Glannon notes, while students who take this approach walk away believing they have "argue[d] both sides," in reality they have argued neither side because they have left unfinished the key business of evaluating the relative strengths and weaknesses of the arguments under the applicable law.[64]

Specific trumps general. I'm not senile. I promise. I remember when I've already said something once. I remember when I've already said something once. Okay, well, maybe not all the time. In any event, in this case, I know I've already told you this twice, but maybe third time's a charm: specific analysis is always superior to general analysis.

When you think you've finished your analysis, add more. Nearly all student exam analysis is too skimpy. Once you think you've fully analyzed the issue, try to go one step deeper. A single added cogent sentence can boost an exam answer above others.

64. *Id.* at 602.

11. Doing the "Monster [Issue] Mash." In October 1962, Bobby "Boris" Pickett had a number one *Billboard* hit with the novelty tune "Monster Mash." The perennial Halloween favorite stars a mad scientist's monster that comes to life in the lab late one night and starts a new dance craze. The law school exam version of the Monster Mash is much less fun.

Legal issues are discrete and should be analyzed as such, even when they're interrelated. Discussion of each issue should be compartmentalized with a topical sentence introducing the issue, followed by a full-blown IRAC attack on that issue and that issue alone. Students often err by attempting to introduce several issues in a single paragraph, then trying to discuss them collectively. It can't be done. Instead of a coherent discussion of each issue, the result is one big monster mash of issues never destined to reach number one.

Here's a way to test yourself on this point. Look at your discussion of a particular issue. Visually cut it out with a pair of scissors. The excised excerpt should be able to stand more or less alone as a complete and coherent discussion of that issue without having to refer to other portions of your answer.

12. Overlooking and, hence, wrongly addressing "givens." Students often waste time analyzing issues they don't need to be talking about because they are "givens" in the question. A given is an assumption either clearly stated in the question (an "express given") or one that is readily inferable from it (an "inferable given"). Often, express givens are inserted for the very purpose of preventing students from talking about the point. If an intentional tort question, for example, says that "A committed a battery against B," there is no need to analyze the elements of battery in connection with A and B because the question is already assuming they have been met. Similarly, if a negligence question states that "A negligently drove his car into B," you can assume A failed to exercise reasonable care in his driving and do not need to discuss that point.

If something is a given, note it as such in your answer and move on to the real issues. For example, in the first illustration, an astute writer would say something like: "It is a given that A committed a battery against B, so there is no need to analyze that point." Overlooking givens is problematic because students end up wasting time writing about non-issues, tangle up the organization of their answers, and convey to the professor that they haven't read the question carefully.

Not all givens are expressly stated assumptions. Often they are inferences that can be readily drawn from the stated facts. For example, the elements of the tort of battery are: (1) a volitional act; (2) intended to cause a harmful or offensive bodily contact; and (3) such a contact results, directly or indirectly. Suppose the question says "During an argument, A pulls a gun from his pocket, points it at B, and pulls the trigger, shooting B in the abdomen." Absent some privilege to shoot B (such as self-defense), this would be a battery. Unlike the example above, however, the battery itself is not an express given (the question doesn't actually say "this is a battery"), but satisfaction of the elements of a battery claim are inferable givens unless other facts call them into question. Accordingly, while you would want to state the elements of battery and briefly note that they are satisfied, you would not want or need to engage in long-winded discussions of whether A pulling out the gun and shooting B constituted a volitional act (it did), whether A intended the shooting (he did), and whether the contact element was satisfied when the bullet entered B's abdomen (it was).

Extensive discussion of an element of a claim is necessary only if particular facts put the element in issue. Thus, for example, to make the volitional act element of battery an issue, we would need facts suggesting that what occurred didn't involve a voluntary act, as in: "A and B, two friends, got in a dispute at a bar one night over which songs to play on the juke box. On the way home, A was still mad and told B, 'I have half a mind to shoot you.' B told A to shut up and sleep it off in the backseat while he drove. A agreed. While A was asleep, he rolled over on a handgun in his coat pocket, causing it to discharge, hitting B." See the difference? Here we have specific facts raising the volitional act element (as well as the intent element) as an issue.

Here's another Torts example of an inferable given from the realm of negligence law. One of the essential elements of a cause of action for negligence is that the defendant was a "but for" cause-in-fact of the plaintiff's injury, meaning the injury would not have occurred absent the defendant's negligence. Because causation is an issue to which Torts profs devote substantial class time, students often search long and hard for causation issues on an exam. But as with all issues, causation is an issue only if the question facts raise it as an issue.

Suppose a negligence essay question states: "A, driving substantially in excess of the speed limit, loses control of his vehicle and collides into the back of B's car. B suffers a broken neck in the collision." Many students will erroneously launch into an elaborate discussion of whether A's negligence was a but for cause of B's injury. Why is it erroneous? Because, absent additional contrary facts, it's a readily inferable given that A's negligence was a but for cause of B's broken neck. While the question doesn't make but for causation an express given (it doesn't specifically say "A's negligence was a but for cause of B's injury), but for causation is clearly inferable from the facts, meaning there's no need to discuss it.

13. Making factual assumptions without saying so or making unreasonable factual assumptions. Exam questions sometimes require students to assume facts that are not specifically stated to fully analyze the issues. If the assumed facts are reasonably inferable from the stated facts, this is perfectly acceptable. For example, if the question states that a relevant event occurred at dusk and the amount of available light is important to resolving an issue (e.g., the reliability of an eyewitness identification in a criminal law or criminal procedure question or the possible negligence of a motorist driving without headlights), it is perfectly appropriate to say something like, "Assuming it was already dark ..." or "Assuming it was still light enough to see at a distance ..." Such assumptions are not only permissible, but necessary to completely and accurately analyze the issue. But you must *clearly state* your assumptions. Don't just make assumptions in your head, even reasonable ones, without noting them in your answer.

Any assumed fact must be reasonably inferable from the given facts. Students sometimes make unreasonable assumptions about facts that lead them far astray. I still remember the student from many years ago who was analyzing a Torts question that said something along the lines of "A shot at B, but the bullet missed him." The student came back with an analysis saying: "A shot at B, but missed him. However, assuming the bullet hit B, it would be a battery." Then he plunged headfirst into an analysis of the law of battery. Assumptions that are *contrary* to the question facts are never reasonable.

14. Being sloppy. This catch-all category includes a number of errors that can be grouped together as general sloppiness: using the wrong exam number or forgetting to include one, making repeated misspellings and grammatical errors, writing illegibly, not following procedural or formatting instructions, and resorting to too many abbreviations.

You want your exam to stand out for good reasons, not bad ones. You want to present your work in its most favorable light and that includes overall appearance. Sloppy errors, even ticky-tacky ones, affect the overall impression your paper makes on that forensic pathologist professor we were talking about, who is already displeased even under the best of circumstances about having to spend his or her holiday or summer break wading into a thick stack of exams. Here are four common types of sloppy errors to avoid:

Using the wrong exam number or forgetting to include one. Most every class will include a couple of students who either forgot to obtain their anonymous exam number from the registrar or lost or forgot it. When these students get to the exam, they just make up a number. When the professor gets ready to grade those exams, literally the first thing noticed will be that the student has a nonconforming exam number (e.g., ten digits instead of three like everyone else), creating an instant bias against that exam. How could the student be so sloppy as to forget his exam number or so lacking in diligence as to overlook obtaining it in the first place? Fair or not, that's going to be the professor's thought process. Using the wrong exam number entails extra hassle for the professor and registrar, sometimes delaying the posting of grades for the entire class. Get your exam numbers right. It's one of the easiest challenges of law school.

Making repeated misspellings and grammatical errors. One of the most common questions students ask about exams relates to misspellings and grammatical errors. "Do they count?" I've heard that question a hundred times. Heck, yes, they count, but not in the way students worry about. Very few professors officially mark down exams for misspelled words and/or grammatical errors. But a paper littered with such errors obviously does not bolster the professor's estimation of the content or the writer. It's not the occasional misspelling or typo you have to worry about. Some students misspell words pervasively—sometimes several words in the same sentence.

Spelling and grammar aren't things to obsess over during an exam, but they are things to pay attention to. If you finish an exam early, go back and reread your work product. Correct typos, insert omitted words, and make other corrections. Good writers spend more time editing and rewriting than composing the initial draft. You won't have that luxury, but you might have time to do a quick proofreading. As mentioned early in the book, you won't be able to rely on your computer spell-check function because schools usually disable it on the exam security software they use.

Writing illegibly. If you don't use a computer for your final examination, you need to be certain that your handwriting is legible. Indecipherable handwriting will hurt you. A professor grading hundreds of pages of exam answers is going to be an unhappy camper if forced to spend three times longer grading your exam because the handwriting is illegible. Handwriting is sometimes so bad that it is literally impossible to decode a word, even when considered in the context of a sentence. At some point, professors will resort to skimming such exams. Distinguish poor handwriting from illegible handwriting. Your handwriting doesn't have to be aesthetically pleasing, just readable.

Failing to follow procedural or formatting instructions. Above I talked about the essentiality of following substantive instructions. Here, I'm talking about less egregious, but still important, procedural or formatting instructions. Many exams contain specific instructions about "how to do things" in terms of formatting your exam (e.g., writing on one side of the page in bluebooks), labeling exam components in a particular way (e.g., numbering your bluebooks "Book 1 of 4, Book 2 of 4," etc.), and turning in the exam (e.g., assembling your exam materials in a designated order). When students fail to follow these instructions, they stand out—in an irritating way.

Using too many or undefined abbreviations. In their rush, some students resort to sloppy and/or indecipherable shorthand and abbreviations. It's permissible to abbreviate the names of the actors you will be repeating many times in your answer, provided you spell out the names the first time and clearly note the abbreviations you will be using. Thus, if you're writing about Greta Garbonski and Henry Flankenhocker, it's okay to say "Greta Garbonski (GG) will sue Henry Flankenhocker (HF) for battery" and then use GG and HF from that point on.

Apart from party names, about the only proper use of abbreviations is when you are faced with an unwieldy legal term that you will be repeating several times. Follow the same rules as for proper names. Thus, in Torts, for example, it would be acceptable to abbreviate "intentional infliction of emotional distress" as "IIED" or "res ipsa loquitur" as "RIL," provided you wrote the terms out the first time, followed by the abbreviations. Do not use abbreviations you learned in other walks of life. I've read exams written by doctors and nurses that were so full of shorthand symbols they looked like hieroglyphics.

15. Writing too little. This last mistake of writing too little subsumes some of the more specific errors already discussed (e.g., leaving out the rules and analysis). It isn't easily and effectively correctable as a stand-alone error, but it does provide food for thought.

Most modern law students take essay exams on notebook computers (e.g., 67 of 74 students in a recent Torts course). The exam-security software spits out a cover page for each exam showing a word count for essay answers. Examining these word counts in relation to performance yields an important, if unsurprising, insight: students who write more tend to do better on law school essay exams. Specifically, on a recent Torts exam, the average word count for the ten highest-scoring answers to a ninety-minute, issue-spotting/problem-solving essay question was 1952, whereas the average word count for the ten lowest-scoring answers was 1163. That's a 40 percent difference!

The moral of this story, of course, is not simply to write more. An essay answer with Tolstoy-esque bulk is worthless if the content isn't accurate and on point. The exam with the highest word count in my little experiment, for example, wasn't in the top ten. On the other hand, the exam with the second highest word count was the top-scoring essay and the exam with the lowest word count was the lowest-scoring essay.

No definitive conclusions can be drawn from my unscientific investigation, of course, but there's no disputing that effective, complete analysis of complex essay questions entails more discussion than most students devote to it. Shorter exam answers tend to be written by students who miss issues, leave out rules, skimp on analysis, or all three.

Hey, Maybe I *Can* Guarantee You Straight *A*s After All ... Nah

Hmm, after rereading all that, I'm thinking maybe I'll change my mind about not being able to guarantee you *A*s if you follow my advice. If you could truly avoid *all* of the above mistakes, you probably would get *A*s. Of course, you won't be able to avoid them all simply by reading this book. Several of them involve skills that need to be developed while you're in law school. At least now you know what to be on the lookout for.

But several of the mistakes *can* be easily avoided. You *can* make yourself be more careful about reading instructions. That alone could change your future. You *can* make yourself spend at least 20 percent of the allotted time for a question studying and thinking about it before starting to write an answer. You *can* make yourself remember not to leave out the rules (assuming you know them). You *can* bring a watch and allocate your time properly during the exam. You *can* stay the entire time of the exam. You *can* be sure to get your exam number right, etc.

Did you notice any common threads in the mistakes? Specifically, did you notice how the CREDO habits carry over even to actual exam-writing? The only one not implicated, because it's too late for it to apply, is being *Consistent*. But notice that avoiding common essay exam mistakes requires one to be:

Rigorous in stating legal rules with precision and completeness;

Efficient in assessing, allocating, and using the allotted time;

Diligent in reading the question carefully, following the instructions, staying for the entire exam period, and proofreading your work; and

Organized in outlining your answer before you begin writing, using subheadings to denote party disputes and issues, following an IRAC framework, and compartmentalizing your issue discussion to avoid the Monster Mash.

Now that you're familiar with common essay exam mistakes, study carefully the sample essay questions and answers in Appendices B and C. Both questions are real questions that I've used on Torts exams. The included model answers are the real answers I used to grade the exams. Appendix B is a classic issue-spotting/problem-solving intentional torts essay question raising several issues. Appendix C is a short essay question addressing a single issue of negligence law.

If you haven't started law school yet or are in its early throes, studying the questions and answers will be of limited value because the law addressed by the questions will be unfamiliar to you. But they'll give you an accurate view of what you can expect to find on a law school exam. Think about the mistakes outlined in this chapter as you study the answers.

CHAPTER 16
TACKLING LAW SCHOOL MULTIPLE–CHOICE QUESTIONS

Back when I attended law school, exams were comprised exclusively of essay questions. Today, many, if not most, professors also include multiple-choice questions on exams. Some professors rely solely on multiple-choice questions. My own exams are split half and half between essay and multiple-choice questions. A couple of good reasons exist for including a multiple-choice component on a law school exam. First, it allows for broader course coverage. As already explained, law school essay questions by their nature usually can touch on only a handful of issues covered during the semester. Adding multiple-choice questions allows the professor to cover a wider array of topics.

A practical benefit of multiple-choice questions is that they provide good practice for the bar exam, which is dominated by multiple-choice questions. The Multistate Bar Examination (MBE), which is administered in forty-eight states and the District of Columbia, is a six-hour monstrous marathon of two hundred multiple-choice questions focusing mostly on first-year subjects (the MBE covers Contracts, Constitutional Law, Criminal Law, Evidence, Real Property, and Torts). The state portion of the bar exam also often includes multiple-choice questions. In some states, as much as 75 percent of the total bar exam is made up of multiple-choice questions. But don't cheer too loudly. It's not as good as it sounds.

Multiple-Guess Mess: Questions
without Right Answers

Legal multiple-choice questions are unlike anything you've encountered in your prior educational experiences, primarily in that they're incredibly difficult and often don't have clear right answers. Probably the closest analogue to anything you've previously seen would be the reasoning questions on the LSAT. You've probably tried to forget the LSAT, but think back. The LSAT reasoning questions test whether a student has the ability to logically reason out which answer is *least wrong* and which answer is *most right*. Law school and bar examination multiple-choice questions test a similar reasoning ability combined with one's knowledge of black-letter law.

MBE-style questions—the model for most law school multiple-choice questions—usually consist of a one- or two-paragraph fact pattern in which events of legal significance transpire among named actors, followed by the "call of the question," followed by four or more answer choices. The "call of the question" is the part that tells you the issue you are to address. With some frequency, a series of two or three questions will be based on the same fact pattern. The succeeding questions in the series may add new facts or change the original facts. If they do, those new or changed facts apply only to that particular question unless otherwise specified.

The call of the question usually asks the reader to predict the most likely resolution of a legal issue raised by the facts. Thus, if the question facts describe actions and interactions between Bob and Jill on Bob's property, the call of the question might be something like "If Bob sues Jill for trespass, Bob will:"—followed by answer choices such as, "Win, because ..." or "Lose, because ...."

The problem for students is that often the choices do not include a clearly right answer. The essence of law school multiple-choice questions is perhaps best captured by an odd piece of advice I remember hearing for the first time many moons ago while taking a review course while studying for the bar exam: "Remember that on the MBE, you're not looking for the right answer. You're looking for the *best wrong answer*." While that might be a bit of an overstatement as applied to all law school multiple-choice questions, the basic point is sound: in law school multiple-choice questions, you're looking for the *best* answer among the choices given, even if you think a better "right" answer exists that's not included.

Ten Multiple-Choice Strategies

Here are some more specific strategies for tackling these beasts:[65]

1.   Read the question carefully. The fact patterns can be complex. As with essay questions, read every sentence asking, "Why was this included?" Not all of the facts in the question will have significance to the "call of the question" (see below), which can be confusing. Reading comprehension is one of the keys to success on all law school exams, including multiple-choice questions. A single word can change the meaning of the question.

2.   Pay attention to the call of the question. Pay close attention to the call of the question (sometimes called the "stem"). The call of the question is the part that immediately precedes the answer choices. It's the part that tells test-takers what they're supposed to analyze. Not infrequently, the fact patterns of MBE-style multiple-choice questions will set forth a scenario seemingly setting up one legal issue, only to surprise test-takers by asking about a different issue in the call of the question.

For example, a question may raise what appears to be an intentional tort issue, such as battery, but then the call of the question will ask about a negligence claim, as in "If Bob sues Jill for negligence . . . ." Students will be reading along thinking *battery, battery, battery,* and wrongly pick an answer addressing a battery claim, overlooking the call of the question. It's a good idea to glance at the call of the question *before* studying the entire question so you'll know what to look for as you read it.

3.   Use a process of elimination. Use a process of elimination to narrow down your answer choices. Usually, there will be one or two answers that are clearly wrong. Mark those out and focus on what's left.

---

65. Some of these tips were adapted from Professor Rogelio Lasso's helpful guide to taking law school multiple-choice questions. *See* Rogelio Lasso, Taking Multiple Choice Exams, *available at* http://www.law.umkc.edu/Students/BarExamInfo/TakingMultipleChoiceExams1.pdf.

4. Don't answer by your "gut reaction." Read all the choices carefully, eliminating the obvious wrong answers, before choosing a selection. It may be that one answer intuitively appeals to you the moment you read it before you've considered all the options, and that may be the answer you ultimately decide on, but don't choose any answer until carefully weighing all the options.

5. Divide your time equally among the questions. Unlike essay questions, which can vary in weight, multiple-choice questions will nearly always be worth the same number of points. Don't get bogged down on one question at the expense of others. Answer it and move on.

6. Beware of absolutes. As you'll learn all too well in law school, very few legal questions have answers that are true all of the time or none of the time. Almost every rule has exceptions and many exceptions have families of baby exceptions. Thus, in answering multiple-choice questions, answers prefaced with words like "always" or "never" usually are wrong answers.

7. Don't skip questions. Even if you're not sure of the answer, you're better off picking an answer than skipping the question with the intention of coming back to it later. Skipping questions poses two risks. First, you might forget you skipped it and start filling in answers for the other questions in the wrong spaces. Second, students frequently skip questions and forget to return to them. Every semester, a couple of students will leave some questions blank on my Torts exam. Since I don't penalize students for wrong answers, the only explanation is that they skipped the questions and forgot to go back and fill them in.

8. Don't be afraid to change your initial answer. You've probably heard the conventional wisdom that you should not change your initial answers to multiple-choice questions because it's more likely you will change an answer from right to wrong than from wrong to right. I heard this advice my entire life, starting in elementary school. Well, guess what? It's completely backwards. Study after study, some of them dating back to the 1920s, consistently show that changing multiple-choice answers is more likely to increase, rather than decrease, test scores. As just one of many examples, a study of upper-level accounting students showed that 95 percent of the students changed answers on their multiple-choice examinations (changing a total of 5.6 percent of the answers). Fifty-six percent of the answers were changed from wrong to right, while only 21 percent were changed from right to wrong. The remaining 23 percent were changed from one wrong answer to another wrong answer.[66] These results are consistent with other studies.

9. Answer all the questions. If time is about to run out and you haven't finished, pencil in an answer for every question. Unless you've been told otherwise by your professor, points won't be deducted for wrong answers. You might be better off choosing the same answer for all unfinished questions (e.g., choose all a-answers or all d-answers). That should assure you of at least some right answers. In case you're wondering, I looked for, but didn't find any research as to whether random guessers are better off picking any particular uniform answer; that is, whether it's better to go, for example, with all d-answers rather than all b-answers.

10. Practice, practice, practice. The best way to get a handle on law school multiple-choice questions is to practice working through a large number of them. Unfortunately, your professors are unlikely to provide you with many, if any, multiple-choice questions as samples because, more so than essay questions, crafting valid, reliable, and fair multiple-choice questions is difficult and time-consuming. (A bit of bad news here: some professors draft really lousy multiple-choice questions and/or borrow questions from other sources without revising them to fit the material the professor covered or the way he or she taught it.) Fortunately, sample multiple-choice questions are available from a number of other sources. CALI (Computer–Assisted Legal Instruction) exercises, which are accessible to law students without charge, are one good option. Several of the study aids listed in Appendix A feature practice multiple-choice questions. Books published for bar review courses, such as Kaplan PMBR and BarBri, contain loads of sample questions. You can sometimes acquire copies of these books from recent graduates who have completed the bar exam. The actual MBE itself is not released to the public on a regular basis, but a couple of previous exams have been made available. Look for them in the law library.

---

66. *See* Marshall A. Geiger, *On the Benefit of Changing Multiple–Choice An-* *swers: Student Perception and Performance,* 117 EDUC. 108 (1996).

Don't get bogged down in fretting about the specifics of practice questions. Some practice questions you encounter may be poorly written or thought-out. Some questions will address the law differently than your professor did. Focus on the format. Your goal in doing practice questions is to get a feel for the nature of MBE-type multiple-choice questions, not to learn the fine points of law.

As with the essay questions included as Appendices B and C, sample multiple-choice questions are of limited usefulness for readers without a background of relevant legal knowledge. Nevertheless, to give you a taste of what to expect, here's a sample Torts multiple-choice question I've used on past exams:

Sample Multiple–Choice Question

Tricia, an eight-year-old girl of below-average intelligence, received a pair of in-line skates for Christmas and couldn't wait to try them out. The moment her family members finished opening their presents, Tricia donned the skates and took off down the sidewalk. Unfortunately, Tricia could not figure out how to fasten the buckles properly. She made it only about 100 yards when the buckles came lose, causing her to lose her balance and careen into the street. June Cleaver had been driving through the neighborhood for some time, trying to locate her ex-husband Ward's new house (Ward was behind on child support and June intended to collect it personally). Many children were outside playing with their new Christmas toys. Seeing the children, June was careful to drive at exactly the 30 mph posted speed limit. She was coming down Tricia's street when Tricia zoomed out into the street on her new skates directly in front of June's car. June slammed on her brakes immediately, but was unable to stop in time to avoid running into Tricia. If Tricia sues June for negligence, the best result is that June should:

(a) Win, because she was going the speed limit.

(b) Lose, because she failed to exercise reasonable care under the circumstances.

(c) Win, because of the emergency doctrine.

(d) Win, because Tricia's actions constituted an unforeseeable superseding cause.

No point in going into an extended analysis of the law, but the correct answer is (b). As you'll learn in Torts, the general standard of care under negligence law is "reasonable care *under the circumstances.*" As circumstances change, the *amount* of care that is required by a person can go up or down. Normally, driving within the speed limit is reasonable care (answer (a)), but the question says that "[m]any children were outside playing." A reasonable person, under those circumstances, would have driven slower than the 30 mph posted speed limit. The emergency doctrine—answer (c)—would be a tempting answer for Torts students. This doctrine recognizes that one acting in response to an emergency situation is not expected to exercise as much care as one who has time to weigh and deliberate the consequences of their conduct. No facts, however, suggest that June behaved or responded differently because of the emergency situation. She simply didn't have time to stop because she was driving too fast. Thus, (c) is not as good an answer as (b). Remember, you are always looking for the *best* answer. As for (d), Tricia's actions do not constitute an unforeseeable superseding cause that would relieve June of liability for her negligence. While the law of superseding causes is complicated, suffice it to say that, given the facts, it was quite foreseeable that a child could dart in front of the car. The facts about Tricia's below-average intelligence are a red herring. They would be relevant only if Tricia's contributory negligence was the call of the question—which is not the case.

Again, this is just to give you a taste of what's coming. Before any of your real exams, you'll want to practice many sample questions.

CHAPTER 17

LEGAL RESEARCH AND WRITING: AN INTERVIEW WITH FIVE EXPERTS

While first-year doctrinal courses differ in content, most of them are extremely similar in format. They each will involve similar daily reading assignments of judicial opinions from a casebook, some mix of Socratic Q and A and lecture about those cases in class, and the same single-exam evaluation method at the end of the semester. Whether it's Civil Procedure, Contracts, Criminal Law, Property or Torts, the quest for first-year success will follow a similar path and require similar tools and strategies. Thus, nearly all of the advice in this book applies equally to each of the traditional doctrinal courses in the first-year curriculum.

But Legal Research and Writing will be wildly different from your other first-year courses. Year after year, a disproportionate amount of the fretting and angst-letting I hear from 1Ls has to do with their legal research and writing courses. For every student gripe about Contracts or Property or Torts, I hear five about Legal Research and Writing.

That the subject commands such out-of-balance attention from students alone makes it a candidate for its own chapter, but there's a more pressing reason for giving extended, separate treatment to legal research and writing courses: *they are the most important courses you will take in law school.* Five legal writing professors from different law schools will help explain why in more detail below, but the reasons are nicely summed up in this observation by Professor David

Walter: "Because this is what lawyers do every hour, every day, every year of their careers—they speak and they write—and when they're not speaking and writing, they're listening and reading."

Legal research and writing courses are part of the mandatory first-year curriculum at nearly every law school. They almost always extend through both semesters (as in Legal Research and Writing I and Legal Research and Writing II). Roughly a quarter of law schools require a third legal writing course in the fall semester of the second year. Legal research and writing course packages travel under a variety of names, including Legal Research and Writing, Lawyering, Legal Method, Legal Skills and Values, and Legal Writing and Analysis. From here on I'll just refer to the courses generically as "legal writing," while recognizing that all legal writing courses also teach legal research skills and most have an oral advocacy component.

Some schools have added other skills components to legal writing courses in recent years, such as negotiation and client counseling exercises. But in all legal writing courses, the fundamental goal is to teach students how to research and analyze legal issues and effectively communicate their analyses in writing and orally. If the purpose of the other first-year courses is to teach students to "think like a lawyer," it could be said that the goal of legal writing is to train students to "write like a lawyer thinks." Legal writing isn't about how to construct sentences. It's about how to conduct and convey legal analysis in a written form.

As a teacher of doctrinal subjects, I'm smarter than to give advice about an area that is so different from my milieu. Hey, I didn't get to be a law professor for nothing. So I asked for, and gratefully received, extensive help with this chapter from five experienced legal writing professors in the form of their answers to a series of pointed questions raising issues common to legal writing courses at all law schools. The Q and A with these five experts is the highlight of this chapter. But before we get to it, here's an overview of some of the common components—and frustrations—of legal writing courses.

An Introduction to Legal Writing Courses
Legal research.

Typically, legal writing begins with a research component, which usually includes exercises designed to train students to find and use different types of legal resources in the law library (e.g., case reporters, digests, legal encyclopedias). Depending on the school, the person teaching you legal research may be a member of the legal writing faculty, a law librarian, a student teaching assistant, a Westlaw or Lexis–Nexis representative or some combination of these folks.

Law schools are still searching for the proper balance between old and new when it comes to teaching legal research skills. Should students continue to be forced to learn the old ways of doing book research in a technological world where legal research is increasingly performed online through computer databases such as Westlaw and Lexis–Nexis? Schools differ in their answers. Some schools limit computer research until students have been taught book research, while others give students keys to the online world of legal research from the beginning.

It's important to first learn how to do legal research with real books, just like it's important that elementary school students learn how to do basic math before giving them calculators. Knowing how to do book research makes students better computer researchers because they better understand the sources with which they're working, which are the same whether the medium is papyrus or megabytes. Moreover, while law students enjoy the luxury of free access to legal research databases (in part to get them hooked), lawyers have to pay substantial fees for these same services. As a result, many law firms still require lawyers to do old-fashioned book research.

The law office memorandum.

Shortly into the first semester of legal writing, students begin working on their first legal writing project: an internal law office memorandum from an associate (you) to a fictitious partner analyzing the law as applied to a given set of facts. These memos, common in real-life law practice, basically ask you to take a client's situation and explain and analyze it so the partner can make informed decisions about the client's case, which may include the decision whether to accept the case or pass on it.

It's common to assign two such memoranda in the first semester, often denoted as the "minor memo" (the first one) and the "major memo" (the second one). Often, the minor memo will be a "closed universe memo," meaning the professor will provide students with all the necessary research, while the major memo will be an "open universe memo," meaning you will do the research yourself. Other first-semester writing assignments can include client letters (i.e., a letter from a lawyer to his or her client) or drafting a contract or pleading.

Researching and composing an office memorandum requires a ton of hard work. As a student consultant wrote: "The mountains of research you find either in the library or online will seem never-ending and you may feel, as I did, that you are often going in circles with very little, if any, direction."

Filleted by feedback.

"You write well, but made a substantive error of malpractice dimensions." Youch! This comment, scribbled by my legal writing instructor on the last page of my major memo assignment introduced me to the harsh realities of law school grading. Like many law students, I was used to As and praise in my previous educational experiences. Now I had a professor telling me that I screwed up so badly I could get sued for it.

One of the biggest practical differences between legal writing and other first-year courses is that students get performance feedback in legal writing, often including letter grades, as they go through the semester. That feedback is often negative and painful.

One can almost hear the self-esteem bubbles bursting when the first wave of legal writing feedback is distributed. Standing in class on those days looking out at rows of morose faces, I feel I should be delivering a eulogy instead of a Torts lecture. As one student put it: "As law students, the majority of us are used to receiving As and when you get that first draft of your first memorandum back with a C- on it (and believe me, this happens even to the students who finish at the top of the class), it can be discouraging." She should know. She's ranked second in her class.

The credit-hour crunch.

The single most iterated 1L gripe (and that's saying a lot) is that the workload required for legal writing is disproportionately heavy compared to the credit hours allocated. Usually, the workload for a law school course corresponds to the number of credit hours for the course. But we reversed everything for legal writing. We require a lot more work for fewer credit hours (usually two). Students complain that this allocation is completely arbitrary, but they're wrong. It's all done according to a highly scientific, mathematical formula:

$$x/y = 2 \text{ credit hours}$$

with x being the number of hours required to master legal writing (rounded to the nearest million) and y being the number necessary to make the answer equal two credit hours.

Hey, just kidding. On the other hand, the real reasons for why legal writing courses get the short end of the credit-hour stick, which our experts discuss below, aren't likely to be much more satisfying to you. Most law schools have or are taking steps to alleviate the disparity. Nevertheless, credit hours allocated to legal writing still lag behind those for doctrinal courses. In 2007, credit hours for legal writing averaged 2.36 hours in the fall and 2.21 hours in the spring, compared to three or four credit hours for the doctrinal courses.

Citation style.

Another component of legal writing courses that students find frustrating is learning legal citation style. "Citation style" refers to the form and format in which legal authorities (such as cases, law review articles, books) are referenced or documented.

The standard legal citation manual is *The Bluebook: A Uniform System of Citation* (18th ed. 2005). The *Bluebook* tells legal writers what citation information to include (e.g., volume, page number, date), what font to put it in (e.g., big and small caps, italics), when to use abbreviations and what they should look like, where to insert commas and periods, and many other details. It's somewhat similar to the MLA (Modern Language Association) style book you might have used in undergraduate school, except far more detailed and complex. Look at the footnotes to this book for samples of what *Bluebook* citation style looks like.

The *Bluebook* is famously hyper-technical and obsessed with minutia. I had to laugh when I read a comment from one of my student consultants advising new students to pay attention to the *Bluebook* because an entire letter grade can be lost on a writing assignment "if you leave off just one comma!" The comment brought back memories of a humor column I published several years ago in the *American Bar Association Journal* satirizing a *Bluebook* rule that required a comma in a particular place under particular circumstances. An excerpt will give you a taste of what you're up against when dealing with the *Bluebook*. The setting for the column was a mock meeting of the board of *Bluebook* editors:

Irving: We need that ******* comma! Rule 15.2 means nothing without The Comma. I'll gladly die for it.

Frieda: *Accord.* [A *Bluebook* reference.]

Dan: *Accord.*

Wendy: Put down the gun, Irving. The *Bluebook* was meant to bring peace.

Irving: Not until I have proof of everyone's commitment to The Comma. I've decided to quit law school and become addicted to amphetamines so I can contemplate The Comma twenty-four hours a day.

Dan: I'm going to have Rule 15.2 tattooed on my thigh, right below the rules for Separately Bound Legislative Histories.

Frieda: I'll cut out my husband's entrails and form them into the shape of one huge comma.

Irving: What about you Wendy?

Wendy: My parents died in a plane crash yesterday. I have to go to the funeral.

Irving: Doesn't The Comma mean anything to you?

Wendy: Alright, I'll send flowers.

While the *Bluebook* is the historically dominant legal citation manual, many law schools use the more recently developed *ALWD Citation Manual: A Professional System of Citation* (3d ed. 2006). When the *ALWD Citation Manual* was first published, its simplified approach to legal citation style earned the book instant acclaim and popularity. Which citation manual to adopt for legal writing courses—*Bluebook* vs. *ALWD Citation Manual*—has been and continues to be a source of debate at many law schools. For a time it looked as though the *ALWD Citation Manual* might overtake the *Bluebook*, but the scale may be tilting back to the old standard.[67]

Several law schools have switched back to the *Bluebook* after adopting the *ALWD Citation Manual* in response to complaints from students who entered the legal job market to find that their bosses—who were schooled in the old classic—expected them to know the *Bluebook*. But as Professor Joan Malmud explains, what most attorneys are looking for is *professional, consistent* citation style that complies with court rules in the particular jurisdiction:

> When most practicing attorneys went to school, only the *Bluebook* existed. The word "Bluebook" is like "Xerox" to many lawyers. "Bluebook" has become a generic word for "citing professionally," just as "Xerox" has become a generic word for "photocopying." If a student were told to go "Xerox" a document, he wouldn't say, "I can't. The office has only Canon copiers." Likewise, when practitioners tell students to "Bluebook" a document, often what they mean is that they want consistent, professional citing, and either the *Bluebook* or the *ALWD Citation Manual* will do that.

Excellent observation, but it should be noted that some lawyers and judges, and nearly all law reviews, really do expect true *Bluebook* citation style. Regardless of which manual is used, it's important to pay attention to citation style and get it right. Not only can bad citation skills lose you points on your assignments in legal writing and other courses with writing requirements, it can haunt you in the real legal world.

The second-semester appellate brief and oral argument.

In the second semester, legal writing usually includes a written and oral advocacy component. Typically, students are required to research and write an entire appellate brief and

67. The Association of Legal Writing Directors 2007 survey showed: 102 directors use the *Bluebook* in their programs, forty-six use the *ALWD Citation Manual* (down from fifty-six in 2005), fifteen use both, and ten leave the decision to the individual professor. ASS'N OF LEGAL WRITING DIRS., *supra*, at 16.

make an oral argument to a panel of mock judges. The brief, which can run upward of fifty pages, is excruciatingly time-consuming and the subject of much complaining by second-semester students.

As for the oral argument, it's the most exciting, but also the most terrifying, event of the first year. It's exciting because the oral argument is often the first law school exercise in which students get to act and feel like "real lawyers" (meaning, in the minds of 1Ls, the lawyers they see on television, who, unlike real lawyers, are always in court). The terror aspect derives from a generalized fear of public speaking accentuated by the fact that oral arguments amount to a public interrogation (they're not monologues—the judges drill students with lots of questions) in which every utterance is critically scrutinized.

It's normal to be nervous about public speaking. Surveys show that public speaking ranks higher than death on lists of people's greatest fears. Seinfeld had a great monologue line about these surveys to the effect that they mean that at a funeral, the average person would rather be the guy in the casket than the one delivering the eulogy. I was so nervous about my oral argument back in law school that I showed up on the wrong day! I arrived at school all spiffed-out in my suit, ready to go, and started freaking out when I couldn't find the correct room. Sweating buckets, I frantically searched the law school for my professor and judging panel only to finally figure out my argument wasn't until the next day. At least I was a day early instead of a day late. I got a good laugh out of it once I was released from the coronary unit.

Looking back, the oral argument still stands out as one of the most memorable, albeit most nerve-wracking, events of law school. A student consultant, quiet by nature, wrote that the "mere thought of having to stand in front of others and argue makes you nauseous." To help her get through the experience, she wrote the reminder to "BREATHE" at the top of her notes. She did fine though, as most students do, in part because they put so much time into the preparation. Sometimes the quietest students shine the brightest in the oral arguments. So don't underestimate yourself. A great oral advocate may be lurking beneath your shy exterior.

Balancing legal writing workloads
with other courses.

One sound piece of advice I can offer—before getting to the advice from our legal writing experts—is to take legal writing seriously and give it your best, but not at the expense of neglecting your other courses. Keep in mind that from a cost-benefit analysis, your doctrinal courses are worth more credit hours, meaning they will weigh more in your cumulative GPA.

On days when major assignments are due in legal writing, class attendance can drop off by a third or more. Professors find such major drop-offs to be irritating and may take them personally. I know professors who intentionally test on material covered in class on days when there are large numbers of absences. At one school, in a faculty email exchange over this issue, a professor commented that the dismal attendance in his class on the due date of a legal writing assignment was "unfortunate" for the students because "[t]oday's materials will find their way onto my exam."

Finding the proper balance can be difficult. In general, I'd say most students err by giving too much attention (much of it in the form of inefficient research and profitless hand-wringing and complaining) to legal writing at the expense of their doctrinal classes, but legal writing profs might disagree.

An Interview with Five Legal Writing Professors

Five outstanding, experienced legal writing professors generously agreed to share their thoughts about a variety of key issues common to all legal research and writing courses. Here's our all-star lineup, in alphabetical order:

Kimberly Boone is the director of the legal writing program at the University of Alabama School of Law, where she graduated Order of Coif and was a member of the law review. She worked several years in employment litigation before joining academia in 2000.

Chris Coughlin is the director of the legal writing program at Wake Forest University School of Law. She holds a joint appointment at the Wake Forest medical school's Translational Science Institute and is a co-director of a university program in bioethics and health policy.

Joan Malmud is a legal writing professor at the University of Oregon. Prior to joining academia, she clerked for a federal judge in California and worked in the litigation department at a corporate law firm in New York City.

Sandy Patrick is a legal writing professor at Lewis & Clark Law School in Portland, Oregon. Previously, she taught at Wake Forest University. Prior to entering academia, she served as a law clerk to a state appellate judge, an assistant state attorney general doing criminal appeals, and as a practicing attorney doing civil litigation.

David D. Walter is a professor at Florida International-al University School of Law (FIU) with nearly twenty years' experience teaching legal writing. Previously, he taught at Seattle University and Mercer University. He also teaches upper-level skills courses and directs an educational center for appellate advocacy and practice skills.

In addition to their other credentials, Professors Coughlin, Malmud, and Patrick are co-authors of *A Lawyer Writes* (Carolina Academic Press 2008), a legal writing book for first-year students. Check out their book for expanded discussion of some of the points they make below.

Our five experts answered a list of fifteen important questions about legal writing courses, including many questions that bear a direct connection to success or failure in those courses.

1. Let's get this one out of the way first. For twenty years as a law prof, I've listened to students gripe that legal research and writing courses require too much time and effort in return for too few credit hours. I recall having the same complaint as a law student and have heard many legal writing professors echo it as well. What's your response to that criticism, what explains the imbalance, and are things changing in that regard?

BOONE: I agree with this criticism and address it with my students. If students view the work they put into legal writing solely as an investment in the two graded credit hours they receive each semester (which is a typical credit-hour allotment), they will be very frustrated. Students should look at the time invested in both legal research and legal writing as learning a new language they will need to be fluent in to do well in all their courses and in future jobs as well.

The imbalance may be explained by the fact that teaching legal writing as a separate course is a relatively new idea. Some law professors still feel strongly that our students should be able to learn legal writing on their own as law students once did. Some doctrinal law profs (i.e., teachers of Torts, Contracts, etc.) may not want to give more credits to legal writing because they feel students already spend too much time on our assignments and don't want students spending even more time away from their traditional first-year classes.

Legal writing professionals across the country continue to push toward more credit hours for our students. It's a slow process, but changes are occurring.

MALMUD: I also agree with the criticism. In their first semester, students have so much to learn about basic legal research and analytical skills. It's all new to them. To develop these skills, they must practice, and practice takes time. The traditional two credit hours are simply not enough.

Academia is a funny world, so explaining why anything happens is a tricky task, but here's my two-part guess: The imbalance reflects, first, the historical distinction the legal academy drew between doctrinal classes and skills classes. Doctrinal classes—classes that teach doctrine, such as Contracts and Torts—were typically viewed as more intellectually complex and, therefore, more worthy of classroom time. Skills classes, by contrast, were seen as less intellectually complex and therefore less needful of classroom time. There may also have been an assumption that students would learn skills on the job—an assumption that no longer holds. As a result, skills classes were allocated fewer credits.

Second, credit hours are like turf. Reallocating credit hours means one faculty member has to cede turf to another faculty member. To the extent that credit hours are seen as reflecting the importance of a class, shifting hours away from one subject to another suggests that one class is less important than another.

Thus, change is a delicate matter. Things are changing for the better, but sometimes change occurs more slowly than we might like.

PATRICK: I always tell my students that their legal writing course will be much like their first job as an attorney—they will work long hours, invest a lot of time and energy into their projects, and probably not get the kind of acclaim (pecuniary or otherwise) they want for the work. I stress that they will, however, get invaluable remuneration of a different kind: Students will learn foundational skills for their legal career, and get plenty of valuable feedback along the way.

Although legal research and writing courses have not historically received the credit hours the subject merits, more and more schools are acknowledging the importance of the course by giving it more credit hours. One reason for the lack of credit hours is that this course of study is relatively new, often being adopted by schools just in the last two decades. Older law school administrators and doctrinal faculty did not have such a course when they attended school. Now we've reached the point where most current law professors took legal writing while they were in school and recognize its importance.

2. For students who recognize they have writing deficiencies, is there anything they can do to help themselves succeed in their first-year legal writing courses before they begin law school?

COUGHLIN: If a student knows he or she has a writing deficiency, I recommend the following—not only to succeed in their first-year legal writing courses, but to succeed in law school and the profession: Start by buying and studying a basic grammar and style book or program. There are many on the market. Accept that learning basic rules of grammar, punctuation, and parts of speech may not be exciting or fun. No "instant gratification" is involved. One student who took it on himself to upgrade his writing skills after his first year of law school analogized his summer remedial writing activities to repeatedly sticking a fork in his knee.

The nature of the deficiency, along with the nature of the individual learning style, must be assessed. Each student is unique and learns differently, and there is no magic pill or process to cure all deficiencies. If the deficiency involves simply a lack of knowledge, step one above might be sufficient. If the deficiency is more serious, the student should consider being tested for a learning difference or disability. If the deficiency rises to the level of a disability, such as dysgraphia (which is a neurological disorder characterized by writing disability), the school may be able to provide reasonable accommodations to help the student succeed. Obviously, any such disability would need to be documented by a medical provider and that information communicated to the law school as soon as possible.

To remedy any deficiency, a student must understand how he or she learns best. To do this, the student should look back on her educational career, and determine whether there is a common denominator in the teachers, environments, situations, and subjects in which she responded most positively and successfully. Everybody learns differently and everybody writes differently.

MALMUD: Learning to write well is a lifelong process that should start well before law school begins and continue long after law school ends. There are no quick fixes.

That said, I recommend that all students read William Strunk and E.B. White's classic *The Elements of Style*. We should probably all read it once a year. Another great book on writing is Richard Wydick's *Plain English for Lawyers*. Both books cover the basics of clear, concise writing.

Once the student gets to law school, if she is still concerned, she should go to her legal writing professor to discuss her concerns. Her professor may have some helpful suggestions, especially if the student has submitted a writing assignment and the professor has had a chance to review the student's writing.

Finally, the student should become a critical reader. During law school, students see a lot of writing—mostly appellate opinions. Some appellate opinions are well written. Others are not. The distinction between work that is well written and work that is not is whether you can understand it. If you can't understand what the writer is trying to convey, the writer has failed. So when you cannot understand what you are reading, ask *why*. What could the writer have done differently? If you find yourself blissfully gliding through your reading, ask *why*. What has the writer done to make the ideas easy to absorb? By asking why some writing is effective and other writing is not, you will begin to develop better judgment about your own writing.

WALTER: Even students with serious writing deficiencies can improve their writing. The first step, of course, is often the most difficult—recognizing that you, the writer, have writing deficiencies. Sure, Cs and Ds in English classes and other courses with major writing requirements are a good clue, but I've seen several writers with serious problems who received Bs and even As in undergraduate courses with extensive writing requirements.

Once the need for assistance is recognized, several avenues are available for students who want to improve their writing. First, there are plenty of professors and tutors in English departments, other departments, and college "writing centers" who are willing to help students correct those writing deficiencies—find them ASAP and ask for their help! Ask them to read samples of your writing. Ask them to look for organizational issues—do your sentences and thoughts seem to flow together in a logical manner? Ask them to check for mechanics issues—are your commas in the right place, is your word usage proper, and is your grammar correct? Ask them to examine the "readability" of your writing—is your writing clear, do you use words precisely, and are you concise in your writing?

Second, as suggested above, find a good "style" book and give it a careful review. That should give you a better idea about some of the topics you'll see in legal writing.

Third, review and critique a few of your writings and the writings of others to evaluate your deficiencies—if you can spot the problems in your past writings or the writings of others, you have taken one more step toward improving your writing in law school and beyond. The idea here is to learn how to read very carefully and with a critical eye.

Even excellent writers will benefit greatly from following the steps outlined above.

3. Is it common for students to enter law school entertaining mistaken assumptions about the nature of "legal writing"? What are those misconceptions?

BOONE: One of the most common misconceptions is that being a strong writer in other fields or being an English major necessarily translates to being good at legal writing.

This is not always the case. Different undergraduate majors both help and hinder you in legal writing. For example, English majors may love to write and know what it means to write in the active voice, but might have a terrible time learning to be more concise and direct. Math and engineering majors may sometimes forget to write in complete sentences, but they may pick up on legal analysis more quickly.

Students may also assume that they can use the same processes they used for college papers on their legal writing assignments. This will not work. The research is different, the citation style is different, and the analysis is new. Let's be brutally honest. Somewhere along the way, many of you wrote a paper shortly before (or even the night before) it was due. If you received a good grade, you may have made a habit of it.

Be forewarned that this will not work in legal writing for several reasons. First, good legal writing may look simple, but it usually requires long hours and multiple drafts to make complex ideas look simple. Second, you may not realize you are lost until you actually start writing. If you start assignments early, you'll have time to ask for help if you need it. And finally, as if you won't hear this enough, all of your law school classmates were at the top of their classes too. Your work will be judged in relation to other good students.

COUGHLIN: One misconception is that legal writing drains your creativity. The reason for this misconception is many legal writing professors require that students use a mnemonic (a specific order) to structure their legal arguments. For example, commonly used mnemonics in legal writing include "IRAC" (Issue, Rule, Application, Conclusion—pronounced similarly but not to be confused with IRAQ)—and "CREAC" (Conclusion, Rule, Explanation, Application, Conclusion).

In reality, using a mnemonic structure should not limit the creative process. Mnemonics are supposed to be flexible tools, not rigid formulas. They provide an effective starting point for drafting a legal analysis. The substance of your analysis—the way you frame your legal arguments and your unique application of the law—is necessarily creative.

To illustrate this point, think of the poetry form of haiku, a Japanese form of unrhymed poetry that is always three lines long, with five syllables in the first line, seven syllables in the second line, and five syllables in the third. While the haiku is written in a strict form, the writer has freedom within the substance of the poem to be creative. Likewise, while the legal writer may use a preset organizational structure, outstanding legal arguments build bridges between prior cases and new sets of facts, a skill that mandates creativity. As my colleague Professor Miki Felsenburg says to her students: "Bore me with your organization and thrill me with your analysis."

PATRICK: I agree with what Professor Boone said that one great misconception about legal writing is that researching and analyzing a legal problem will mirror the work students did for term papers in undergraduate school. This misconception arises in large part because new law students don't understand that legal writing is not just about "writing." It's about something much more complex—legal *thinking*. Committing sound analysis to paper requires far more skill than knowing the parts of a paragraph, how to use commas, or whether the period goes inside the quotation mark (it does). Legal writing requires students to find the law that governs a client's issue, discern the relevant parts of the law, weave those parts into a cohesive explanation, and apply it to a client's fact situation. Doing all of those things requires the student to mentally engage the material with critical reading, thinking, and questioning.

4. I commonly tell students that their legal research and writing courses may be the most important courses in law school and I'm sure you would agree. How would you explain to students why that is so?

MALMUD: Legal writing teaches the must-have skills to be a successful attorney. I promptly forgot most everything I learned in Contracts, Civil Procedure, and Constitutional Law within hours of taking the exams. On the job, though, that wasn't a problem. I worked for big fancy law firms and for government agencies but none of my employers expected me to remember much substantive law. My employers did expect me to know how to research the substantive law, synthesize it into a coherent explanation of the law that would apply to a client's problem, and then write my analysis in a clear and compelling way. I learned those skills primarily in my legal writing class.

PATRICK: From their first day of orientation, my students hear the proclamation that legal writing is the most important class they will have in law school. They initially hear those words from me (whom they might not believe), but soon hear them echoed by upper-division students, practicing attorneys, and prospective employers. Each year I invite guest speakers to class—upper-level students, law clerks, or attorneys. Invariably, without my solicitation, they confirm the notion that legal writing is the most important class in law school. Why? Because it teaches students the core skills for legal learning: how to assess law, think about law, and communicate law to someone else. Effective lawyering requires those skills. An attorney can know everything there is to know about tort law, but if he cannot assimilate law relevant to a client's issue and communicate his analysis, that attorney will not effectively represent his client.

WALTER: I do agree! I tell my 1Ls on the first day that legal writing courses are the most important courses in law school. Written and oral communication skills are so critical to everything lawyers do. In two American Bar Foundation studies, the lawyers polled overwhelmingly identified oral communication skills and written communication skills as the two skills/knowledge bases that are most important to lawyers. They ranked "knowledge of substantive law" as seventh in importance.[68]

The researchers also surveyed hiring partners to determine the most important skills students should learn in law school. The top three skills? Library legal research, oral communication, and written communication. Knowledge of substantive law came in a distant eleventh place.[69]

Why are oral and written communication skills more important than knowledge of the substantive law? Because this is what lawyers do every hour, every day, every year of their careers—they speak and they write—and when they're not speaking and writing, they're listening and reading.

5. The standard major assignment in most first-semester legal writing courses is the law office memorandum written from junior associate to senior part-

---

68. *See* Bryant G. Garth & Joanne Martin, *Law Schools and the Construction of Competence*, 43 J. LEGAL EDUC. 469, 473 tbl.1 (1993).

69. *Id.* at 490 tbl.11.

ner. **Why is the office memorandum still seen as the most effective or important vehicle for teaching legal writing to 1Ls as opposed to, say, drafting pleadings or legislation or some other type of assignment? Related to that question, I'm sure 1Ls often wonder what drives the content of legal writing courses. Any insights on that point?**

BOONE: The *process* required to write the memorandum is what makes it a good first-semester tool. The office memo, at least as we teach it, requires the students to research two legal issues and analyze them objectively. We ask the students to write an interoffice memo (from associate to partner within the same firm) to train students to fully and objectively evaluate legal issues, rather than argue for or against a certain result. For example, in a civil suit, we may ask the student to evaluate two issues to help determine whether the firm (the student's fictitious employer) should take the case. Even with an assignment structured this way, most first-year students struggle with the notion that we aren't seeking a single "right answer." In other words, I could usually care less whether the student concludes the firm should take the case. I'm much more concerned with whether the student has thoroughly researched and analyzed the issues and fully explained the reasons both for and against taking the case.

The content of our legal writing course is driven in part by a desire to prepare students well for their first summer jobs. An in-house memo is the type of assignment our students are most likely to be assigned in those jobs.

Learning to explain legal rules and apply them to a fact scenario also helps students develop the skills they will need to write effective exam answers.

COUGHLIN: While some students complain that the office memo is dated, it remains the optimal vehicle for beginning law students to develop analytical skills. It is also important, of course, to learn to effectively draft pleadings and legislation, but those skills are more sophisticated, technical, and require knowledge of litigation and/or legislative processes. Such exercises are better taught after the students have completed Civil Procedure and/or a legislation or administrative law course or seminar.

Typically, most legal writing programs begin by assigning an office memorandum with a closed universe of research (that means that three or four cases are provided to the students and the analysis is limited to using those materials). The students must critically read and parse the cases, extract the governing rules, and distinguish between relevant and irrelevant facts from the prior cases. These are fundamental skills all lawyers must develop.

Among other things, composing a law office memorandum teaches students two types of basic legal reasoning skills: (1) *rule-based reasoning*, where the student applies the language of a rule to a client's facts to predict an outcome; and (2) *analogical reasoning*, where the student shows that the client's case is sufficiently similar to, or different from, previous cases that the outcomes in the previous cases either should or should not control the client's case.

PATRICK: Legal writing professors still use the legal memorandum as the primary vehicle for a writing assignment because it requires engaged analysis and exemplifies the type of assignments students will most likely be doing early in their legal careers.

Legal memoranda require law students to analyze a legal issue by going through the same process they will use as attorneys. Attorneys typically will research the issue, assess how the law fits together, and then apply that law to the client's case. This type of direct analysis and application of law to facts often requires a deeper level of critical reading and thinking skills that are not always necessary when drafting pleadings, regulations, or statutory text.

Attorneys, particularly those in the private sector, will likely draft more legal memos than they can count during their first years of practice. In two years as an associate at a large law firm, I drafted three times more legal memos than I did pleadings, briefs, interrogatories, and other documents combined.

Legal memoranda are relevant to students for another reason: A memorandum assignment simulates what the students will be asked to do on most of their first-year exams. Most exams during the first year ask students to predict an outcome for a factual scenario and support their decision with the law they know. Although exams have certain differences from the office memo, both assignments ask students to assess a problem, discern and apply the relevant law, and communicate a cogent answer.

6. If you had to list just three hallmarks of an outstanding law office memorandum, what would be they be? Conversely, if you had to list three hallmarks of a poor law office memorandum, what would they be?

COUGHLIN: "The Outstanding Office Memorandum" is:

1. A direct and precise response to the question being asked. The writer tells the reader up front what the specific issue is being analyzed, as well as the predicted outcome. The body of the memorandum—the analysis—does not go off on tangents but builds bridges between each point to reach a conclusion.

2. A clear, concise response using plain English. As my colleague Professor Barbara Lentz puts it, if you wouldn't use the word when ordering at McDonald's, don't use it in your office memorandum. So just as you wouldn't say "Herewith my hamburger, french fries would be a most effective side dish and, accordingly, supersize me," when ordering at the drive-thru, do not use that type of language or sentence structure in your memorandum. For maximum clarity and effectiveness, use the KISS theory (Keep it Simple, Stupid).

3. A response that shows all steps of the analytical process. An outstanding office memorandum can be thought of as a math problem in elementary school. Simply getting to the correct solution or prediction is not enough. You must show your work.

Conversely, "The Not So Outstanding Office Memorandum" is:

1. A response that is overly formal in style. Students sometimes think that if they write formally their reader will not realize the writer did not take enough time or did not understand the analysis. When students are confused, they think that if they use eighteenth-century prose, the professor will not realize that they did not spend enough time to understand the links between the cases and/or build the necessary analytical bridges between them.

2. A response that is written in the passive voice. While there are strategic uses of the passive voice (i.e., "mistakes were made" rather than "the defendant made a mistake"), consistent use of the passive voice is a red flag that tells your legal writing professor one of the following: (1) I haven't

spent enough time on this memo. One can think back to Samuel Clemens' (Mark Twain) famous quote "I apologize for the length of this letter, but I didn't have time to make it shorter."; or (2) I don't understand this analysis, but if I use really complex language maybe my legal writing professor will think I am really smart.

3. A response that is fraught with *Bluebook* errors, typographical errors and formatting errors. Typically, there is a correlation between a lack of precision in analysis and a lack of precision in style. Errors with these "finer points" distract a reader from the analysis and limit the amount of confidence a reader has in the writer's prediction of the outcome.

PATRICK: I agree wholeheartedly with Professor Coughlin's comments regarding the hallmarks of a good memo, so let me concentrate on the hallmarks of a bad one. Local attorneys at large law firms in our city recently asked our Legal Writing and Analysis department to conduct a seminar instructing young associate attorneys on how to improve their writing. The partners articulated a fairly consistent list of problems with which associates struggle. Those problems mirror the hallmarks of a poorly written law office memorandum:

1. Poor organization. Often neither the overall presentation of issues nor the component substantive parts within each issue are presented in a logical, clear order that the reader can follow, absorb, and understand.

2. The legal substance of the memo is not clearly communicated to the reader. The paragraphs fail to signal their points, leaving the reader lost as to what each paragraph will prove. The law may not be fully explained. Additionally, the memo may be organized around cases instead of legal points, with the writer failing to show how the cases fit together. The application of the law to the client's facts often has leaps in logic, leaving the reader unclear about how legal precedent requires a particular outcome for the client's case.

3. The product is not professional. Often, because of time constraints so prevalent in law practice, memos are rife with errors—typographical errors, poor grammatical choices, inappropriate punctuation, and poor citation. The overall effect of the errors paints the attorney as either lax or incompetent.

Ironically, writing an outstanding memorandum does not take that much more time than writing a poor one. A little extra time spent organizing the research, mapping out the most logical flow of arguments, and polishing the final draft can transform a mediocre memorandum into a great one.

WALTER: First, the most important hallmark of an outstanding office memo is its selection and development of the law (i.e., relevant cases, statutes, regulations, and so forth). Accuracy is critically important because the writer is flying solo—no one else is researching and analyzing the issues—so the writer must get it right the first time. If the writer fails to find or discuss a key case, or if the writer explains the case or the legal rule poorly, the attorney relying on the memo may give the client inaccurate legal advice. Thus, the writer's most important task is to find the appropriate law and explain it accurately.

The second hallmark of an outstanding memo is its organization. The large-scale organization of an outstanding memo will be perfect from beginning to end: from the memo heading, to the framing of the legal questions presented, to the brief answers to those questions, to the statement of the facts, to the discussion, and finally to the conclusion. The mid-scale organization of an outstanding memo also will be near perfect. For example, the discussion section will be organized into appropriate sub-sections, each one starting with a conclusion, followed by explanation of the law, application of the law to the facts, and ending with mini-conclusions. Finally, the small-scale organization of an outstanding memo will be excellent, with nearly every sentence and idea leading to the next idea in a logical manner, like climbing a staircase step by step to reach the logical conclusion at the top of the landing.

The third hallmark of an outstanding memo is superb application of the law to the facts; that is, clear explanation of the legal arguments.

7. What characteristics or personality traits can you spot in 1Ls early on that you consider predictors of success in their legal research and writing courses? Conversely, what characteristics or personality traits can you spot in 1Ls early on portending a lack of success in their legal research and writing courses?

BOONE: Students who are open to constructive criticism are much more likely to be successful in my class. They seek feedback, discuss the feedback they receive without being defensive, and try to fully implement that feedback. Students who actually enjoy the research and writing process and understand that both processes continue throughout an assignment also do well.

I am most concerned by the student who sets a conference with me early in the semester and says, "Look, I just want an *A*. Tell me what I need to do to get an *A*, and I'll do it." These students are much more concerned with the result than the process, and my whole class is about the process. These students are very frustrated that I can't give them ten specific steps to follow to get an *A* or a sample memo they can use as a template. At the other end of the spectrum, students who are unwilling or unable to ask for help generally don't do very well either. When a student comes to a conference and has no questions at all, I am very concerned.

MALMUD: Openness to learning. If a student is open to learning, that student will be successful to one degree or another. If a student believes that he is already a good writer and, therefore, has nothing to learn from a legal writing class, that student is likely to fail. Students must remember that writing in different contexts requires different skills. For example, while I can write a compelling memorandum or brief, no one would want one of my short stories or poems. Although some skills do cross over, success in one writing context does not necessarily mean success in the other. The key is for each student to learn what attorneys expect in legal writing, and then determine which skills will cross over and which new skills will need to be developed.

WALTER: Three closely related attributes go far in predicting a student's success in legal writing and in law school overall: work ethic, caring, and attention to detail. The students who earn the top grades in legal writing are those who have an excellent work ethic and are truly dedicated to turning out a superb work product.

Successful students *care* whether they have found the best cases to make their law and application sections work. They *care* whether they have eliminated every last punctuation and grammatical error. They *care* about citation style. They pay attention to details, such as whether there should be a period after the *id.* in a short-form citation to authority, as in *"See id.* at 737." (To satisfy the burning curiosity of the uninitiated, there should be a period after the *id.*)

These students also tend to read the cases and statutes more carefully and critically, pulling out facts and arguments that other students typically miss. They also tend to ask more questions about the materials than other students, again, trying to discover as much relevant detail within the material as possible.

I recently conducted a two-year study at our law school to determine how well undergraduate GPAs and LSAT scores correlate with legal writing grades and overall law school grades. Somewhat surprisingly, neither LSAT scores nor GPAs were useful in predicting how students would fare in law school (although undergraduate GPAs were somewhat more helpful). Very interestingly, scores on the fifty-question, multiple-choice legal research exam we use in our first-semester legal writing course proved to be a far better predictor of students' future grades in first-year courses (including legal writing) than either the LSAT or undergrad GPA! How's that possible? Students who scored higher on the exam typically read the assignments more carefully, took better notes in class, reviewed the books more closely in the library, and put much more effort into making certain they understood the material. In short, they worked harder, they cared, and they paid close attention to everything.

8. Some students mistake functional writing (e.g., coherent sentences, good grammar, etc.) with good legal writing. They don't realize how important the analysis is or even what analysis is. How would you define "analysis" in a way that law students can understand what it means?

BOONE: Everyone can read the rules (cases, statutes, etc.) and most students can learn the rules well enough to predict accurate answers to many legal questions. But analysis goes further than that. Analysis is not about the answer. It's about the process of reaching that answer. Some have analogized it to long division: if you don't show all your work, you get no credit. For example, if you are asked to "analyze" what time it is, you would first explain to the reader the "rules" of time zones, identify the important fact regarding what time zone you are located in, and apply the time zone rules to the specific time zone to reach an answer.

COUGHLIN: Analysis is the process of evaluating the law on a particular topic. In a legal analysis, the writer will show how an established rule of law will function given a new set of facts (i.e., rule-based reasoning) or explain why a client's case is like or unlike a previous case and how those comparisons work to yield a particular result (i.e., analogical reasoning). In other words, it is deducing a likely outcome considering prior law and new facts. Analysis is where a student's creativity and brain power truly come to light.

Analysis is like the fixings in a sandwich. While two pieces of bread may be homemade and quite good, it isn't enough unless you add the meat, veggies, cheese, and condiments. Before all the fixings are added, there is no sandwich. There are simply two pieces of bread. Likewise, in your memorandum, the analysis is the fixings—it is the most important component of the memorandum.

MALMUD: In the typical fall-semester memo, there are three analytical components that distinguish functional writing from really good, insightful legal writing. The first analytical component involves separating the whole into its parts. Every legal analysis will begin with a governing rule. Almost all legal rules are made up of component parts known as "elements" or "factors." For example, the tort of negligence has four elements (duty, breach of duty, causation, and injury). Part of analysis is breaking down broader rules and principles into their constituent elements or factors and examining each of them one by one.

The second important analytical component is the explanation of the law. For each element or factor that is at issue to a client's problem, law students must coherently explain the relevant law. Doing so is difficult because students must pull together the law from numerous, disparate sources. But that's the analytical challenge: assembling a group of relevant disparate legal snippets into a seamless whole. This component of legal writing is analytical in that it requires students to understand both the whole and the parts and explain their relationship to the reader.

Finally, students must apply the law to a particular fact pattern in order to predict an outcome in the client's case. This part of the argument is analytical in the sense that students must think precisely about why the law will lead to one outcome and not the other and then articulate their thinking in a compelling way. Law professors commonly refer only to this last part—applying law to facts—as "the analysis." But please know that the first two parts are also analytical in their own way.

9. If we divide the process of composing a law office memorandum or other legal writing assignment into three parts—researching, writing the initial draft, and rewriting/editing the final product—which part commonly gets the short end of the stick from students? In other words, which of the three steps do less successful students regularly not devote enough time and attention to?

MALMUD: Editing—it's key to a professional work product. A study by Anne Enquist of Seattle University showed that successful legal writing students spend approximately three-fifths of their writing time revising and proofreading, while less successful students divide their time more equally between writing the first draft and revising and proofreading it.

But to say "edit more" is unhelpful. One has to know *how* to edit. Effective editing requires first a big-picture understanding: What's my goal? If you understand your goal, you can step back from your project and ask yourself, does this work achieve my goal? For example, if you are writing an objective memo, the goal is to educate and inform. Understanding that goal allows you to step back and ask yourself, have I educated the attorney receiving this memo about all the relevant law? Have I done so clearly? Have I informed the attorney about the areas where the law favors our client and the areas where our client will struggle to make her case? Have I clearly explained why those strengths and weaknesses exist?

Second, effective editing requires you to understand the problems that typically get in the way of achieving your goal and actively look for those problems. Essentially, you have to create a checklist out of your legal writing class. Let's say in class you've discussed that a well-organized legal argument states a conclusion, explains the law, applies the law, and then concludes again. Well, have you done that? Be sure to go back and check. Let's say your professor has pointed out that your sentences tend to be wordy. Well, that needs to be added to your checklist, and with each memo you write, you'll need to check your sentences for wordiness.

Because editing often seems like such drudgery, I'd like to put in a personal plug for editing. Editing is about creating a synchronized, lucid solution to a complex problem. The reward and "fun" comes from seeing the improvement.

Let's say I want to build a machine that will squirt just the perfect amount of mustard onto a hotdog. The parts lay before me. I start trying to fit them together. I discover at the end of my first attempt that I've done pretty well, but the machine has a leftward tilt, so that all the mustard winds up on the conveyor belt to the left of the hotdog. I tinker until the mustard is hitting dead-on, but there's too much of it. I tinker a little bit more so that just the right amount of mustard is hitting the hotdog. Finally, for a flourish, I adjust the machine so that instead of the mustard running in a straight line, it has an S-shaped flow down the hotdog's spine. I did it! I created the perfect mustard-hotdog combination. To me, that's the pleasure in editing. It's the time when I sync up all the parts to create exactly the product I want to deliver. There's beauty in that.

PATRICK: Without a doubt, students spend the least amount of time revising and polishing the final product. Realizing that the revising and polishing steps can often take longer than the research and drafting steps is a secret to success.

The research phase is often the most enjoyable because students can wander mindlessly, breezily, through library stacks or online databases—working, yes, but minimally engaging difficult material. Research can be a delightful black hole, allowing students to save the thinking for later.

Once some thinking has occurred and the student has slogged through statutes and cases and mapped out some kind of tangible structure, students are willing to devote some time to hashing out that draft—what they hope will be the *only* draft. That draft is like painting the walls of a room; we all paint expecting immediate gratification and hoping that two coats will not be necessary. And maybe even that we can skip doing all that difficult trim work! Likewise, some students hope one slapdash draft will be enough.

When students finally finish the first two laborious stages (research and writing the first draft), they are spent—from both a time and a mental standpoint. They rationalize that the first draft is good enough, and submit it.

Early in my legal writing career, colleagues introduced me to Anne Lamott's book on writing, *Bird by Bird*. Lamott's ideas on fiction writing transfer quite easily to legal writing. In one chapter she accurately captures the three stages of composing a written document. The first draft is the "down draft," where the goal is just to get the words down on paper. The second draft is the "up draft"—you fix it up and "try to say what you have to say more accurately." The final draft is the "dental draft," where you check "every tooth to see if it's loose or cramped or decayed, or even, God help us, healthy."[70]

My students love this analogy, although sometimes they add their opinion that the final draft is called a dental draft because getting it done is worse than having a root canal. Despite the pain involved, revising and polishing are the pivotal steps needed to reach that dental draft. Revising takes time. The task also requires that the writer engage the text in a hypercritical way, making sure every statement is accurate and complete, every sentence is soundly constructed, every paragraph flows logically to the next. Polishing is an equally arduous task requiring writers to move beyond spell-check to look at each word, each piece of punctuation, and each citation.

Students who are willing to complete that third step—revising and polishing until they get a dental draft—usually are very successful.

WALTER: While all three aspects of the research and writing process often get the "short end of the stick," I think the legal research process gets "shorted" most often, causing great damage to students (and their clients) in the long run.

Here's what frequently happens. After the students are given the facts for the open memo problem (i.e., a memo where students have to do the research themselves), most of them begin their legal research. Some perform in stellar fashion, devoting the necessary hours in the books and on-line, carefully researching the issues, closely reading the

70. *See* Anne Lamott, Bird by Bird: 25–26 (First Anchor Books 1995).
Some Instructions on Writing and Life

cases, and finding nearly all of the relevant law. Many students, however, underestimate how long it will take to locate the relevant law, and some underestimate how frustrating it can be to find the law. In both instances, these students do not complete the research task. Unfortunately, and as surprising as it might sound, there are a few students who never start their research, figuring instead that they'll simply rely on another student, or the professor, to tell them which statutes and cases are important.

Once the research phase ends and the drafting phase begins, the students typically discuss the law both in and out of class, and most students will then learn which cases and statutes should be included in the memo. Even if a student did not do a great job during the research phase, at this point it's still possible for a student to earn a good grade on the draft and final project by "borrowing" the research and ideas of others, without going back and completing the research on their own.

Students know they have to turn in high-quality drafts and final versions of the memo to do decently in the course, so built-in incentives exist for these phases. In the long run, however, students who shirk quality research will earn lower grades in legal writing courses, as well as future courses, such as seminars, that require research. And because they never develop efficient research skills, they'll actually spend more time earning those lower grades than their classmates. But the bigger harm will befall the clients of these students, as less effective and less efficient researchers pass the short end of the stick to their clients.

10. One would assume a correlation exists between the amount of time spent on a major legal writing assignment and the result. But we all know students who fruitlessly pour in tons of time inefficiently. What are some of the ways time devoted to a major legal writing assignment is not time well spent?

BOONE: I don't think this should count as time devoted to the assignment, but apparently an amazing amount of time is spent worrying about the assignment and complaining about how hard (or how simple) it is to one's classmates. I would not want students to completely miss this chance to bond with their fellow 1Ls, but they should try not to waste too much time commiserating. Inefficient research and the quest for a perfect outline also take up untold hours. If students have been lost for hours or days in the research or the writing process, they should stop and ask for help. Finally, searching relentlessly for a very clever turn of phrase is probably not the best use of your time.

COUGHLIN: Many law students are competitive. Because many law schools grade on a curve, this population of students want to make sure they are on the top end of that curve. For many students, instead of focusing on answering the question asked by the assignment, they try to go above and beyond the facts and relevant authorities to try to find alternate areas and authorities to explore so as to make legal arguments that other students are not making. While students may spend inordinate amounts of time researching to come up with unique arguments that no one else may make, it is time that would have been better spent proofing and editing their papers or relaxing with a cup of coffee and newspaper.

While researching all arguments thoroughly is commendable, and spending time thinking about alternative arguments is helpful, students tend to go down tangents and waste a lot of time for minimal or no return. An analogy is going to the doctor and telling her that you have a runny nose, cough, and are achy. You would expect the doctor to say you have a cold and that you need rest and lots of fluids—not to send you in for a full-body MRI in search of any possible ailment.

In legal writing, to maximize time and effort, spend sufficient time researching, writing, editing and proofreading so that you feel comfortable that you have done the best you can. The rest will take care of itself. Even if all the students use the same authorities, every student's thought process is unique. So, be strategic with your time. While you want to consider all viable arguments, don't create arguments that really aren't there.

PATRICK: Students become the most inefficient at two points in time: when they postpone thinking until *after* the research process and, similarly, when they start writing before they've developed a map of how the pieces of the legal argument should be arranged.

Research can seem like a productive time, but it can actually be a waste of time when students avoid critically reading and thinking about the sources *before* wasting time and resources printing them. Thinking during research makes the task a little more difficult, but understanding early on how each source will (or will not) contribute to the answer will certainly save the student a lot of time later in the process. I encourage students to use charts or diagrams along the way to see how the legal authorities relate to each other and how the authorities together answer the legal question.

Once the authorities are compiled, students too frequently want to jump into the writing without first organizing the law around the points they need to explain. Many students have never outlined assignments before writing them, and they utterly resist this step. Outlining or mapping the structure of the arguments saves the writer time and aggravation. Students normally find that once they understand the document's overall organizational structure and the organizational structure within each issue, the writing is not so difficult. To the contrary, students who try to figure out the organization as they write hit a lot of dead ends and usually must discard a lot of what they wrote along the way.

The most successful students quickly learn that producing a solid piece of legal analysis is a multi-step process. Skipping steps inevitably backfires and makes the student's effort less efficient.

11. Related to the above question, research obviously is a key ingredient of successful legal writing, but ineffective or inefficient research can go on with no end in sight and little to show for it. Any tips for how students can improve the efficiency of their research? How does a student know when he or she has done enough research?

BOONE: To effectively research a legal issue, students must understand two things. First, if there were an easy answer to the question, they probably would not have been asked to research and write about that issue. Second, students must make sure they understand the question. For example, if I ask my students to predict how a California state court will rule on a particular issue, a student who answers only with law from other states has not answered my question effectively. The most relevant law would, of course, be California law. If you are thinking that this student simply failed to follow my instructions, you are partially right. My students don't intentionally disregard the instructions, but they often end up with poor research results because they got lost somewhere in the process. This tends to happen when the students are trying too hard to come up with the "perfect" case to answer my question. When there isn't one, they tend to start changing the question. They are, after all, going to be lawyers, right?

Seriously though, students can research much more efficiently if they keep in mind that there is usually no "golden egg" in the treasure hunt. Students often spend days looking for the "perfect" case to resolve their issue. They quickly discard cases that are fairly similar and provide good rules in the relevant jurisdiction, because they just know that there is a better case out there if they just keep looking. Surely, some court somewhere has addressed this exact issue before! These are great students, and they just know they can find THE answer—even if I have told them there is not one. Once they are completely exhausted and the deadline for the assignment is fast approaching, they realize that those cases they discarded might have been exactly what they needed. That leads us to another suggestion. Students should carefully track their research paths. This allows the exhausted student to avoid further frustration because he can at least go back and find those sources he discarded earlier.

A student has probably done enough initial research when he begins to see the same sources over and over again. When a student starts noticing that all of her sources seem to be citing each other, rather than citing sources the student has not yet seen, she is probably done with this round of research.

COUGHLIN: Take advantage of all training opportunities from Westlaw and Lexis. Not only will you enhance your research skills, you'll have the opportunity to win prizes and eat lots of free pizza.

But do not rely on computerized legal research as your only option. It is important to know how to research in the books because many smaller law firms or public service entities may not have access to computerized legal research or the funds to pay for it. Also, understanding print resources will provide you with a better idea of the scope of information you are researching. In addition, computerized legal research has the drawback of being only as good as your search terms. If your search term does not precisely appear in the document, you may miss a big case. You are more likely to get a wider breadth of relevant materials when you combine computerized and print research.

It is difficult to be efficient in legal research at first. Initially, the best way to begin is to use a flow chart and make sure that you document each step or source that you find for easy retrieval in the future. There are many such flow charts or decision trees for basic case law and statutory research skills that will be available in the legal research materials you receive in class or on the web.

As far as knowing when you are completed, a good rule of thumb, as Professor Boone said, is to continue with your initial research until you start seeing the same sources appear over and over again and the cases or sources begin to cite each other.

PATRICK: Efficient and thorough research requires a student to do four things: know the question being asked, follow a methodical process of reviewing sources, keep a trail of where you have been, and above all, think as you go.

Students, and even young lawyers, can be horribly inefficient at research because they do not adhere to those four mandates. Research can be deliciously mindless as one prints off stacks of cases to read later or as one follows tangential queries down a cyberspace rabbit hole. But once that illusion of productivity wears off and that young student or attorney realizes he is no closer to answering the legal question than he was hours or days ago, frustration and panic erupt.

Using a methodical process for research can foster efficient and thorough research. First, always know the exact legal question you are being asked to answer. Usually clients pose narrow legal questions; understanding the question before you delve into myriad sources can save time and energy.

Next, establish a logical method for going through the various sources of authority. Most research texts students will see in law school set out some sort of step-like process to use in research. Understand that process and use it consistently.

Keeping a trail of where you have been and the sources you have checked can be crucial for a successful research project, particularly in real-life practice. Whether in school or practice, finishing a research project at one sitting will not likely happen. In reality, a research project may take several days or weeks and may be interrupted by competing tasks. Keeping a detailed list of search terms, sources, queries, will prevent duplicative research efforts later in the project.

Finally, think as you go. Never print a stack of "possibly relevant" cases to read later when you have time. No one, not even an experienced attorney, can read and assimilate two dozen cases at once. I warn my students to print a source *only* after they know what part of the legal puzzle that source solves. Thinking as you go through the research process is more difficult (and sometimes not as much fun), but saving time and finding the answer efficiently is well worth the effort.

I also echo that research is finished when either your search efforts start to yield the same legal authorities time and again or you run out of time on the project.

12. I'm always all over my seminar students about typos, *Bluebook* errors, formatting mistakes, and other fine points. They think I'm just being a nitpicker. You've touched on this, but could you elaborate about how important these finer points are when it comes to evaluating either a student's or lawyer's writing product?

COUGHLIN: The finer points mentioned in the question are essential. While my students may consider my strict attitude toward citation, formatting, etc. frustrating, they generally come to appreciate that precision and attention to detail make the difference in being invited onto the moot court board or law review, or getting a job offer.

Specifically, many times I take a point off the student's final grade for any *Bluebook* error. My philosophy is that these finer points represent the area of your writing product over which the student has the most control. You do not have control over your client's facts, and you do not have control over the state of the law. You can not control what your professor, judge or senior partner will think of your legal argument because of personal bias or prior life experiences or simply because the law may be against you. You can control, however, citation, formatting, and proofreading.

If you are sloppy with these finer points, your reader will think that your analysis is likewise imprecise. If you are not precise with your typing, your proofreading, your citation, your punctuation, how then will your reader have confidence in your work? For example, when I was in practice, a colleague sent out a letter that was supposed to read "return receipt requested" but instead read "rectum receipt requested." One can imagine recipients having a difficult time placing confidence in the substance of a letter when the heading makes an illicit proposition.

MALMUD: You are being a nitpicker, and your students should thank you for it. Let's fast-forward to the question of how important these finer points are in the real world. Imagine you are a lawyer interviewing two job candidates. One candidate walks in wearing a suit and presents you with a crisp, clean resume. The other walks in wearing jeans, flip-flops, and presents you with the same resume content-wise, but full of typos. Which one would you hire? Whether we like it or not, those reading our work make judgments about our capabilities based on its appearance, just as people make judgments about us based on our appearance. Sloppy citations, punctuation, grammar, or formatting will make your reader skeptical about the quality of your analysis.

Because attention to these details matters in the real world, we pay attention to them in legal writing classes. Although legal writing grades are always more dependent on the legal analysis than on mechanics, they will ultimately be lower if the student doesn't pay attention to the "finer points" of grammar, typos, punctuation, and citation errors.

WALTER: The "fine points"—punctuation, usage, grammar, spelling, citation, and formatting—are very important to the overall grade on a legal writing memo and may be even more important in the real world. In my legal writing classes, I give a specific point value for the errors listed above, a value that is typically about 10–15 percent of the overall assignment grade. Committing too many of these errors will cost a student about one-third letter grade, dropping a $B+$ to a B, for example.

For legal writing professors who use a more "holistic" grading system rather than a specific point system, I think that the grading penalty for such errors is likely to be even more severe. Why? Because of something called "heuristics."

The concept of heuristics is pretty straightforward: when decision-makers are short on time or information, they often make judgments based on more observable factors, even if those factors don't necessarily lead to a purely rational decision. In other words, heuristics is a decision-making shortcut often based on appearances.

In practice, it might operate like this: A trial judge, looking over a three-foot tall stack of court documents so that she can make decisions on dozens of pending motions, begins reading the plaintiff's memo. It's full of typos, the cases are cited incorrectly, and some of the sentences don't make sense because of grammar and usage problems. Frustrated, the judge picks up the defendant's memo. It's perfect. There are no misspellings or typos, the cases are properly cited, and the memo is well written. The defendant could very likely prevail on the motion even if the law actually favors the plaintiff.

It works the same way in legal writing courses. Poor mechanics may cause the grader to undervalue the substance of the writing, giving a lower grade than the substance might otherwise dictate.

13. What complaint do you hear from students year after year that you think is justified? Conversely, what complaint do you regularly hear that is unjustified?

BOONE: I think student complaints that they receive too few credit hours for the work they do in legal research and writing are justified. On the other hand, I think students' complaints about our strict deadlines in legal writing are unjustified. With very few exceptions, my students lose significant points on major assignments if they are even a few minutes late. If an assignment is over twenty-four hours late, I will not grade it. The policy may seem harsh, but the practice of law runs on deadlines. Students may as well get used to it.

PATRICK: One justified criticism is that students do not get enough research instruction. With the explosion of online legal sources on the internet in recent years, we cannot begin to teach all of the research skills that students may need for their legal careers. Sources expand or change so quickly we do well to cover the basic sources of law and the easiest ways to find them. I encourage students to take an upper-division course we offer in advanced legal research taught by our skilled librarians. I also would encourage law students to lobby their administrators for more research-oriented classes and to take those classes to improve their research skills.

WALTER: I hear three complaints on a frequent basis, and I think two are probably quite justified. Many students complain that their professors don't return writing assignments as quickly as they should. Ideally, feedback would be immediate. Students would know exactly what they did right and wrong and be able to correct the wrongs on the next version. Unfortunately, with so many students and so many papers, it often takes longer than ideal to critique and grade memos and other assignments.

Second, I often hear students say that their professors don't grade consistently, and third, I hear related comments that legal writing professors grade unfairly and play favorites (i.e., grading someone down or up based on the prof's dislike or like for the person).

I think it's true that some profs don't grade consistently. Perhaps they're grading without a grade sheet or list of key points, perhaps they're grading too many papers at one sitting, or perhaps they're grading at 3 a.m. Whatever the cause, the effect is often the same: inconsistent grades. For example, two students make the same mistake, but only one student gets dinged, or a student corrects an error made on a prior draft in the final version (at the prof's suggestion), but then the professor grades the change negatively. Or just as frustrating, the prof finds something wrong on the second draft that passed un-criticized on the first draft. If a student thinks the professor has missed something or graded inconsistently, the student should talk with the professor. Fortunately, most grading inconsistency does not affect the student's overall course grade, even if it affects the individual assignment grade. If, for example, the professor mistakenly gives one student eighty points on a memo when the student should have received seventy-six points, the four-point error should not affect the overall grade in the course.

As for that third criticism, I think it is mostly unfounded. Over my nearly twenty years as a legal skills teacher, I have worked with thirty to forty legal writing professors. I don't think I have personally met any legal writing professors who graded anyone up or down based on their like or dislike of the individual student.

14. **I've seen many incidents of plagiarism arise in legal writing courses over my years as a professor. Some of them have been egregious. A common defense is that the student didn't know what he or she did constituted plagiarism. The first few times I heard this defense raised, I found it lacking in credibility. As the years have passed, I'm less sure. It seems that some students simply don't grasp what plagiarism is and isn't. Can you give readers of this book some clear guidance as to what constitutes plagiarism and how to avoid it?**

BOONE: This question arises so frequently that the Legal Writing Institute has created a plagiarism brochure. Students can find it at http://www.lwionline.org/publications/brochure.asp. The brochure defines plagiarism, explains how it arises most often in the law school setting, and provides five basic "Rules for Working with Authority." The brochure also gives sample sources and excerpts from student papers and asks the reader to decide whether the writer has avoided committing plagiarism. The answers explain how the student writers have followed or failed to follow the five basic rules. Students may be surprised by some of the answers. The brochure also discusses how the rules tend to operate differently in the practice of law. Finally, the brochure reminds students to ask their professors if they have any doubts about whether attribution is required. I recommend that students consult this plagiarism brochure.

Students must make sure they understand their legal writing professors' rules about collaboration. Most of our plagiarism problems arise when students misunderstand or choose to ignore those rules.

MALMUD: Plagiarism is appropriating the ideas of another and presenting them as your own without attribution.

For the most part, plagiarism in legal writing classes should not be a problem. Before entering law school students should know that they cannot use the ideas of another student or other source without providing attribution. By the second week of school, students know they must cite every proposition appropriated from another source.

One difficult question for new legal writers is knowing when a sentence needs both a citation and quotation marks. Quotation marks signal that not only the *idea* comes from another source, but also the specific words and their unique sequencing. Here's a rule to follow: If you have appropriated not only the substantive idea from another source but also its unique sequencing of specific words, use a citation *and* quotation marks to show you borrowed both.

For new legal writers, knowing when to use quotation marks can be difficult because lawyers appropriate key legal phrases without providing quotation marks. For instance, lawyers might write that a police officer had "reasonable suspicion of criminal activity" without using quotation marks. That language is a statement of a legal standard. Essèntially, it's "public language." By way of example, a quick search of federal cases in the past year showed that twenty-seven federal judicial opinions used this exact phrase, and none used quotation marks. Pay attention to the cases you read. If a phrase repeats itself in many cases, you can likely use that phrase without quotation marks, but a citation of where it came from would still be required.

WALTER: I ask students to follow two simple rules to avoid plagiarism. First, if a writer is borrowing the exact words (three words or more, or just one very unique word), the writer must use quotation marks (or, as you'll learn, if a quotation is fifty or more words, it should appear as an indented block without quotation marks). A surprising number of students fail to use quotation marks when they quote from cases, statutes or other legal sources. Why is that? It's true that some writers knowingly and intentionally plagiarize the original source, hoping they won't be caught. But often, there's an innocent explanation. Some students are not careful when they copy or download the original source, and they lose track of what they wrote and what they borrowed from other sources. Regardless of the explanation, I still deduct substantial points for the failure to use quotation marks. Plagiarism is a serious offense.

The second rule is also pretty straightforward. If a writer: (a) borrows exact words (again, usually three or more, but it can include just one unique word); (b) borrows an idea (the writer paraphrases from the source); or (c) borrows the organization or structure from the original source, the writer must provide a citation to that source and that citation must include the exact page number(s) of the borrowed material. The last point is a bit tricky and one that escapes even some conscientious students. Borrowing a writer's *organization or structure of ideas* without full attribution is also plagiarism, even if you use your own words. This issue tends to come up more in upper-level seminars than in first-year legal writing courses.

15. What's the silliest mistake one of your students has ever committed?

COUGHLIN: The silliest mistake a student committed happened during a closed universe office memorandum (where we provide the students all the law they have to work with) assignment involving only two cases that the student had to compare and contrast. The issue was a very narrow one: whether, given our client's facts, the element of the tort of slander known as "publication" (a term of art meaning that the slanderous remark was disclosed to at least one person other than the defendant) was satisfied. One case held that the element was satisfied and the defendant was liable for the tort. The other case held that element was not satisfied and the defendant was not liable.

The problem facts the students were wrestling with were intentionally drafted to fall right in the middle of the two cases. During the first few weeks of my class, I practically hold my students' hands. I had walked them through the analysis and flowcharted it on the board. We had discussed the issue *ad nauseum*. Unfortunately, one student disregarded the first two weeks of class (including orientation week, which included twelve intensive classroom hours of legal research and writing instruction) and wrote a paper not about the narrow element of publication in a slander case, but about First Amendment rights to free speech! While it was an interesting essay on the history of the First Amendment, I had no choice but to fail the paper.

MALMUD: Well, let's see. Here are a few to choose from:

Students not realizing they might need their professors for a reference one day.

Students who assume everyone but them "gets it"—not realizing all the other students are thinking the same thing.

Students who think that after reading forty identical papers I won't notice the condensed font they tried to slip in to get around the page limitation.

I love this one: I once explained to my students that prepositions often signal excess language and so if they can cut out prepositions, their sentences are likely to be more concise and vigorous. A student then handed in a paper containing literally no prepositions! Quite an accomplishment.

WALTER: Silly mistakes come in all shapes and sizes. The big ones usually do not seem very humorous to the student who suffers grade-wise. For example, a silly error, using the wrong font size or exceeding the page limit, could result in a grade reduction. It's a "silly" mistake because the instructions on font sizes are clear, but one with serious consequences.

Many smaller mistakes are quite humorous, for both prof and student, especially when they don't result in a severe grade penalty. One semester I used an environmental law problem for a memo assignment, and one student wrote in his memo: "My client has discussed whether he will fill the chemical basin with his partners." We all had a good laugh over that one.

Perhaps the silliest mistake occurred in my fifth year of teaching (I still remember it well). In connection with a search and seizure issue, we were discussing the Fourth Amendment to the United States Constitution and its prohibition against "unreasonable searches and seizures."

One of my students boldly asked during class where she could find a copy of "that statute." A bit confused, I asked, "What statute?" And she replied, "The one you've been discussing for the last thirty minutes."

Stifling a gasp, I asked her, "By statute, are you referring to the Fourth Amendment?" I was hoping she would say no and point to some statute mentioned in one of the cases. Unfortunately, she said, "Yes, that's the one. Is that a federal statute?" At that point several students laughed aloud, but I quieted them with a quick look. In case you've missed the joke, the Fourth Amendment is part of the United States Constitution—not a statute. If you avoid making that mistake because of reading this, I'd say your investment in McClurg's book was worthwhile.

CHAPTER 18

MAINTAINING WELL-BEING

Can't put it off any longer. I said in the beginning I'd be honest about the good, bad, and ugly of law school, so it's time to share the news that law students, especially 1Ls, typically are not a happy, contented group. One law professor offered this grim assessment:

> Law students get sick more frequently than others: headaches, stomachaches, colds, allergies. They have problems in their relationships with friends or family. They worry more than they work. They are continually agitated or lethargic. They gain or lose weight. They take up or increase their chemical crutches, such as caffeine, nicotine, alcohol, or cocaine. They often become angry and bitter—especially at their teachers, sometimes at their colleagues or at the profession—or they withdraw, dropping out, skipping classes, or simply avoiding getting to know their classmates. When called upon in specific stressful situations to use reserves of courage and confidence, they may be debilitated; and they often have no reserves to call upon.[71]

Well, that doesn't sound good. Let's see what she's talking about.

The Bleak Side of Law School: Stress, Anxiety, and Depression

Law students suffer disproportionately from stress, anxiety, and depression. Of course, one might expect that people

---

71. B.A. Glesner, *Fear and Loathing in the Law Schools*, 23 CONN. L. REV. 627, 631 (1991).

enrolled in a competitive, demanding professional degree program like law school would be a bit more stressed out than your Average Joes and Josephines, but the problem goes beyond that. Studies have found that psychological distress in law students significantly outpaces not only the general population, but other graduate student populations, including medical students.

Way back in 1957, a study comparing law students and medical students found that law students scored higher on an anxiety scale, both in the first year and also at graduation.[72] A 1980s study of University of Arizona law and medical students found that law students scored significantly higher than both the general population and medical students in nearly every category of psychological dysfunction measured, including anxiety, depression, feelings of inadequacy and inferiority, hostility, and obsessive-compulsiveness.[73]

While law school may attract some people already inclined toward emotional distress (including over-achieving obsessive-compulsive types), evidence suggests a causal relationship between law school and psychological dysfunction. One study found that law students begin school with psychopathological symptom responses similar to the general population, but that those symptoms become substantially elevated during law school and after graduation. On depression scales, for example, 17-40 percent of law students were found to suffer from depression compared to 3-9 percent of the general population.[74] A more recent study reached similar conclusions about 1Ls, finding "large increases in negative affect, depression, and physical symptomology" between the beginning and end of the first year.[75]

These gloomy patterns continue after graduation. A Johns Hopkins University study found that lawyers ranked fifth in the overall prevalence of depression out of 105 occupations.[76]

72. *See* Leonard D. Eron & Robert S. Redmount, *The Effect of Legal Education on Attitudes*, 9 J. LEGAL EDUC. 431 (1957).

73. *See* Stephen B. Shanfield & G. Andrew H. Benjamin, *Psychiatric Distress in Law Students*, 35 J. LEGAL EDUC. 65, 67–68 (1985).

74. *See* G. Andrew H. Benjamin, Alfred Kaszniak, Bruce Sales & Stephen B. Shanfield, *The Role of Legal Edu-*

cation in Producing Psychological Distress Among Law Students and Lawyers, 1986 AM. B. FOUND. RES. J. 225 (1986).

75. Kennon M. Sheldon & Lawrence S. Krieger, *Does Legal Education have Undermining Effects on Law Students? Evaluating Changes in Motivation, Values, and Well–Being*, 22 BEHAV. SCI. & L. 261, 280 (2004).

76. *See* William W. Eaton, James C. Anthony, Wallace Mandel & Roberta

When the data were adjusted to focus on the association between depression and the particular occupation (by taking into account non-occupational factors contributing to depression), lawyers moved into first place.[77] We're number one! We're number one!

A later study of lawyers in Arizona and Washington found that 21 percent of male lawyers and 16 percent of female lawyers exceeded the clinical cut-off measure for depression, significantly higher than depression rates found in the general population. The same study found that 30 percent of male lawyers and 20 percent of female lawyers exceeded the clinical cut-off for measuring generalized anxiety disorder, as compared to 4 percent of the general population.[78]

Hey, it might not be too late to get your law school deposit back. Just kidding. Well, not completely. My goal certainly isn't to discourage anyone from getting a legal education. On the other hand, this information is worth considering if you're on the fence about attending law school.

To the extent law school is responsible for causing emotional distress in law students, one doesn't have to look far for plausible explanations: the heavy emphasis on grades and corresponding worries about failure, the competitive environment, high student-teacher ratios, intimidating instructional methods, professors who are sometimes imperious and distant, brutal workloads, burdensome debt-loads, lack of performance feedback, the adversarial nature of the legal system in which law students are constantly immersed, the emphasis on objective analytical thinking over personal values and emotions, strains on personal relationships, doubts about whether law school is the right career path, and, of course, for 1Ls, general fear and uncertainty about what to expect.

Stress isn't inherently bad. In proper doses, it can be a good source of motivation. As a law student, for example, I felt tremendous pressure to not "look stupid" in front of my peers. That made me work harder in preparing for class—not a bad thing. On the other hand, the stomach problems I developed as a 1L were not a good thing. Nor were the

---

Garrison, *Occupations and the Prevalence of Major Depressive Disorder*, 32 J. OCCUPATIONAL MED. 1079, 1082 tbl.1 (1990).

77. *Id.* at 1085 tbl.3.

78. Connie J.A. Beck, Bruce D. Sales & G. Andrew H. Benjamin, *Lawyer Distress: Alcohol–Related Problems and Other Psychological Concerns Among a Sample of Practicing Lawyers*, 10 J.L. & HEALTH 1, 49–50 (1995).

sleepless nights ... or the panic attack when I got called on in Constitutional Law ... or the fact that all I ever talked about outside of law school was law, law, and more law ... or that I let law school change some of my values and goals.

Stress, of course, is a natural part of many of life's undertakings and challenges. Some degree of "law school stress" is inevitable and unavoidable, just as "medical school stress" is unavoidable for med students, "military stress" for service members, "relationship stress" for couples, "parenting stress" for mothers and fathers, etc. Not only is it impossible to eliminate stress while in law school, it's not even desirable. Perhaps tellingly, the least-stressed law students I've encountered in my career, while perhaps happier than most other students, are rarely top performers academically. The key is to keep stress within manageable bounds.

But how does one go about that? How can first-year students endure the demands of law school while maintaining a healthy sense of well-being? Is it even possible? First, some heartening news on that point. Although studies suggest that psychological distress in law students isn't limited to 1Ls, actual *law school* distress ameliorates considerably after the first year. In my experience both as a student and in dealing with many law students as a professor, the first year of law school is by far the most overwhelming and stressful of the three years in terms of school itself.

There's truth in the old law school adage: "In the first year they scare you to death. In the second year they work you to death. In the third year they bore you to death." Upper-level students acquire new sources of stress. Anxieties stemming from uncertainty, the Socratic method, etc., are replaced by worries about finding a job, juggling the time demands of part-time clerking jobs, law review, and moot court with course work, taking and passing the bar exam, and entering the real world once and for all. But in terms of day-to-day law school, most third-year students, as the adage holds, appear to be more bored than distressed.

Recognizing that it's neither possible nor desirable to eliminate all stress, let's look at some tips for keeping your stress in check and raising your overall well-being as a 1L.

A Dozen Tips for Managing Stress
and Promoting Well–Being

1. Take care of yourself physically. The first year of law school is part academic test and part endurance test. It will tax your mind and body to the limits. As one commentator said, "Physical and psychological exhaustion are, I think, programmed into the first year."[79] As the first semester progresses past the halfway mark, classrooms start sounding like tuberculosis wards as more and more students begin showing up sick. The reasonable apprehension about missing class and, hence, important material that could be on the exam, keeps students coming to class—and spreading germs—when they'd be better off at home in bed. One student consultant shared this tale, which is at once funny, disconcerting, and a revealing statement about law school:

> During the second semester, it seemed like everyone in our class was coming down with the flu. When I felt that familiar achy, feverish feeling one morning, I cried. Literally, I cried because I knew there was no way I could skip class or slow down. So I struggled through that day and the next and finally went to the health clinic on campus. When the nurse practitioner asked if I had been exposed to anyone who had the flu, I said, "Well, three people who sit next to me have it." She asked if they had been coming to class and I said, "Yeah. I mean, we are in law school. You can't miss class." She got this very frustrated look on her face and said emphatically, "Well, if that's the case then maybe we should make the entire law school get flu shots next year so you don't infect the whole campus!"

And you thought I was exaggerating back in the CREDO chapter when I said consistent students miss class only if they're on their deathbeds. I felt guilty reading this story because I know I'm part of the problem. In any event, although you can't control the sick people next to you, you can help yourself by arriving at law school in good physical shape and determined to stay that way.

Exercise is a proven stress reliever and promoter of physical and mental well-being. Indeed, a list of the benefits from

---

79. Stephen C. Halpern, *On the Politics and Pathology of Legal Education,* 32 J. LEGAL EDUC. 383, 388 (1982).

regular exercise resembles a cure-all prescription for many of
the ailments suffered by law students. Exercise reduces depression and anxiety, increases energy, strength, and stami-
na, improves mental acuity, enhances the immune system,
promotes better sleep, and increases self-esteem.

Join the university's fitness center. Memberships usually
are available at low cost to students, or even included as part
of their student fees. Use the stairs instead of the elevator at
law school. Do bicep curls with your Contracts and Property
casebooks. Just find a way to work exercise into your weekly
routine. Also concentrate on maintaining a healthy diet (it's
very easy to fall into a fast-food habit in law school), go to bed
at a reasonable time, and at least *try* to avoid germs. Most
illnesses are spread through hand to mouth contact. Wash
your hands frequently. Carry and use an anti-bacterial hand
sanitizer. They come in a variety of dispensers, including
wipes.

Staying healthy will enable you to stay consistent, and
staying consistent will help prevent you from falling behind,
which, as discussed below, is one of the major causes of stress
in law students.

2. Beware of alcohol and other substance abuse.
Lawyers like to drink. Alcohol flows freely whenever and
wherever they gather socially. Several studies have documented alcohol problems in the legal profession. A survey of
North Carolina lawyers found that nearly 17 percent reported consuming three to five drinks a day. A study of Washington lawyers concluded from a random sample that 18 percent
of practicing lawyers were "problem drinkers." One research-
er of alcoholism among lawyers estimated that at least 15
percent of lawyers are alcoholics, compared to 7-8 percent of
the general population.[80] Although the data are less extensive,
statistics also show that abuse of other chemical substances is
prevalent among lawyers.

Alcohol and other substance abuse are involved in from
50-75 percent of all disciplinary actions against attorneys.[81]
Small wonder that every state bar organization maintains a

80. Patrick J. Schiltz, *On Being a Happy, Healthy, and Ethical Member of an Unhappy, Unhealthy, and Unethical Profession*, 52 VAND. L. REV. 871, 876–77 (1999) (collecting and reporting on these studies).

81. Betty Reddy & Ruth Woodruff, *Helping the Alcoholic Colleague*, PROF. LAW., May 1992, at 4.

lawyer assistance program for substance abuse and other mental health problems.

Law students enjoy alcohol as well. In one survey, more than one-third of law student respondents answered affirmatively to the question: "Do you think you drink too much?"[82] And those were the ones who recognized they had an alcohol issue. Many people don't. A George Mason University study found that 11 percent of law students experienced eight or more hangovers during the previous semester, while 36 percent experienced one to three hangovers.[83]

Law schools may contribute to the problem by maintaining and fostering structures and activities that emphasize the consumption of alcohol. In addition to teaching students "to think like a lawyer," law school culture could be accused of teaching students "to drink like a lawyer." At some schools, student government associations sponsor weekly social events for students at local bars that amount to little more than drinking-fests.

Following a Torts class discussing the potential liability of individuals and businesses for providing alcohol to persons who then drive drunk and cause injury, a student I'll call John asked if he could speak with me privately. Since first-semester grades had just come out, I was expecting a sad story about his Torts grade. Instead, he said something like: "Professor, I didn't want to bring this up in the class discussion because I didn't want the class to turn against me, but I don't understand how or why law schools encourage so much drinking."

He described a social event promoted by the student government organization in which the local bar association offered free drinks at a bar during a happy hour. "Everyone just came for the free drinks," he said. "Because they were free, people were pouring them down as fast as they could. When the free drinks ended, everyone just got in their cars and drove somewhere else." He went on to describe ugly scenes at other law school social events where some students get "falling-down drunk." "You'd never recognize them from class, Professor," he said.

---

82. Heins et al., *supra*, at 521.

83. *See* Gerald W. Boston, *Chemical Dependency in Legal Education: Prob-* *lems and Strategies*, 76 MICH. B.J. 298, 299 (1997) (discussing this study).

Substance abuse is an issue at all law schools, just as it is at all undergraduate institutions. This is not surprising since most law students are only shortly removed from undergraduate school. But the stakes are higher in law school. Students learning to become professionals have to face the fact that, whether they like it or not, they can't continue behaving like undergraduate party animals.

Not all substance abuse is for partying. I hear scary tales from law students about the widespread use of Adderall around exam time. Adderall, a drug approved for treating attention-deficit disorder and narcolepsy, is an amphetamine. According to one source, so common is its use that students excitedly announce, "I found someone to sell me the 15 mgs for four bucks instead of five. Only seven bucks for the 20 mgs!" In addition to obvious health concerns, taking prescription drugs without a prescription is illegal.

Excessive drinking or other substance abuse is problematic for law students on several fronts. First, alcohol is a depressant, so while it might provide short-term relief for stress, it actually feeds depression. A close association between depression and heavy alcohol use is well-established by research. Second, the adverse consequences of an arrest for drunk-driving or other substance-related illegalities are substantially enhanced for law students, who have a much stronger interest in maintaining a good reputation and clean record than they did as undergraduate students. State bar organizations conduct thorough background checks of applicants. Misconduct in law school that might have been excused as youthful indiscretion had it occurred in undergraduate school will be more carefully scrutinized and harshly judged.

Drinking too much in public carries its own pitfalls. Not uncommonly, intoxicated students embarrass themselves in front of their colleagues and professors, unwisely pose for party pics that later get posted on the internet, and even become victims or perpetrators of sexual assaults. You can count on the fact that any untoward behavior at a law school social gathering will be quickly and widely circulated among your peers. Stick to a "two-drink rule" as a good rule of thumb at law school social gatherings.

You have only one reputation. You don't want to lose your self-respect or the respect of your classmates because of a drunken incident. Remember, you're stuck with these people for three years. You'll have enough anxieties to contend with. You don't need a regretted intoxicated moment adding to your troubles.

3. Be on the lookout for signs of depression and seek help if you think you're suffering from it. As noted above, law students suffer disproportionate rates of depression. Professor Joan Malmud at the University of Oregon prompted me to highlight this serious issue. Corresponding about the legal writing chapter (Chapter 17), she slipped this paragraph into an email:

> I don't know if you're considering a section on depression in law school, but if it's a section that would fit, I would include it. For the first several years of teaching, I would find out when the year was over that several of my students had suffered depression. As their teacher, I sometimes saw odd behavior but I never ascribed it to depression; sometimes, though, I saw no remarkable behavior. I felt so sad that my students had been suffering, and I hadn't known about it and was unable to reach out to them.

Her email made me sad too because it got me thinking about all of the students suffering from depression that I no doubt overlook year after year. Indeed, many depressed students are probably unaware of their own plight. Be alert for signs and symptoms of depression. Among those listed in the diagnostic manual for mental disorders published by the American Psychiatric Association (DSM–IV, as it's usually called) are:

- Loss of interest or pleasure in activities you normally enjoy.
- Social withdrawal.
- Reduced (or sometimes increased) appetite.
- Decreased energy.
- Feelings of worthlessness or guilt.
- Persistent irritability or anger.
- Feeling "blah."
- Brooding.
- Obsessive rumination about minor failings.
- Difficulty concentrating.

- Memory difficulties.

- Insomnia or other changes in sleep patterns.

- Loss of interest/desire in sex.

- Recurrent thoughts of death or suicidal ideation.[84]

If you're suffering from depression, or think you might be, seek help. Virtually all universities have counseling departments where students can obtain free, confidential counseling services. Call and make an appointment. Don't delay. Don't accept depression as a normal consequence of law school. Just recently, I had a student who came to me very upset about law school. We talked about some of her issues and I gave her the number of the university counseling department. Within a couple of weeks, I noticed she looked much happier. When I finally had a chance to talk to her again, she said the counseling had helped her.

4. Don't fall behind. One of the surest ways to ratchet up your anxiety level, and one of the most dangerous pitfalls to avoid in law school, is falling behind. Not only are consistent students who stay current more academically successful, they can justifiably feel more confident and less stressed-out because they don't have to go to bed every night worrying about how far they are behind. Believe what I've said several times: once you fall behind in law school, it's impossible to catch up. There are no restful gaps in law school semesters that one can use to get up to speed. Every day brings new cases, new concepts, and new rules in each course. Weekends are needed for outlining and periodic review. Sad as it may sound, my greatest joy of the Thanksgiving holiday in my first year of law school was that I had two full extra days to study. Previous chapters have emphasized the importance of being a consistent, organized law student (i.e., one who doesn't fall behind) and offered specific suggestions on how to stay that way.

5. Find and maintain a healthy support network of positive-minded classmates. We all need the support of loved ones when we're going through an ordeal and law school is quite the ordeal. It's well-established in academic literature that social support promotes well-being.[85] Being

---

84. *See* AM. PSYCHIATRIC ASS'N, DIAG-NOSTIC AND STATISTICAL MANUAL OF MENTAL DISORDERS 349–52 (4th ed. 2000).

85. Beck et al., *supra*, at 6–7.

involved in a happy intimate relationship, for example, has been shown to have positive effects on overall well-being—all the more reason to pay attention to and take care of your preexisting relationships when you arrive at law school, as discussed back in Chapter 2.

Unfortunately, your non-law school loved ones aren't going to be able to help with some of your law school travails because they won't understand what you're going through (unless they're lawyers). To the contrary, they might be or seem overtly unsupportive because they feel neglected and jealous of the time you're devoting to your new endeavor. So in addition to your non-law school champions, you'll need a social support network within law school. As one student wrote in extolling the benefits of her law school friends:

> Having someone who knows exactly the stresses and hardships that you are going through is helpful. Your boyfriend/girlfriend, husband/wife do not care to hear about your school experience, nor can they relate to how hard it is. Friends are a great support system who help me through school every day.

Fortunately, making friends in law school is easy because of the psychological bonding effect of group terror. In a famous social psychology experiment, researchers put a group of monkeys in the same cage with a group of lions. Monkeys and lions usually don't socialize because the lions eat the monkeys, which causes hard feelings. Early in the experiment, it appeared events would follow this customary pattern as the lions began chasing the monkeys and the monkeys began bonking the lions on the heads with coconuts.

At this point, the researchers inserted a Contracts professor into the cage who began conducting a Socratic dialogue about the doctrine of promissory estoppel. An amazing transformation occurred. The lions and monkeys immediately locked paws and began singing pub songs. Within a few minutes, the lions were giving the monkeys foot massages and the monkeys were encouraging the lions to get in touch with their inner cubs.

Okay, this wasn't a real experiment, but I'm confident it would work out this way. That's what happened to me. Normally, I'm quite shy, but on the first day of law school orientation I was anxious and desperate to make a friend. We were packed like matchsticks into an auditorium, sitting in alphabetical order. Speaker after speaker took the podium, but the only thing I remember them emphasizing was the lack of bathroom facilities in the law school. I'm sure they talked about other things, but that's what stood out. The way people went on and on about it, adequate restroom facilities seemed to be the most important issue in legal education.

After the speeches, we were divided into groups, still in alphabetical order. A 3L took us on a tour of the law school. We traipsed in single file down hallways, through classrooms and finally into the library, where in a narrow aisle between the stacks a large puddle on the floor blocked our passage. Everyone, including our 3L tour guide, stood stymied staring at the puddle until the guy behind me deadpanned, "I guess they weren't joking about the bathrooms." In the stress of the circumstances, this struck me as hilarious. I turned and introduced myself to James H. "Mac" McCarty, Jr. We went on to form a study group together and even became room- mates. We spent many law school days and nights working and playing together. To this day, good old Mac is one of my favorite people in the world. The friends you make may be the single best feature of the entire first year of law school. Some of them will go on to become best friends who last a lifetime.

Your law school friends can be a lifeline to maintaining your well-being. They will give you someone you can vent to (don't overdo it), borrow notes from, ask clarifying questions of, laugh, cry, mourn, and celebrate with. Hold on to them for dear life and treat them well. You'll need them and they'll need you.

In forming your inner circle, seek people who are general- ly optimistic about life, even if cynically so. Nattering Nabobs of Negativism, described in Chapter 4, should be avoided, less they pull you down into their pit of pessimism and despair.

6. Don't take on stressful situations that can be avoided or postponed. With law school supplying plenty of stress already, avoid situations that will predictably add even more psychological distress. Common ones that come to mind include starting or ending intimate relationships and getting involved in confrontations with classmates. Starting a new romantic relationship can be exhilarating, of course, but it's also a huge distraction. Who can concentrate on *Pennoyer v. Neff* when they're worrying about things like, "Does she like me like me or does she LIKE me like me?" There's a reason why Little Anthony and the Imperials' 1964 hit, *Goin' Out of My Head* has sold more then four million copies and been performed more than six million times. And while ending bad relationships can be a blessing, they cause pain, longing, and general distraction even when termination is in everyone's best interests. So long as the relationship is tolerable (i.e., blah rather than harmful), I recommend maintaining the status quo at least until you're between semesters.

Then, of course, there are law school intimate relationships. Insert a large group of bright, interesting, and attractive young men and women in a closed setting and, well, you know what's going to happen. Some of them are going to hook up. Sometimes this can be a good thing, as I've known many students who met in law school and went on to get married. But for every fairy tale law school romance that ends in wedded bliss, a dozen messes occur that never should have seen the light of day.

Romantic relationships between first-year law students are particularly problematic because unlike most other intimate relationships, when they fail, you can't escape from the person. In a normal breakup, parting sentiments such as "I never want to see your ugly face again!" can be enforced. Not so in law school. Even if you end up detesting your former paramour, you'll be trapped in the same room with him or her every day for at least one year and in the same building for three years. When I asked a group of 1Ls nearing the completion of their first year what advice they would give to new law students, one student wrote back:

> I have some ideas of what not to do. This lesson I found very important. I got sucked into the social scene of school too much the first semester. It is reflected in my grades. I started off strong but after a couple of weeks I chased a girl around and we had a relationship but when it was over and exams rolled around I found that I couldn't concentrate on my studies. If I had to do it over I would focus on school and not worry too much with going out during the week (or weekend). Though hanging out with classmates is a good thing, too much can be very bad. It clouds the mind.

In addition to being careful about romantic entangle-
ments, avoid arguments (other than legal arguments) and
other confrontations with classmates (as well as professors, of
course). If a confrontational situation arises, which isn't
uncommon due to the tension, competition, and claustropho-
bic setting of the first year, take the high road and walk away
from it. You're better off losing a little pride than being
goaded into in a petty dispute. Most people who go to law
school are good folks, but many law students have large egos,
some are very immature (not surprising given their ages),
and every large entering class is bound to have a couple of
jerks in it.

**7.   Use study aids to bolster confidence, especially
in courses where the professors don't clarify the law.**
As discussed in Chapter 3, one of the greatest law student
fears is that they won't understand the material. It's scary to
feel like you're in the dark about what you're supposed to be
learning. In a normal higher-education environment, students can rely on the course textbook and the professor,
together, to teach them what they need to know. But, of
course, we've seen that law school is not a normal learning
environment. The case method and nature of casebooks pre-
clude your textbook from being a reliable place to turn to for
answers and the Socratic method of teaching can interfere
with your professors being an in-class source of enlightenment and understanding.

These are key reasons why supplemental study aids like
those listed in Appendix A are so popular in law school. In
undergraduate school, you didn't have to buy extra books to
explain the book assigned for the course. In law school, you'll
have to, at least for some courses. In addition to helping you
learn the law for exam purposes, study aids can bolster your
confidence and sense of self-efficacy by flipping on light bulbs
in your dark confusion.

Study aids are particularly helpful for reducing anxiety
(and enhancing performance) in classes taught by professors
who either rely exclusively on Socratic questioning or who
simply are poor or disorganized communicators. Most law
professors supplement Socratic dialogue with explanatory
lecture, but not all professorial presentations are models of
clarity. Whether due to their own non-linear thinking patterns, lack of preparation or an intentional design to "hide

the ball," some professors are magicians of obfuscation. Even clear, well-organized professors won't be able to explain everything in class thoroughly, in part because imparting information is not the sole goal of first-year classes and in part because there's just not enough class time.

One student consultant recommended reading the relevant sections of reliable study aids *prior* to attending classes on the theory that it allows one to enter the room with more confidence, already possessing a mental framework for processing the material covered that day. The downside of such an approach is that students may enter the classroom with preconceived notions of what they should be getting out of the day's presentation, which might conflict with the professor's goals. But if it helps to substantially promote confidence and well-being, as she swears it does for her, that risk might be an acceptable trade-off.

One type of study aid warrants specific mention: "canned briefs." Canned-brief study aids contain case briefs of every case in a particular casebook. Many law professors hate them and will *not* want to see them in the classroom (of course, they can't see the digitized versions uploaded on student computers) because some students rely on canned briefs in lieu of briefing, and sometimes even reading, the cases themselves. I could get kicked out of the legal academy for admitting this, but as a law student I found canned briefs helpful in preparing for certain classes, as a *supplement* to (not substitute for) my own conscientious reading and briefing of the cases. Canned briefs can be helpful in clueing you in on what to look for in a case and in summarizing complex fact patterns. But you have to be very careful about how you use them. Historically, not all the briefs in canned-brief series have been completely accurate and law professors have been known to take great delight in hammering students who spout incorrect information in class in reliance on a faulty canned brief.

8. Establish contact with a faculty member you like and respect. In their study documenting elevated psychological distress in law students, Benjamin and colleagues noted that one cause may be the high student-teacher ratios that exist at most law schools. They speculated that the resulting distant relationship between law students and faculty is "related significantly" to student dissatisfaction.[86]

Back in 1975, 84 percent of law students responding to a survey said they had no faculty member who took an interest in their academic progress and 71 percent said they had no faculty member to turn to for personal advice.[87] Some recent data suggest the situation has improved at least somewhat. The 2007 Law School Survey of Student Engagement, to which more than 27,000 students responded, indicated that more than half of students used email to communicate with a faculty member, nearly half had discussed assignments with a faculty member, and roughly a quarter talked with a faculty member or other law school advisor about career plans.[88]

Having a faculty contact could make you feel more comfortable, connected to, and at home in your law school environment, as well as give you a person to turn to for advice and other help. In Chapter 9, I encouraged you to make efforts to get to know your law professors and offered specific suggestions about how to do it.

9. Don't give up your primary hobby/interest. All law students need a healthy non-law school related outlet for their energy, something they find fun and that requires focus in a way that preempts obsessive thinking and worrying about law school. One of the neat things about law students is how multi-faceted they are. On my entering-student questionnaire, I ask students to list their outside interests. Reading about their interesting hobbies and hidden talents always leaves me impressed. As a conversation point, when I run into students outside of class, I'll ask, based on their questionnaires: "So do you still like to [play Frisbee golf/write poetry/collect lunch boxes/build cabinets, etc.]?" More often than not, the answer is something like, "No, I had to give that up when I started law school. There wasn't enough time."

Wrong answer! There *is* enough time to continue a fun, non-law related recreational pursuit if you develop and implement effective time-management skills. Maybe not to the

86. Benjamin et al., *supra*, at 249.

87. Carl A. Auerbach, *Legal Education and Some of Its Discontents*, 34 J. LEGAL EDUC. 43, 57 (1984).

88. *See* LSSSE, LAW. SCH. SURVEY OF STUDENT ENGAGEMENT: 2007 ANNUAL SURVEY RESULTS (2007), *available at* http://www.lssse.iub.edu.

same degree you engaged in it prior to law school, but enough time to enjoy the benefits of it. If it's an activity you're good at, so much the better. Because law school can inflict such a beating on one's sense of self-worth, it's comforting, confidence-boosting, and relaxing to partake in a hobby you know you're better at than your classmates and even your professors.

Nearly every day for my entire three years of law school, I carved out an hour or so in the evening to just sit around playing my acoustic guitar. It helped me stay sane and took my mind off my troubles. Whether your passion is a musical instrument, chess, rugby or bird-watching, make an agreement with yourself before you start law school that you will not give it up.

10. Treat yourself to a night off. Related to the above, all work and no play makes Jack and Jill Law Student not only dull boys and girls, but candidates for early mental health intervention. Set aside at least one day or night a week to relax and unwind. If you have a significant other, this is vital not only to you, but to your partner and to you both as a couple, for the reasons explained in Chapter 3. Don't feel guilty about it or look at a night off as wasted time. Look at it as recharging your batteries so you'll be more effective when you get back to work the next day.

Make it a point to avoid conversation of law school during these R & R breaks. This is much easier said than done, particularly if your night off involves socializing with law students. Turn it into a contest: first person who mentions anything about law school has to pay a penalty of some type. At the end of a recent semester, I held a party at my house for my first-year Torts students. One of the student party organizers came up with a game in which each student was issued three clothespins on arrival. If a student mentioned anything about law school, anyone who overheard the statement could take one of their clothespins. Students with the most clothespins at the end of the party received prizes. Being competitive, the students really got into the contest. Nevertheless, even the most determined players regularly slipped up. All afternoon, I heard cries of "Gotcha!" and "Darn!" as students snatched clothespins back and forth. (Particularly amusing were the lengthy legal debates as to whether certain comments were or weren't actually about law school.) Watching that game unfold reminded me of the extent to which law school permeates the souls of poor 1Ls.

11. Remember that only a few people can finish at the top and that consistent, diligent effort pays rewards in the long run. Most students, even if they deny it, arrive at law school hoping they can be one of the top students in the class. Professor Lawrence Krieger, who researches law student well-being, asked his first-year class how many of them wanted to be in the top 10 percent of the class. Ninety-percent of the students raised their hands. As Krieger noted, herein lies a major obstacle to law student well-being. If the "want" to be on top is perceived as a "need," most everyone in the class is going to end up perceiving themselves as a failure.[89]

Just because you're not in the top 10 percent doesn't mean you're not a good law student or won't be a great lawyer. Compare law student class rankings with the annual rankings of law schools themselves by the *U.S. News & World Report*. The rankings, on which many students rely in choosing a law school, are a source of tremendous stress and pressure on law schools. All schools would like to be nearer to the top, and many think they deserve to be in the top 10 percent. Law schools devote enormous resources to improving their *U.S. News* rankings, but in the end, only about twenty law schools (out of 196 ABA-accredited schools) can finish in the top 10 percent.

Does that mean the other schools are "failures"? That they're not any good? Of course not. To the contrary, all accredited law schools are of very high quality. The problem is that the rankings don't take into account and reflect many of the attributes that make a law school good. Same thing with law school grades. Law school exams measure only a limited set of skills. They don't measure oral facility, resourcefulness, dedication, heart, grit, integrity or even necessarily the amount of knowledge a student has acquired.

In 2006, a majority of law school deans signed an open letter to LSAT-takers warning them not to put too much stock in the *U.S. News* rankings (even as they worked hard to bolster the ranking of their own schools). The letter said:

---

89. *See* Lawrence S. Krieger, *What We're Not Telling Law Students—And Lawyers—That They Really Need to Know: Some Thoughts–In–Action Toward Revitalizing the Profession from Its Roots*, 13 J.L. & HEALTH 1, 11 (1999).

"The idea that all law schools can be measured by the same yardstick ignores the qualities that make ... law schools unique ...." Substitute "law students" for "law schools" and the statement rings just as true. Hmm, maybe it's time for law schools to reevaluate how we evaluate students.

I'm not suggesting that you shouldn't care about your grades. Of course grades are important. High grades open more doors to more jobs than lower grades. But recognizing grades are important and that it's worth doing your best to improve them is different from letting grades define who you are. People come to law school to get a professional degree and a license to practice law. No one sits down and says, "I think I'll go to law school so I can try to rack up three more years of good grades!" Job opportunities in law are not limited to the top 10 percent of the class. Quite the contrary is true. For the past decade, the job market for law school graduates has been largely strong and stable, with roughly 90 percent of all law graduates finding employment within nine months of graduation.

Students bear part of the blame for grade competition and anxiety by obsessively comparing their grades and talking about the grades of others. Grades are awarded anonymously. If all law students kept their grades—good, bad or medium—to themselves, it would lessen their environmental impact. If you tell your grades to even one person, many others will find out what they are. Compete only against yourself. If you work diligently and consistently, your grades will improve. Hard-working students will earn the respect of their classmates and professors regardless of their class rank.

12. Cling tightly to your personal values. Many law students come to law school thinking that law is about liberty and justice for all. They're in for a disillusioning awakening when they discover that legal rules and their application do not always lead to fair or just results. In the first year, professors concentrate on training students to *objectively* analyze and solve legal problems. Just as medical students must learn to detach themselves emotionally from their patients, law students must learn to detach their analyses from their personal feelings about a case.

While not intentional, law school's emphasis on objective analytical thinking, as shown by Professor Krieger's work in the area, can cause students to become disconnected from

their values and compassion. Thinking from the heart, regrettably, is not regarded as a pathway to either academic or
financial success as a lawyer.

As a byproduct of this corrosion, law school has a way of
forcing students to substitute law school's values for their
own. The competitive process of legal education conveys,
inadvertently, the message that the most important rewards
in the legal profession are extrinsic (e.g., high grades, high
salaries), rather than intrinsic (personal growth, helping others). As Krieger explains:

> Scientific research for the past 15 years has consistent-
> ly shown that a primary focus on external rewards and
> results, including affluence, fame, and power, is unful-
> filling. These values are seductive—they create a nice
> picture of life but they are actually correlated with
> relative unhappiness. Instead, people who have a more
> "intrinsic," personal/interpersonal focus—on personal
> growth, close relationships, helping others, or improv-
> ing their community—turn out to be significantly hap-
> pier and more satisfied with their lives.[90]

I attended law school with dreams of becoming a great
civil rights lawyer. My hero was Clarence Darrow, the Chicago criminal defense lawyer known for championing unpopular causes. He was my hero because he was my mother's hero
and she told me stories about him when I was growing up.
Before I even knew what a lawyer was, I knew that there was
this great man out there, this *lawyer*, who always stood up
and fought for the underdog.

Somewhere along my law school journey, I took a wrong
turn and got lost. I either forgot or sublimated by dream. I
allowed the culture of law school to inculcate a new value
system in me, one in which prestige, high salaries, expense
accounts, and other perks became the most valuable prizes of
becoming a lawyer. My success as a law student made matters worse in that regard. With high grades and law review
membership, all signs pointed in one direction. When I started interviewing at law firms in the second year of my federal
judicial clerkship, I contacted only firms considered to be
prestigious and that paid the highest salaries. I didn't contact
a single civil rights firm. On receiving an offer from a highly

---

90. Lawrence S. Krieger, The Hidden
Sources of Law School Stress: Avoiding
the Mistakes that Create Unhappy and
Unprofessional Lawyers 4 (2006).

regarded commercial litigation firm, I accepted it even though I didn't enjoy the interview or think I wanted to work there. Everything turned out fine in the end, but I'll always regret never having made an attempt to be that civil rights lawyer I dreamed about.

A study suggests I followed a predictable path. It found that law students who attain high grades in the first semester demonstrate significant shifts away from service-oriented career preferences toward high-stress, money-oriented, prestige opportunities.[91] I think I would have been a happier law student and *know* I would have been a happier lawyer if I had not lost sight of why I wanted to go to law school and be a lawyer in the first place.

On the questionnaire I give to first-year students, I ask why they came to law school. A substantial percentage of students give sincere answers about wanting to help people, often targeting specific groups such as children, the elderly or the disabled. Very few law students, however, end up pursuing those original goals once they become lawyers. Words to live by from Shakespeare: "To thine own self be true." Don't let law school corrupt your values or reasons for being there.

Complicating this advice is that, much more commonly than in other graduate programs, law students either don't know why they came to law school or came for uninspired reasons such as "What else was I going to do with a degree in medieval history?" or "I figured it would be a decent way to make a living." The well-being of such students, of which there are a large number, is perhaps even more at risk. It's one thing to put up with the workload and stress of law school if you have a good reason and strong motivation for being there, but quite another if you don't know why you're there or arrived only with a vague goal of improving your career options. Anecdotal evidence suggests that the happiest lawyers are those who wanted to be lawyers for a long time before enrolling in law school.

Hang on to the person you were before you got to law school. Stay connected to your heart and follow it in planning your career. "Follow your heart" is the most essential piece of advice I give to my students. Money and fame don't make

91. Sheldon & Krieger, *supra*, at 281.

people happy. Some of the richest people I know are the most wretchedly empty and unhappy people I know.

Good Advice, But Will You Follow It?

Hearing advice and following it are two different things. That's a particular problem with the recommendations in this chapter, some of which constitute "lifestyle advice" as applied to law students. Admittedly, some of my tips for maintaining well-being fall under the "I didn't need to buy a book to tell me that" category. Will couch-potato readers start an exercise regimen because it's suggested above? Will law students with drinking issues become teetotalers because of the alarming statistics cited regarding law student/lawyer alcohol abuse? Will 1Ls keep up with their hobbies because a law professor said it's a good idea? Maybe, but I'm not counting on it. My goal in this chapter is more modest: to alert you to recurring issues that contribute to higher stress and lower well-being among students and offer you some ideas for dealing with them. It's up to you, of course, to manage your life.

CHAPTER 19

WELCOME *BACK* TO THE JUNGLE: THE PERILOUS SECOND SEMESTER

In a way I kind of feel as though the first semester was like me going into a burning building to pull somebody out of the fire. I wanted to go and was happy to do it, and after coming out I was glad I did it, but felt like I wouldn't want to do it again. Now for the next semester I feel as though there is somebody else in the house and the fire has gotten worse. I groan and make myself go in again, and part of me wants to go back in, but in the back of my mind I'm aware of how tired I am from the first time and am a little more worried about whether or not I will get out of the building alive this time.

1L's comment about starting
the second semester

Virtually all of the advice in this book up to this point applies equally to the first and second semesters, including advice about study and exam techniques. This chapter focuses on the particular issues and obstacles that the second semester raises for students. Knowing and understanding the obstacles should lessen the blow of smacking into them and make it easier to navigate around them.

The second semester, particularly in the opening days and weeks, is one of the most daunting challenges in all of law school. How students respond to it is a crucial determinant of their long-term success. This is the juncture where, for reasons described below, students make judgments and decisions about themselves and law school that play a large role in determining and defining their ultimate "law school selves."

The Second Semester has Upsides

It may seem counterintuitive that many law students find the second semester more difficult and dispiriting than the first. With three months experience under their belts, one might think the second semester would be a "been there, done that" relative breeze for students. In the first semester, students are lost in a maze of uncertainty and bear the weight of the fear and stress that stumbling blindly carries with it. Beginning law students must acclimate themselves to an entirely new educational world. They spend forever preparing for class only to arrive feeling unprepared because the professors are asking questions they hadn't thought about. Many live in paralyzing fear of the Socratic method. For first-semester students, an entirely new vocabulary converts reading a single paragraph of a case into a marathon exercise in using *Black's Law Dictionary*. It's in the first semester that students who arrive at law school in search of "the right answers" must succumb—sometimes kicking and screaming the whole way—to the frustrating ambiguity of legal doctrine. All of this must be accomplished in strange surroundings full of strangers. Aggravating matters, students have no clue if they're doing anything right because everything transpires in a vacuum of feedback.

These conditions are vastly improved come the second semester. Students know how to prepare for class. They're much more efficient at reading and briefing cases. The Socratic method is less intimidating. To their pleasant surprise, students saw that no one got tortured or executed for giving a wrong answer in the first semester. The physical environs students return to after the holiday break are familiar. Some of those strangers from the first semester are now good friends and at least some of the professors are known quantities. Students know what to expect on law school exams. After receiving their first-semester grades, they finally have the feedback they craved so desperately. They've made it through the first crucible of law school. Full-time students are one-sixth of the way to becoming lawyers. Part-time students are one-eighth of the way home.

Nevertheless, Student State of Mind is Mixed

So what's not to like about the second semester? Plenty. It's true that all of the reasons listed above work to alleviate some major causes of stress and anxiety in students. But the second semester brings its own set of new problems. Before considering them, let's take a glimpse at the state of mind of 1Ls returning after the holiday break for their second semester. For the past couple of years, I've polled my Torts students at the start of the second semester with this online question:

What is your dominant feeling as you begin the second semester?

- Excited

- Tired

- Bored

- Depressed

- Rested and ready

Very few students select "Excited" and "Rested and Ready." The most common answers by far are "Tired" and "Depressed." A couple of students even pick "Bored"—definitely not a good sign since they still have years of law school to go, followed by a lifetime of being a lawyer.

Recently, I probed more deeply into student sentiments about starting the second semester. Just before classes began, I asked a section of Torts students to comment on, among other things, their: (1) state of mind; (2) motivation level; and (3) happiness level in comparison to the first semester. The responses showed that, while some students feel better off in the second semester, a significant segment are less happy and less motivated. In between is a large group of students who are ambivalent about their feelings.

Students expressing positive feelings about their state of mind, motivation level, and happiness level emphasized many of the improved conditions listed above: more efficient study skills, a larger comfort zone from knowing what to expect, new friendships, increased confidence from having made it through the first semester, and excitement about being on their way to becoming lawyers. Here are some sample positive responses:

- Overall, I am happier than at the start of first semester. I am one-sixth of the way through! If the second semester goes as fast as the first, the three years should fly by. I feel engaged by all of my professors and am genuinely happy to be *learning.* (Cheesy, I know, but it's true.)

- I am definitely happier! I know now that I made the right decision in coming to law school. I have met many great friends and am very impressed with the law school and the professors. I learned that law school wasn't as horrifying as I was told it would be, and after a semester of it, it really boosted my confidence.

- Excited. I worked at a large law firm for a year before coming to law school and had lunch with a few attorneys there while home on break. I made a crack that I was one-sixth of a lawyer. One of the attorneys who has been practicing for three or four years cracked back "I'm not even one-sixth of a lawyer." I think that hammered home the point that there is so much that I don't know. Part of me wanted to come back to start filling in the blanks.

- I might actually be a little more motivated now that I know what to expect. I was so nervous at the beginning that I couldn't concentrate on anything else. Now that I know what to expect from the finals, I feel like I have more of an opportunity to improve my study skills and just my performance in general.

Unfortunately, these feel-good vibes were more than offset by a strong current of discontent among many students. Note the similarity in these responses from three students to my questions regarding, respectively, state of mind, motivation level, and happiness level:

Student 1:

1. My general state of mind as I start this semester is unmotivated.

2. I am definitely less motivated at the start of this semester than I was at the beginning.

3. I am also unhappier than I was during the first semester.

(The student added a post script: "Though this sounds depressing, I'm not depressed. Just struggling a little at the moment.")

Student 2:

1. Unhappy and sullen.

2. Much less motivated—I'm already convinced I failed out of school, so the last thing I want to do is continue to work hard.

3. The same amount of light unhappiness, but it's for different reasons. In the beginning it was fear and anxiety. Now I just feel defeated.

Student 3:

1. I generally feel depressed to be quite honest.

2. I am less motivated now than when I started the first semester.

3. I am a bit unhappier than when I began.

Potential Pitfalls of the Second Semester

Difficulties in the second semester that contribute to feelings like those described above are largely overlooked in advice given to first-year students. I make an effort to give my students relevant advice as they progress through law school, but, honestly, until composing this book, had never fully comprehended the pitfalls of the second semester or discussed them with students. Let's take a look at them:

Ignorance can be bliss.

The uncertainty of the first semester is a substantial cause of strain on 1Ls, but unveiling law school can be problematic as well. In the second semester uncertainty about law school is replaced by a disquieting *certainty* that it can be exhausting, onerous drudgery. In his 1709 *An Essay on Criticism*, eighteenth-century English poet Alexander Pope coined the phrase "A little learning is a dangerous thing." Law students might modify it to say a little learning can be a depressing thing. Look at how some 1Ls weighed in on their newfound awareness in response to the questions about starting the second semester:

- Now I know exactly what I'm walking into. First semester there was a bit of excited anticipation, etc.

Now I know I'll be in the library for the next four
months.

- In some ways I'm happier because I really enjoy the
  process of learning and have really enjoyed school,
  but in other ways I am unhappier because I now
  know how hard I will have to work this semester.

- I am unhappier than I was starting the first semester because I now understand the toll that law
  school can take on my personal life.

- The hardest thing to me about starting the second
  semester is knowing that I have to go through the
  whole exam process at the end again, and not only
  one more time, but five more times.

- The hardest thing about starting the second semester is realizing that we have five more semesters to
  go.

The thrill is gone.

As suggested by some of the comments, the realization of
what a long haul law school will be is worsened by the fact
that the excitement and adrenalin that fueled students
through the first semester has evaporated. Students arrive at
law school brimming with anticipation and energy. Seeing
and feeling it is one of the great joys of being a 1L law
teacher. But like romances that lose their dizzying effects
when the newness wears off, law school becomes more of a
chore than an adventure after the ebullience of the first
semester subsides.

Students start the second semester with a hangover effect
of physical and emotional exhaustion from the first semester.
The holiday break is just long enough to remind students
what it's like to live like a free person, but not quite long
enough for students to fully recharge their batteries. As
bluesman B.B. King would put it, "the thrill is gone."

Be prepared for this letdown at the beginning of the
second semester. Know that it's completely normal, natural,
and, happily, usually transitory. Within a couple of weeks,
most students bounce back to their old selves. While they
never quite regain that exhilaration that comes with newness, they do get their second wind and perk back up substantially.

The double-edged grade blade.

Depending how they turn out, first-semester grades can be either a major boost or impediment to starting the second semester. You've heard the aphorism "Be careful what you wish for." It applies to law school feedback big-time. We've discussed how most students begin law school with at least some hope of finishing near the top of their class, but also the mathematical reality that only a small percentage of students can fulfill that goal or dream.

For those who performed well, first-semester grades can infuse new energy and confidence. It shows up in class. Every year, in the early days of the second semester, students who never raised their hands the first semester start volunteering in class. When they do, I smile inside as I call on them, thinking: "Ah, good for you. You must have done better than you expected."

But for every student whose confidence gets a jolt from grades, three or four others get their egos electrocuted. High expectations, previous educational success, mandatory grading curves, and an abundance of talented people create a perfect storm for dashed hopes. The storm is unleashed the moment first-semester grades are released. Suddenly, students who rarely have seen a grade below an *A* in sixteen-plus years of education would be willing to trade 100,000 shares of Microsoft stock for a *B*. A *B-* might be worth 75,000 shares. *Anything* without the dreaded *C* in front of it (or, of course, *D* or *F*). I tell students, truthfully, that no meaningful difference exists between a *B-* and a *C+* exam, but there's no assuaging their disappointment.

Here's a particularly vivid indicator of the impact of first-semester grades on student perspective. One student answered my questions about state of mind and happiness and motivation levels before receiving his grades and said he felt compelled to re-answer them after receiving grades, explaining "I feel vastly different now." Compare his pre-and post-grade answers:

State of mind before grades:

Not so much depressed, but unexcited. I believe this is due simply to the fact that I don't know how I did. If I knew how I did, even if it was bad, I would feel a little more excited than I do now. At this moment, it's all just uncertain, and that definitely has made me less excited to get started this semester.

State of mind after grades:

Excited. Objectively speaking, I did well first semester, but subjectively speaking, I didn't do as well as I want to. I feel reassured that I'm in the place I am called to be and I am excited at the prospect of doing even better this semester than I did last semester.

Motivation level before grades:

Less motivated.

Motivation level after grades:

More motivated now that I have received grades. I did well, although not as well as I wanted to. But I feel like I have the ability to do even better now, because I have the experience of the first semester.

Happiness level before grades:

Happier, because I know what's coming. While there is uncertainty in the grades from the past semester, I know what's going to hit me as far as work in this upcoming semester. That is a little more reassuring than the absolute uncertainty I felt when I began the first semester.

Happiness level after grades:

Happier now that I have grades. I feel some sense of accomplishment, something that I didn't have first semester or before I got some of my grades back. I think students are wired to feel stressed before they get those grades back. They are reassurance that the work was worth something. They are what we were aiming at; our goal.

Making lower-than-hoped-for grades more demoralizing is the fact that most students work their tails off in the first semester. It undermines spirit and confidence to work harder than one has ever worked before and come up short, at least (or perhaps especially) in one's own eyes. Many students just don't see a connection between their hard work and the results. One student comment to my happiness question touched thoughtfully on this point. When he submitted it, he included a note saying he wrote it mostly for his own benefit:

You are told when you come to law school that, more likely than not, you will not be the best of the best. That's fine. From my personal experience, everyone lies if they tell you they do not wish in their heart that when grades are posted they will be perched towards the top of their class. Reality dictates that many of us will be disappointed—seriously disappointed in some cases. Personally, I did "fine" this semester. I had grades that I am proud of and one in particular that I am not happy with. I am, at the moment, your everyday Average Joe law student. Middle of the pack or a notch or two above.

I have many deep and close friends here, and I know that I worked very hard the previous semester. I know that I worked harder than some of my dearest friends. I know that several of them did better than me—some did tremendously well. It's difficult to describe the frustration that causes. You are happy for the individuals that did well, yet you are mystified and deeply frustrated that the hundreds (thousands?) of hours that you worked did not provide the reward you sought.

How students respond to first-semester grades is crucial to their remaining law school existence, as well as their post-law school lives. Far too many students define themselves by their first-semester grades. If they received Cs, they tell themselves: "Well, I guess I'm only a C student." Then many of them proceed to behave like C students by not working as hard from that point on.

It bears repeating: Law school is a marathon, not a sprint. Suppose you really were a serious marathon runner. A marathon is roughly 26 miles. The one-sixth mark—that is, the equivalent mark of finishing one of the six semesters of law school for a full-time student—would be 4.3 miles. Suppose you came to that point of the race and realized you were in the middle of the pack (i.e., the C student of marathon runners). Would you give up? With so much ground still remaining, so much time and terrain to gain on the competition, would you tell yourself, "Well, I guess I'm no good as a marathon runner. I might as well slow down."?

It's *way* too early to give up on law school after just one semester. For people who continue working hard, grades generally go up. For people who start working less, grades generally go down. I've seen it happen a hundred times. Think back to the student mentioned in Chapter 9 for whom I wrote the strong recommendation letter even though she received a *D* in Torts I. One reason I was willing to endorse her so strongly was because after she received the *D*, she came to me and said she intended to work even harder in the second semester. She got a *B-* in Torts II, a five-step increase. And I'll never forget the student who broke down crying in my colleague's office after receiving a *D* on his Contracts midterm exam—his very first law school exam. He went on to graduate number one in his class and serve as editor-in-chief of the law review.

Law school exam-taking is a learning process for most students. It's true that a few people in each class have a natural knack for it right off the bat. Sadly, it's also true that a small number of students never get the hang of it and are academically dismissed. But for most students, as with any new skill, it's a matter of improving through repetition. You're only at the one-sixth mark of the race at the beginning of the second semester. Don't slow down. Turn it up a notch.

Getting back in the groove.

A universal challenge of starting the second semester is simply getting back into the routine of daily classes and class preparation. After going and going like the battery bunny on meth for three months, students finish that last exam of the first semester and everything suddenly stops. Many students don't know what to do with themselves during the holiday break. They're not used to having so much free time. Many report that they can't enjoy the break at the beginning because they feel guilty about not studying. Then, just about the time they readjust to an unstructured lifestyle full of leisure time, it's time to get back to the grind.

Included in my "starting the second semester" survey was this question: "The hardest thing for me about starting the second semester is [fill in the blank]." The dominant response was getting refocused to do it all over again. Look at the commonality—indeed, near identicalness—in the following responses, and there were many more just like them:

- The hardest thing for me about starting the second semester is getting refocused to do it all over again. The first semester felt so draining both emotionally and physically. It is hard to adjust to getting back and getting refocused.

- The hardest thing for me about starting the second semester is getting back into the habit of doing all of the reading on a consistent basis.

- The hardest thing for me about starting the second semester is getting back into the habit of studying and being in that building for several hours on end.

- The hardest thing for me about starting the second semester is getting back into the mindset (you have to get into a certain mindset, I think, to get into the habit of briefing, etc.).

- The hardest thing for me about starting the second semester is feeling like I'm back at the beginning. I felt so good about finishing that first semester, and even though I was unsure about my grades I was still pretty proud of myself for making it. Now I feel like I have to start all over again. But I'm sure once I'm back in the swing of things, the semester will begin to fly by just like the first semester did.

And in that last sentence we find the saving grace of this challenge. This too shall pass. Once students do get back into the swing of things, the second semester flies by just like the first one did and like the third, fourth, fifth, and sixth ones (and seventh and eighth for part-time students) will.

Key to your success is forcing yourself back into the groove *at the very beginning*. Don't squander the opening weeks of the second semester moping or dawdling. If you'll forgive the mixed metaphor, you must come out swinging to get back in the swing. The CREDO (Consistent, Rigorous, Efficient, Diligent, Organized) outlined in Chapter 10 applies to each semester of law school. It's important to be consistent from the get-go in the second semester, just as in the first semester. Warm-up class sessions are even less likely to occur than in the first semester. Profs generally come in and start teaching new law in the opening minutes of the first class. Hit the ground running or you can lose ground quickly.

Increased competitiveness.

Before you start law school, you're likely to hear stories about how competitive law students are, to the point where many are alleged to be "cutthroat." The classic repeated story is a variation on students hiding the case reporter volume containing the key case that everyone needs to complete their memos for Legal Research and Writing—or even more egregiously, tearing the case out of the book. The latter actually happened to me in law school. I tracked down the reporter volume in the library containing the essential case for my memo, but when I turned to the case, it was missing. Someone had actually ripped out the pages!

In general, my experience as a professor has been that law students are quite supportive of one another. Of course, like all human experiences, the level of competition in law school varies depending on the particular group and individuals. I frequently observe students going out of their way to help and support their classmates, sometimes to astonishing degrees, but also hear occasional ugly stories of ruthless competitiveness.

To the extent competitiveness is an issue with which to be concerned, students tell me it gets worse in the second semester. I think much of it relates back to that first set of grades having been issued. In the first semester, everyone is in the same boat, struggling to stay afloat. The shared experience creates a communal bond. But once first-semester grades have been issued, there may be a feeling—both among some high achievers and some lower-than-hoped-for achievers—of "Hey, you're in *that* boat and I'm in *this* boat."

Some students with high grades may consider themselves superior to their classmates and project, or be perceived to project, that image to others. In turn, some lower-performing students may resent the students at the top, particularly if they flaunt their success. Meanwhile, students who may not have appreciated the importance of class rank and GPA in the first semester become all too aware of it as the second semester progresses and they see the top-ranked students landing the good summer law firm jobs, research assistant positions, etc.

To say this is unfortunate would be an understatement. The fact is you and your 1L mates are all in the same boat. There's not much meaningful practical advice I can give you on this issue other than to put you on notice that over-competitiveness is not an attractive quality. If you do well your first semester, keep it to yourself. People will find out about it anyway, and respect you all the more for it. If you brag about your high grades, people will hate you—as they should.

Enhanced workload.

Depending on the law school, a major cause of second-semester stress is an increased workload. Some schools add an extra course in the second semester. And, of course, an extra exam accompanies the extra course. Some professors also move at a quicker pace in the second semester, which means more material and longer reading assignments.

And then there's the appellate brief and oral argument, one of the heaviest burdens of 1L existence. As discussed in Chapter 17, most students' second semester loads in Legal Research and Writing will include having to write an appellate brief and engage in an oral argument before a mock appellate court. No reason to rehash the subject, except to note that these requirements add substantially to second-semester workloads. It takes more time and effort to research and write an appellate brief than to compose the law office memoranda assigned in first-semester legal writing courses. Additionally, the oral argument consumes tremendous emotional energy. One plus is that increased efficiency in class preparation resulting from lessons learned in the first semester helps to counterbalance the additional workload of the second semester.

Second-guessing life as a lawyer.

One obstacle some students face in the second semester is much larger than the second semester and even law school itself. It's the global issue of wondering whether one made the right choice in sacrificing everything (e.g., time, effort, financial resources, relationships, other opportunities) to come to law school. Should I be here? Is this what I really want to do with my life? In the first semester, students are struggling just to keep up, giving them little time to ponder the long-term wisdom of their career choice. In the second semester, nagging doubts kept at bay in the first semester start to creep into consciousness.

Most students come to law school with very little understanding of what lawyers actually do. For many, their exposure to the law has been limited to glamorized media accounts. They're disappointed to find that the first year of law
school is consumed with the study of un-scintillating, often
archaic, and rarely inspiring rules and doctrines.

Adverse possession? Attractive nuisance? Who cares about
those? When do we get to learn how to conduct those great
television-lawyer 'gotcha' cross-examinations that extract
confessions from murderers just in time for the last commercial break? And what's up with all these very un-John Gris-
ham-like cases? Where's the intrigue, the suspense, the romance?

In the second semester, if not sooner, students are hit
with the realization that being a lawyer, while potentially
rewarding on many levels, is anything but glamorous. Instead
of inspiring students about practicing law, professors may
actually dampen student enthusiasm, although not intentionally. Mid-second semester, I again surveyed a section of Torts
students, asking the question: "How are you feeling about
your career choice itself (i.e. becoming a lawyer)? Any sur-
prises (either positive or negative) on that front?" One student replied:

> I think professors focus too much on the negative
> aspects of the job. Many professors make it seem like
> our lives are going to be terrible when we get out and
> start practicing. I've heard some of my classmates
> asking why we're doing this if it's such a horrible job.

Oops. Sorry about that. He might have been referring to
me. While I try to inspire my students about the institution
of law, I feel an obligation to be candid about the sometimes
harsh reality of actually practicing it. To do otherwise, I
think, would be a disservice. But I might go overboard in my
candor, which admittedly leans toward the negative. My four
years as a practicing lawyer were marked by long hours, high
stress, and an intense hatred of billable hours, which require
a lawyer to keep track of and document every moment of the
day.

I suspect a fair number of other law profs are guilty of
being naysayers as well. While law professors hold the institution of "being a lawyer" in high regard, they may have less
fondness for the actual practice of law, especially private

practice. Many law professors fled the practice of law for what they saw as a better life in academia. Consequently, we might be the wrong people to be talking to our students about the pros and cons of private practice.

The good news is that studies of the legal profession show that most lawyers are satisfied with their career choice. In the first installment of the *After the JD* project, a comprehensive study that will track the careers of 5,000 lawyers for ten years, researchers reported that 80 percent of lawyers surveyed two to three years after graduating from law school were either "moderately or extremely satisfied with their decision to become a lawyer."[92] The report found no evidence of pervasive unhappiness in the legal profession.

If you have doubts about your career choice, stop and ask why? First, understand that it's normal and appropriate to reevaluate such a life-changing decision as going to law school. Unfortunately, an informed evaluation isn't possible prior to actually attending. The second semester is a good time to pause and size things up.

Some students decide they simply don't like or enjoy law school or the law or the prospect of being a lawyer—or all three—and withdraw. There's nothing wrong with such a decision if it's made for the right reasons. One recent student concluded in the second semester that she wasn't going to find true happiness being a lawyer, so she decided to withdraw from law school after the first year and enroll in a graduate psychology program. She wryly answered my above career-choice question by stating: "I'm feeling great about my career choice [i.e., her choice to quit law school]."

If you feel quite certain you don't want to be a lawyer, it's better to cut your losses by figuring that out sooner rather than later. I'll never forget the student who showed up at my office the Monday after her law school graduation and asked if I would write a letter of recommendation for her to enroll in a graduate program in social work. Surprised, I asked what prompted her decision. She said she knew from the beginning of law school that she didn't want to be a lawyer, but felt pressure to complete her legal education so she wouldn't be seen as "a quitter" by her family and in her own eyes.

92. NALP FOUND. FOR LAW CAREER RESEARCH & EDUC./AM. BAR FOUND, AFTER   THE JD: FIRST RESULTS OF A NATIONAL STUDY OF LEGAL CAREERS 47 (2004).

The key in making this assessment is to be sure you're looking at the long-term prospects for happiness in the legal profession, rather than at the frustrations or stress of the moment. Law school itself will pass, more quickly than you realize. In my first year, I did not enjoy law school, but I did like the law itself. I loved that every case was different. I was awed by the power of law to affect people's lives for better or worse. I found the mental challenge of unraveling the complexities of law to be thrilling. My love for and appreciation of "the law" kept me going when law school times got tough. When students come to me second-guessing whether they want to be a lawyer, the first question I ask is: "Do you enjoy the law itself?" If the answer is a clear "no," I suggest that maybe law isn't the field for them. But if the answer is yes, I usually encourage them to hang in there.

Take heart in the fact that many students absolutely *love* law school and many lawyers *love* the practice of law. Here are some glowing endorsements of law school and the prospect of becoming a lawyer that I received from second-semester students in response to my question about their career choice:

- I'm excited! I know this is what I was meant to be!

- I love the career. I do love the law. I'm surprised with how much I actually enjoy reading the cases, even the cases that I'm reading for the appellate brief.

- I have always wanted to be a lawyer, since I was in sixth grade. I cannot see myself in any other profession, so I feel like this is the right career choice for me. Also, I really enjoy talking about the law and politics, and I enjoy being in law school where I don't have to feel like a dork if I get excited to talk about something related to the law, like the difference between assault and battery. I feel that being a lawyer is a respected profession, and even though as you know, we are always made fun of, when someone finds out I am in law school, there is definitely a respect there.

Related to questions about whether they want to be lawyers, some second-semester 1Ls begin stressing over *what kind* of lawyer they want to be. They get worried when they don't know the answer. In response to my career-choice question, one student wrote he was happy he came to law school, but added: "I just wish that when everyone asked what kind of lawyer I want to be I had an answer. When I answer with 'I don't know,' they look at me like I have been wasting my time. That is really getting annoying." Certainly, it's a good question to start considering. But it's nothing to get agitated about. There's no reason most 1Ls should know what kind of lawyers they want to be because they haven't been exposed either to enough law or to the real world sufficiently to develop informed opinions.

As previously mentioned, I thought I wanted to be a civil rights lawyer before I got to law school, but once I arrived and discovered so many different interesting subject areas, I was back to square one. When I graduated, I still didn't know what kind of law I wanted to practice. My judicial clerkship gave me two extra years to think about it, but even with that extra time, I still chose the wrong path. I decided to be a commercial litigator, only to find I hated it. It wasn't until six years after law school when I became a professor that I knew I had found my place.

Finding the right fit—both in terms of the field of law and the particular place and people you work with—is arguably the most important decision you will ever make in terms of your long-term happiness. You'll spend more time working than doing any other activity in your life, even sleeping. Better to make the decision correctly than quickly, while also recognizing that you might not get it right the first time.

So cross this worry off your list. Unless you came to law school to be a specific type of lawyer, keep your mind open to all options and trust that you will find your way. The students who follow their hearts in making the decision end up much happier than the many who don't. In the meantime, when someone asks what kind of lawyer you want to be, just say, "A great one! But I need to do more exploring before deciding on a particular type of practice."

Financial issues.

Many students get panicky, or at least very concerned, about financial issues in the second semester. Students often arrive having saved enough money to get them through the first semester only to realize they need to start borrowing more heavily starting in the second semester.

Debt load, in turn, takes on greater prominence as a source of anxiety as students begin to realize that the lawyer salary data they read about prior to attending law school—and which, unfortunately, draws many students to law school—is skewed. Those $160,000 starting salaries and lavish annual bonuses splashed across the media go to only a small percentage of top-performing students who land jobs at large law firms in big cities. Entry-level salaries for most law graduates are likely to be in the $40-$50,000 range. Not bad, but not enough to live comfortably on *and* pay off the massive debt many students acquire in law school. (The Association for Legal Career Professionals website—http://www.nalp.org—is a good place to find current information about salary trends for lawyers.)

Only one sensible answer exists to these financial issues: manage your debt responsibly. Keep it as low as possible. I'm always amazed at the standard of living many students maintain while living on borrowed money. They drive nicer cars than I do, eat out frequently, dress well, and even take vacations. Some years ago a student confided to me that she used student loan money to pay for breast augmentation surgery!

Thankfully, I escaped law school with minimal debt, in large part because my law school mates and I lived at a very low standard of living. Several of us shared a ramshackle house, so rent was cheap. We didn't use the air conditioning even though it's hot as Hades in Gainesville, Florida for much of the year. We never ate out, so food was cheap. For lunch, I took a can of tuna and a piece of bread to school on most days. We picked our entertainment based on cost. Our big nights were parties in our backyard or a couple of pitchers of cheap beer during happy hour. We didn't take vacations. Our cars were falling apart. We didn't buy clothes. This isn't a sob story. To the contrary, we were probably happier then than we've ever been. If you know you're going to be dependent on borrowed money for living expenses, start scaling down your lifestyle in advance. That way you won't miss it as much when the time comes. My guess is that students could easily trim their debt by twenty percent if they simply lived more frugally.

News flash. Remember what I said at the beginning that you should consciously avoid trying to learn any law before law school? I take it back. Here's some law that is definitely worth investigating: In 2007, Congress passed the College Cost Reduction and Access Act (CCRAA). The program will cap student loan payment amounts based on a formula that takes into account factors such as the borrower's income and family size. If the borrower makes payments for twenty-five years, remaining qualifying loan balances will be forgiven. For law students going into a "public service" position (a term not yet specifically defined), the borrower need only make payments for ten years before qualifying loan balances will be forgiven. The program, which is a godsend to debt-financed law students, goes into effect in 2009 and applies to all government-guaranteed loans. Consult a financial-aid counselor for advice and details.[93]

Finally, as an aside, you need to know that anyone who attends law school as part of a "get rich" plan is making a huge mistake. That is not a good reason to become a lawyer. Most lawyers do earn decent livings, but it usually takes several years to get to that point. Even if you get rich, the money will not make you happy if you hate what you're doing. I took a big pay cut many years ago in leaving private practice to become a law professor and never regretted it for even one second.

Summer job anxiety.

Related to the above is anxiety about obtaining a summer legal job at the conclusion of the first year. Students feel tremendous pressure in their second semester to land summer clerkships (also called "summer associate" positions) at law firms. In many cases, this pressure arises from pressing financial needs, but it also stems from an expectation that getting summer legal jobs is something 1Ls are *supposed* to do.

Usually to no avail, I try to reassure students that this is not the case. I tell them not to worry about summer clerkships, particularly in the summer between their 1L and 2L years, explaining that I never had a summer clerkship and everything turned out fine for me. They respond that lawyers and upper-level students tell them that getting a summer

---

93. *See* Kristi Lemoine, *New Legislation Puts Loan Forgiveness Within* *Reach*, STUDENT LAW., Apr. 2008, at 22.

clerkship is the only entryway to a permanent job with a law firm.

It's true that many firms hire associates from the ranks of former clerks who performed well. But it's certainly not an absolute rule. Most students who perform well academically are able to obtain good permanent jobs after graduation regardless of whether they clerked at a law firm. Lower-performing students might need to prove themselves more to a firm before the firm will take a chance on them, but they're also the least likely to be hired for summer clerkships, at least the well-paying ones, which come almost exclusively from large firms. In any event, the summer after the second year of law school—not the first—is the clerkship window from which most permanent job offers flow. Many law firms won't hire students after their first year on the theory that 1Ls haven't learned enough yet to be of great value.

The lack of clerking opportunities after the first year is particularly disheartening to students who were counting on high-paying summer jobs to offset their financial burdens. Similar to the stories about stratospheric starting salaries, many students have heard about high-paying, cushy summer law clerk positions prior to attending law school. These positions do exist (the largest firms pay up to $3,000 a week), but like those six-figure starting salaries, they usually are reserved for that same group of top-performing students. And, again, they're usually doled out to 2Ls rather than 1Ls. Remember also that glitzy summer clerkship positions often require one to relocate, meaning that living expenses eat up a lot of the largess.

The long and short of it is: don't feel tremendous pressure to obtain a legal job in your first summer. If you need money, consider non-legal jobs as a way to get a hiatus from law school. Many students can earn more waiting tables than they could earn clerking for a law firm. If you don't need the money, summer school is a good option. Getting a couple of courses out of the way in the summer will lighten your burden during the regular academic year. It's even possible to graduate a semester early if that's your goal. Volunteering in a legal capacity for a non-profit organization is a great way to affirm your decision to attend law school. If you have the resources, consider a summer abroad program. Law schools sponsor summer abroad programs in every corner of the world. I've never had a student attend one who didn't come back saying it was one of the greatest experiences of his or her life.

In the meantime, concentrate on doing the best you can in law school and trust that things have a way of taking care of themselves.

CHAPTER 20

LAW REVIEW, MOOT COURT, AND OTHER CO- AND EXTRACURRICULAR ACTIVITIES

Your courses will consume most of your time, but a variety of co-curricular and extracurricular activities also take place in law schools. No, I'm not talking about the keg parties. I'm talking about serious academic stuff like law review, moot court, and student organizations. While deep involvement in these activities is reserved largely for upper-level students, the first year is when students usually face decisions as to which of these paths, if any, to follow.

These activities are voluntary, yet some require the dedication of hundreds of hours of labor. Wait! Don't flip ahead yet. While seeing "voluntary" and "hundreds of hours of labor" in the same sentence might seem like an excellent reason to skip this chapter, you'll be amazed by the large number of students who actively pursue these extra commitments. Why? Because they give students opportunities to sharpen their lawyering skills, enrich their law school experience, find and create a distinct legal identity for themselves, meet and spend time with like-minded students and develop mentoring relationships with faculty who serve as coaches or advisors, and, importantly, bolster their resume credentials.

Law Review

Every law school publishes a "law review," a student-run, student-edited journal of scholarly legal articles written primarily by law professors, but also by judges, lawyers, and students. Law reviews typically publish four to six issues per year, with each issue containing a few primary articles by outside authors and a few works written by student members of the law review. Some law review articles become extremely influential in the development of the law, while many others are read only by the authors and a few close relatives.

Being on law review has long been the holy grail of law school success. The law review stamp defines its holder as an elite academic performer. Traditionally, this was necessarily the case because the only students permitted to participate on law review were those with high GPAs and class rank. For example, back in the day, I received an automatic invitation to join the *Florida Law Review* in my first year based on being ranked in the top 5 percent of my class. Under this "grade-on" system, still in place at some schools, the rich get richer. Students with high grades already have better and wider job opportunities than their classmates. Put them on law review and those opportunities expand even more.

Today, the vast majority of law reviews have become more egalitarian in their selection process. Instead of having students automatically grade-on to law review, most schools have a "write-on competition," usually at the conclusion of the first year. At some schools, any student can participate in the write-on competition, but most schools impose a minimum GPA requirement to participate, generally in the *B*-range. Competition details vary, but write-on competitions typically entail a time-limited writing assignment such as an analysis of a recent case, often accompanied by a test on *Bluebook* citation-style. The competition submissions are evaluated anonymously. Students who perform well in the competition are extended an offer to participate on law review. Sometimes the offers are based on a combined assessment of the write-on competition results and the students' GPAs. Some law reviews split membership invitations between automatic grade-on qualifiers and write-on participants.

One drawback of write-on competitions is that they discourage many worthy applicants from trying out, especially since the competitions often take place shortly after the completion of first-year exams. Understandably, the last thing most students want to take on immediately after concluding their exhausting first year is a grueling writing competition.

To achieve law review membership status—and, hence, the privilege of listing law review as a resume credential— students must successfully complete one and sometimes two major writing projects that travel under the names "casenote," "note," and "comment." A casenote is an extensive analysis of a noteworthy case. Notes and comments (essentially the same thing with different labels) have a broader focus, addressing a topical legal issue rather than an individual case. These works are lengthy and time-consuming, usually running more than fifty double-spaced pages with at least two hundred footnotes. The best of these student works get selected for publication in the law review.

In addition to the writing requirements, staff members are required to do painstaking "cite-checking" of articles that have been accepted by the law review for publication. This involves verifying the accuracy of footnote citations as to both proper *Bluebook* format and substantive content. While anything but fun, these assignments really force students to sharpen their citation skills, which is a valuable, underappreciated asset for the reasons discussed in Chapter 17.

Particularly ambitious and well-qualified students go on to become law review editors (rather than just staff members), which is considered an especially high honor. The editor-in-chief of the law review occupies a status roughly equivalent to being captain of a starship.

Each year the current board of editors selects, through an application process, the editors for the next year. The student editors run the whole operation, much to the chagrin of law professors, who submit the bulk of article manuscripts for publication consideration. In the ultimate role reversal of legal education, students accustomed to being lorded over by law professors in every aspect of their law student existence suddenly have the upper-hand as professors from around the country—desperate to publish or perish—come begging to have their articles published. Law reviews at elite schools receive literally thousands of manuscript submissions a year, accepting only a handful of them. Making matters even more topsy-turvy, once an article is accepted for publication, the students edit it. So now we have law students who only recently were enrolled in first-year legal writing courses telling professors how to write. Classic!

Other than that devilish pleasure, what does law review have to offer students other than a lot of hard work? A few things. Students usually earn a few credit hours for law review. Some schools give partial tuition waivers or scholarships to editors. Also, virtually all law schools require students to complete one substantial writing project as a graduation requirement and law review student works usually are held to satisfy that requirement. To varying degrees dependant on the quality of the faculty advising and student-editor supervision, law review helps members advance their skills as legal researchers and writers. A few students get their student works accepted for publication in the law review, which is a pretty neat deal.

And you're going, yeah, well, I guess that stuff sounds okay, but I still can't see how it justifies voluntarily taking on hundreds of hours of extra work. I agree. Honestly, I found law review to be a tedious, largely unfulfilling experience. Cite-checking assignments were dreadful. Other important duties assigned to me included making coffee for the editors on Tuesday mornings and printing and collating student course outlines that the law review sold to other students for profit. The editing supervision I received on my casenote and note was unexceptional—not surprising since it came from untrained student editors with only slightly more experience than I had.

Would I do it all over if I had the chance? Absolutely, because of one other benefit not described above: being able to write "law review" on my resume. Law review is still viewed as the ultimate academic credential of legal education. Law review status operates as a kind of VIP-admission ticket into the world of legal employment. I used to live in Miami, home of many popular nightclubs in famous South Beach. At the hot clubs, long lines of people form behind a rope every night and bouncers at the door pick and choose who gets to come inside. As my students explained it to me, the only ones ever invited past the rope are the "beautiful people." Well, being on law review makes you one of the beautiful people in the legal job market.

Large law firms favor applicants who served on law review. Many federal and some state judges limit consideration of applicants for judicial clerkships to law review members. And law review status is pretty much a standard credential for becoming a law professor. Being a member of the law review helped me obtain all three of my principal legal jobs: federal judicial law clerk, associate at a highly regarded law firm, and law professor. As I tell my students, while it involves a lot of unglamorous work, law review is the gift that keeps on giving.

If you're a strong writer and especially if you enjoy writing, I encourage you to give the law review write-on competition a try. Depending on the situation, the odds may be in your favor. The number of invitations extended annually is determined by current needs of the law review. Sometimes those needs are large. If the law review is seeking, for example, to fill twenty slots and only thirty students enter the write-on competition, your chances of making law review are pretty good.

If you don't make or try out for the primary law review, consider participating on a "secondary journal," as they're called. In addition to the main law review, many law schools publish other journals focusing on particular subject areas. Large, elite schools may publish several secondary journals. Pick a legal topic and there's a good chance a law school is publishing a specialized journal devoted to it. Art law, civil rights law, elder law, health law, international law, media law, race, gender and sexual identity law, sports law, tax law, technology law—there are secondary journals devoted to all of them. At last count, U.S. law schools were publishing 321 secondary journals in addition to their primary law reviews.

The abundance of secondary journals is good news for law students because they substantially increase the opportunities for students to serve on a scholarly journal. While being a member of a secondary journal is not considered quite as prestigious as serving on the primary law review, it still carries resume weight. Moreover, if the secondary journal focuses on a subject area in which you have a genuine interest, the experience might be more enjoyable and meaningful than serving on the primary law review. The selection process for secondary journal membership typically is similar to that for the primary law review—some combination of a write-on competition and minimum GPA—although the GPA requirement may be relaxed or even eliminated.

Moot Court

Not considered quite as prestigious, at least traditionally, as law review, but a lot more fun and exciting, is moot court. "Moot court" is basically "mock court" in an appellate setting, as opposed to a trial setting. Like law reviews, moot court has been around legal education for a long time, beginning at Harvard Law School in the mid–1840s. Until fairly recently, however, moot court lagged far behind law review in terms of stature both within law schools and in the job market. But things have changed on that front in the last decade or so. Moot court has made tremendous strides in legal education both in popularity and prestige.

Most law schools have a moot court program. While they vary considerably in their structures, the programs sometimes begin at the ground level with a first-year intramural appellate argument competition. Participants receive a package of materials containing an abbreviated appellate record of a fictitious case that is pending on appeal before a high court, often the U.S. Supreme Court. Students work in teams of two. Each team must argue the legal issues raised by the problem against other student teams in front of three-person panels of mock appellate judges, which might include law professors, lawyers, real judges or law students. Because students always work in teams, the problems usually raise two legal issues, enabling each student to argue one issue during the mock appellate proceeding.

After each set of arguments, the panel of judges declares a winning team. The competitions may be structured as either single- or double-elimination. The March Madness of legal education, intramural moot court competitions generate a lot of excitement within the law school as everyone watches to see who progresses and who gets knocked out of the tourney. The winners and other high-performers often have the upper-hand in being selected to be members of the school's moot court board.

Members of the moot court board get to participate in regional and national moot court competitions, of which there are many, against teams from other law schools. The major competitions attract teams from more than 100 schools. Like law review, moot court requires a lot of work. Before even getting to the long rounds of practice arguments leading up to a competition, each competition team must research and write an appellate brief of up to fifty pages arguing one side of the issues. In oral argument, however, students have to be able to argue both sides. Thus, in round one they may argue "on brief" (i.e., taking the same positions they argued in their written brief), while in round two they may be required to switch positions and argue "off brief." In judging practice rounds, I'm always amazed by the ability of students to accomplish this complete frame-of-mind switch with just a few minutes in between arguments. Teams are judged both on their briefs and oral arguments.

Moot court carries some of the same benefits as law review, along with some extras. Like law review, moot court participation, especially at the board level, usually carries some credit hours. Board members may get a partial tuition waiver or scholarship. A moot court brief often satisfies the upper-level writing requirement. Additionally, moot court forces students to develop both writing *and* oral advocacy skills. It trains students to think on their feet and work as a part of a team. Accomplishments in moot court are more visible and easily recognized. Winning or placing highly in a moot court competition is a heady honor, one that schools usually feature on their websites and in other marketing materials.

After reading about law review and moot court, you may be wondering, as many students do, "If I have to choose between law review and moot court, which one should I pick?" It's possible to do both, although I don't recommend it. Something has to give when a student commits to doing both because they each devour so much time. The choice may seem obvious: "Hmm, let's see. I can spend my time writing and checking hundreds of footnotes or I can argue a case before the Supreme Court. I wonder which would be more fun?"

You couldn't go wrong with either choice, but if my daughter came to me and asked which one to pursue, I'd go with law review. Why? Because law review still has the edge in terms of the prestige and marketability factor. The last time one of my research assistants checked the online directory for the Association for Legal Career Professionals, substantially more law firms listed law review as a desirable credential than listed moot court.[94]

---

94. *See* NALP Directory of Legal Employers, http://www.nalpdirectory.

Anecdotal evidence from former students in the job market also suggests a higher value is placed on law review, at least by larger firms. One top student wrote me that "during my gauntlet of interviews with big firms earlier this year, many of the lawyers interviewing me said they valued law review more highly than moot court." In the narrow market for judicial law clerks, which are highly sought prestigious positions, law review gets the clear nod. The 2000 NALP Judicial Clerkship Study found that grades and law review membership were the most important predictors of success in the clerkship application process. No mention is made of moot court.[95]

Many professors would dispute my assertion that law review is the superior resume credential, especially those who are involved in the moot court programs at their schools. As I said, both law review and moot court are excellent credentials and you couldn't go wrong with either one.

Other Competitions

In addition to moot court, law schools often sponsor teams in other types of skills competitions. Trial competitions are the most common type after moot court. Trial competitions generally involve two- or three-member student teams who compete against other student teams, either from the same school or other schools, in mock trial proceedings. Moot court, remember, involves appellate proceedings. Thus, instead of simply making legal arguments to judges, students examine and cross-examine witnesses, make opening and closing statements to juries, etc.

Opportunities may also exist to participate in negotiation and client counseling competitions. The ABA sponsors national competitions in both areas. Negotiation competitions pit law students, acting as lawyers, against other students in attempting to resolve legal problems through negotiation, rather than adversarial legal proceedings. Client counseling competitions involve students, again acting as lawyers, interacting with mock clients. The competitions simulate a first consultation with the client at which the student lawyers seek to extract legally relevant information related to the

com (directory data reviewed Jan. 8, 2008).

95. *See* NALP, COURTING CLERKSHIPS: THE NALP JUDICIAL CLERKSHIP STUDY

(2000), *available at* http://www.nalp.org/content/index.php?pid=135#overview.

client's problem and analyze and discuss possible courses of action. These competitions offer some of the same rewards as moot court, although they usually are less prominent in the law school landscape and are seen as less prestigious.

Student Organizations

All law schools permit students to form organizations related to particular student interests. Student organizations enable students to pursue and explore legal causes and subjects about which they are passionate, while providing a social outlet and opportunity to network with like and like-minded people. Joining a student organization is a great way to meet people and enrich your law school experience. Especially if you feel alienated or isolated, as many law students do, a student group can provide a real boost to your spirits and morale.

The range of law school student organizations is limited only by a lack of student interest to start one and keep it active. I asked a research assistant to surf through law school websites and compile a list of law student organizations. She returned with a list of more than 300 organizations, and it wasn't even complete. Turns out there's a little something for everyone out there. Student organizations exist representing just about every imaginable racial, ethnic, and religious group, political viewpoint (from conservative Republicanism to anarchy), social cause (from animal rights to reproductive rights), and legal subject area (from environmental law to national security law). Student organizations devoted to recreational pursuits include those appealing to interests in sports and hobbies (boxing, hockey, surfing, target-shooting), games (bridge, chess), even culinary tastes (cooking, wine-tasting, single-malt scotch).

Assuming sufficient student interest can be shown (usually by compiling a petition), it's feasible at most schools to start a student organization by following a few simple requirements such as drafting a constitution and compiling a proposed budget. One way to gauge the level of student involvement at a school is to check out the school's website for a list of student organizations, although be cognizant of the correlation between the number of student organizations and size of the law school. Larger law schools, particularly well-funded ones, usually have the most student organizations.

Most law schools also maintain active chapters of the two largest national law school fraternities: Phi Delta Phi and Phi Alpha Delta. Expect to have upper-level students hitting you up to join one or both of them. While both fraternities promote themselves as professional and social organizations, Phi Delta Phi is generally seen as the more academically oriented of the two, while Phi Alpha Delta is known more for its social activities. Visit their websites for more information: Phi Delta Phi, http://phideltaphi.org, and Phi Alpha Delta, http://www.pad.org.

One other student organization warrants special mention: student government. All law schools have a student government association (SGA) made up of elected officers. These usually include a president, vice-president, treasurer, secretary, and representatives for each class. Most SGA presidents I've known have been concerned more with organizing social events than with using the SGA to improve academic life or the reputation of the law school. When it comes time to vote for SGA officers, don't just vote for your friends, smooth talkers, or the candidates who hand out free candy. Vote for the folks you think will be truly committed to improving the quality of your law school.

Outside Speakers

Law schools and student organizations often bring in outside speakers, many of them prominent in their fields, to enrich the intellectual life of the school. These can be either individual speakers or groups of speakers brought in for a symposium. The Environmental Law Society, for example, may bring in an expert on global warming for a luncheon talk. Or the law review may sponsor an entire symposium devoted to climate change, inviting several speakers for a daylong event.

Regrettably, because law students are so busy, these events often are poorly attended, which doesn't reflect well on the school. Professors sometimes require students to attend presentations in lieu of class, both as a way to enrich the students and to ensure a good turnout. Many individual presentations are held during lunch and include free food for attendees. If that's the case, take a break from your studies, go to the presentation and grab a bite and gain some extra knowledge.

CHAPTER 21

RECAPPING LAW SCHOOL'S FIRST YEAR IN THE WORDS OF STUDENTS

I think it's much easier to tell someone else that, to succeed in law school, "You've got to do this, you've got to do that, etc." than it is being the incoming student and having an appreciation for and actually listening to and implementing what someone else is telling you.

> 1L nearing completion
> of the first year

One of the frustrating aspects about giving advice on how to succeed in law school is the certain knowledge that many students won't follow it. This is true no matter how great the advice. As we near the end of our figurative 1L ride, I thought the best way to reinforce the advice for law school success and well-being that you've been reading would be to hear it retold in the words of those who had just labored through the real 1L odyssey. Paraphrasing humor writer Dave Barry, I'm hoping that reading the same advice coming from law students will assure you that "I was not making this stuff up" and help drive home the key points.

In writing this book, I took the pulse of a class of 1Ls via periodic emailed lists of questions as they progressed through their first year from beginning to end. Many of their replies are sprinkled throughout the book. Two weeks before the end of their dizzying 1L trip, I sent my students a final set of questions:

1. Name one thing you know now (other than the law) that you wish you had known when you started law school.

2. Imagine your brother/sister/partner/best friend is starting law school. What advice would you give them?

3. What is your dominant feeling or sentiment (e.g., relief, nostalgia, boredom, frustration, exhaustion) as you near the end of law school's first year?

4. Now that you've nearly reached the end of the first year, would you do it again knowing what you know now?

Reading their answers to questions 1 and 2, I was surprised—pleasantly so—by how closely their comments track the advice in this book. Their answers to questions 3 and 4 are also enlightening for those about to begin their own 1L journey. Below are select answers to each question, which I've grouped under subheadings to give them some structure. As you read the student advice, think back and try to connect it to the specific sections of this book where you first heard it. Specifically, think back to the CREDO chapter (Chapter 10) and take note of how many of the tips relate to the CREDO habits (Consistent, Rigorous, Efficient, Diligent, and Organized). Although these comments come from only one group of law students at one school, I can tell you with confidence that they are representative of every group of law students I have ever taught.

QUESTION 1: Name one thing you know now (other than the law) that you wish you had known when you started law school.

Law school will be one of the most difficult challenges of your life.

- I think the one notion that students have about the law school experience is that it will be difficult. This is universal. I think students underestimate tremendously the type of difficulty that they will encounter. It is not necessarily that the material is always exceptionally difficult to understand, but that the process by which you learn and the sheer quantity of work required to learn—let alone master—the subject matter is overwhelming. I wish that I had some understanding of that before I started the whole deal.

- I wish I had known how mentally taxing law school was going to be. Beyond "learning the law" there is the stress of getting good grades, legal writing assignments, moot court, etc. Further, trying to balance this stress with the normal stress of life (family, relationships, money, etc.) is a challenge in and of itself.

- I wish I'd known how easy it is to fail out. I just assumed law school would be slightly harder than college—I was way off.

But it can be done, so take heart!

- I wish I'd had the confidence in my abilities at the beginning of the year that I have now. I'd stress to readers that if they have been accepted to law school, they are fully capable of doing well in law school. They didn't get there by some mistake in the admissions process. They didn't get someone else's letter of acceptance. I think there's a tendency to assume that because we've never done something, we "can't" do it. We say this sort of thing all the time. If a person has never learned to cook, they'll say, "I can't cook." In law school, it might be "I can't argue a case" because they've never done it. I'd recommend that new students do their best to put a stop to that way of thinking and say instead, "I haven't learned *yet* to cook" or "I haven't learned *yet* to argue a case" or whatever.

- That law school is not as insurmountable as one would think. Sure it's a lot of work, but it's not particularly hard work. It's what you would be doing in a job if you weren't in law school. The difference is, here, you don't get paid for it!

- I wish I had known that law school is not really as scary or difficult as people make it out to be.

"It's a brave new world."

- I wish I'd known that the way I'd studied in undergraduate school and graduate school would bear no resemblance to the way I needed to study in law school if I wanted to pass my exams.

- I wish I would have known just how different the whole law school experience was going to be from anything else I had ever done. I honestly feel that there is nothing in undergraduate school that could possibly have prepared me for law school. The only way to be successful is to try to adapt quickly.

- I wish I had known how to *study*. In undergrad I felt like things came fairly easy and other than writing papers I didn't actually have to sit down and dedicate my time to school material. I had never before *really* reviewed material from class or outlined and these are vital skills you need to apply in law school.

Everyone has the same fears.

- That everyone else was just as nervous about some aspect of the whole new experience as I was. Someone very well may have told me that before I started. If they did, I didn't believe them. But it's true. It has taken me two semesters of getting to know others well enough to realize that they are all nervous too. The basis for the nervousness varies drastically, but we all feel it. For some it will be about speaking in class or doing an oral argument. Others are nervous about not being liked, flunking out, or going broke. Amazingly to me, some of the most intelligent students seemed to struggle the most at first. Perhaps because they have always been the shiniest fish in their ponds, they were unaccustomed and uncomfortable with being surrounded by so many true peers. Everyone is struggling with some aspect of the law school experience!

Don't fall behind!

- You have to stay on top of your obligations and responsibilities EVERY DAY. I don't just mean your reading assignments. You have to make sure to check your email daily and stay on top of other obligations such as signing up for Westlaw training and adding to your outlines on a regular basis. This was a big transition from my undergraduate experience. I would go weeks without checking my email and just cram for a few days before a big test without suffering any dire consequences. If your undergraduate experience was anything like mine, you cannot get away with adhering to the same habits once you start law school.

- I wish that I would have known that everything moves one step ahead in law school. If you are ahead in your readings/preparations, then you are where you need to be.

- If you are merely prepared for each class on a "just-in-time" strategy, you are behind. And if you fall behind, it is impossible to catch up. Although you can get notes from others, double a reading assignment for a class, etc., you simply cannot replace the actual learning process that comes from actual preparation in advance.

Conscientious outlining and periodic review are critical.

- How important outlining is and how important it is to keep up with it as you go along. Outlining is a major part of the learning process for me and I did not realize how important it was until I really did it. It doesn't just help you study the material. It allows you to organize the concepts in a logical manner that helps you see the bigger picture.

- Fall semester would have been so much less stressful if I had kept a running outline that was updated biweekly, instead of waiting two weeks before exams to begin making the outline.

- I wish I would have known just how much time it took to study for exams. I wish I would have known that if I put just an hour into studying after class each day it would have made things easier.

Law school is competitive.

- I think that competition is the white elephant in the room in terms of discussion of the law school experience. Everyone is in a marathon race against the other. Everyone is aware of this—some simply care more than others. However, there is something to be said for being considerate and helpful to your peers.

There are people who will go out of their way not to help you lest they give up some tiny thread of comparative advantage. Those students are rarely liked and respected even less. I think it would do our profession and our peers a great deal of good to realize that in the end it does not matter what grades you made or what awards you won. These are important, no doubt. But the relationships that you make now stay with you forever.

- To believe people when they warn how competitive law school is. Looking back, college was like running a 5K for a cause where everyone wanted you to succeed. People are there along the way giving you water and cheering you on. Even the slowest runner is praised for participation. Law school feels more like roller derby. While racing to the finish line, your competition is beating on you, intentionally tripping you up and pulling your hair out all in an effort to pass you by.

- I wish that I had known exactly how competitive law school is. I think that I kind of knew, but I had no real understanding of the fierceness of the whole system.

Being organized and managing time efficiently will make your life easier.

- I think the one thing that I wish I had a better working knowledge of when I started law school is that organization can make the most monumental task attainable.

- Organization makes work easy. It sounds simple, but I never realized I was disorganized. Your desk can be clean and everything can appear perfect, but if you don't know what the fourteen things you have to do at your computer are, then you're wasting time. Simply knowing what needs to be done and when makes it easy to crank out high-quality work quickly. So much time is wasted figuring out what to do and getting the tools to start.

- That it is really all about time management. I was told then, but I really know now.

Case briefs should be brief.

- Case briefs should be concise! Really concise. Read
  the case carefully and underline/highlight important
  parts but don't waste your time typing every point
  into a brief. The professor will highlight in class the
  important points you should get out of the case.
  Then you can go back and copy anything into your
  brief that you may not have covered fully in your
  notes.

Don't be a transcriber.

- Do not transcribe everything the professor says into
  class notes. The professors' words are important, of
  course, and if they make a point to slow down and
  state a specific point of law, transcribe it. But you
  need to filter their words into notes that you can
  understand.

Women experience law school differently than men.

- Women tend to underestimate their abilities, while
  men seem to overestimate theirs. Most girls are just
  not complimented on their intelligence that often.
  I'm trying to make a point of doing that more with
  my daughter and downplaying her appearance, but
  it's just so second-nature with girls to say "What a
  pretty dress!" or "Your hair looks so nice today!"
  and so on. The students who come to mind who I
  consider lacking in the confidence they fully deserve
  to have are all female. Many women students have
  said, "I want to be in a back office" or "I don't want
  to do litigation" and so on. There's certainly no
  more competence in being male, but there is definitely more confidence. Even with many law schools
  having a 50–50 gender balance, the de-emphasis on
  intelligence that girls experience in relation to the
  boys they later end up competing against has an
  effect. This brings us back to what I wished I'd
  known. Having made it through several scary things
  in law school (the final exams, the papers, the oral
  argument) and seeing now that I have the ability to
  do them, I could have spared myself a lot of needless
  stress if I'd had a bit of this confidence back in
  August.

Exercise!

- I wish I would have known how wide my backside was going to get from sitting around studying all the time (point: find time to exercise).

QUESTION 2: Imagine your brother/sister/partner/best friend is starting law school. What advice would you give them?

Of all the questions I asked students while writing this book, I think I like this one best because, by casting the advice recipient in the role of a close loved one, it made many students think beyond the more typical "how to succeed" advice and get down to the heart of the matter. Some of the answers to this question fall into the realm of "soul searching." Most of the practical advice again hammers home the same fundamental points discussed above and throughout this book.

Think hard about whether law school is really the place for you.

- Talk to attorneys, consider the financial debt, sit in on a law school class, read a Supreme Court decision, pray/meditate/contemplate about it, understand the pressure involved, do a cost-benefit analysis (even though you may not understand that concept well yet), know that this will be far different from your undergraduate experience, consider the community you are moving to and will be living in for three years.

- I would advise anyone starting law school to make sure that it is truly where you want to be and that you are going *when* you want to be there. I was fortunate enough to take a year after graduation to work, relax, and refocus my energy. Several classmates of mine (including one who decided to withdraw after fall semester) regretted not taking time off. I think timing is so important to overcome the amount of work that is required in law school.

- It is said so often that it sounds cliché, but you have to find in yourself the reason that you want to be here. You have to commit to yourself that you will do this, without fail, no matter what. Kind of like rescuing a baby from a burning building. Once you commit to do it, you follow through with it to the bitter end.

- Oh dear. Well, I don't know. First, I'd ask if they really wanted my advice. I wouldn't try to talk anyone out of it, but I'd advise that they sit in on some classes, talk to a lot of law students, talk to a lot of lawyers, if possible. I'd advise that if they do all those things, they can find out what law school entails and what a legal career entails, and then consider carefully whether it is something they would enjoy. I would say to ask themselves why they're going to law school. If they said something like, "It's all I can do with my degree," I would advise that they think about it some more.

- First I would say, "Are you crazy? You saw what I went through!" Ha ha! And then I would seriously tell them to really give law school a lot of thought. This isn't just something to do just because you can't get a job or you want to stay in school for another three years. If you want to get the most for your money and your time, law school really does become your life. But if law school is your dream, it is worth it. You can't just come to law school to get a quick and easy career, because it's not quick and it's not easy. Law school takes more work than you can imagine, as well as time and patience. There will be days when you want to quit. But if you're there for the right reasons, you will realize that in three years you will have fulfilled your dream and have a degree that will give you a better life. Then all the hard work will seem worth it and you can get right back to the books!

- Before you actually accept that first loan check and commit yourself, attend a week of classes. Listen. Try to picture yourself doing this for three years. Then try to imagine yourself out in the real world tackling the "hypotheticals" you heard the professors pose. Decide if that's really what you want out of your life for the next forty years. If it still seems okay, and you handle stress tolerably well, then go for it. You'll meet intelligent people from every field of study and from every possible avocation. It's fascinating. But you have to be sure it's what you want to do.

Enjoy your time before you start.

- Take a really long vacation before starting school.

Approach law school like a job.

- When I started law school, I was told to treat school as a 9 to 5 job and to just stay at school and work for that amount of time whether in class or not. This method didn't really work for me, because I like naps, breaks, etc., but the basic point was helpful. It made me realize that as long as I put in around seven to eight hours of work a day, whether it's preparing for class, being in class, or outlining, I would be fine.

- I've treated school like a job and work as soon as I get home from class until I am done for the next day. I think that helps.

- Treat it like a job, with a fixed schedule. Stop when it's time to sleep.

Get your life in order.

- Clear your life of unnecessary distractions and commitments as much as possible before the first day of class. Be organized from day one and never let yourself fall behind. It appears to me that the destructive feelings of being overwhelmed and scared about having fallen behind will finish you off long before you ever have a chance to make a bad grade on an exam.

- Get your life in order because you won't have time for disorganization once you start law school. Have a game plan in advance about when you are going to study, and be prepared to do it religiously.

Everyone struggles.

- I would tell them that everyone struggles in their own way, be it a bad grade, getting called on when you are unprepared for class, showing up late, or just personal issues. No one's journey through law school is easy, so any struggles you have, remember there are many other students who feel the exact same way as you.

- I think the biggest thing to realize and remember is that there are going to be days when you have mental, physical, and emotional breakdowns. Trust me, I probably have two or three a month. And there are going to be days when you really want to hit that person who's ranked in the top ten who keeps talking about his or her grades in front of everyone not ranked in the top ten.

You'll get out what you put into it.

- Law school really becomes what you make of it. If you start with a goal of finishing in the top 25 percent of your class, then you'd better accept that studying is going to be a continuous and very large part of your life. If you do, you'll probably meet your goal. If you start law school just as a way to get another degree and procrastinate the career-search process, then just do what you have to do to get by, but don't be disappointed when you aren't in the top of your class. I think every single person has a different perspective on law school and a different way of tackling it. You just have to make it your own!

Be prepared to work harder than you ever have before.

- Study twice as hard as you think you need to be studying.

- Be ready to spend a lot of time to do a lot of work. Do not go into law school with the attitude that it is anything like undergraduate school. Anyone can do well if they are willing to put in the time and effort.

- Law school is going to be the most serious and difficult task you have ever taken on. You have to go into it wholeheartedly and devote most of your time to it.

- Take a quiet week [before you start] and try to find that one kernel of motivation that will get you through when you have no energy, desire or drive left upon which to rely. You will need it.

Relax, try to enjoy, and do the best you can.

- Relax. Don't worry about using six colors of high-lighter to try to absorb every piece of every case. Do the work, try to understand the situation and the rule, and then be willing to put it down and watch a movie. Your ability to produce results is directly proportional to your ability to relax. One of my closest friends is busy burning herself out over law school. Another good friend of mine is doing the same thing at a different law school. They are making their lives hell, ruining their health, and they're frustrated with their understanding. There is a time for work and a time to stop and let your brain recover. Understand the difference.

- Relax. Although law school is a very stressful time, have fun with it. The classes are interesting, you will make amazing friends, and it really can be fun.

- Just do the best you can. Don't try to compare yourself with anyone else or stress too much about the competitive nature of law school because it will only wear you down. The only thing you really have control over is your own performance.

- Approach law school as a learning/training mission rather than as a contest for grades. The second I stopped trying to learn the material enthusiastically and started strategizing as to how to get the best grades, law school became less fun and the stress tripled.

Realize that non-law students aren't interested in hearing about the law and law school.

- I'd probably tell them that they are about to have their entire lives consumed with the law and conversations about the law. Most of all I would remind them that no matter how interested everyone at the law school is in this stuff, nobody else really cares about it. Try to keep it to yourself because the law does not make for good conversations with friends and family. You'll just come off as boring and weird. I mean outside of lawyers and judges, who could possibly care if a "dog sniff" constitutes a search within the meaning of the Fourth Amendment?

- Be careful about mixing your non-law school friends with your law school friends. Only mix your non-law school friends with law school friends who are capable of conversing about interests other than law school. No non-law school friend wants to be stuck at a table with five law students who only want to talk about law school.

Sort through advice carefully.

- Advice to 1Ls: do not listen to anyone else's opinion about professors. Before each semester, I heard that Professor X was pure concentrated evil, or that you can sleep through Professor Y's class, etc. Some information has been helpful, such as what to expect in terms of assignments and exam prep, but most of rest has been so far off base as to now seem comical.

Don't miss classes.

- Do not miss any classes. I have only missed one class since the beginning of the semester and it was for a court date for a traffic ticket. I felt really behind and confused missing just that one lecture. In undergrad it might have been fine to skip every now and then, but I would definitely advise anyone coming to law school not to miss any classes unless they absolutely have to.

Keep your emotions in check.

- You're not as smart as you think you are, nor are you as useless as you think you are. You'll go through periods of elation and periods of doubt. Both extremes are false and should be promptly dismissed.

- Don't be afraid of law school. While a little bit of fear is good motivation, too much can be crippling. There is no need to fear your professors, colleagues, or assignments. Most everyone is nice and helpful and most of the assignments and cases are straightforward.

- Do not beat yourself up about things that you cannot control. You will walk into a class and, by design, not know all that you need to know. Recognize that you cannot win every battle. Most of all enjoy the experience.

- Don't stress yourself out over grades because stressing out won't get you anywhere. There will be people a lot calmer than you who will make better grades, so don't waste your time worrying about grades and how much studying you are doing. Everyone will be studying hard and stressing gets you nowhere.

Make Friends. Develop a support network.

- Start introducing yourself to other students and try to make friends at orientation. Cliques begin forming then and cliques translate to study groups (which can be a very useful tool, depending on the group). When I say cliques, it's not so much a social thing as a way of finding others who have something in common with you and who, like you, also have no idea what they've gotten themselves into.

- Make as many friends as possible because in order to survive law school the best support system is people who know exactly what you are going through. Plus, friends are helpful for group study sessions and sharing outlines.

- Meet nice people. It helps so much to have a group of friends that can be your sounding board or help you feel like you aren't the only one who is stressed or overwhelmed.

- Make friends because you need people who understand what you are going through to keep you sane.

- Get to know your classmates—they are not the enemy. Do not hide books or hoard outlines—share!

Start outlines early. Engage in periodic review.

- Start outlining early. If you don't then it's almost impossible to do it at the end of the semester.

- If my little sister was starting law school, I would tell her to review her notes daily or weekly. My problem is that I waited until it was time to outline before I looked back at my notes, and was very unfamiliar with some of the concepts at that point.

- Outline early, at least two weeks before everyone else is starting. If you don't procrastinate, you'll have it all done with a week of class left and you won't be freaking out trying to desperately outline when you should be studying for exams.
- Review your notes after every class before starting your homework for the next day.
- Start your outlines on day two of law school. I think it saved me first semester.

Do your own outlines.

- "Legendary outlines" by former students do exist, but they won't get you an *A*. Going to class, reading the material, taking your own notes, and studying will do that. There is no cramming in law school. Spacing out in the back playing video games will earn you a fast ticket out.

Sit up front.

- Sit in the front. This is productive for a couple of reasons. First, I tend to space out a lot and this prevents this. If you're in the first few rows you're visible to the entire class and to your professor. Not only will this ensure you're attentive at least most of the time, but also that you study hard so as not to be embarrassed by being called on. Another benefit is you get to know your professors a bit better and they get to know you. They're a lot less intimidating if you know them as someone other than just a professor. They're usually pretty cool.

Stay in shape.

- Drop the Ho–Ho's and back away from them. They are not your friend. True, they whisper nice, sweet things in your ear, and call out to you in the middle of the night, but when you have to get all gussied up for your oral argument, you're going to look like a fat man in a little suit.

Seek help from your profs.

- If something comes up that is beyond your control, go to your professors and ask for help. That's one thing I have always been too proud (or too dumb) to do. I always try to do things on my own. It's okay to sit down with someone and explain that you are overwhelmed.

Back up your work!

- Back up your computer work in many places!

Don't give up.

- Keep your head down and plow through it. At times it will be fun, but at times it will really suck. If you really want to do it, it will be worth it. Just keep pushing through the difficult times.

- Never give up! Repeat after me: "This too shall pass!" And keep smiling.

Take practice exams under simulated conditions.

- To study for exams, use professors' old exams. Take them like real exams, including timing yourself.

Don't be a Know–It–All.

- Don't become a know-it-all thinking you know everything about the law after a month of law school. Your friends will hate you if you do.

Use study aids to clarify.

- There are some teachers who are simply unclear about what they are teaching in class and what you should be learning in the course as a whole. If you find yourself with a teacher like that, don't hesitate to get a study aid or a canned outline to learn the material on your own. Read the assignments, because you need to be familiar with the material, but if the teacher is not getting the job done, make sure you get an understanding from somewhere.

Don't obsess about "looking stupid" in class.

- Don't freak out about getting called on in class. Everyone gets called on and everyone feels like they look stupid. However, no one ever remembers but you.

Don't fall behind.

- I would tell them that when they have extra time, try to get ahead in their work. There is never

enough time to get things done in law school, so
what you think is free time, really isn't or shouldn't
be. Mostly, I would just try to encourage them to
stay focused and organized so that they won't get so
stressed out.

- DO NOT GET BEHIND ON YOUR WORK. PLAN
  AHEAD. Six hours over two Saturdays is much
  better than six hours the weeknight before something is due.

- Keep up! Don't fall behind in your reading. Do your
  best work at all times. Don't ever cop out and just
  "phone in" a class hoping that the professor won't
  call on you.

Don't give up your hobbies/outside life.

- [Law school is difficult and requires a lot of work,
  but] you cannot give up every aspect of your life for
  law school. It's important to find something you
  enjoy outside of school with which to fill the limited
  free time you have. I would not have been able to
  make it as far as I have, and I realize I still have a
  long way to go, without being able to do something
  to relax when I have finished working for the day. I
  found that playing church-league basketball, playing
  a round of golf on the weekend, or just hanging out
  with my friends for a night made opening up my
  book and diving back into the intricacies of the law
  the next morning much easier to cope with.

- Make sure you have an outlet outside of school—
  whether it is tutoring a child, running, playing the
  guitar, yoga, sewing—just something to do other
  than study!

- Don't work ALL of the time, only most of it.

- Find time in every day to relax.

- Balance your academic life with your personal life.
  Don't give up all the things that make you who you
  are to provide more time for school. There is no way
  you can be happy if you completely sacrifice the
  things you do outside of school. If you are unhappy
  in general your performance in class will suffer.

QUESTION 3: What is your dominant feeling or sentiment (e.g., relief, nostalgia, boredom, frustration, exhaustion) as you near the end of law school's first year?

Silly me. I naively expected cheerful answers to this question, not taking into account the fact that with five exams still looming, the students weren't really thinking—like I was—that they were at "the end" of the first year yet. Disproportionately, the answers reflected anxiety and exhaustion. But some students were able to look ahead and feel excitement, pride, relief, and a sense of accomplishment for what they'd been through. I'm sure if I asked the same question after exams were finished, the answers would have been a lot more upbeat. More than anything else, these answers constitute proof beyond a reasonable doubt of the physical, mental, and emotional toll that the first year of law school takes on the participants. Since many of the answers expressed the same basic feelings, I've selected representative responses for each category:

Anxiety/Stress

- I'm full of anxiety. I didn't do well last semester and I have to do much better to remain in school for another year. For the last three weeks or so I have been waking up with nightmares and I have had a difficult time sleeping because I am so nervous about finals.

- My grades weren't very good (and I mean really not good, not "dork"-not good where you get all *B*s and one *B*- and think you're failing law school), so I'm very nervous and scared because failing out of school is a legitimate concern.

- I could moan and cry about not doing as well as I had hoped, but nothing will change that fact now. I'm also rather anxious about second year. I've heard the adage repeated several times, "First year, they scare you to death. Second year, they work you to death. Third year, they bore you to death." What is exactly involved in being worked to death? Because I honestly can't imagine that it could get worse than this.

- I know I am exhausted, but can't feel it because I am under so much pressure and stress while preparing for exams.

Despair

- "Dear God! I have two more years of this?" It's kind of like being sent to war and then getting wounded in battle. You start to think you are finally going to get sent home after you heal only to find out you're being sent back to the front line, with even less chance of survival because now you're wounded.

Exhaustion

- Exhaustion. I am ready for a good night's rest after finals. I haven't slept in my bed three nights since I've been in law school. The rest of the time, I fall asleep studying in the living room or at the computer.

- EXHAUSTION. I have reached a new level of mental exhaustion I did not know existed.

- Exhaustion. Sheer, unrelenting exhaustion. The panic of finals hasn't yet hit me. I think I'm in denial.

Frustration

- Frustration. Effort = Results. Plain and simple. I wish I would have spent more time studying and enjoying what I was learning—and less time analyzing what I could do to ensure a decent class rank.

- Frustration for not being as motivated as I think I should be, which makes me think that I chose the wrong career path. I see how passionate my friends are about finishing law school and I'm sad that I don't share the same feelings. It makes me worried that I'm not really supposed to be here because honestly at this point, I can't really see myself in the future as a lawyer. Coming straight from undergrad into law school makes me wish that I'd taken at least a few months off to get my priorities straight and make sure law school was the right choice for me.

Excitement/Happiness

- Excited about being a 2L, but still nervous about exams.

- I am energized. I feel excited that I now understand things better. Last semester I was planning a wedding, selling a house, etc. This semester I am focused on school only. That makes ALL the difference in the world. I now enjoy classes more, because I understand things more clearly. I am also at peace now that I have finally accepted the fact that I have no social life outside of classes. I am moving towards the realm of nerd-dom at a steady pace.

- Excitement. I really just want it to be over so I can go home for a bit.

- Anticipation. I figured out I can do the law school thing pretty well. Now it is time to make some waves, make a name, and see just how well I can do it.

Indifference

- I guess I really feel kind of indifferent about it. I am relieved that the first year is coming to a close, but I know there are still two difficult years ahead. I don't really buy into the claim that school gets a lot easier after the first year. I think the students just become accustomed to the demands of the routine.

Numbness

- I am basically numb at this point. I'm looking forward to spending a summer away from law school so I will actually have time to reflect on and re-evaluate my choice to attend.

Pride

- As the year ends, I think I mainly feel proud. Proud of myself for moving across the state, living by myself for the first time, and taking on a world of new responsibilities. Proud for getting through the first year, doing well in my classes, and finding a way to balance school and studying and a social life. Proud to go back home this summer and tell every-

one that I just finished my first year of law school
... and survived!

Relief

- Relief. It is impossible to believe that in just under
  three weeks I will have survived a WHOLE YEAR of
  law school. But at the same time there is definitely
  the end of the year stress as exams approach.

- My dominant sentiment is relief. I do not hate law
  school, but I will thoroughly enjoy a break from it
  this summer. I look forward to spending an entire
  afternoon drinking beer at a pool, playing guitar, or
  watching movies without feeling guilty about school
  work I should be doing!

- My dominant sentiment is relief. Ending this year
  will be a wonderful thing. However, there is a certain level of anxiety still present due to the impending exams.

Shock/Surprise

- Shock. I cannot believe it went by so fast. It doesn't
  feel like I'm one-third of the way prepared to be a
  lawyer.

- Surprise that two semesters have flown by already.
  Last August, with three years looming ahead of me,
  it seemed like it would be a very long time before I'd
  be finished. Doesn't feel quite as distant now that
  this first year seems to have gone by so quickly.

All of the Above/Mixed feelings

- I feel all of those things—each of them intensely at
  different times. Probably the most powerful ones are
  fear (before exams) and relief (after exams). I still
  worry every day that I'm not smart enough.

- My answer would be "(E) All of the above." I guess
  the most dominant feeling would be that of exhaustion. At this point in the semester, it is hard to feel
  relieved with the impending doom of finals lurking
  two weeks away. With so much to do, I am rarely
  bored, and if I am, I embrace the downtime. Any
  frustration that I feel is with myself, for failing to
  start outlining earlier in the semester.

- Such a mix of emotions ... Relief and exhaustion, but mostly a sense of accomplishment. So amazing to realize that, "Yes, I can do this!"

- A lot of mixed emotions. I know I'm not going to know what to do with myself when exams are over. In a weird, sick way, I know I'll miss the routine. Ha, I guess you've seen *Shawshank Redemption*? Maybe, like Red, I've become a bit institutionalized.

- A little bit of relief because I have made it through my first year, and definitely a lot of exhaustion from making it through that first year. It could be nostalgia because I know that I will never be in this position again and it is all downhill from here. I think being in the same class with the same people the whole year has made us a very close class and it is sad to think that those same people might not be in your classes the next year.

QUESTION 4: Now that you've nearly reached the end of the first year, would you do it again knowing what you know now?

After reading the above answers, you might be surprised at the responses to this last question. Despite all the stress, anxiety, frustration, exhaustion, and other less-than-positive feelings, the vast majority of the students who responded to question 4 said they would do the first year all over again even knowing what they know now. Many said they would do so enthusiastically, as reflected in answers such as "Absolutely!" and "Hell yes." But not all. Some students said they wouldn't do it again and others were ambivalent. Also, not all students responded, so we don't know what their feelings were. Below I set forth just a few of the more interesting answers. Don't be misled by the absolute number of responses. Remember, most students said they'd do it again.

Would do it again.

- I would definitely do it again. I have had a wonderful time in law school. Although I have struggled through my first year, I would do it again no questions asked. My 1L experience has solidified my desire to be a part of this profession. Who knows, after I receive my grades I may be begging to do it again, seriously!

- Absolutely! It was definitely hard and a new way of studying and preparing for classes, but I wouldn't do anything else. In this first year, I realized that I made the right choice. I can't imagine spending the last year in any job or any other type of grad school.

- Absolutely I would do it again. I may have to still. Ha, ha! It's a great experience and knowing what I know now, at the very least, I'm a more rounded person.

- Yes, I would do it a thousand times over. I have wanted to go to law school and be an attorney since eighth grade and have told people that I was going to do it for just as long.

- Definitely. Only I would like to go back in time and smack myself in the face for not studying more.

- Yes. No regrets. Life is an adventure. Even if I hated law school, I wouldn't change it. It is easy to look back and regret. It is better to learn, plan for the future, and accept the lessons you've learned. Don't go to law school unless you're sure you want to. Don't waste money and time if you're just unsure of your future or just because you feel like you're good at arguing and need a respectable career. But once you're in, accept the choice. If you are miserable, learn what you can. Maybe law is too combative for you. Maybe you don't want to feel like your morals are for sale. Maybe you just prefer more creative work. The people who spend time regretting their choice just make themselves less happy and take their focus away from their futures.

Ambivalent

- Knowing what I know now, I think that I would do it again, but I would do it differently. Law school is nothing like undergrad. I would come in with the understanding that I have to work four times harder than what I did before.

- Honestly, I'm not sure. But I'm also glad I didn't know what I know now, because I might not be here if I did. And I'm glad I'm here.

- Let me put it this way: WOULD YOU? Well, only if I didn't remember the first time.

Would not do it again.

- If what you mean by "what you know now" is the knowledge of the experience itself, then probably not. I think that's the only way anyone actually makes it through the misery of it all: you really can't and don't know what you're getting into until you're doing it. It's probably best to keep it that way.

- Honestly? Probably not. At this point, however, I am very emotionally and financially dedicated to this pursuit and feel like I should see it through to completion.

- No. Not sure what else I would have done, but I wish I'd heard and followed the advice I would give others about being sure this is what you want to do before accepting that first loan check.

* * *

Here's a final, very apt closing remark from a student who said he would *not* do the first year again knowing what he knows now: "Most of what I know now, I had been told at the beginning of the first semester. The problem is I didn't put it to use. Therefore, I believe that I could fall into the same traps."

You now have the information and advice you'll need to avoid falling into those traps and succeeding in law school. It may seem far off, but it won't be long before you'll be finishing your own 1L adventure. Like the rest of life, your time in law school will fly by.

When you reach the end of it, I hope you won't find yourself in the position of the student quoted above, bemoaning not heeding advice. I'd rather picture you smiling and thinking, "You know, that book I read about the first year gave some really good advice. I'm glad I followed it!"

Epilogue: The End of a Long and Grinding Road

I still remember the day of my last exam of my 1L year. What a feeling! It was like being released from prison. I walked out of the law school into bright sunshine and felt light as air. That night some of my non-law school friends staged a big party at a subterranean den called (and painted to resemble) Middle Earth, located beneath a block of dorms on the University of Florida campus. (Tolkien was popular on college campuses long before the *Lord of the Rings* movie trilogy.) We listened to music, watched a weird home movie some of my pals created, drank potent punch, and just hung out.

I was the only law student there. I doubt I mentioned law school the entire night, having learned months earlier that non-law students could care less about it. I did think about it though. I have a distinct memory of sitting in a chair watching the hubbub around me, sipping punch, and feeling blissfully happy, thinking: "I'm done! I can't believe I'm actually done!" Temporarily forgetting, I guess, that I still had two more years to go.

But human nature is funny that way. While I definitely would not want to repeat the first year, like many lawyers, I look back at it with nostalgia and fondness. For better or worse, there has never been another year of my life resembling my 1L experience. I've never learned as much or experienced as much camaraderie in any one year. I'm not sure I ever experienced as much stress either, but, thankfully, the human psyche seems designed to remember the good over the bad.

Your experience is likely to be similar. For most readers, the first year of law school may still be an abstraction. I hope I succeeded in giving it some shape in these pages, but, when all is said and done, what I said at the beginning of the book is true. The only way to truly understand and appreciate the

392

1L experience is to live it yourself. Good luck on your journey! Here's wishing you a smooth ride.

* * *

APPENDIX A

LIST OF LAW SCHOOL STUDY AIDS

As discussed in Chapter 2, law students searching for help in the form of outside study aids will find no shortage in supply. Virtually all law students use some study aids for at least some courses. Below is a list of the available law school study aid series, just so you'll know what's out there. No attempt is made to rank or evaluate them, but it bears emphasizing that they are by no means equally popular with law students. I had never heard of many of them until compiling this list.

Some of the series are classics that have been around forever. You may recall my story about how the *Gilbert* in Criminal Law helped me get my first *A* in law school three decades ago. Other longtime staples in the study aid industry include the West *Hornbook Series*, *Emanuel* outlines, *Law in a Flash* flashcards, *Legalines*, and *Casenotes* briefs. Many series on the list are relative newcomers.

Increasingly, study aids are available as computer downloads. Some are even available in audio format, so if you get tired of cruising to your favorite tunes in your car, you can rock out to a professor droning on about the mailbox rule or the elements of first-degree murder.

It's often the case that an individual entry in one series will stand out as the superior choice for a particular subject while entries in other series will be the best choice for other subjects. In general, I recommend going with study aids written by professors. Professor-authored series are noted below.

Generally speaking, law school study aid series break down into four different types: (1) outlines of the law in particular subject areas, sometimes keyed to popular case-books; (2) treatise-like works that explain the law of a subject area in a non-outline format; (3) exam-prep series containing practice essay and/or multiple-choice questions and analysis (many of the outline series also contain practice questions); and (4) "canned brief" series containing case briefs of all of the cases appearing in particular casebooks. CALI computer exercises, an excellent resource available to law students at no charge, are kind of in a category by themselves.

As I cautioned in the beginning of the book, don't rush out and buy any of these. Wait until you get to law school and hear what upper-level students and professors have to say about particular study aids for particular courses. Finally, remember that all study aids should be used only as a supplement to your own diligent work.

Aspen Publishing

- *Casenotes Legal Briefs Series.* With 150 titles available, entries in the *Casenotes* series contain briefs of all the cases in major casebooks keyed to the particular book. Available as a digital download at aspenlaw.com.

- *Crunch Time Series.* Titles in this series contain flow charts, capsule summaries of major points of law, exam tips, and sample exam and essay questions with model answers. Available as a digital download.

- *Emanuel Law Outline Series.* As the name suggests, *Emanuel Law Outlines* provide legal explanation of particular subjects in outline form. Each title includes both capsule and detailed outlines, exam questions with model answers, and a cross-reference table of cases keyed to leading casebooks. Available as a digital download.

- *Essentials Series* (**written by professors**). This is a new treatise-type series designed to give law students a big-picture view of their law school classes. The books are written in a narrative style by law professors and utilize examples to demonstrate the major concepts in each area of law. Each volume is from 150–250 pages. Each chapter addresses a major issue in the subject area, including discussion of the principal cases related to that issue that students are likely to read in their courses.

- *Examples & Explanation Series* (**written by professors**). This popular series provides explanations of the law, followed by hypothetical questions that test your understanding of the explanations, followed by detailed answers to the questions. I recommend Joseph Glannon's Torts entry in this series to my students. Available as a digital download.

- **Friedman's Practice Series.** This series focuses on exam preparation with practice essay and multiple-choice questions along with model answers and analysis. Available as a digital download at StoreLaw.com.

- **Glannon Guide Series (written by professors).** This new counterpart to the *Examples & Explanations* series is geared toward multiple-choice exam questions. The series takes students through legal concepts with concise discussions, followed by practice multiple-choice questions with answers and analysis.

- **Introduction to Law Series (written by professors).** Titles in this series offer an overview of a law school subject, with particular attention paid to explaining difficult concepts.

- **Law in a Flash Series.** The "flashcard series" reviews legal subjects point by point using cards that contain a question on the front, often in the form of a hypothetical fact pattern, and the answer on the back. The cards resemble question and answer cards for board games like *Trivial Pursuit*. Available as a digital download.

- **Professor Series (written by professors).** This is an advanced outline series focusing on elective upper-level subjects, rather than required 1L subjects, so you can cross this one off your list of consideration for the first year.

- **Siegel's Series.** This series is for self-quizzing. Each title works through key topics in a question and answer format with both multiple-choice and essay questions with model answers.

CALI.org

- **CALI Lessons (written by professors).** CALI (Center for Computer–Assisted Legal Instruction) lessons are on-line instruction that include summaries of the law in each course by specific topics along with interactive questions and answers. CALI lessons are accessible without charge to law students.

Carolina Academic Press

- **Concept and Method Series (written by professors).** This series examines and explains the "elemental building blocks" of different subject areas. Each chapter includes practice problems.

- *Mastering Series* **(written by professors).** The *Mastering* series is a treatise-type series written in a student-friendly fashion that de-emphasizes footnotes and citations. The books contain a roadmap at the beginning of each chapter and a list of points to remember at the end of the chapter.

- *Starting Off Right Series* **(written by professors).** This series focuses on first-year courses. Each title examines the basic concepts of the course, and seeks to help students learn how to analyze fact patterns and develop skills such as case-reading, organization, outlining, and exam-writing.

Fleming's Fundamentals of Law

- *Exam Solution Series.* This series includes audio and video CDs/DVDs that contain a combination of lectures, outlines, practice exam questions, and instruction on issue-spotting, exam-writing, and memory retention devices.

Foundation Press

- *Concepts and Insights Series* **(written by professors).** These books offer explanation in treatise form of the concepts behind legal rules. The publisher describes them as "a teacher's manual for students."

- *Foundations of Law Series.* Not really a study aid, but sometimes listed as one. Each title contains a collection of readings excerpted from articles and books in the subject area, followed by notes and questions. Some professors assign these books as supplemental course texts.

- *Turning Point Series* **(written by professors).** Rather than focus on an entire law school subject as do most study aids, these compact books focus on particularly complex areas within a subject, such as "takings" under property law and the First Amendment religion clause under constitutional law.

Gilbert Publishing

- *Gilbert Law Summaries* **(written by professors).** Titles in this series follow an outline format that explains the law in both a concise capsule summary form and a more comprehensive form. Titles also feature examples, exam tips, multiple-choice and essay questions with answers, and a chart keying the outline to the most popular casebooks in the subject area.

- **Law School Legends Audio Tapes (lectures by professors).** This series features audio lectures by professors. Each lecture includes examples and exam tips along with written materials that track the lecture.

- **Legalines.** Each title in this large, long-running series is adapted to a particular casebook, containing detailed briefs of all the major cases in the book, as well as explanation of the black-letter law in an outline format. The series is now available under *E-Legalines* as customizable digital books, allowing students to add class notes and delete cases that are not covered.

- **Quizzer Software.** These CD–ROMs cover the main 1L subjects and are designed to help students practice for exams. The *Quizzer Flashcard* software gives students more than 1500 true/false, multiple-choice, and short-answer questions in flashcard format along with detailed answers and scoring explanations. The *Quizzer Essay Workshop* software gives students 125 essay questions to test their essay-writing skills.

InteractiveLegalTools.com

- **Interactive Series (lectures by professors).** This multimedia series is quite different from other law school study aids. Titles include video and audio lectures, interactive multiple-choice and essay questions, and a fill-in-the-blank, downloadable outline.

Law Review Publishing

- **E-Z Review.** This series of condensed outlines features visual step-by-step organizational flow charts, concisely stated rules, and short case briefs.

Lexis-Nexis

- **Question and Answer Series (written by professors).** Titles in this series are made up principally of multiple-choice and short-answer questions that allow readers to test their understanding of the law in a subject area by applying it. The multiple-choice questions include analyses explaining which answer option is the best one and why the other options are not as good. The short-answer questions also include model answers.

- *Understanding Series* (**written by professors**). This series offers titles in a wide variety of subject areas that explain the law in a compact treatise-like format.

McClaren Legal Publishers

- *Legal Path Series.* Similar to *Casenotes*, titles in this series contain case briefs keyed to major casebooks.
- *Legal Trail Series.* This series purports to "translate" codified rules and statutes, such as the *Federal Rules of Civil Procedure*, into plain and simple English. The books follow up the rules and statutes with outline explanation.
- *Spark Law Series.* This series provides a condensed version of the *Legal Trail Series* in outline format with flowcharts to help understand how the rules or statutes work together.

MultiState Legal Press

- *Finals Law School Exam Series.* Each title in this series provides both detailed and capsule subject outlines and multiple-choice and essay questions with detailed answers.
- *PMBR Audio Series.* This series offers concise audio lectures in both tape and CD format.

Nailing the Bar Publications

- *How to Write Law School Exams Series.* Finally, a book that tells professors how to write law school exams! Kidding, but that's what the title makes it sound like. These books focus on preparing students to successfully answer essay questions. The books break the issues down, offer recommended answers, and discuss how to avoid falling prey to red herrings and other non-issues.
- *Tyler's Simple Outline Series.* Written in an accessible style, these concise outlines include brief explanations of black-letter law.

StoreLaw.com

- *Casebriefs Digital Briefs.* This series offers case briefs in digital format.

- *Blond's Law Guides* (**written by professors**). No, these were not written by Elle Woods, fictional star of *Legally Blonde*. This series includes concise black-letter law outlines, flowcharts, mnemonics, and case summaries from leading casebooks. Each book comes with a license to download the book and a free software program for organizing notes, briefs, and outlines.

- *Blond's Software.* This new series of downloads features *Blond's Flashcard Series*, *Blond's Multiple Choice Series*, and *Blond's Essay Exams*. Available as a package download of all 1L subjects or individually by subject, the software also includes a program allowing students to customize the content and to test and score themselves.

- *EssayWriter Series* (**written by professors**). This software download series integrates *Friedman's Practice Series* content into an interactive product that helps you work through essay questions.

- *IPod & MP3 Lectures* (**lectures by professors**). These one-hour audio lectures are presented by law professors on specific topics rather than entire subjects. For example, rather than covering the entire subject of property law, a lecture is available addressing only servitudes and easements on land. As the name suggests, these lectures can be downloaded directly to your mp3 player. Add "servitudes and easements" to your party playlist and watch those law students flood the dance floor.

West, a Thomson Reuters business

- *Black Letter Outlines* (**written by professors**). Titles in this mainstay series follow an outline format that explains legal rules and exceptions. Each entry includes both a comprehensive and capsule outline, as well as practice questions and answers.

- *Concise Hornbook Series* (**written by professors**). We could call this the "Hornbook–Lite" series. The entries are abbreviated versions of the thicker, more in-depth, and heavily footnoted traditional hornbooks described below.

- *Exam Pro Series* (**written by professors**). Titles in this series contain practice exams with questions in a variety of formats. The questions are designed to simulate real law school exams.

- *High Court Case Summaries.* This is another canned brief series. The titles are keyed to the most widely used casebooks in the particular subject area. Other features include graphic depictions to aid in remembering the cases, headnotes that summarize the importance of the cases, definitions of legal terms, and perforated pages that can be incorporated into a binder.

- *Hornbook Series* (**written by professors**). Entries in this classic series provide comprehensive, authoritative coverage, including both historical development and contemporary application, in treatise format. All explanation is supported by citations.

- *Nutshell Series* (**written mostly by professors**). With more than 130 titles, this series provides succinct summation of the law in different areas. The books are compact, both in content and size.

- *Quick Review Series.* This series provides both main and capsule outlines for each subject. The main outline includes explanation, as well as exam strategies, charts, tables, and study tips. Each title also contains multiple-choice and essay practice questions and a "10–5–2 hour" study guide suggesting what you should study with ten, five, and two hours left to prepare for the exam.

- *Sum and Substance Audio Series* (**lectures by professors**). This audio series features lectures by professors in different subject areas.

- *Sum & Substance Quick Review* (**written by professors**). These books provide a primary outline with explanations, exam hints, charts, tables, and study tips. They also contain a consolidated outline to give students a big-picture overview of the subject and sample essay and multiple-choice questions.

APPENDIX B

SAMPLE ISSUE–SPOTTING/ PROBLEM–SOLVING ESSAY QUESTION WITH MODEL ANSWER

Below is an essay question I once included on a Torts exam and now use as a practice midterm exam. Following the question is the model answer I would use to grade the exam. It's a classic issue-spotting/problem-solving-type law school essay question. The question addresses a handful of issues in the arena of intentional torts, a relatively easy-to-understand area of law.

The issues and legal standards are explained in the model answer, but don't worry about the specifics of the law. The sample essay questions in this appendix and Appendix C are included to give curious readers an authentic feel for what law school essay questions and answers look like in terms of both content and structure. If I were starting law school, that would be one of my first questions: "What are exams really like?" I recommend reading these essay question appendices in conjunction with Chapter 15, which analyzes fifteen common mistakes students make on law school essay exams.

I resisted the temptation to insert commentary and analysis dissecting the questions and answers for you, as I think that would unhelpfully complicate matters at this stage of your law school life. Other prep books focus exclusively on law school essay exams. Consult them for more in-depth exploration.

Intentional Torts Essay Question
(Total possible points: 120; recommended time: 70 minutes)

Sheila and the Shingles (S & S) is a highly successful rock group. Sheila is actually Sheldon Ferndale, lead singer and songwriter for the group. Sheldon decided early on that to be successful in the rock music world, one has to be outrageous

402

and the more outrageous the better. Bizarre and unpredictable stage shows thus became a hallmark of S & S concerts.

At a concert date in Omaha during their 2006 world tour, S & S appeared onstage in military fatigues. Halfway through their hit song, "Take Me Hostage," Sheldon pulled a semiautomatic handgun from his belt, pointed the gun at the crowd and screamed, "Nobody move or I'll shoot."

Most of the audience cheered, thinking this was just another S & S theatrical trick, but some audience members believed it was real and froze in fear. Bernard Boone, sitting in the front row, was not familiar with the reputation of S & S and believed the threat was real. Fearing for his and other audience members' safety, he pulled a handgun from inside his coat and shot at Sheldon. The bullet missed Sheldon, but struck the bass player, Lucky Chord, wounding him in the thigh. None of the band members saw this happen and, in fact, did not realize Lucky had been shot. (The fact that he was writhing on the floor did not tip them off because Lucky frequently played the bass in that position.)

As it turned out, Sheldon was not just engaging in theatrics. Many years of abusing controlled substances had finally caught up with him. He was suffering from an insane delusion in which he believed he was on the front line of the Iraq war and that the audience was a human wave of terrorists about to attack and kill him. He aimed the gun into the crowd and pulled the trigger.

He shot Matt Madrigal, a 13–year-old boy who was attending the concert with his best friend and his best friend's mother, Wilma. Sheldon then immediately put down the gun and fled the stage, where he was quickly apprehended.

Fortunately, Matt's injury was not serious. He recovered fully. Wilma, however, was traumatized from witnessing Matt's shooting. Wilma went to see a psychologist numerous times in the months following the incident to help her deal with the trauma.

After recovering from his psychotic episode, Sheldon gave a sworn statement to the police that said: "I did not wish to hit anyone when I shot that gun."

This is an intentional torts question. Do not discuss negligence, even though potential negligence claims exist. Fully discuss and analyze all claims and issues among all potential plaintiffs and defendants arising from this unfortunate series of events, except for potential claims by one band member against another band member. Use subheadings to delineate different claims among different parties (e.g., A v. B, C v. D, etc.).

Model Answer

Below is a model answer to the question, including the point range for each issue to give you an idea of how points are tied to the relative difficulty of the issue and the amount of discussion required to address it. Points denoted per issue represent the range of possible points that could be awarded. Thus, for the first issue regarding the effect of Sheldon's insanity on his intent, a student could receive anywhere between zero to fifteen points. Note that not all professors grade by a point system. Here's the answer:

Several lawsuits are likely to arise out of this unfortunate series of events. They will be discussed separately.

Audience members v. Sheldon

Members of the concert audience who believed Sheldon's threat have viable claims against him for assault and false imprisonment.

Intent/Sheldon's insanity (point range: 0–15). A preliminary issue applicable to these and other intentional tort claims against Sheldon is his insanity. Sheldon will assert that his insanity prevented him from forming a tortious intent. In his delusional, paranoid state, he was acting in self-defense, thinking the audience was going to attack and kill him. But as we learned in *McGuire v. Almy*, insane people are generally held responsible for their intentional torts. More specifically, insanity does not operate to negate the intent element. As the court in *McGuire* said, for policy reasons such as deterrence and fairness, the law will not inquire into the subjective state of mind of the insane person with a view toward excusing his intentional conduct if it turns out he was acting pursuant to an insane delusion.

Assault (0–10). Audience members *who believed* Sheldon's threat was real should prevail in an assault claim against him. An assault occurs where there is a volitional act intended to cause imminent apprehension of a harmful or offensive bodily contact, and such imminent apprehension results. Sheldon volitionally pointed the gun and expressly threatened to shoot audience members. His intent to create an apprehension could be inferred from his conduct. Any audience member who experienced imminent apprehension of a shooting should prevail. Of course, those audience members who believed it was simply a stage antic would not have sound claims because they were not in imminent apprehension of a harmful contact. Thus, an essential element of assault—the result element—would be missing.

False imprisonment (0–15). Similarly, audience members who believed the threat was genuine may have viable claims for false imprisonment against Sheldon. A false imprisonment requires a volitional act, an intent to confine unlawfully, and a resulting unlawful confinement. When Sheldon wielded the gun, he said, "Nobody move or I'll shoot." The facts state that some audience members "froze in fear." Sheldon acted volitionally, his intent to confine can be inferred from his express statement ordering the audience not to move, and a confinement resulted with regard to any audience member who obeyed the command. A confinement can occur through a threat to use physical force. No actual force is required. The audience members were not required to "test the threat." As with the assault claim, only those audience members who believed the threat was real and did not move because of it would have viable claims.

Lucky Chord v. Bernard Boone

Battery (0–5). Lucky will sue Bernard for battery for shooting him in the leg. Battery requires a volitional act intended to cause a harmful or offensive bodily contact and such a contact results. Here, we had a volitional act and harmful contact, but Bernard may have a defense, one that also calls into question the intent element.

Self-defense and defense of others (0–15). Bernard will assert the privileges of self-defense and defense of others. Self-defense and defense of others apply when one reasonably believes the use of force is necessary to prevent a threatened battery against himself or others and uses a reasonable amount of force under the circumstances. A proportionality rule applies to determine the reasonableness of the amount of force. Thus, one is permitted to use deadly force in self-defense or defense of others only when he reasonably believes deadly force is threatened.

Bernard will argue he was privileged to use deadly force because he reasonably believed Sheldon was about to use deadly force against either him or other audience members. The facts state that he acted "[f]earing for his and other audience members' safety." Given S & S's reputation for bizarre stage shows, one could argue persuasively that an audience member would not have reasonably believed Sheldon's threat was real. Thus, if Sheldon had been engaged in a stage prank, there's a strong chance a court would find the privileges inapplicable. As it turned out, however, the threat was real. Thus, the privileges may very well apply.

No transferred intent (0–15). Lucky may argue that even if Bernard was privileged to use deadly force against Sheldon, he wasn't privileged to shoot Lucky, and that Bernard's intent to shoot Sheldon transferred to Lucky under the doctrine of transferred intent. Transferred intent holds that if one intends to commit an intentional tort, such as a battery, against one person and ends up committing the tort against a different person, the actor's intent is deemed to transfer to the other person (thereby satisfying the intent element).

However, transferred intent would apply only if it was determined that Bernard was *not* privileged to act in self-defense or defense of others. If Bernard's conduct was privileged, there would be no tortious intent to transfer. Thus, Lucky would fail in his battery claim against Bernard if the privileges of self-defense or defense of others are found applicable, which they should be under these circumstances.

Matt v. Sheldon

Battery (0–3). Matt will sue Sheldon for battery for shooting him. The elements of battery have already been stated.

Belief intent (0–12). The only issue would be Sheldon's intent. As already discussed, his insanity would not negate his intent. However, after the incident, Sheldon gave a statement saying "I did not wish to hit anyone when I shot the gun." This statement, assuming it's true, would suggest he did not desire to shoot anyone. Two kinds of intent exist, however: desire intent and belief intent. Even if Sheldon lacked desire intent (that is, even if he honestly did not desire to cause a harmful contact), he could still be liable for battery if he had "belief intent," meaning that when he shot the gun he believed to a substantial certainty that he would hit someone. The facts say Sheldon "aimed the gun into the crowd and pulled the trigger." Thus, a fact-finder could infer that he knew to a substantial certainty that someone in the audience would be hit even if he didn't desire to shoot anyone. Sheldon will be liable to Matt for battery.

Wilma v. Sheldon

Intentional infliction of emotional distress (0–15). Wilma will sue Sheldon for intentional infliction of emotional distress (IIED) based on her trauma from witnessing Matt getting shot. IIED allows one to recover against an actor who through extreme and outrageous conduct intentionally or recklessly causes severe emotional distress to another. Although the standard for what qualifies as extreme and outrageous conduct is high, Sheldon's conduct—pulling out a gun and opening fire on a concert audience—probably satisfies it. It is conduct likely to be found to be beyond the bounds of all decency and utterly intolerable in a civilized society. Threatening people with physical violence, as we learned in *Siliznoff*, can constitute extreme and outrageous conduct.

As to the fault element, section 46(1) of the *Restatement (Second) of Torts* adopts a dual intent-recklessness fault standard for IIED. Thus, even if Sheldon didn't intend to cause emotional distress, he was probably at least reckless. Recklessness is conduct that creates a high probability of a harmful consequence as judged by an objective standard. A reasonable person would know that shooting someone at a concert would create a high probability of causing severe emotional distress to a third party.

Whether Wilma's distress qualifies as "severe" would be an issue. She obviously suffered distress, as evidenced by her numerous visits to the psychologist. The fact-finder would have to determine the severity of her distress, probably assisted by expert witnesses. Further fact development would be required.

Bystander limitation (0–10). But Wilma has another problem. As we learned, section 46(2)(b) of the *Restatement (Second) of Torts* imposes an additional limitation in non-family member "bystander" IIED cases such as this one: the requirement that the plaintiff suffer bodily harm flowing from the emotional distress. Matt was unrelated to Wilma and we don't have any facts indicating that Wilma's distress caused her bodily harm. If she didn't suffer bodily harm from her emotional distress, her claim would fail under the *Restatement* test. This issue also would require additional factual development.

Non-bystander IIED claims (0–5). It's possible that Wilma or other audience members could have their own non-bystander IIED claims based on Sheldon's conduct in threatening them with the gun if they suffered severe emotional distress as a result of the incident. No facts, however, indicate anyone except Wilma suffered severe emotional distress.

APPENDIX C
SAMPLE SHORT ESSAY
QUESTION WITH
MODEL ANSWER

Below is a "short essay question" that I included on a recent Torts exam, followed by my model answer to the question. The question raises a single issue that is identified in the question. Because they don't present major issue-spotting or organizational challenges, short essay questions are relatively "easier" than issue-spotting/problem-solving questions of the type in Appendix B.

The question below addresses an area of tort law known as "negligent infliction of emotional distress." Courts have long been reluctant to recognize claims for negligent (as opposed to intentional) infliction of emotional distress because of a fear of opening the so-called "floodgates of litigation" to lawsuits every time someone negligently causes another to suffer emotionally.

As you'll see from the question and answer below, over time, courts adopted tests that gradually expanded the right to recover money damages for negligently caused emotional distress. We cover three approaches to the issue in class. Generally, if your professor covers different legal tests that courts apply to the same issue, students should address all of them in answering a question raising that issue unless the question expressly indicates otherwise. In this case, I went ahead and included explicit instructions to that effect in the question. The legal standards are explained in the model answer, but again, don't worry about the specifics of the law. This question and answer are included simply to show you what a short essay question and answer can look like.

Essay Question
(Total possible points: 60; recommended time: 35 minutes)

Ted went to the grocery store with his five-year-old daughter, Alice. They had just finished shopping and were in the parking lot. While Ted was loading the groceries into the back of his SUV, Alice, being a little scamp like most kids, took off running around the parking lot without Ted noticing. It wasn't until Ted closed the hatchback on his SUV and said, "Let's go, Alice," that he realized she was missing. Frantic, Ted scanned the parking lot, but could not see Alice. He jumped into his vehicle and began driving around the lot looking for her. He also called 911 in a panic, thinking someone might have abducted her. He turned the corner and drove along the south side of the store. He was looking to his left when he heard tires screeching, followed by a thud. He turned to his right and there, lying on the pavement approximately 100 feet away, was Alice. She had been struck by a negligent truck driver who backed into her without looking. Blood was on the pavement around her. Tragically, she died almost instantly. Ted fainted. He suffered severely disabling emotional distress, with accompanying physical consequences, as a result of the incident. Six months later, he filed a lawsuit against the negligent truck driver, Rafe, for negligent infliction of emotional distress. Using separate subheadings, analyze Ted's chances of recovery in: (1) a jurisdiction following the impact rule; (2) a jurisdiction following the zone of danger rule; and (3) a jurisdiction following the *Dillon v. Legg/Thing v. La Chusa* approach. Note: Ted's possible comparative negligence is not part of this question.

Model Answer

Here is the model answer I used to grade the exam:

Ted's chances for success don't look good regardless of which of the three approaches is followed:

Impact rule

The impact rule, now followed by only a small number of states, limits negligent infliction of emotional distress (NIED) claims to those who suffer a physical impact of some type from the defendant's conduct. The impact rule was intended to draw a tight circle limiting claims for NIED and it did. The ostensible purpose of the rule was to weed out trivial and feigned claims, the idea being that the impact assured some degree of genuineness to the claim, although courts often strained to find the rule satisfied by even minor, trivial contacts. Under the impact rule in its pure form, "bystander claims" for NIED, such as Ted's, did not exist because all viable claims were on behalf of "direct victims." Ted did not suffer any physical impact with his person from the negligent truck driver. He would have no claim in a jurisdiction adhering to the impact rule.

Zone of danger

Ted's NIED claim also would fail in a jurisdiction following the zone of danger (ZOD) rule. The zone of danger rule allows recovery for emotional distress only to persons who were themselves within the zone of *physical* danger threatened by the D's conduct. The facts state Ted was safely in his SUV approximately 100 feet away from the accident scene. He was not within the zone of physical danger created by the D's negligent backing up. Accordingly, he would not be able to recover under the ZOD approach unless the court stretched the zone of danger to exorbitant lengths.

Dillon v. Legg/Thing v. La Chusa approach

Ted's best chance for recovery would be if he were in a jurisdiction following the *Dillon v. Legg* approach. In *Dillon*, the California Supreme Court abandoned the zone of danger test and replaced it with a foreseeability test limited by three guidelines. Those guidelines were: (1) whether the P was located near the scene as contrasted with one who was a distance away; (2) whether the shock resulted from a direct emotional impact upon the P from the sensory and contemporaneous observance of the accident, as contrasted with learning about it afterwards from others; and (3) whether the P and victim were closely related.

The *Thing* court slightly modified the *Dillon* guidelines and converted them into fixed rules. Those rules allow recovery in bystander NIED cases if: (1) the P was closely related by blood or marriage to the victim; (2) the P was present at the scene and contemporaneously perceived the injury as it occurred; and (3) the P suffered emotional distress beyond that which would be expected in a disinterested observer.

The first and third factors are clearly met here. Ted was Alice's father, so he obviously was in a close blood relationship with Alice. As to the third factor, Ted fainted and suffered severely disabling emotional distress accompanied by physical consequences. His emotional distress went beyond that which would be expected in a disinterested observer.

Ted may have a problem with the second factor. Ted was close to the scene, but did not witness the accident and was not aware Alice was being injured until after the fact because he was looking the other way.

Whether Ted would prevail in a *Dillon/Thing* jurisdiction would depend on how liberally or stringently the court interpreted the contemporaneous perception element. Certainly, Ted seems to fit within the spirit of the factor. He was only 100 feet away, heard the accident occur, and immediately turned to see the gruesome aftermath. As we learned, however, the *Thing* court was very concerned with drawing reliable lines to help keep the lid on a potentially expansive tort claim. Unless the court considered Ted's auditory perception of the event to be the equivalent of witnessing it visually, Ted would lose even in a *Dillon/Thing* jurisdiction.

Index

413

INDEX

Curriculum—Cont'd
>First-year, 53–67
>Legal Research and Writing. *See* Legal Research and Writing.
>Property. *See* Property.
>Semesterization of first-year courses, 55
>Skills courses in, 54, 56
>Slow evolution of, 53–55
>Torts. *See* Torts.

Day planner, need for. *See* Being organized.

Depression, 315–17, 323–24. *See also* Mental distress in law students; Substance abuse.

"Designated hitter" method of calling on students. *See* Socratic method.

Diligence, importance of to success, 161

Doctrinal courses. *See* Curriculum.

Drug abuse. *See* Substance abuse.

Educating Lawyers: Preparation for the Profession of Law. *See* Carnegie Foundation report on legal education.

Efficiency
>Importance of to success, 155–60, 373
>In allocating time on exams, 244–48
>In Legal Research and Writing, 302–07
>Tips for enhancing generally, 155–60

Erie Railroad Co. v. Tompkins, 58

Essay exams
>Average length of answers to, 228, 264–65
>Fifteen most common student mistakes in answering
>>Being sloppy, 262–64
>>Doing the "Monster [Issue] Mash," 259
>>Failing to be precise, 252–53
>>Failing to follow IRAC, 253–55
>>Failing to read and follow instructions, 241–43
>>Giving a general dissertation on the law, 256–57
>>Leaving out the relevant rules of law, 255–56
>>Making improper factual assumptions, 261–62
>>Misreading key facts, 250–52
>>Not managing time properly, 244–48
>>Omitting or skimping on application/analysis, 257–58
>>Overlooking and wrongly addressing "givens," 259–61
>>Starting to write too soon, 243–44
>>Writing about non-issues or overlooking issues, 248–50
>>Writing too little, 264–65

Essay exams—Cont'd
>Inability to provide broad course coverage with, 150–51
>Legibility, importance of, 21–22, 263
>Sample issue-spotting/problem solving essay question and model answer (Appendix B), 402–08
>Sample policy essay question, 239
>Sample short essay question and model answer (Appendix C), 409–12
>Types of essay questions
>>Issue-spotting/problem-solving questions, 74, 227, 238 (defining), 240, 254–55, 264, 402–08, 409
>>Miscellaneous types, 238–40
>>Policy questions, 206, 238–39 (defining), 254
>>Short essay questions, 151, 238 (defining), 240, 255, 266, 409–12
>*See also* Exams; Grades/grading.

Exams
>Anonymity of, 133–34, 262
>Essay. *See* Essay exams.
>Exam-security software for, 21, 235
>Multiple-choice questions. *See* Multiple-choice questions.
>Plotting study grid for, 229–31
>Practice exams, importance of taking, 231–34, 271–73, 383
>Preparing for, 226–36
>Sample questions. *See* Essay exams; Multiple-choice questions.
>Single-exam format, explanations for, 226–28
>Supplies for, 234–35
>Use of computer for, 21–22
>*See also* Essay exams; Grades/grading; Multiple-choice questions.

Extracurricular activities, 160, 358–67. *See also* Co–Curricular activities; Outside speakers; Student organizations.

Failing/failure. *See* Fear/fears.

Falling behind, need to avoid, 37, 72, 161, 219–20, 319–20, 371–72, 377, 381–82, 383–84

Fear/fears
>As shared by all students, 27–38, 371
>Most common in law students
>>Failure/failing to meet personal expectations, 27–32, 370
>>Interference of law school with outside relationships, 34–37
>>Not keeping up with workload, 37–38

415

INDEX

INDEX

Sample case briefs. *See* Case briefs/briefing.

Sample essay exams. *See* Essay exams.

Sample multiple-choice question. *See* Multiple-choice questions.

Sample Socratic dialogue. *See* Socratic method.

Sample student class notes. *See* Notetaking.

Seat selection. *See* Classroom seating.

Second semester
- Advantages of, 338
- As a crucial juncture for students, 337–38, 345–46
- Difficulty of getting back into the groove in, 346–47
- Effect of first-semester grades on attitudes toward, 343–46
- Financial worries arising in, 353–55
- Increased workload in, 349
- Pitfalls of, 341–57
- Reevaluating decision to attend law school in, 349–53
- Student reaction to, 339–47

Secondary law journals, 362. *See also* Law review.

Semesterization of first-year courses. *See* Curriculum.

Skills courses. *See* Curriculum.

Socrates. *See* Socratic method, Origin of.

Socratic method, 28, 31, 68, 71, 75, 77, 79, 110, 112, 113, 116, 117, 128, 129, 131, 139, 159, 170, 172, 173, 200, 205, 274, 318, 325, 328, 338
- As an inefficient method for conveying information, 101–02
- As involving "cold-calling" on students, 104–05
- Benefits of, 93–95
- Criticism of, 92, 93–95
- Current status in U.S. legal education of, 88, 92, 93
- Effect of on women and minority students, 107–09
- Facts and myths about, 100–09
- How it works, 90–92, 94–95
- Importance of listening to classmates, 201–02
- Odds of getting called on, 105–06
- Origin of, 89
- "Panel" or "designated hitter" system of calling on students in lieu of, 104–05
- Percentage of professors using, 92–93
- Purposes of, 89–90, 101
- Sample Socratic dialogue, 95–99
- Student fear of, 32–33, 100–01, 104, 106–07, 114
- *See also* Case method; Langdell, Christopher.

Sorting through law school advice, 14, 73–74

Stress. *See* Depression; Fear/fears; Mental distress in law students; Substance abuse.

Student Bar Association. *See* Student Government Association.

Student fears about law school. *See* Fear/fears.

Student loans/debt, 317, 353–55

Student Government Association, 321, 367

Student organizations, 366–67

Students. *See* Law students.

Statistics, Studies, and Surveys
- ABA Curriculum Study, 54–55
- Anonymous grading in legal writing courses, 134
- Attrition rates, 28–29
- Average credit hours for legal writing courses, 278
- Average first-year section size, 41
- *Bluebook* vs. *ALWD Citation Manual*, number of legal writing programs using each, 280
- Case reading, 176
- First-year course offerings, 54–55
- Law professors, data regarding, 124–25
- Law student alienation, 333–35
- Lawyer job satisfaction, 351
- Lecturing, percentage of time class time devoted to, 102
- Legal writing, percentage of effort successful students devote to revising and proofreading in, 299
- LSAT, correlation between scores and first-year grades, 147
- Memory retention, 209
- Mental distress in law students, 315–18
- Multiple-choice questions, changing answers to, 270–71
- Multitasking, negative effects on cognition, 84–85
- Note-taking, 202, 203, 204, 217
- Relationship of computer use to exam performance, 22
- Research and writing as most important lawyering skills, 290
- Seat location and academic performance, 75–77
- Socratic method, percentage of professors using, 92–93
- Student contact with faculty members, 330
- Substance abuse among law students and lawyers, 320–21

419

INDEX

†